Emerging Global Trade Governance

T0270806

Mega free trade agreements (FTAs) are being formed to fill the gap created by new developments in global governance and are reshaping the world economic order. The Trans-Pacific Partnership (TPP) agreement is one of such 21st century FTAs.

This book highlights three trade-related issues covered by the TPP that greatly concern emerging countries – investment, intellectual property rights (IPR), and state-owned enterprises (SOEs). It contains rigorous economic, legal, and political analyses on the final text of the agreement, combined with country-specific policy discussions focusing on Indonesia, the Philippines, Thailand, and Viet Nam, giving readers insights into the establishment of global rules and regulations for 21st century trade. The book also outlines the requirements for emerging Asian countries to better formulate trade policies in the new era of international trade and promote regional integration in ASEAN and East Asia.

Lurong Chen is an Economist at the Economic Research Institute for ASEAN and East Asia (ERIA). He obtained his PhD in International Economics from the Graduate Institute of International and Development Studies, Geneva.

Shujiro Urata is Professor of Economics at the Graduate School of Asia-Pacific Studies, Waseda University; Faculty Fellow at the Research Institute of Economy, Trade and Industry (RIETI); Research Fellow at the Japanese Centre for Economic Research; and Senior Research Advisor, Economic Research Institute for ASEAN and East Asia (ERIA). He received his PhD in Economics from Stanford University.

Junji Nakagawa is Professor of International Economic Law at the Institute of Social Science, University of Tokyo. He obtained his PhD in Law from the University of Tokyo.

Masahito Ambashi is an Economist at the Economic Research Institute for ASEAN and East Asia (ERIA). He received his PhD in Economics from the University of Essex.

Routledge-ERIA Studies in Development Economics

For more information about this series, please visit www.routledge.com/Routledge-ERIA-Studies-in-Development-Economics/book-series/ERIA

Emerging Global Trade Governance

Mega Free Trade Agreements and Implications for ASEAN

Edited by Lurong Chen,
Shujiro Urata, Junji Nakagawa
and Masahito Ambashi

Routledge
Taylor & Francis Group

LONDON AND NEW YORK

Economic Research Institute
for ASEAN and East Asia

First published 2019
by Routledge
2 Park Square, Milton Park, Abingdon, Oxon OX14 4RN

and by Routledge
605 Third Avenue, New York, NY 10017

First issued in paperback 2020

Routledge is an imprint of the Taylor & Francis Group, an informa business

British Library Cataloguing-in-Publication Data
A catalogue record for this book is available from the British Library

Library of Congress Cataloging-in-Publication Data
Names: Chen, Lurong, editor. | Urata, Shūjirō, 1950– editor. |
    Nakagawa, Junji, 1955– editor. | Ambashi, Masahito, editor.
Title: Emerging global trade governance : mega free trade agreements
    and implications for ASEAN / edited by Lurong Chen, Shujiro Urata,
    Junji Nakagawa and Masahito Ambashi.
Description: Abingdon, Oxon ; New York, NY : Routledge, 2019. |
    Series: Routledge-ERIA studies in development economics ; 13 |
    Includes bibliographical references and index.
Identifiers: LCCN 2018042738| ISBN 9781138484764 (hardback) |
    ISBN 9781351051309 (ebook)
Subjects: LCSH: Free trade—Pacific Area. | Trans-Pacific Strategic
    Economic Partnership Agreement (2005 June 3) | ASEAN.
Classification: LCC HF2570.7 .E44 2019 | DDC 382/.911823—dc23
LC record available at https://lccn.loc.gov/2018042738

ISBN 13: 978-0-367-50439-7 (pbk)
ISBN 13: 978-1-138-48476-4 (hbk)

Typeset in Galliard
by Apex CoVantage, LLC

Contents

Figures

Tables

Boxes

Contributors

Masahito Ambashi is an Economist at the Economic Research Institute for ASEAN and East Asia (ERIA). He received his PhD in Economics from the University of Essex.

Riza Noer Arfani is Chair, WTO Chairs Programme and Senior Lecturer, the Department of International Relations, Faculty of Social and Political Sciences, Universitas Gadjah Mada, Indonesia. He received his PhD in International Relations from Ritsumeikan University.

Lurong Chen is an Economist at the Economic Research Institute for ASEAN and East Asia (ERIA). He obtained his PhD in International Economics from the Graduate Institute of International and Development Studies, Geneva.

Ramon L. Clarete is a Professor at School of Economics, the University of the Philippines. He has a PhD in Economics from the University of Hawaii in Honolulu.

Maharani Hapsari is a Lecturer at the Department of International Relations, Faculty of Social and Political Science, Universitas Gadjah Mada, Indonesia. She obtained her PhD in International Development from Nagoya University.

Akiko Kato is Associate Professor of Intellectual Property Law at the College of Law, Nihon University, Japan. She obtained her PhD in International Law from the International Christian University.

Tsuyoshi Kawase is Professor, Faculty of Law, Sophia University; Faculty Fellow at Research Institute of Economy, Trade and Industry (RIETI); Chairman of Subcommittee on Trade Remedies, Industrial Structure Council, Ministry of Economy, Trade and Industry (METI), Government of Japan. He obtained his LLM from Georgetown University Law Center, USA.

Jakkrit Kuanpoth is the Advisor for Law for Development at the Thailand Development Research Institute (TDRI); Of Counsel at Tilleke and Gibbins International, Thailand and Visiting Professorial Fellow of the University of Wollongong, Australia. He obtained his PhD in Law from the University of Aberdeen.

Junji Nakagawa is Professor of International Economic Law at the Institute of Social Science, University of Tokyo. He obtained his PhD in Law from the University of Tokyo.

Anh Duong Nguyen is Senior Economist, Director of Department for Macroeconomic Policy and Integration Studies, Central Institute for Economic Management of Vietnam; Convener of Corporate Law and Governance group, APEC Economic Committee. He obtained his Master of Economics from the Australian National University, Canberra.

Glenda T. Reyes is a freelance consultant. She obtained her Master in Public Administration with specialisation in public policy from the National College of Public Administration and Governance of the University of the Philippines and received her Post Graduate Diploma in Economics from the University of Melbourne.

Shujiro Urata is Professor of Economics at the Graduate School of Asia-Pacific Studies, Waseda University; Faculty Fellow at the Research Institute of Economy, Trade and Industry (RIETI); Research Fellow at the Japanese Centre for Economic Research; and Senior Research Advisor, Economic Research Institute for ASEAN and East Asia (ERIA). He received his PhD in Economics from Stanford University.

Tri Thanh Vo is Senior Economist, Central Institute for Economic Management of Vietnam; Chair of Vietnamese Committee for Pacific Economic Cooperation. He obtained his PhD in Economics from the Australian National University, Canberra.

Poppy S. Winanti is Senior Lecturer at the Department of International Relations, Faculty of Social and Political Sciences, Universitas Gadjah Mada, Indonesia. She received her PhD in Politics from the University of Glasgow.

Acknowledgements

The idea for this book emerged from the ERIA research project on '21st Century Regionalism, Mega FTAs, and Asian Regional Integration'. The project brought together nearly 20 experts in area of international relations, economics, and law to conduct rigorous economic, legal, and political analyses on the final text of the agreement of Trans-Pacific Partnership, combined with country-specific policy discussions.

With a wide range of papers developed from the project, we decide to bring them together into a major statement in the form of this editorial volume – *Emerging Global Trade Governance: Mega Free Trade Agreements and Implications for ASEAN.*

Support from ERIA colleagues, in particular, Hidetoshi Nishimura, Fukunari Kimura, Izuru Kobayashi, Shigeki Kamiyama, Shimpei Yamamoto, Maria Rosario, Stefan Wesiak, Fany Trianingsih, and Chrestella Budyanto, is gratefully acknowledged.

Throughout the compilation of the book, we have the support from Yongling Lam and Samantha Phua of Routledge. Their encouragement and patience have been critical to the completion of this project.

Last, but not least, we are indebted to all contributors to this book: their enthusiasm has been unwavering, from the involvement in the initial research project and through the subsequent dialogues to complete this book.

Lurong Chen
Shujiro Urata
Junji Nakagawa
Masahito Ambashi

Introduction

Mega FTAs in the 21st century global trade governance

Lurong Chen, Shujiro Urata, Junji Nakagawa, Masahito Ambashi

1. GVCs and the emergence of mega FTAs

The second unbundling of globalisation and global value chains (GVCs) have been producing changes that alter international relations, especially in the economic dimension. With the international fragmentation of production, competitiveness is increasingly determined at the level of sub-stage activities, rather than the whole production processes. As the characteristics and productivity of labour are now defined in great detail and in various categories, the expansion of global production sharing leads to a finer division of labour and a new pattern of international trade. The new global economy calls for fundamental reforms of global governance on international trade and investment to ensure the efficiency and sustainability of GVCs.

The current world trade system is facing challenges – there are mismatches between what we need and what we have now. On one hand, the current multilateral framework of global trading system was designed and constructed mostly in the second half of the 20th century. The World Trade Organization (WTO) rules in effect are not sophisticated enough to regulate the complex, multilayered network of GVCs in the new century. On the other hand, although there are a large number of regional trade agreements (RTAs) that have been established and implemented aiming to complement multilateralism, their influence is generally limited due to their small size relative to the wide extension and coverage of GVCs. There is a need for a solution that is wide enough in scope and sophisticated enough in content.

The basic motives and objectives underlying the signing of mega free trade agreements (FTAs), which involve a large number of members, are twofold. First, to consolidate and expand market access. In this regard, what motivates countries to pursue mega FTAs is not very different from what motivated them to pursue multilateral trade negotiations, RTAs, or FTAs. Countries' exporters are hoping for better access to foreign markets, particularly those that are fast growing or have a big potential to grow.

Second, another important motive for seeking to conclude mega FTAs is to set the rules for the 21st century. What distinguishes mega FTAs from others is the pursuit of rules and regulations that go beyond traditional free trade. Mega FTAs are intended to cover sectors not addressed in multilateral trade negotiations under the auspices of the WTO, such as regulatory and competition issues, protection of investments, and standards for environmental protection and workers' rights.

In the literature, the related exploration of mega FTAs is still at an early stage; most existing studies provide only conceptual or general discussions on mega FTAs. Links between the analysis of the provisions and policy implications, especially those taking into account country-specific conditions, are missing.

This book aims to fill the gaps in the existing literature. The essays making up this volume are based on a technical analysis and interpretation of the officially published text of the Trans-Pacific Partnership (TPP), which serves as a real-world example of how mega FTAs approach new global economic rule-making in the Asia Pacific. By combining the examination/discussion on the related legal framework and economic conditions in selected Asian countries, the book offers deeper insights into the potential impact of mega FTAs, the kinds of domestic reforms a country needs to undertake to meet the requirements of new international regulations, and the possible policy options to seize the opportunities and tackle the challenges arising from mega FTAs.

It is worth noting that the transition from the TPP to the Comprehensive and Progressive Agreement for Trans-Pacific Partnership (CPTPP), which was signed after the withdrawal of the United States (US) from the TPP, does not affect the fundamental analyses and discussions in this book that directly address the text of the TPP agreement. This is because the CPTPP was established by the other 11 TPP member states, and it retains the core content of the TPP agreement. Although most analyses directly address the final text of the TPP agreement, with some referring to the CPTPP text, related conclusions and policy recommendations retain their validity and should be applicable to mega FTAs in general.

2. Structure and chapter synopsis

Mega FTAs aim for high global standards in disciplining international trade and investment. For the member states, it is necessary to clarify the content of domestic legal reforms that will have to be conducted once the agreement has been implemented, while those countries that have expressed an interest in or the intention to accede to the partnership are bound to accept the obligations already set out. In either case, a deep understanding of these new rules and their effect compared with the domestic legal system will be useful.

This book focuses on three specific topics closely relevant to GVCs and the 21st century trade governance – investment, intellectual property rights (IPR), and state-owned enterprises (SOEs). The book first investigates the investment-related provisions in one thematic chapter (Chapter 1) and two country reports (Chapter 2 and Chapter 3). The second part, Chapters 4–8 explore how Association of Southeast Asian Nations (ASEAN) Member States could raise the standards of IPR protection under their domestic laws to meet the required level as set out in Chapter 18 of the TPP. And finally, the discussion in the third part of the book (Chapters 9–12) centres on the TPP disciplines on SOEs.

2.1. Part I – rules and regulations on investment

International capital flows and investment have deep implications for 21st century trade. For that reason, the TPP provides for a higher degree of openness and a wide range of rules for streamlining international trade and investment amongst the parties. Chapter 9 of the TPP agreement (the 'investment' chapter) has 30 Articles and 12 Annexes, trying to clarify the obligations on the liberalisation and protection of foreign investment. The TPP agreement adopted the negative list approach to induce each member state to liberalise foreign investment as a rule. But it also includes exceptions enumerated in its country-specific list of non-conforming measures (Annexes I, II, and III). To understand these regulations and their implications, it is helpful to adopt a three-stage approach of study – (i) the analysis of the general obligations as provided in Chapter 9, (ii) the analysis of country-specific obligations with respect to liberalisation of investment, which are provided in country-specific lists of non-conforming measures, and (iii) the comparison of country-specific obligations and the existing restrictions on foreign investment of each member state.

In Chapter 1, 'Investment in the Trans-Pacific Partnership: Possible Impacts on ASEAN Member States', Junji Nakagawa conducts a comprehensive comparative analysis of the general obligations as provided in Chapter 9 with those of the ASEAN Comprehensive Investment Agreement (ACIA), including the substantive obligations, the procedural obligations on the investor–state dispute settlement (ISDS), and the approaches to country-specific lists of non-conforming measures.

Nakagawa points out that although the TPP's definition of investment is similar to that in the ACIA, it covers not only the provisions that the ACIA already has, but also many provisions that the ACIA does not cover (so called 'ACIA-plus' provisions). This gives readers a real-world example of the high standards of a typical mega FTA that ASEAN Member States, either TPP or non-TPP parties, are faced with. In particular, the TPP's procedure for ISDS contains several 'ACIA plus' elements, especially in the area of arbitral proceedings. Moreover, the TPP agreement combines the liberalisation commitments in its investment chapter and the chapter on trade in services. This can solve most of the caveats[1] of the ACIA because of the latter's sole focus on the liberalisation commitments in investment.

Chapter 2 by Riza Noer Arfani and Chapter 3 by Glenda T. Reyes provide country-specific insights into Indonesia and the Philippines, respectively. They both reach a conclusion similar to that of Chapter 1: to meet mega FTA's high standards on investment, ASEAN member states will have to make substantial domestic legal reforms to facilitate and protect foreign investment by removing a wide range of performance requirements and barriers to domestic market access.

Arfani's chapter, 'The Investment Chapter of the Trans-Pacific Partnership and Indonesia', not only reviews Indonesia's current legal framework, but also outlines its regional obligation to the ACIA and in the schedules of specific commitments in the ASEAN Framework Agreement on Services (AFAS) packages regulating foreign investment. In the case of Indonesia, in addition to Law No. 25 (2007) on Investment that stipulates categorical restrictions on foreign investment, there are also non-categorical restrictions – stipulated in other relevant laws and rulings applied in either strategic sectors or business sectors associated with Article 33 of the State Constitution – that need to be considered. The study suggests that the categorical and non-categorical features of restrictions imply different approaches to implementation and policymakers should be aware of these when entering into investment-related obligations.

Reyes' chapter, 'An Assessment of the Philippines' Readiness to Mega New Generation Agreements: Investment', maps and assesses the existing national laws, rules, and regulations in the Philippines that affect foreign investment and the potential pros and cons of adopting the TPP investment scheduling approach to investment liberalisation for the country. The analysis reveals that for the Philippines to join an agreement like the TPP, the country needs to deal with a significant number of domestic measures that are inconsistent with the new framework, structure, and obligations for investment that mega FTAs will require. This will be a big challenge because the Philippine Constitution and national statutes prohibit or limit foreign participation in certain areas, industries, and activities.

2.2. Part II – rules and regulations on IPR

Chapter 18 of the TPP agreement contains provisions on IPR protection that surpasses the level under the Trade-Related Aspects of Intellectual Property Rights (TRIPS) Agreement of the WTO ('TRIPS-plus'). For those countries seeking sustained economic growth and development, joining GVCs is indispensable, and for this providing a high level of IPR protection should be a requirement. It is one of the reasons that IPR protection was one of the most controversial areas during the TPP negotiation.

Chapter 4 by Akiko Kato, 'Understanding the IP-related Contents of the Trans-Pacific Partnership Agreement,' provides a thematic analysis of the provisions contained in Chapter 18 of the TPP. Kato characterises Chapter 18 as a reflection of US interests and the power relations amongst the negotiating countries. This characterisation is salient in the TRIPS-plus approach and the single-undertaking approach, under which the TPP member states agreed to adopt rules that are (i) more stringent than those provided by the TRIPS Agreement, (ii) applied to all the TPP parties, and (iii) enforced through the dispute settlement system.

Kato then provides a detailed analysis of selected provisions of Chapter 18 in Section 2. Here are her major findings. First, the TPP introduces many TRIPS-plus provisions on substantive and procedural aspects of patent and undisclosed test data protection. They include patentable subject matter (Article 18.37), patent term adjustment for pharmaceuticals (Article 18.48), protection of undisclosed test data for pharmaceuticals (Article 18.50) and biologics (Article 18.51), and introduction of a patent linkage system (Article 18.53). Second, the TPP introduces several TRIPS-plus provisions on copyrights and related rights. They include the term of copyright (70 years, Article 18.63), regulation against actions circumventing technological protection measures (TPMs) (Article 18.68), and protection of rights management information (RMI) (Article, 18.69). Third, the TPP introduces detailed TRIPS-plus obligations on the enforcement of IPR. They include methods of calculating damages (Article 18.74), provisional measures (Article 18.75), border measures (Article 18.76), and criminal procedures and penalties (Article 18.77). Fourth, TPP Article 18.83 provides for transitional periods for some of the TPP parties in implementing the provisions of Chapter 18. Fifth, although the CPTPP has suspended the application of some of the aforementioned TRIPS-plus provisions of Chapter 18, this does not change the general characteristic of Chapter 18 of the TPP as a model for the IP chapters of 21st century trade agreements.

Chapter 5 by Nguyen Anh Duong, 'Intellectual Property Rights in TPP Agreement: Commitments and Implications for Viet Nam', discusses the implication of Chapter 18 of the TPP for Viet Nam. Nguyen emphasises that Viet Nam's aim to improve its IP system was closely associated with its attempt to integrate itself with the world economy. The first major push was the Viet Nam-US FTA in 2001, which incorporated comprehensive provisions on IPR. The second push was from Viet Nam's negotiation to join the WTO in 2007. To prepare for WTO accession, Viet Nam had to establish and enforce IP laws that meet the standards of the TRIPS Agreement. Despite these efforts in improving IPR protection, Nguyen admits that there is still much room for improvement, partly due to the weak enforcement of existing IP laws. The CPTPP may, therefore, lead to substantial additions to and changes in the IP laws of Viet Nam, even though some of the provisions that require a high level of IPR protection under the original TPP have been suspended under the CPTPP. Most important, Nguyen argues, Chapter 18 of the CPTPP imposed substantial requirements to strengthen the enforcement of IPR in Viet Nam.

Learning form the country's commitments in Chapter 18, Nguyen points out that meeting TPP's IP standards is neither simple nor easily fulfilled for Viet Nam. Nonetheless, the demand for long-term credible commitment can enhance investors' confidence in the implementing country and reduce the risk of inconsistency in IP management. This can translate favourably in terms of the impact on the performance of the Vietnamese economy. In conclusion, Nguyen recommends that Viet Nam should start preparing for implementing its commitments under Chapter 18 even before such commitments are yet to take effect or remain suspended. In particular, Viet Nam should dedicate efforts to regulatory preparations (ratification of a number of international agreements related to IPR protection and cooperation, amendment of existing laws on IPR protection and, most important, improvement of the enforcement structure for IPR protection) and capacity development (training for domestic enterprises, training for IP-related government authorities and enforcement agencies, and improvement of information and telecommunication technology capacity for IPR protection).

Chapter 6 by Poppy S. Winanti, 'Regulatory Framework on IPR in Indonesia: Overview and Preliminary Assessment on the TPP's IP Chapter', provides an overview of Indonesia's existing IPR laws, and on the basis of this, evaluates the country's domestic IPR situation in the context of TPP obligations. In Indonesia, a meaningful IP policy reform was pursued by the government only after the country became a WTO member and was obligated to implement the TRIPS Agreement. Unfortunately, Winanti argues, Indonesian society has not fully acknowledged the benefits of IPR protection. The number of residents' patent applications in Indonesia remains considerably lower than non-residents' patent applications. Indonesia ranked poorly in the Property Rights Index from 2010 to 2016, and it has been on the US Trade Representative's Priority Watch List from 2010 to 2017.

Winanti concludes that even though Indonesia's existing IPR laws are in compliance with the TRIPS Agreement, if Indonesia intends to join the TPP, it will have to reform parts of its existing IP laws to make it compatible with Chapter 18, which has a number of TRIPS-plus provisions. More precise, it will have to work on various areas of the domestic legal system of IPR protection, including the administration and cancellation procedures for geographical indications (GIs) (Articles 18.31 and 18.32), definition of inventions (Article 18.37.2), patent term adjustment (Article 18.46 and 18.48), protection of undisclosed test data for pharmaceuticals (Article 18.50) and biologics (Article 18.51), definition of new pharmaceutical product (Article 18.52), facilitation of cross-border acquisition of industrial designs (Article 18.56), enforcement of trade secret infringement by state owned enterprises (Article 18.78), and ratification of selected multilateral agreements on IPR protection (Article 18.7).

In light of their compatibility with Chapter 18 of the TPP, Winanti categorises the existing domestic IPR laws of Indonesia into three groups. The first category consists of those that are fully compliant with Chapter 18, the second is the TPP minus with minor revisions, and the third is the TPP minus with major revisions. Though revision of the second category will be beneficial to Indonesia, Winanti argues that it is uncertain whether the revision of the third category will benefit Indonesia. Moreover, amending national laws involves a long procedure so cannot be done within a short time.

Chapter 7 by Ramon L. Clarete, 'Access to Medicines and Plant Seeds: The Challenges the Philippines Faces with the TPP's Intellectual Property Rights Rules', takes stock of the changes that the Philippines may need to undertake to comply with the obligations of the TPP if it decides to accede to it. After briefly sketching the differences between the TRIPS-compliant domestic IPR laws of the Philippines and the provisions under Chapter 18, Clarete's chapter takes up two issues that may define the public acceptability of Chapter 18 of the TPP in the Philippines – access to medicines and plant patents.

First, by delaying the entry of generic drugs in the territory of its parties, the TPP is leaning more to the interests of innovator drug companies. Although nothing in the TPP can prevent the continued access of Filipinos to cheaper generic medicines that are locally available, the TPP would make users wait from 5 to 8 years before new generic medicines can become available.

Second, with respect to the TPP provisions on IPR, parties are allowed to choose the modality of protecting the intellectual property in plant technologies.

If the Philippines decides to accede to the TPP and it decides to use a *sui generis* system instead of patents to protect the rights of plant variety owners, it has to become a member of the UPOV 1991 Act. The treaty recognises an optional exception to the practice of farmers saving and using their own seeds. But there may be a clash if genetically modified plant varieties are open pollinated.

Chapter 8 by Jakkrit Kuanpoth, 'Intellectual Property Protection under the Trans-Pacific Partnership Agreement: From Thailand's Perspective', undertakes a regulatory impact analysis (RIA) to determine the potential impact of Chapter 18 of the TPP on Thailand's IPR laws and policies if it decides to join the TPP. After providing a brief overview of Thailand's IPR laws, Kuanpoth points out major TRIPS-plus provisions of Chapter 18 that may affect Thailand's IPR laws when it decides to join the TPP. They include a new use of known pharmaceutical products (Article 18.37.2), exclusivity protection over test data or other data of pharmaceuticals (Article 18.50) and biologics (Article 18.51), a requirement for a new party to join the UPOV 1991 Act on plant variety protection (Article 18.7.2), specific obligations on the administrative procedures for the protection or recognition of GIs (Article 18.31), legal remedies against circumvention of TPMs (Article 18.68), protection of RMI (Article 18.69), patent term adjustment (Article 18.46), and international cooperation (Article 18.13).

In conclusion, Kuanpoth expresses concern that joining the TPP may have a negative socio-economic impact on Thailand. In particular, the restrictions on local companies and their ability to use and produce new products have been a matter of concern in Thailand, as the growth of the Thai pharmaceutical industry is being slowed because of patent protection. The provisions of Chapter 18 may also increase the monopoly rights of patent holders and increase the prices of medicines, agricultural chemical products, and seeds. They will also have severe negative effects on the societal, cultural, and educational development of Thailand, particularly when the new copyright rules are introduced.

2.3. Part III – rules and regulations on SOEs

In the TPP agreement, Chapter 17 is said to be 'exploratory' given its effort to expand and deepen the multilateral trading rules to discipline the behaviour of both SOEs and government agencies in trade and investment. It requires SOEs to be independent economic units in the market and operate on a non-discriminatory basis; and it disciplines the support of government agencies to SOEs to ensure fairness and avoid any competition distortion effect.

Chapter 9 by Tsuyoshi Kawase and Masahito Ambashi, 'Disciplines on State-Owned Enterprises under the Trans-Pacific Partnership Agreement: Overview and Assessment', provides a thematic analysis of the SOE rules agreed in Chapter 17. Their chapter provides a comprehensive review of the major disciplines of SOEs stipulated by the TPP Agreement and a comparison with the current rules in the multilateral framework or other FTAs.

Kawase and Ambashi's work also considers the implications of signing the CPTPP agreement for the SOE rules after the US withdrawal from the TPP and attempts to provide guidance for prospective parties to meet the requirements upon their accession to the agreement. Kawase and Ambashi come to the conclusion that the TPP's disciplines on SOEs have various exceptions and may, therefore, be very limited in the scope of application. Despite its limited scope of application, one could still expect the SOE chapter to have a 'ground-breaking' effect in terms of improving the competitive environment in the Asia-Pacific region.

Chapter 10 by Vo Tri Thanh, 'TPP and State-Owned Enterprises in Viet Nam', provides an interpretation of the SOE chapter from an economic-legal perspective by comparing the related legal framework and other investment agreements in effect in Viet Nam. In particular, Vo highlights the key commitments to the TPP made by Viet Nam and those rules and regulations set by the TPP agreement anticipated to be the foundation of new global standards.

Vo believes that joining the TPP will give a boost to SOE reforms in Viet Nam. The direct impact on Viet Nam could be modest given the limited scope of the Agreement, while the indirect impact depends on whether the government will in fact adopt the TPP-standard rules it committed to. Vo suggests that TPP can be an external driving force to push forward domestic reform efforts, by minimising preferential treatment of SOEs; improving regulations on oversight, monitoring, evaluation, information disclosure, and transparency of SOEs; strictly enforcing budget constraints; and enhancing the institutional and technical capacity of the Vietnam Competition Authority.

Chapter 11 by Ramon L. Clarete, 'State Trading Rules in TPP: Implications for the Philippines', explores the implications of the rules for Philippine SOEs. Clarete finds that similar to what Vo has discovered in the case of Viet Nam, most SOEs in the Philippines are outside the scope of the TPP's rules because their activities do not actually affect international trade and investment or the revenues they generate from international trading are below the *de minimis* rule of the agreement. Indeed, although the government corporate sector in the Philippines is relatively large, only 13 out of over 100 SOEs are covered by the TPP rules. Clarete further illustrates why the TPP rules on SOEs alone will be insufficient to stimulate SOE reforms in the Philippines. In case of the National Food Authority, a better solution could be to combine them with the multilateral regulation on quantitative import restrictions in agriculture.

Chapter 12 by Maharani Hapsari, 'Disciplines on State Owned Enterprises in Indonesia vis-à-vis the Trans Pacific Partnership Agreement', gives an overview of the national regulatory framework governing Indonesian SOEs with reference to the TPP agreement. Hapsari's work shows gaps between the existing regulatory frameworks that govern SOEs in Indonesia and the normative vision that the TPP agreement introduces to discipline markets with a view to equalising the treatment received by SOEs and private enterprises. For Indonesia to put in place the SOE disciplines required by Chapter 17 of the TPP agreement, the country will have to combine domestic and international aspirations, especially in improving the availability, transparency, and accountability of public information on SOEs.

3. Implications for regional integration in ASEAN and East Asia

Some studies suggest that the success of mega FTAs could be a stepping stone towards multilateralism. For instance, WTO (2011) suggests that mega FTAs could 'work from the bottom' by multilateralising bilateral agreements while WTO could 'work from the top' to consolidate mega FTAs. But it is not an easy task to bring together several big arrangements, especially when considering the wide range of issues these arrangements contain. It will not be easy for mega FTAs to be either merged with others or for new participating countries to enrol. Newcomers need to negotiate with each individual current member state and reach agreements bilaterally, and the enforcement of treaties will require beyond-the-border actions. Some countries may not want to or have the capacity to join mega FTAs.

Alternatively, a more practical solution would be to squeeze out the topics that are largely common to mega FTAs and get the WTO involved in negotiations on specific issues and topics such as the government procurement agreement (GPA) and information technology agreement (ITA). This will require 'flexibility' on the part of the WTO in talks on new trade and trade-related issues, with a view to establishing a framework with a maximum degree of openness to facilitate the enrolment of new participants and the inclusion of new topic(s). The ambition here is to either make these agreements part of the comprehensive WTO rules, or at least pave the way for further negotiations. It is crucial for the two processes to learn from each other and eventually become complementary.

The effectiveness of this strategy relies on the involvement of developing countries in the rule-making of mega FTAs. Developing countries have as a group contributed half of the world gross domestic product, and they have outpaced developed countries in terms of exports in goods and services. The process of new rule-making needs developing countries' voices, particularly the emerging economies in Asia, otherwise the success of mega FTAs may actually increase the difficulties in returning to WTO negotiations.

In a nutshell, mega FTAs work on higher standards and higher quality. They require not only so-called at-the-border liberalisation (such as free trade in goods, trade in services, and foreign investment), but also beyond-the-border economic reforms or regulatory coherence in areas such as enforcing IPR protection, involving SOEs in international trade and investment, and regulating the digital economy. Accordingly, such agreements contain WTO-plus and WTO-extra provisions. The former refers to the deepening or extension of commitments that member states have already made at the multilateral level, whereas the latter refers to those new trade-related issues that are not currently covered or regulated by the WTO. Very often, those WTO-plus and WTO-extra provisions have some overlap with each other (Horn, Mavroidis, and Sapir, 2009).

Mega FTAs aim to develop an extensive set of rules and regulations in global economic governance. It is critical for developing countries to keep a close eye on these issues. Asian economies should be encouraged to become more deeply involved in the process of new rules setting as long as it does not go against or is incompatible with multilateral trade liberalisation. This would enable them to not only defend their interests and negotiate better terms in any agreement, but also contribute to a better and development-friendly world trading system.

The region has enough reasons to be confident in its roles in global governance. On one hand, Asia is already the world factory of manufactured goods. Its contribution to the efficiency of GVCs and the global economy should not be underestimated. On the other hand, the region hosts the world's largest potential market. It is predicted that by 2030, over two-thirds of the world's middle class will be in Asia, and the region will account for over 60 percent of the world's total middle-class consumption.

The consequent impact of mega FTAs on individual countries and regions may vary due to differences in the stages of development, the legal framework, the political system, and so on. First, mega FTAs will affect not only the regional trade order, but also the global trade order. Second, they tend to have a deep impact on both member and non-member states of the agreements. From a country's perspective, this requires more in-depth investigation of the related issues in the context of the general global tendency and each country's unique situation.

As for mega FTAs, Asian countries should at least observe the progress of negotiations and implementation of the agreements and follow up the issues that are under discussion or in fashion so to speak. For instance, reduction of non-tariff measures (NTMs) will be highlighted in the negotiations of mega FTAs. Generally speaking, the worldwide tariff rates are already very low or even zero for some products – 98 percent of traded goods that the TPP agreement covers are already or will be duty free. The issue of removing NTMs has been discussed in the WTO but has not seen much progress. Mega FTAs will make greater efforts to achieve reductions in NTMs.

Similarly, trade in services is an increasingly important part of the global economy. Global trade in services has been growing much faster than trade in goods since 2005. In 2015, 80 percent of US gross domestic product was generated by the service sector. Service exports reached US$716 billion, half as much as total goods exports. Despite the country's trade deficit in goods, there was a surplus of over US$200 billion for service trade in that year. Rules and regulations on trade in services in mega FTAs may complement those of the General Agreement on Trade in Services (GATS).

More important, those new trade issues, either WTO-plus or WTO-extra, such as those relating to IPR, SOEs, and the digital economy, need to be given greater attention.

As mega FTAs are re-levelling the playing field, it is important for Asian countries to understand what the new rules and regulations are that mega FTAs ask for, what is the 'gap' between the countries' current legal situation and market situation, and what kind of standards mega FTAs are trying to enforce.

For example, the beyond-the-border measures will be associated with social and economic adjustment costs. This will be sourced from the cross-border regulatory harmonisation and/or the mutual reorganisation of standards, and from connecting to the issues of current account balancing, public budget balancing, job displacement, and so on. The effective policy intervention calls for collaboration between the administrative and legislative agencies as well as cooperation amongst different government branches, particularly between foreign affairs departments and those in charge of domestic market regulation (Kimura and Chen, 2016).

Emerging Asian countries still need to be careful to avoid economic marginalisation. It does matter whether they will participate in the global governance as individuals or as a group that represents the 'third pillar' of the world economy (alongside North America and the European Union). In the long run, it will be a multipolar international system that can maximise the space of development, not only for small economies, but also for the big actors in the region, such as Japan and China.

In this regard, the Regional Comprehensive Economic Partnership (RCEP) has a special meaning for Asia. The RCEP is indeed part of Asian countries' efforts to collaborative explore regional governance avenues and should be seen as an extension of the construction of an integrated ASEAN community that provides the region with a platform, from which ASEAN Member States can act collectively on the global economic stage (Chen, 2016).

Note

1 Such as the limited sectoral coverage of reservation lists, the flexibility of modification, and the difficulties of identifying existing restrictions in the related domestic laws and regulations.

References

Chen, L. (2016), 'RCEP Is Not the Anti-TPP', *The Diplomat*, 3 December.

Horn, H., P.C. Mavroidis and A. Sapir (2009), 'Beyond the WTO? An Anatomy of EU and US Preferential Trade Agreements', *Bruegel Blueprint Series*, 7.

Kimura, F. and L. Chen (2016), 'Implications of Mega Free Trade Agreements for Asian Regional Integration and RCEP Negotiation', *ERIA Policy Brief* No. 2016–03.

WTO (2011), *The WTO and Preferential Trade Agreements: From Co-existence to Coherence (World Trade Report 2011)*. Geneva: World Trade Organization.

Part I

Rules and regulations on investment

1 Investment in the Trans-Pacific Partnership

Possible impacts on ASEAN member states

*Junji Nakagawa**

1. Introduction

This chapter analyses Chapter 9 of the Trans-Pacific Partnership (TPP) document titled 'Investment'.[1] Its main purpose is to clarify the obligations of the TPP parties on the liberalisation and protection of foreign investment so that member states of the Association of Southeast Asian Nations (ASEAN), which are parties to the TPP, may prepare domestic legal reforms to meet these obligations when the TPP enters into force. For ASEAN member states that are not parties to the TPP, this chapter will serve as a useful reference in considering what kind of domestic legal reforms will be needed when they join the TPP.

The United States (US), which initiated the negotiations on the TPP, intended to make the TPP 'a new kind of trade agreement for the 21st century',[2] with a high level of trade and investment liberalisation and a wide range of rules for streamlining trade and investment amongst the parties. The TPP investment chapter builds on the 2012 US Model Bilateral Investment Treaty (BIT),[3] and carefully calibrates balance between providing strong investor protections and preserving the government's ability to regulate in the public interest. It also promotes the liberalisation of foreign investment through the negative list approach, whereby each party liberalises foreign investment, as a rule, with the exceptions enumerated in its country-specific list of non-conforming measures. Accordingly, three stages of analysis are needed.

The first is the analysis of the general obligations as provided in Chapter 9. The second is the analysis of country-specific obligations with respect to liberalisation of investment, which are provided in country-specific lists of non-conforming measures. The third is a comparison of country-specific obligations and the existing restrictions on foreign investment of each member state. This chapter focuses on the first stage of analysis, leaving the second and third stages of analysis to separate country-specific surveys.

This chapter (i) conducts a comprehensive analysis of the general obligations as provided in Chapter 9; (ii) briefly explains the structure of Chapter 9 and compares it with that of the ASEAN Comprehensive Investment Agreement (ACIA),[4] as the latter can serve as a common framework of reference for ASEAN member states, regardless of whether they are parties to the TPP; (iii) analyses the substantive obligations of the TPP parties on the liberalisation and protection of investment, as provided under Section A of Chapter 9, and compares the provisions of Chapter 9 of the TPP with those of ACIA so that the potential impact of Chapter 9 on ASEAN member countries may be clarified; (iv) analyses the procedural obligations of TPP parties on the investor–state dispute settlement (ISDS), using ACIA as a reference to clarify the real impact of TPP Chapter 9 on ASEAN member countries with respect to the ISDS; and (v) explains the basic structure of the country-specific lists of non-conforming measures, and presents an analytical framework for the country-specific survey of investment liberalisation under the TPP.

2. Structure of the TPP investment chapter

2.1. Article headings of the TPP investment chapter

Chapter 9 of the TPP is composed of two sections consisting of 30 articles. Section A covers definitions of terms, scope, and substantive obligations regarding liberalisation and protection of investment. Section B provides for the procedure of the ISDS. Table 1.1 shows the article headings of Chapter 9, including annexes.

Table 1.1 Article headings of chapter 9, including annexes

Section A	
Article 9.1	Definitions
Article 9.2	Scope
Article 9.3	Relation to Other Chapters
Article 9.4	National Treatment
Article 9.5	Most-Favoured-Nation Treatment
Article 9.6	Minimum Standard of Treatment
Article 9.7	Treatment in Case of Armed Conflict or Civil Strife
Article 9.8	Expropriation and Compensation
Article 9.9	Transfers
Article 9.10	Performance Requirements
Article 9.11	Senior Management and Boards of Directors
Article 9.12	Non-conforming Measures
Article 9.13	Subrogation
Article 9.14	Special Formalities and Information Requirements
Article 9.15	Denial of Benefits
Article 9.16	Investment and Environmental, Health, and Other Regulatory Objectives
Article 9.17	Corporate Social Responsibility
Section B	*Investor–state dispute settlement*
Article 9.18	Consultation and Negotiation
Article 9.19	Submission of a Claim to Arbitration
Article 9.20	Consent of Each Party to Arbitration

Section B	*Investor–state dispute settlement*
Article 9.21	Conditions and Limitations on Consent of Each Party
Article 9.22	Selection of Arbitrators
Article 9.23	Conduct of the Arbitration
Article 9.24	Transparency of Arbitral Proceedings
Article 9.25	Governing Law
Article 9.26	Interpretation of Annexes
Article 9.27	Expert Reports
Article 9.28	Consolidation
Article 9.29	Awards
Article 9.30	Service of Documents

Annexes to Chapter 9	
Annex 9-A	Customary International Law
Annex 9-B	Expropriation
Annex 9-C	Expropriation Relating to Land
Annex 9-D	Service of Documents on a Party under Section B (Investor–State Dispute Settlement)
Annex 9-E	Transfers
Annex 9-F	DL600
Annex 9-G	Public Debt
Annex 9-H	No title (exceptions to the dispute settlement provisions under Section B, Investor-State Dispute Settlement, or Chapter 28, Dispute Settlement)
Annex 9-I	Non-conforming Measures Ratchet Mechanism
Annex 9-J	Submission of a Claim to Arbitration
Annex 9-K	Submission of Certain Claims for Three Years after Entry into Force
Annex 9-L	Investment Agreements

To elucidate on the legal impact of Chapter 9 of the TPP on ASEAN member states, this chapter compares Chapter 9 with the provisions of ACIA because the latter can serve as a common framework of reference for ASEAN member states. Tables 1.1 and 1.2 compare the article headings of Chapter 9 of the TPP and ACIA. Article headings of the US 2012 Model BIT are also listed to show their similarity with those of the TPP. Table 1.1 compares the general provisions and substantive obligations while Table 1.2 compares the procedures for an ISDS.

We may draw two observations from these tables. First, there are many similarities between the article headings of Chapter 9 of the TPP and ACIA. These similarities exist both in the general provisions and in the substantive obligations, and in the ISDS procedures. Second, an elaborate comparative analysis of these two documents is needed to clarify the real, legal impact of implementing Chapter 9 of the TPP amongst ASEAN member states. There may be differences in their scope and content – even if they use similar terms or have the same subject matter, such as 'national treatment' or 'submission of a claim to arbitration'.

Table 1.2 Comparison of the contents of chapter 9 of the TPP, ACIA, and the US US 2012 Model BIT

Part 1: General provisions and substantive obligations

Topic	TPP	ACIA	US 2012 Model BIT
Objectives		Article 1	
Guiding principles		Article 2	
Scope of application	Article 9.2	Article 3	Article 2
Definitions	Article 9.1	Article 4	Article 1
National treatment	Article 9.4	Article 5	Article 3
MFN treatment	Article 9.5	Article 6	Article 4
Minimum standard of treatment	Article 9.6	Article 11	Article 5
Treatment in case of armed conflict or civil strife	Article 9.7	Article 12	
Expropriation and compensation	Article 9.8	Article 14	Article 6
Transfers	Article 9.9	Article 13	Article 7
Performance requirements	Article 9.10	Article 7	Article 8
Senior management and board of directors	Article 9.11	Article 8	Article 9
Non-conforming measures	Article 9.12	Article 9	Article 14
Subrogation	Article 9.13	Article 15	Article 15
Special formalities and information requirements	Article 9.14	Article 20	Article 17
Denial of benefits	Article 9.15	Article 19	Articles 12, 13
Investment and environment, health, and other regulatory objectives	Article 9.16		
Corporate social responsibility	Article 9.17		
Measures to safeguard the balance-of-payments	Article 29.3	Article 16	
General exceptions		Article 17	
Security exceptions	Article 29.2	Article 18	Article 18
Transparency		Article 21	Articles 10, 11
Entry, temporary stay, and work of investors and key personnel		Article 22	
Promotion of investment		Article 24	
Facilitation of investment		Article 25	

Part 2: Investor–state dispute settlement

Topic	TPP	ACIA	US 2012 Model BIT
Consultation and negotiation	Article 9.18	Article 31	Article 23
Submission of a claim to arbitration	Article 9.19	Articles 32, 33	Article 24
Consent of each party to arbitration	Article 9.20		Article 25
Conditions and limitations on consent of each party	Article 9.21	Article 34	Article 26
Selection of arbitrators	Article 9.22	Article 35	Article 27
Conduct of the arbitration	Article 9.23	Article 36	Article 28
Transparency of arbitral proceedings	Article 9.24	Article 39	Article 29
Governing law	Article 9.25	Article 40	Article 30
Interpretation of annexes	Article 9.26		Article 31
Expert reports	Article 9.27	Article 38	Article 32
Consolidation	Article 9.28	Article 37	Article 33
Awards	Article 9.29	Article 41	Article 34
Service of documents	Article 9.30		Article 36

Note:
ACIA = ASEAN Comprehensive Investment Agreement
BIT = US Model Bilateral Investment Treaty
TPP = Trans-Pacific Partnership

Source: Author.

2.2. *Annexes to Chapter 9*

Chapter 9 has 12 annexes. Some of these annexes complement the texts. For instance, Annex 9-B provides details on the substantive obligations on expropriation (Article 9.8) for better understanding of the parties.[5] The others provide the country-specific exceptions or special rules. For instance, Annex 9-C provides the exceptions to the obligations under Article 9.8 that are applicable to Singapore and Viet Nam on expropriation relating to land. In conducting an elaborate analysis of Chapter 9, the author considered all the annexes. Table 1.3 shows the list of the annexes.

2.3. *Liberalisation commitments*

TPP Annexes I, II, and III combine the list of commitments of each party to the TPP regarding the liberalisation of investment. Annex I presents the existing restrictions of each party that may not be strengthened in the future, or imposed restrictions with ratcheting obligations.[6] Annex II presents the existing restrictions of each party that may be strengthened in the future, or imposed restrictions without ratcheting obligations. Annex III presents the existing restrictions of each party in the financial services sector, including both provisions – with and without ratcheting obligations.

3. Liberalisation and protection of investment: substantive rules of the TPP investment chapter

Section A of Chapter 9 covers the general provisions and substantive obligations in the TPP. The following subsections analyse the major provisions of Section A.

Table 1.3 Annexes to chapter 9 of the TPP agreement

Annex 9-A	Customary International Law
Annex 9-B	Expropriation
Annex 9-C	Expropriating Relating to Land
Annex 9-D	Service of Documents on a Party under Section B (Investor–State Dispute Settlement)
Annex 9-E	Transfers
Annex 9-F	DL600
Annex 9-G	Public Debt
Annex 9-H	No title (exceptions to the dispute settlement provisions under Section B, Investor-State Dispute Settlement, or Chapter 28, Dispute Settlement)
Annex 9-I	Non-conforming Measures Ratchet Mechanism
Annex 9-J	Submission of a Claim to Arbitration
Annex 9-K	Submission of Certain Claims for Three Years after Entry into Force
Annex 9-L	Investment Agreements

Source: Author.

3.1. Scope

Article 9.2 provides for the scope of Chapter 9. It applies to measures adopted and maintained by a party relating to (i) investors of another party and (ii) covered investments (Article 9.2.1). Article 9.1 defines the following terms:

- **Investor of a Party** means a Party, or a national or an enterprise of a Party, that attempts to make, is making, or has made an investment in the territory of another Party; and
- **Covered investment** means, with respect to a Party, an investment in its territory of an investor of another Party in existence as of the date of entry into force of this Agreement for those Parties or established, acquired, or expanded thereafter.

To clarify the scope of these terms, we must refer to the definition of 'investment' under Chapter 9. Article 9.1 defines 'investment' as follows:

- **Investment** means every asset that an investor owns or controls, directly or indirectly, that has the characteristics of an investment, including such characteristics as the commitment of capital or other resources, the expectation of gain or profit, or the assumption of risk.

Although this is a comprehensive definition, it serves as a useful reference as it points out three characteristics of an investment, namely, (i) the commitment of capital or other resources, (ii) the expectation of gain or profit, and (iii) the assumption of risk. The definition of 'investment' in ACIA is almost identical to that of Chapter 9. Article 4(c) of ACIA defines investment as 'every kind of asset, owned or controlled, by an investor', and footnote 2 thereto clarifies that where an asset lacks the characteristics of an investment, that asset is not an investment regardless of the forms it may take. It then explains the characteristics of an investment as 'the commitment of capital, the expectation of gain or profit, or the assumption of risk'. We may, therefore, conclude that the TPP and ACIA adopt the same comprehensive definition of 'investment'.

To illustrate the term, Article 9.1 of the TPP enumerates examples of an investment. It must be noted that this is an illustrative list and it allows for other forms of investment such as

1 an enterprise;
2 shares, stocks, and other forms of equity participation in an enterprise;
3 bonds, debentures, other debt instruments and loans;
4 futures, options, and other derivatives;
5 turnkey, construction, management, production, concession, revenue-sharing, and other similar contracts;
6 intellectual property rights;
7 licences, authorisations, permits, and similar rights conferred pursuant to the party's law; and
8 other tangible or intangible, movable or immovable property, and related property rights, such as leases, mortgages, liens, and pledges.[7]

Article 9.2.2 provides for the personal scope of 'measures' covered by Chapter 9. A party's obligations under Chapter 9 shall apply to measures adopted or maintained by the central, regional, or local governments or authorities of that party (Article 9.2.2[a]). Measures adopted or maintained by any person, when it exercises any government authority delegated to it by central, regional, or local governments or authorities are also within the scope of Chapter 9 (Article 9.2.2[b]). ACIA provides for the same personal scope of 'measures' (Article 4[f] [i] and [ii]).

3.2. National treatment

Article 9.4 contains provisions that relate to national treatment. Each party shall accord to investors of another party treatment no less favourable than what it accords, in similar circumstances, to its own investors regarding the *establishment*, *acquisition*, expansion, management, conduct, operation, and sale or other disposition of investments in its territory (italics provided by the author, see Article 9.4.1). The same treatment shall be accorded to covered investments as well (Article 9.4.2). Article 5 of ACIA on national treatment adopts an almost identical language.[8] This means that both treaties belong to a so-called pre-establishment model (Jouvin-Bret, 2008, p. 13), whereby they grant foreign investors a positive right to national treatment not only once the investment has been established but also on admission, entry, and establishment of the investment.

Essentially, under this model, each host state accepts a limit on its sovereign right to regulate the inflow of foreign investment. However, this is subject to the right of host states to adopt or maintain exceptions to this general commitment. Thus, the TPP and ACIA include country-specific lists of exceptions (negative lists) to national treatment (see section on 'Liberalisation Commitments under the Country-Specific Schedules of Non-conforming Measures)'.

A unique provision is found in footnote 14 to Chapter 9 on 'like circumstances'. It states that the treatment accorded in similar circumstances under Article 9.4 or Article 9.5 (Most-Favoured-Nation Treatment) depends on the totality of the circumstances. This includes the relevant treatment that distinguishes between investors or investments based on legitimate public welfare objectives. This footnote implies that a party to the TPP may accord a less favourable treatment to investors of another party based on legitimate public welfare objectives, even when such treatment has not been listed on its negative list. There is no similar footnote in ACIA, which nonetheless contains Article 17 (General Exceptions), where it states that an ASEAN member state may adopt or enforce measures that would constitute a violation of Article 5 (National Treatment) if this is necessary to pursue public policy objectives, such as protection of public morals and protection of human, animal, or plant life or health. The only difference is that footnote 14 to Chapter 9 provides for differential treatment based on legitimate public welfare objectives, without specifying what such objectives may be, whereas Article 17 of the ACIA enumerates a limited number of exceptions to Article 5. Whether this difference will result in substantive difference in practice is not clear.

3.3. Most-favoured-nation treatment

Article 9.5 provides for a most-favoured-nation (MFN) treatment. Like Article 9.4 on national treatment, this applies at both the establishment and post-establishment stages. 'Each Party shall accord to investors of Another Party treatment no less favourable than that it accords, in like circumstances, to investors of any other Party or of any non-Party with respect to the *establishment*, *acquisition*, expansion, management, conduct, operation, and sale or other disposition of investments in its territory' (italics provided by the author, see Article 9.5.1). The same treatment shall be accorded to covered investments as well (Article 9.5.2). Article 6 of ACIA on MFN treatment adopts an almost identical language.[9] Like Article 9.4 on national treatment, both the TPP and ACIA allow exceptions to this requirement, which are enumerated in the country-specific negative lists (see Section 5).

It must be noted that the MFN treatment under Article 9.5 of the TPP allows a party to accord more favourable treatment to investors or covered investment of another party than what is accorded under the TPP when such treatment is accorded under a treaty[10] with a third party, both at present or in the future. This rule also applies to MFN treatment under Article 6 of ACIA.[11] However, Article 9.5.3 provides that MFN treatment not encompass international dispute settlement procedures or mechanisms, such as those included in Section B of Chapter 9 (Investor–State Dispute Settlement). This precludes a possibility of 'importing' a more favourable ISDS settlement procedure, such as the rules relating to dispute settlement *ratione temporis* (temporal coverage, retrospective application) or *ratione materiae* (subject matter coverage), that will be provided under a treaty that a TPP party will conclude in the future. The MFN treatment, therefore, applies only to substantive rules, not to procedural rules. The same principle applies for ACIA.[12]

3.4. Minimum standard of treatment

Article 9.6 provides for the so-called minimum standard of treatment under customary international law. Article 9.6.1 states that '(e)ach Party shall accord to covered investments treatment in accordance with applicable customary international law principles, including *fair and equitable treatment* and *full protection and security*'.

An obligation to accord fair and equitable treatment (FET) to foreigners and their property began to appear in US treaties on friendship, commerce, and navigation in the late 1940s.[13] The specific obligation to accord FET to foreign property was then included in the 1959 Abs-Shawcross Draft Convention on Investments Abroad[14] and in the 1967 Draft Convention on the Protection of Foreign Property of the Organisation for Economic Co-operation and Development (OECD).[15] From these draft international instruments, the obligation passed into the model bilateral investment treaties (BITs) of developed countries. The obligation to accord FET is now contained in most investment treaties.[16]

Before 2000, however, no publicly available arbitral award applied the FET standard. Since 2000, investors alleged a breach of the FET standard in almost every claim brought under an investment treaty. The popularity of the FET standard can be explained by its two characteristics: (i) a government may breach the standard even if a foreign investment is treated as well or better than local investment, and (ii) a broad range of governmental measures can be challenged for failure to meet the standard.[17] Hence, to counter this trend of frequently resorting to the FET standard in ISDS, recent investment treaties, notably US treaties, adopted a narrow definition of the standard. The TPP follows this practice.

First, Article 9.6.2 provides that the FET standard under Article 9.6.1 does not create additional substantive rights beyond those provided by the customary international law minimum standard of treatment of aliens.[18] Second, Article 9.6.2 adds explanations of the terms 'fair and equitable treatment' and 'full protection and security', as follows:

i   'fair and equitable treatment' includes the obligation not to deny justice in criminal, civil, or administrative adjudicatory proceedings in accordance with the principle of due process embodied in the principal legal systems of the world; and
ii 'full protection and security' requires each party to provide the level of police protection required under customary international law.

Third, Articles 9.6.3 to 9.6.5 provide for additional clarifications to restrict the application of the FET standard, as follows:

i   9.6.3 A determination that there has been a breach of another provision of this Agreement, or of a separate international agreement, does not establish that there has been a breach of this Article.
ii 9.6.4 For greater certainty, the mere fact that a Party takes or fails to take an action that may be inconsistent with an investor's expectations does not constitute a breach of this Article, even if there is loss or damage to the covered investment as a result.
iii 9.6.5 For greater certainty, the mere fact that a subsidy or grant has not been issued, renewed or maintained, or has been modified or reduced, by a Party, does not constitute a breach of this Article, even if there is loss or damage to the covered investment as a result.

While provisions like Article 9.6.3 are found in many of today's investment treaties,[19] Articles 9.6.4 and 9.6.5 are rare provisions. These intend to circumscribe the possibility of applying the FET standard in ISDS procedures beyond those instances strictly defined under this article. Specifically, Article 9.6.4 reflects the investor's *legitimate* expectation as an element of the FET standard,[20] and emphasises that merely failing to meet an investor's expectation does not constitute a violation of the FET standard. Article 9.6.5 reflects the recent surge of investment arbitration cases challenging the reform of host states' subsidies on renewable energies,[21] and clarifies that such subsidy reform does not *per se* constitute a breach of the FET standard.

Compared with these detailed provisions of Chapter 9, the provisions of the ACIA on minimum standard of treatment are less extensive, but its contents are much the same as those in Chapter 9. First, Article 11.1 of the ACIA is almost identical to Article 9.6.1 of Chapter 9.[22] Second, Articles 11.2(a) and (b) are almost identical to Articles 9.6.2(a) and (b) of Chapter 9.[23] Third, Article 11.3 is almost identical to Article 9.6.3 of Chapter 9.[24] However, ACIA does not contain provisions that correspond to Articles 9.6.4 and 9.6.5. Accordingly, Articles 9.6.4 and 9.6.5 should be regarded as 'ACIA plus' provisions of the TPP investment chapter.

3.5. Treatment in case of armed conflict or civil strife

Article 9.7 requires each party to accord national treatment and MFN treatment to investors of another party and to covered investments on the measures it adopts or maintains that relate to losses suffered by investment in its territory owing to armed conflict or civil strife.

Under customary international law, damage to the alien during armed conflict or civil strife has long preoccupied arbitral tribunals. Emerging from these cases is the principle of non-responsibility of the host state. However, this principle is qualified by a duty of the host state to exercise due diligence, that is, to use the police and military forces to protect the interests of the alien to the extent feasible and practicable under the circumstances.[25] When a host state finds itself in a situation that makes it impossible to perform the duty of due diligence, the principle of *force majeure* may apply. This is reflected in Article 23.1 of the International Law Commission Articles on State Responsibility, as follows:

> The wrongfulness of an act of a State not in conformity with an international obligation of that State is precluded if the act is due to force majeure, that is the occurrence of an irresistible force or of an unforeseen event, beyond the control of the State, making it materially impossible in the circumstances to perform the obligation.[26]

In many investment treaties concluded by European countries, however, the parties decided not to include the principle of *force majeure*, though they tacitly accept the applicability of the principle. On the other hand, US treaty practice has been more inclined to address the principle explicitly.[27] What most European and US treaties have in common is that they require national treatment and MFN treatment in compensation schemes adopted *voluntarily* by the host state to deal with the consequences of the armed conflict or civil strife,[28] and Article 9.7 of the TPP followed this treaty practice. It must be noted, therefore, that this provision does not require the payment of compensation for losses or damages caused by armed conflict or civil strife. It is up to the host state to decide whether to pay compensation in such cases, based on its deliberation of the circumstances according to the principle of *force majeure*. However, if it decides to pay compensation, Article 9.7 requires the host state to make the payment according to the principles of national treatment and MFN treatment. A similar requirement is provided in ACIA.[29]

Article 9.7.2 of the TPP provides for two exceptions to the general principle that the host state may voluntarily decide whether to pay compensation in case of armed conflict or civil strife. It requires a party to pay compensation if an investor of another party suffers a loss in the territory of the former resulting from the following:

i   Requisitioning of its covered investment or part thereof by the former's forces or authorities; or
ii Destruction of its covered investment or part thereof by the former's forces or authorities, which was not required nor a necessity during that situation.

As these exceptions are not provided by ACIA, this is another 'ACIA plus' provision of the TPP investment chapter.

3.6. Expropriation and compensation

Article 9.8 provides for expropriation and compensation. It is based on the classical requirements for a lawful expropriation under customary international law, that is, a public purpose; non-discrimination; and prompt, adequate, and effective compensation,[30] or the so-called Hull rule. It is also based on the principles of due process that some treaties explicitly require regarding the procedure of expropriation.[31] Accordingly, Article 9.8.1 requires that expropriation of a covered investment shall be (i) for a public purpose; (ii) in a non-discriminatory manner; (iii) upon payment of prompt, adequate, and effective compensation; and (iv) in accordance with due process of law. Article 14.1 of ACIA provides for almost identical requirements.[32] Note that these four requirements are applied cumulatively.

Of the four requirements that must be met for an expropriation to be considered legal, the principle of compensation has been by far the most controversial. Accordingly, many investment treaties provided for additional rules to elaborate on the principle of compensation. The TPP and ACIA followed this practice. Article 9.8.2 provides that compensation shall (i) be paid without delay, (ii) be equivalent to the fair market value of the expropriated investment immediately before the expropriation took place, (iii) do not reflect any change in value occurring because the intended expropriation had become known earlier, and (iv) be fully realisable and freely transferable. Article 14.2 of ACIA provides for almost identical requirements.[33] Article 9.8.3 provides for the payment of interest in case of delay, such that the compensation shall be no less than the fair market value on the date of expropriation plus interest at a commercially reasonable rate for the currency, if the fair market value is denominated in a freely usable currency. Article 9.8.4 provides for a similar requirement when the fair market value is denominated in a currency that is not freely usable. Similar requirements are provided under Articles 14.3 and 14.4 of ACIA, though the latter does not explicitly require the payment of interest at commercially reasonable rate.[34]

A question of prime importance is the legal status of the regulatory measures of the host state under the rules of indirect expropriation. Emphasis on the host state's sovereignty supports the argument that the investor should not expect compensation for a regulatory measure of the host state, particularly when such measure is taken in pursuit of public welfare objectives. A current prevailing treaty practice is to elaborate rules to distinguish legitimate regulatory measures of the host state from indirect expropriation that must be compensated.[35] The TPP and ACIA follow this practice.

First, Article 9.8.5 provides for a specific case of regulatory measure as exempt from the payment of compensation, that is, the issuance of compulsory licences in relation to intellectual property rights in accordance with Chapter 18 (Intellectual Property) and the TRIPS Agreement. Article 14.5 of ACIA provides for a similar exemption.[36]

Second, Annex 9-B to Chapter 9 confirms the shared understanding of the TPP parties on expropriation, including indirect expropriation. Section 3 refers to indirect expropriation, in cases where an action or series of actions by a party has an effect that is equivalent to direct expropriation without the formal transfer of title or outright seizure. The ensuing provision, which is almost identical to Section 3 of Annex B to the 2012 US Model BIT, elaborates conditions for determining indirect expropriation, as follows:

a   The determination of whether an action or series of actions by a Party, in a specific fact situation, constitutes an indirect expropriation, requires a case-by-case, fact-based inquiry that considers, among other factors:

  i   The economic impact of the government action, although the fact that an action or series of actions by a Party has an adverse effect on the economic value of an investment, standing alone, does not establish that an indirect expropriation has occurred;
  ii   The extent to which the government action interferes with distinct, reasonable investment-based expectations; and
  iii The character of the government action.

b   Non-discriminatory regulatory actions by a Party that are designed and applied to protect legitimate public welfare objectives, such as public health, safety, and the environment, do not constitute indirect expropriation, except in rare circumstances.

As Sections 3 and 4 of Annex 2 to ACIA provide for almost identical conditions for determining indirect expropriation, there is no 'ACIA plus' in the TPP investment chapter.

3.7. Transfers

The TPP contains liberal rules on the transfer of funds by investors that are essentially like those of ACIA. Article 9.9.1 provides that each party shall permit *all transfers* relating to a covered investment – to be made freely and without delay into and out of its territory. Article 13.1 of ACIA is almost identical to this provision. Likewise, both articles list examples of such transfers, which are also almost identical. What follows are the types of transfers enumerated under Article 9.9.1. This is an illustrative list and other forms of transfer may be allowed under Article 9.9.1.

i   Contributions to capital;
ii   Profits, dividends, interest, capital gains, royalty payments, management fees, technical assistance fees, and other fees;
iii Proceeds from the sale of all or any part of the covered investment or from the partial or complete liquidation of the covered investment;
iv   Payments made under a contract, including a loan agreement;
v   Payments made pursuant to Article 9.7 (Treatment in Case of Armed Conflict or Civil Strife) and Article 9.8 (Expropriation and Compensation); and
vi   Payments arising out of a dispute.

Article 9.9.2 deals with convertibility and exchange rates. It prescribes that each party permit transfers that relate to a covered investment – to be made freely in a usable currency at the market exchange rate prevailing at the time of transfer. An identical rule is provided under Article 13.2 of ACIA.

Article 9.9.3 provides for a specific type of transfer that must also be permitted, such as returns in kind. It prescribes that each party permit returns in kind on a covered investment, to be done as authorised or specified in a written agreement between the party and a covered investment or an investor of another party. As no provision in ACIA corresponds to this, this should be classified as 'ACIA plus'.

Freedom of transfer is not an absolute right. Article 9.9.4 provides for circumstances where the host state may prevent or delay a transfer when this applies to the laws on (i) bankruptcy, insolvency, or the protection of the rights of creditors; (ii) issuing, trading, or dealing in securities, futures, options, or derivatives; (iii) criminal or penal offences; (iv) financial reporting or record keeping of transfers when necessary to assist law enforcement or financial regulatory authorities; or (v) ensuring compliance with orders or judgements in judicial or administrative proceedings. Footnote 22 in Chapter 9 adds another circumstance for the host state to restrict a transfer. This is the application of laws relating to its social security, public retirement, or compulsory savings programmes. Article 13.3 of ACIA contains an almost identical list.

A notable difference exists between the TPP and ACIA on the restriction of transfer during periods of severe balance-of-payments crises, external financial difficulties, or other exceptional circumstances. Article 13.4(c) of ACIA provides that a member state may impose restrictions on any capital transactions in exceptional circumstances, such as when movements of capital may cause, or threaten to cause, serious economic or financial disturbances in the host member state.[37] On the other hand, the TPP has no such provision. In Chapter 29 (Exceptions), Articles 29.3.1 and 29.3.2 provide for temporary safeguard measures in the event of serious balance-of-payments and external financial difficulties and threats thereof, but Article 29.3.4 provides that measures referred to in these paragraphs shall not apply to payments or transfers relating to foreign direct investment. In Chapter 11 (Financial Services), Article 11.11.3 provides that, despite Article 9.9 (Transfers), a party may prevent or limit transfers by a financial institution or cross-border financial service supplier through prudential measures,[38] but this does not cover restriction of transfers to *investors or covered investments in general, in exceptional circumstances.* Judging from these provisions, we conclude that the TPP does not allow parties to restrict transfers even in exceptional circumstances.[39] This liberal stance towards transfers is an important 'ACIA plus' of the TPP.

3.8. Prohibition of performance requirements

Performance requirements refer to obligations imposed by the host state on the investor to conduct its business in a prescribed manner. While the World Trade Organization (WTO) Agreement on Trade-Related Investment Measures (TRIMs) prohibits performance requirements that violate the principle of national treatment (General Agreement on Tariffs and Trade [GATT] Article III) and the principle of the prohibition of quantitative restrictions (GATT Article XI), investment treaties, notably the US BITs, prohibit a wider range of performance requirements.[40] The TPP follows this practice. It sets out two types of performance requirements that are prescribed under the TPP.

The first type refers to *general* prohibition of performance requirements (Article 9.10.1). The second type refers to *conditional* prohibition of performance requirements, where performance requirements are prohibited even as a precondition to the receipt of an advantage that an investor enjoy (Article 9.10.2). Normally, the first type prohibits a wider range of performance requirements than the second type. Table 1.4 compares the first type of prohibition of performance requirements under the TPP and the WTO TRIMs Agreement. As Article 7.1 of ACIA incorporates the TRIMs Agreement, *mutatis mutandis*, the difference between the TPP and the TRIMs Agreement is the 'ACIA plus' of the TPP on the prohibition of performance requirements.

Article 9.10.2 enumerates four types of conditional prohibition of performance requirements. These are to (i) achieve a given level or percentage of domestic content; (ii) purchase, use, or accord a preference to goods produced in its territory, or to purchase goods from persons in its territory; (iii) relate in any way the volume or value of imports to the volume or value of exports or to the amount of foreign exchange inflows associated with the investment; or (iv) restrict the sale of goods or services in its territory that the investment produces or supplies by relating those sales in any way to the volume or value of its exports or foreign exchange earnings. These four performance requirements correspond to those listed under the WTO TRIMs Agreement and ACIA, except for (iv) on services.[41] On the basis of these comparisons, there is no significant 'ACIA plus' on conditional prohibition of performance requirements.

Table 1.4 Prohibition of performance requirements under the TPP and the WTO TRIMs

Performance requirements prohibited under Article 9.10.1 of the TPP	TPP	TRIMs
(a) To export a given level or percentage of goods	Yes	Yes
(a) To export a given level or percentage of services	Yes	No
(b) To achieve a given level or percentage of domestic content	Yes	Yes
(c) To purchase, use, or accord a preference to goods produced in its territory, or to purchase goods from persons in its territory	Yes	Yes
(d) To relate in any way the volume or value of imports to the volume or value of exports or to the amount of foreign exchange inflows associated with the investment	Yes	Yes
(e) To restrict sales of goods in its territory that the investment produces by relating those sales in any way to the volume or value of its exports or foreign exchange earnings	Yes	Yes
(e) To restrict sales of services in its territory that the investment supplies by relating those sales in any way to the volume or value of its exports or foreign exchange earnings	Yes	No
(f) To transfer a particular technology, a production process, or other proprietary knowledge to a person in its territory	Yes	No
(g) To supply exclusively from the territory of the party the goods that the investment produces or the services that it supplies to a specific regional market or to the world market	Yes	No
(h)(i) To purchase, use, or accord a preference to, in its territory, technology of the party or of a person of the party	Yes	No
(h)(ii) To prevent the purchase or use of, or to accord preference to, in its territory, a particular technology	Yes	No
(i)(i) To adopt a given rate or amount of royalty under a licence contract	Yes	No
(i)(ii) To adopt a given duration of the term of a licence contract	Yes	No

Note:
TPP = Trans-Pacific Partnership
TRIMs = Trade-Related Investment Measures
WTO = World Trade Organization

Source: Author.

While the TPP has a wide range of prohibition in performance requirements, Article 9.10.3 sets out several instances where a host state may impose specific categories of performance requirements, either generally or conditionally (Table 1.5). Thus, to estimate the impact of the TPP on the prohibition of performance requirements on its domestic legal system, a TPP party shall consider the combined effects of Articles 9.10.1, 9.10.2, and 9.10.3.

Finally, Articles 9.10.4 to 9.10.6 set out three conditions on the prohibition of performance requirements. First, a party may impose requirements to employ or train workers in its territory if such employment or training does not require the transfer of a particular technology, production process, or other proprietary knowledge to a person in its territory (Article 9.10.4). Second, the prohibition of performance requirements under Articles 9.10.1 and 9.10.2 is exclusive,

Table 1.5 Allowable performance requirements under Article 9.10.3 of the TPP

(a) Allowable conditional requirements	To locate production, supply a service, train or employ workers, construct or expand particular facilities, or carry out research and development, in its territory.
(b) Allowable requirements relating to technology and licensing	(i) If a party authorises the use of an intellectual property right in accordance with Article 31 of the TRIPS Agreement, or to measures requiring the disclosure of proprietary information that fall within the scope of, and are consistent with, Article 39 of the TRIPS Agreement (ii) If the requirement is imposed or the commitment or undertaking is enforced by a court, administrative tribunal, or competition authority to remedy a practice determined after judicial or administrative process to be anticompetitive under the party's competition law
(c) Allowable requirements relating to licensing	If it is imposed or the commitment or undertaking is enforced by a tribunal as equitable remuneration under the party's copyright laws
(d) Allowable requirements relating to local content, local purchase, and technology transfer	(i) Measures that are necessary to secure compliance with law and regulations that are consistent with the TPP (ii) Measures that are necessary to protect human, animal, or plant life or health (iii) Measures related to the conservation of living or non- living exhaustible natural resources
(e) Allowable requirements relating to export performance, local content, and local purchase	Qualification requirements for goods or services with respect to export promotion and foreign aid programmes
(f) Allowable requirements relating to local content, local purchase, supply location, technology, and licensing	Requirements with respect to government procurement
(g) Allowable conditional requirements relating to export performance and local content	Requirements imposed by an importing party relating to the content of goods necessary to qualify for preferential tariffs or preferential quotas
(h) Allowable requirements relating to technology and licensing	Measures to protect legitimate public welfare objectives, provided that such measures are not applied in an arbitrary or unjustifiable manner, or in a manner that constitute a disguised restriction on international trade or investment

Note:
TPP = Trans-Pacific Partnership
TRIPS = Trade-Related Aspects of Intellectual Property Rights

Source: Author.

allowing a party to employ any requirements that are not enumerated there (Article 9.10.5). Third, Article 9.10 does not apply to requirements between private parties (Article 9.10.6). As these provisions confirm the admissibility of several types of requirements, there is no 'ACIA plus' in them.

3.9. Senior management and board of directors

Article 9.11 relates to a specific category of performance requirement, which is the nationality of senior management staff and board members. Article 9.11.1 prohibits a party from requiring a senior manager who is a natural-born person of a particular nation to be appointed within an enterprise that is considered a 'covered investment'. On the other hand, Article 9.11.2 allows a party to require that the majority of the board of directors, or any committee thereof, of an enterprise of that party that is a covered investment, be of a particular nationality or resident in the territory of the party, if that requirement does not materially impair the ability of the investor to exercise control over its investment. As Articles 8.1 and 8.2 of ACIA set out rules identical to Articles 9.11.1 and 9.11.2, respectively, there is no 'ACIA plus' on this.

3.10. Special formalities and information requirements

Another category of performance requirements is on specific legal formalities where a host state requires investors to meet in connection with investments and disclose information. Articles 9.14.1 and 9.14.2 set out rules on them.

Article 9.14.1 allows a party to require special formalities in connection with a covered investment, such as a residency requirement for registration, or that a covered investment is legally constituted under the laws of the party.[42] Article 9.14.2 allows a party to require an investor of another party or its covered investment to provide information concerning that investment solely for information or statistical purposes. At the same time, it requires the party to protect confidential information from any disclosure that would prejudice the competitive position of the investor or the covered investment. Finally, as a rule, a party may obtain or disclose information for the equitable and good faith application of its law.

Article 20 of ACIA sets out the same rules as Article 9.14; there is, therefore, no 'ACIA plus' on this.

3.11. Subrogation

Modern investment treaties provide for subrogation of the claims of the foreign investor in the home state. This enables the home state to take over the investor's claims against the host state after paying the claims through the investment insurance or guarantee schemes run by the home state.[43] Article 9.13 provides for this, as follows:

> If a Party, or any agency, institution, statutory body or corporation designated by the Party, makes a payment to an investor of the Party under a

guarantee, a contract of insurance or other form of indemnity that it has entered into with respect to a covered investment, the other Party in whose territory the covered investment was made shall recognise the subrogation or transfer of any rights the investor would have possessed under this Chapter with respect to the covered investment but for the subrogation, and the investor shall be precluded from pursuing these rights to the extent of the subrogation.

Article 15 of ACIA provides for subrogation. Although the language of Article 15 is different from that of Article 9.13 of the TPP, there is no 'ACIA plus' in the latter, as both articles have the same substantive requirement on subrogation.

3.12. *Denial of benefits*

States have devised methods to counteract strategies of foreign investors that seek the protection of particular investment treaties by acquiring a favourable nationality. One such method is the insertion of a so-called denial of benefits clause in the investment treaty. Under such a clause, states reserve the right to deny the benefits of the treaty to a company incorporated in a state but with no economic connection to that state.[44] Article 9.15 is a case in point. Under Article 9.15.1, a party may deny the benefits of Chapter 9 to an investor of another party that is an enterprise of that other party and to investments of that investor if the enterprise (i) is owned or controlled by a person of a non-party or of the denying party,[45] and (ii) has no substantial business activities in the territory of any party other than the denying party. Article 19.1(a) and (b) of the ACIA set out the same rule as Article 9.15.1.

Another case of denial of benefits occurs when the denying party adopts or maintains measures that prohibit transactions with the non-party, and a person of that non-party owns or controls an enterprise of another party to circumvent those measures. A typical case is a circumvention of economic sanction by a person of the targeted non-party. Article 9.15.2 refers to that case. As Article 19 of ACIA does not refer to this case, this is an 'ACIA plus' provision.

On the other hand, Article 19 of ACIA refers to two cases where the TPP does not consider a denial of benefits. First is when the denying party does not maintain diplomatic relations with the non-member state to which the person belongs (Article 19.1[c]). Second is when the investor has made an investment that breached the domestic laws of the denying member state, which reserves areas of investment for natural or juridical persons of the denying member state (Article 19.2). These should be regarded as 'ACIA minuses' of the TPP.

3.13. *General exceptions and security exceptions*

Article 17 of ACIA provides for general exceptions to the substantive obligations that member states agree to uphold, which are like those enumerated under Article XX of the GATT 1994.[46] On the other hand, Chapter 9 of the TPP does not contain the provisions of general exceptions. It only states in Article 9.16

that '(n)othing in this Chapter shall be construed to prevent a Party from adopting, maintaining or enforcing any measure *otherwise consistent with this Chapter* that it considers appropriate to ensure that investment activity in its territory is undertaken in a manner sensitive to environmental, health or other regulatory objectives'. But this does not provide for any exceptions to Chapter 9. It is worth noting that the lack of general exceptions, therefore, could be regarded as an 'ACIA minus' of the TPP investment chapter.

In what are regarded as security exceptions, Article 29.2 applies to the TPP *as a whole* including Chapter 9. This article provides that nothing in the agreement shall be construed to (i) require a party to furnish or allow access to any information if the disclosure of it is determined to be contrary to its essential security interests, or (ii) preclude a party from applying measures that it considers necessary for the fulfilment of its obligations for the maintenance or restoration of international peace or security, or the protection of its own essential security interests. Article 18 of ACIA provides for similar security exceptions, except that the ACIA allows a member state to take any action pursuant to its obligations under the United Nations (UN) Charter for the maintenance of international peace and security (Article 18[c]). Although this exception is not present in Article 29.2 of the TPP, the parties to the TPP should implicitly accept this because they intend for the TPP to coexist with their other international agreements, including the UN Charter, under Article 1.2. Accordingly, there should be neither 'ACIA plus' nor 'ACIA minus' in the TPP on security exceptions.

3.14. *Corporate social responsibility*

Corporate social responsibility (CSR) has recently captured the attention of civil society and the business world, and recent international documents refer to the CSR as a recommendable policy for foreign investors. A notable example is the 2011 version of the Organisation for Economic Co-operation and Development (OECD) Guidelines for Multinational Enterprises (OECD, 2011). The guidelines provide the principles and standards for responsible business conduct based on the CSR. The TPP may be the first trade agreement to refer to the CSR. Article 9.17 sets out the importance of each party encouraging enterprises operating within its territory or subject to its jurisdiction to incorporate voluntarily into their internal policies those internationally recognised standards, guidelines, and principles of the CSR that have been endorsed or are supported by the party. Reference is also made to the CSR in Article 19.7 on labour issues and in Article 20.10 on the environment. As drawn from the language of Articles 9.17, 19.7, and 20.10, these provisions do not create any legal obligations for a party to the TPP. Rather, they intend to express the common political will of the TPP parties to pay due regard to the CSR. ACIA does not refer to the CSR, but this should not be regarded as an 'ACIA plus'.

Table 1.6 summarises the major 'ACIA plus' and 'ACIA minus' elements of the substantive obligations of the TPP investment chapter drawn from the comparative analysis of the TPP Chapter 9 and ACIA in Section 3.

Table 1.6 Major 'ACIA pluses' and 'ACIA minuses' of the TPP investment chapter – substantive obligations

Substantive obligations	ACIA pluses	ACIA minuses
National treatment	A party may distinguish, based on legitimate public welfare objectives	None
MFN treatment		None
Minimum standards of treatment	Merely failing to meet investor's expectation does not constitute violation of FET standard	None
	Subsidy reform does not, per se, constitute breach of the FET standard	None
Treatment in case of armed conflict or civil strife	Obliges a party to pay compensation to a loss resulting from requisitioning of investment	None
	Obliges a party to pay compensation to a loss resulting from destruction of investment, where it was not required by the necessity of the situation	None
Expropriation and compensation	None	None
Transfers	A party shall secure free transfer of investor's funds even in exceptional circumstances	None
Prohibition of performance requirements	See Tables 4 and 5	None
Senior management and board of directors	None	None
Special formalities and information requirements	None	None
Subrogation	None	None
Denial of benefits	A party may deny benefits to prevent circumvention of the prohibition of transactions	Denial of benefits of a person of a country with whom a member state does not maintain diplomatic relations
		Denial of benefits to prevent circumvention of the reservation of investment for its nationals
General exceptions	None (but see ACIA pluses on national treatment and MFN treatment)	Article 17 of ACIA
Security exceptions	None	None
Corporate social responsibility	None	None

Note:
ACIA = ASEAN Comprehensive Investment Agreement
FET = fair and equitable treatment
MFN = most-favoured-nation
TPP = Trans-Pacific Partnership

Source: Author.

4. Investor–state dispute settlement under the TPP

Section B of Chapter 9 (Articles 9.18–9.30) outlines the procedure in the settlement of investment disputes between foreign investors and host states,[47] frequently referred to as ISDS. The TPP's procedure for ISDS is largely based on the 2012 US Model BIT[48] and contains several 'ACIA plus' elements, such as provisions for securing transparency in ISDS procedures.[49] The following subsections explain the TPP's procedure for ISDS according to the procedural steps of the ISDS, with occasional reference to their 'ASIA plus' nature.

4.1. Consultation and negotiation

Article 9.18.1 provides that parties to an investment dispute should initially seek to resolve the dispute through consultation and negotiation, including the use of good offices, conciliation, or mediation.[50] In Article 31.1, the first sentence of ACIA provides for a similar requirement, though the latter uses the term 'shall' instead of 'should'. This means the requirement to seek to resolve the dispute through consultation and negotiation is legally binding under ACIA, whereas the corresponding requirement under the TPP is not. However, this is not a significant difference in practice because Article 9.19 of the TPP requires that disputing parties seek to resolve it through consultation and negotiation *as a legal precondition* for the submission of a claim to arbitration.

The claimant (the foreign investor) shall deliver to the respondent (the host state) a written request for consultations, setting out a brief description of facts regarding the measure or measures at issue (Article 9.18.2).

4.2. Submission of a claim to arbitration

4.2.1. Subject matter coverage

If the dispute has not been resolved within *6 months* from the request for consultations, the claimant may submit the claim to arbitration. The claim consists of two components. First, there must be a breach by the respondent of (i) an obligation under Section A, (ii) an investment authorisation, or (iii) an investment agreement. Second, the claimant must have incurred loss or damage because of that breach (Article 9.19.1[a]). This is the case where the claimant submits a claim on its own behalf. The claimant may also submit a claim on behalf of an enterprise of the respondent that the claimant owns or controls (Article 9.19.1[b]). When the claimant submits a claim arising from a breach of an investment agreement,[51] the subject matter of the claim and the claimed damages must directly relate to the covered investment in reliance on the relevant investment agreement (Article 9.19.1, *proviso*).

Article 32 of ACIA provides for a similar temporal requirement for an investor to submit a claim. If the dispute has not been resolved within *180 days* from the request for consultations, the investor may submit a claim to arbitration. On the other hand, subject matter coverage of the claim under ACIA is narrower than under the TPP. While the TPP covers any breach of the respondent of an obligation under Section A, ACIA covers only the breach done by the member state on an obligation arising under Article 5 (National Treatment), Article 6 (MFN Treatment), Article 8 (Senior Management and Board of Directors [SMBD]), Article 11 (Treatment of Investment), Article 12 (Compensation in Cases of Strife), Article 13 (Transfers), and Article 14 (Expropriation and Compensation). Accordingly, a member state's breach of an obligation under Article 7 (Prohibition of Performance Requirements), Article 9 (Reservations), and Article 10 (Modification of Commitments), amongst others, are outside the domain of the ISDS under ACIA. In addition, while the breach of an investment authorisation or an investment agreement by a host state falls within the scope of the ISDS under the TPP, these breaches are not, *in themselves*, the subject matter of a claim for arbitration under ACIA. These are important 'ACIA pluses' of the ISDS under the TPP.

4.2.2. Tobacco carve-out

A party may elect to deny the benefits of the ISDS proceedings on claims challenging a tobacco control measure[52] of the party (Article 29.5). This so-called Tobacco carve-out is inserted in the TPP upon Australia's request, which has a series of investment disputes with Phillip Morris and, therefore, insisted on either inserting this or totally excluding itself from the TPP ISDS procedure until the final stage of the TPP negotiation.[53] This is an 'ACIA minus' element of the TPP on the subject matter coverage of the ISDS. It is reported that Australia and New Zealand expressed their intent to apply this provision.[54]

4.2.3. Procedural requirements

The TPP sets a couple of procedural requirements for an investor to submit a claim. First, at least 90 days before submitting any claim to arbitration, the claimant shall deliver a written notice of its intention to submit a claim to arbitration (notice of intent) to the respondent (Article 9.19.3). Article 34.1(b) of ACIA provides for the same requirement. Second, no claim shall be submitted to arbitration if more than *3 years and 6 months* have elapsed since the date the claimant had first known of the alleged breach under Article 9.19.1 (Article 9.21.1). ACIA requires the claimant to submit a claim to arbitration within *3 years* from the time the claimant had known of the alleged breach (Article 34.1). This is another 'ACIA plus' of the ISDS under the TPP.

The claimant may submit a claim under one of the following alternatives (Article 9.19.4):

i   The International Centre for Settlement of Investment Disputes (ICSID) Convention[55] and the ICSID Arbitration Rules[56] provided that both the respondent and the party of the claimant are parties to the ICSID Convention;

ii   The ICSID Additional Facility Rules[57] provided that either the respondent or the party of the claimant is a party to the ICSID Convention;
iii   The United Nations Commission on International Trade Law (UNCI-TRAL) Arbitration Rules[58]; or
iv   If the claimant and respondent agree, any other arbitral institution or any other arbitration rules.

Article 33 of ACIA provides that the claimant may submit a claim to any of the previous four alternative arbitration procedures *plus*:

v   the courts or administrative tribunals of the disputing member state, provided that such courts or tribunals have jurisdiction over such claims; and
vi   the Regional Centre for Arbitration at Kuala Lumpur or any other regional centre for ASEAN.

While the latter is an alternative to ACIA ('ACIA minus' for the TPP), the former is also provided for by Article 9.21.2[b] of the TPP, which provides for the claimant's right to initiate any procedure before any court or tribunal of the respondent as an alternative to arbitral proceedings. Article 34.1(c) of ACIA provides for the same rule. Hence, both the TPP and ACIA provide that the claimant may choose between domestic court procedures of the respondent and one of arbitral proceedings. Once the claimant chooses one of them, it may preclude from bringing the claim to the other alternative (the so-called fork in the road principle).[59]

4.3. Arbitral proceedings

4.3.1. Selection of arbitrators

Procedure for selecting arbitrators: Unless the disputing parties agree otherwise, the tribunal shall comprise three arbitrators – one arbitrator is appointed by each of the disputing parties, and the third, who shall be the presiding arbitrator, is jointly appointed in an agreement by the disputing parties (Article 9.22.1). ACIA provides for the same rule (Article 35.1[a], [b]). If a tribunal has not been constituted within 75 days after the claim is submitted, the Secretary General of the ICSID, at the request of a disputing party, shall appoint the arbitrator(s) not yet appointed (Article 9.22.3). Article 35.3 of ACIA provides for a similar rule, but the appointing authority differs depending on the arbitral tribunal selected.[60]

Consolidation: If two or more claims have been submitted separately for arbitration and the claims have a question of law or fact in common arising out of the same events or circumstances, any disputing party may seek a consolidation order with the agreement of all the disputing parties (Article 9.28.1). Unless otherwise agreed by all disputing parties, a consolidated tribunal shall be constituted by (i) one arbitrator agreed by all the claimants, (ii) one arbitrator appointed by the respondent, and (iii) the presiding arbitrator appointed by the Secretary General of the ICSID (Article 9.28.4). Article 37 of ACIA also provides for consolidation but does not set out rules for the constitution of the consolidated tribunal.

4.3.2. *Conduct of arbitration*

Preliminary objections: A tribunal has the authority to address objections on its jurisdiction as preliminary question apart from the merits of the claim. If it decides that the claim is not within the jurisdiction of the tribunal, it shall render an award to that effect (Article 9.23.4, first sentence). Articles 36.2 and 36.3 of ACIA provide for the same rule.

Place of arbitration: The disputing parties may agree on the place of arbitration under the applicable arbitration rules. If they fail to agree, the tribunal shall determine the place according to the applicable arbitration rules, provided that the place shall be in the territory of a state that is a party to the New York Convention[61] (Article 9.23.1). Article 33.5 of the ACIA provides for the same rule.

Frivolous claims: Article 41(5) of the ICSID Arbitration Rules provides for an expeditious procedure for dismissing frivolous claims or claims that are manifestly without legal merit.[62] The TPP investment chapter sets out a similar procedure. The respondent may file an objection to a claim that is manifestly without merit (Article 9.23.4). Such an objection shall be submitted to the tribunal as soon as possible after the tribunal is constituted, and no later than the date the tribunal fixes for the respondent to submit its counter-memorial (Article 9.23.4[a]). On receipt of an objection, the tribunal shall suspend any proceedings on the merits, consider the objection, and issue a decision or award on it, stating the grounds for such action (Article 9.23.4[b]). If the respondent so requests, within 45 days after the tribunal is constituted, the tribunal shall decide on the objection on an expedited basis no later than 150 days after the request (Article 9.23.5). When the tribunal decides on the respondent's objection, it may award to the prevailing disputing party reasonable costs and attorney's fees – in submitting or opposing the objection (Article 9.23.6). Articles 36.2 to 36.4 of ACIA provides for a similar procedure to deal with frivolous claims.

Third-party involvement: A non-disputing party to the TPP may join the arbitration proceedings and make oral and written submissions to the tribunal regarding the interpretation of the TPP (Article 9.23.2). This is aimed at securing the TPP parties' interest in the interpretation of the TPP.[63] There is no corresponding provision in the ACIA, but it contains a special provision by which a non-disputing member state may join the arbitration if a disputed measure is a taxation measure (Articles 36.6 to 36.9). Accordingly, this is a limited 'ACIA plus'.

Amicus curiae submissions: After consulting with the disputing parties, the tribunal may accept and consider *amicus curiae* submissions on a matter of fact or law within the scope of the dispute if this can assist the tribunal in evaluating the submissions/arguments of the disputing parties from a person or entity that is not a disputing party but has a significant interest in the arbitral proceedings (Article 9.23.3). As there is no corresponding provision in the ACIA, this is another 'ACIA plus'.

Expert reports: A tribunal, upon request of a disputing party or, unless the disputing parties disapprove, of its own motion, may appoint one or more experts to report on any factual issue concerning scientific matters raised by a disputing party (Article 9.27). Article 38 of ACIA provides for a similar procedure.

Interim measure of protection: A tribunal may order an interim measure of protection to preserve the rights of a party, including an order to preserve evidence in the possession or control of a disputing party (Article 9.23.9). As there is no corresponding provision in the ACIA, this is an 'ACIA plus'.

4.3.3. Transparency of arbitral proceedings

The transparency of ISDS procedures is one of the most important issues in today's practice and academic discussions,[64] as the subject matter of ISDS proceedings occasionally touches on the public policy of host states, such as environmental protection. The investment chapter of the TPP, as well as ACIA, set out detailed rules for securing transparency in the arbitral proceedings. In the TPP, first, the respondent shall transmit the documents of the arbitral proceedings (e.g. pleadings, memorials, and briefs) to the non-disputing parties and make them available to the public (Article 9.24.1). Second, the tribunal shall conduct hearings open to the public and shall determine, in consultations with the disputing parties, the appropriate logistical arrangements (Article 9.24.2, first sentence). Third, the tribunal shall make appropriate arrangements to protect confidential business information of the claimant from disclosure (Article 9.24.2, second sentence; Articles 9.24.3–9.24.5). Article 39 of ACIA provides for the transparency of arbitral proceedings, but the level of transparency achieved under ACIA is lower than that under the TPP. First, the disputing member state *may (not shall)* make publicly available all awards and decisions produced by the tribunal (excluding pleadings, memorials, and briefs) (Article 39.1). Second, ACIA does not require the tribunal to conduct hearings open to the public. Third, the tribunal shall make appropriate arrangements to protect confidential business information of the claimant from disclosure (Articles 39.2 to 39.4). This is an important 'ACIA plus'.

4.4. Arbitral awards

4.4.1. Content of an award

When a tribunal makes a final award, it may award, separately or in combination, only (i) monetary damages plus interests; and (ii) restitution of property, in which case the award shall provide that the respondent may pay monetary damages plus interests in lieu of restitution (Article 9.29.1). A tribunal may also award costs and attorney's fees incurred by the disputing parties in connection with the arbitral proceeding and shall determine how and by whom those costs and fees shall be paid, according to the applicable arbitration rules (Article 9.29.2). A tribunal shall not award punitive damages (Article 9.29.6). Articles 41.2, 41.3, and 41.4

of ACIA provide for the same rules, respectively, though it does not provide for cost burden.

4.4.2. Enforcement of an award

Each party shall provide for the enforcement of an award in its territory (Article 9.29.10). If the respondent fails to abide by a final award, on request by the home state of the claimant, a panel shall be established under the TPP state-to-state dispute settlement procedure (Chapter 28) (Article 9.29.11). Regardless of whether Article 9.29.11 applies, a disputing party may seek enforcement of an arbitral award under the ICSID Convention, the New York Convention, or the Inter-American Convention (Article 9.29.12). Articles 41.8 and 41.9 of ACIA set out similar provisions on the enforcement of an arbitral award, but it does not provide for resorting to state-to-state dispute settlement procedure. This last point should, therefore, be regarded as an 'ACIA plus' (see Table 1.7).

Table 1.7 Major 'ACIA pluses' and 'ACIA minuses' of the TPP investment chapter – ISDS procedure

Stages of the ISDS procedure	ACIA pluses	ACIA minuses
Subject matter of ISDS	Breach of an obligation under Section A, Breach of an investment authorisation, and Breach of an investment agreement (ACIA limits to Articles 5,6,8,11,12,13, and 14)	Tobacco control measure may be excluded from arbitral proceedings (v 29.5)
Available forums	None	Regional Centre for Arbitration is not available
Selection of arbitrators	None	None
Consolidation	Detailed procedure is set out	None
Preliminary objections	None	None
Place of arbitration	None	None
Frivolous claims	None	None
Third-party involvement	A non-disputing party may join the proceedings (ACIA allows third-party involvement solely on disputes on taxation measure)	None
Amicus curiae submissions	Available	None
Expert reports	None	None

(*Continued*)

Table 1.7 (Continued)

Stages of the ISDS procedure	ACIA pluses	ACIA minuses
Interim measures of protection	Available	None
Transparency of arbitral proceedings	Documents of arbitral proceedings shall be made public (Awards/ decisions may be made public under ACIA); hearing shall be open to the public	None
Enforcement of an award	State-to-state dispute settlement available	None

Note:
ACIA = ASEAN Comprehensive Investment Agreement
ISDS = investor–state dispute settlement
TPP = Trans-Pacific Partnership

Source: Author.

5. Liberalisation commitments under the country-specific schedules of non-conforming measures

5.1. Liberalisation commitments under the TPP

Both the TPP and ACIA adopt the so-called negative list approach in making liberalisation commitments. Each party lists exceptions to their investment liberalisation commitments in their country-specific list of non-conforming measures, generally called Schedules of Commitments, or simply Schedules. Following the treaty practice of the US, the TPP combines the liberalisation commitments in both investment chapter and trade in services chapter, while ACIA focuses solely on the liberalisation commitments in investment. There are three groups of lists, or Schedules, for the TPP: Annexes I, II, and III. Annex I refers to the lists of non-conforming measures that may not be strengthened in the future, or those with ratcheting obligations (Article 9.12.1). Annex II refers to the lists of non-conforming measures that may be strengthened in the future, or those without ratcheting obligations (Article 9.12.2). Annex III refers to the lists of non-conforming measures on financial services sector, comprising both those with and without ratcheting obligations. The following is a detailed explanation of each annex.

5.1.1. Annex I

Annex I compiles the Schedules of each party that sets out a party's existing measures that are not subject to some or all of the obligations imposed by Articles 9.4 or 10.3 (National Treatment), Articles 9.5 or 10.4 (MFN Treatment), Article 9.10 (Performance Requirements), Article 9.11 (SMBD), Article 10.5

(Market Access), or Article 10.6 (Local Presence).[65] Each Schedule entry sets out the following elements: (i) **sector** refers to the sector where the entry is made; (ii) **sub-sector** refers to specific sub-sector where the entry is made; (iii) **industry classification** refers to the activity covered by the non-conforming measure according to the provisional central product classification codes;[66] (iv) **obligations concerned** specify the aforementioned obligations of the TPP that do not apply to the listed measure(s); (v) **level of government** indicates the level of government that maintains the measure(s) (central, regional, or local government); (vi) **measures** indicate the laws, regulations, or other measures where the entry is made; and (vii) **description** sets out the non-conforming measure(s) where the entry is made. As an illustration, the following is the first entry in Malaysia's Schedule in Annex I.

Sector	All
Obligations concerned	National treatment (Article 9.4)
Level of government	Central government
Measures	*Registration of Business Act 1956* [Act 197]
	Limited Liability Partnership Act 2012 [Act 743]
	Co-operative Societies Act 1993 [Act 502]
Description	*Investment*
	Only Malaysian nationals or permanent residents can register a sole proprietorship or partnership in Malaysia. Foreigners can register a limited liability partnership in Malaysia, but the compliance officer shall be a citizen or permanent resident of Malaysia that resides in Malaysia. Foreigners are not allowed to establish or join cooperative societies in Malaysia.

For those measures listed in the Schedule of a party, the party may continue to amend them, to the extent that the amendment does not decrease the conformity of the measure, as it existed before the amendment, with the obligations (Article 9.12.1[b] and [c]). The party, therefore, bears a ratcheting obligation in these amended measures.

5.1.2. Annex II

Annex II compiles the Schedules of each party that sets the sectors, sub-sectors, or activities for which that party may maintain or adopt new or more restrictive measures that do not conform with the obligations imposed by Articles 9.4 or 10.3 (National Treatment), Articles 9.5 or 10.4 (MFN Treatment), Article 9.10 (Performance Requirements), Article 9.11 (SMBD), Article 10.5 (Market Access), or Article 10.6 (Local Presence). As no ratcheting obligation in the measures is listed in Annex II, each party has a complete regulatory freedom to maintain, introduce, or change such measures. Each Schedule entry sets out the same elements as those used in Annex I. As an illustration, the following is the second entry in Malaysia's Schedule in Annex II.

Sector	Oil and gas
Obligations concerned	National Treatment (Articles 9.4 and 10.3)
	Performance Requirements (Article 9.10)
	SMBD (Article 9.11)
	Market Access (Article 10.5)
	Local Presence (Article 10.6)
Description	Investment and Cross-Border Trade in Services
	Petroliam Nasional Berhad (PETRONAS) and its successors are vested with the entire ownership and the exclusive rights, powers, liberties, and privileges, which shall be irrevocable in exploring, exploiting, winning, and obtaining petroleum whether onshore or offshore of Malaysia.
	PETRONAS, in its role as the exclusive owner of the petroleum resources, decides on the form and conditions of contractual arrangements available for foreign participation and selection of the contract parties.
Existing measures	*Petroleum Development Act 1974* [Act 144]

5.1.3. Annex III

Annex III compiles the Schedules of each party on the financial services sector. Section A refers to the measures with ratcheting obligations while Section B refers to the measures without ratcheting obligations. Each Schedule entry sets out the same elements as those used in Annexes I and II. As an illustration, the following is the third entry in Malaysia's Schedule in Annex III, Section A.

Sector	Financial Services
Sub-sector	All
Obligations concerned	SMBD (Article 11.9)
Level of government	Central
Measures	Section 122 of the *Companies Act 1965*
Description	At least two directors of a company incorporated in Malaysia must be ordinarily resident or have principal residence within Malaysia.

Finally, as an illustration of Annex III, Section B, the following is the first entry in Malaysia's Schedule in Annex III, Section B.

Sector	Financial Services
Sub-sector	All
Obligations concerned	MFN Treatment (Article 11.4); Cross-Border Trade (Article 11.6)
Level of government	Central
Description	Malaysia reserves the right to adopt or maintain any measures related to the non-internationalisation of the ringgit, which include:

(a) the requirement for international settlement to be made in foreign currency,

(b) limitation on the access to ringgit financing by non-residents for use outside Malaysia, and

(c) limitation on the use of ringgit in Malaysia by non-residents.

Existing measures   *Central Bank of Malaysia Act 2009*
Financial Services Act 2013
Islamic Financial Services Act 2013
Notices on Foreign Exchange Administration Rules

5.2. *Liberalisation commitments of ASEAN member states under ACIA*

ASEAN member states committed to an investment liberalisation under ACIA.[67] ACIA also takes a negative list approach, whereby each member state commits itself to liberalise foreign investment except those measures listed in its reservation list (Article 9.1, ACIA).[68] Each member state's reservation list is, therefore, an important source of information on its existing restrictions on foreign investment. There are, however, several caveats. First, the sectoral coverage of reservation lists is limited. Article 3.3 of ACIA provides that for the purpose of liberalisation and subject to Article 9 (Reservations), this shall apply to the following sectors: (i) manufacturing; (ii) agriculture; (iii) fishery; (iv) forestry; (v) mining and quarrying; (vi) services incidental to (i) through (v); and (vii) any other sectors, as may be agreed upon by all member states.[69] Services, except those incidental to primary and secondary industries, are not covered by the reservation lists of ACIA. This is because liberalisation of investment in services sector falls within the scope of the ASEAN Framework Agreement on Services (AFAS) of 1995.[70] It is, therefore, necessary to check the liberalisation commitments of each member state under AFAS to identify existing restrictions on investment in the services sector, and the second caveat applies here.

Second, as AFAS adopts a positive list approach, the liberalisation commitments do not directly indicate restrictions. Under a positive list approach in the liberalisation of services, a country commits itself to liberalise a specific mode of service in a specific sector. However, it does not necessarily mean that those mode(s)/sector(s) that are not on the positive list are not liberalised, as the country has the discretion to decide whether and to what extent it will liberalise those mode(s)/sector(s). To identify existing restrictions under AFAS, a comprehensive survey of domestic laws and regulations that restrict investment in services sector is needed.

Third, the reservation lists of ACIA sets out solely exceptions to Article 5 (National Treatment) and Article 8 (SMBD), and they do not cover exceptions to Article 6 (MFN Treatment) and Article 7 (Prohibition of Performance Requirements). This means that there may be restrictions on investment not on the reservation lists that are either applied to non-members of ASEAN or are related to the prohibition of performance requirements.

Fourth, a member state does not bear ratcheting obligations on restrictions in its reservation list. During the 12 months after submission of the reservation list, a member state may adopt any measures and modify or withdraw its list provided that such measures or modification shall not adversely affect any existing investors and investments (Article 10.1 of ACIA). This implies that as far as such measure or modification applies to future investors and investments, it may have adverse effects. After the expiration of 12 months, a member state may adopt any measure, modify or withdraw its list, by negotiation and by agreement with any other member state, including the provision of compensatory adjustments (Article 10.2 of ACIA). Again, such measure or modification may have adverse effects as far as it applies to future investors and investments.

5.3. Tips for the analysis of the impact of the TPP on investment liberalisation

To assess the impact of the TPP on investment liberalisation on an ASEAN member state, three stages of analysis should be undertaken: (i) analysis of the existing measures of a member state that restrict foreign investment; (ii) analysis of the allowable restrictions of the member state under the TPP; and (iii) comparison of the outcomes of the first two stages of analysis. The differences between the existing restrictions and the allowable restrictions under the TPP are the real impact of the TPP on investment liberalisation. This is because the member state must abolish existing restrictions to the extent that there are no differences between them and the allowable restrictions under the TPP. The following discussions explain how to conduct each stage of the analyses.

5.3.1. First stage: analysis of existing restrictions

All ASEAN member states are parties to ACIA and have liberalisation commitments under said agreement. To clarify existing restrictions on foreign investment, we must analyse the content of the reservation list of each member state. The first step is to draft a table of restrictions that are on the reservation list of each member state, specifying sector(s) and sub-sector(s), obligations concerned, level of government, description of the measures (restrictions), and their domestic legal sources.

In light of the caveats on the reservation lists of ACIA in Section 5.2, the table should be complemented with an analysis on the existing restrictions on investment in services sector. To guide the conduct of such an analysis, see also Section 5.2.

In addition, as the reservation lists of ACIA do not cover restrictions on investment applied to non-members of ASEAN, we should investigate the following two issues. The first will determine if those restrictions that are on the reservation lists are also applicable to non-members of ASEAN. The second will determine if other restrictions are applicable to non-members of ASEAN other than those on the reservation lists.

5.3.2. Second stage: analysis of allowable restrictions under the TPP

The next stage is to draft a table of allowable restrictions under the TPP. Such restrictions are on the three Schedules of each party that are annexed to the TPP. For the explanation on the three annexes, see the section on 'Liberalisation Commitments under the Country-Specific Schedules of Non-conforming Measures'. The table should be organised as two sets of tables. One is a table of restrictions with ratcheting obligations and the other is a table of restrictions without ratcheting obligations. Restrictions on financial services (Annex III) should be combined with other services and investment.

5.3.3. Third stage: analysis of the difference between existing restrictions and allowable restrictions

Compare the two tables. The differences between them are the real impact of the TPP, that is, these are the restrictions that the party must abolish to implement its liberalisation commitments under the TPP. The differences may diverge depending on each party's liberalisation commitments under the TPP and under ACIA. In general, three observations are in order. First, due to the difference in the obligations, differences will be prominent in the field of prohibition of performance requirements. Second, due to the difference in the sectoral coverage, differences may be more prominent in the field of services sector than in other industrial sectors. Third, in light of many 'ACIA pluses' in the ISDS procedure, ASEAN member states, particularly their government authorities in charge of government litigation, should prepare for the ISDS procedure of the TPP, which is substantively different from the ISDS procedure of ACIA.

6. Conclusion

This chapter analysed Chapter 9 of the TPP on investment. Its main purpose was to clarify the obligations of the TPP parties on the liberalisation and protection of foreign investment so that ASEAN member states may prepare domestic legal reforms to meet these obligations when they join the TPP. After an elaborate textual analysis of Chapter 9, results showed that ASEAN member states will have to make substantive domestic legal reforms in the liberalisation of foreign investment, particularly on performance requirements and investment market access. The content of such domestic legal reforms should be clarified by analysing the existing restrictions on investment of each ASEAN member state and the allowable restrictions under the TPP. Section 5 briefly explained how to conduct such country-by-country analysis. In addition to the substantive domestic legal reforms that ASEAN member states will have to make when the TPP enters into force, this chapter concludes that ASEAN members, particularly their government authorities in charge of government litigation, must prepare for the ISDS procedure of the TPP, which is substantively different from the ISDS procedure of ACIA.

Notes

* Professor of International Economic Law, Institute of Social Science, University of Tokyo. Email: nakagawa@iss.u-tokyo.ac.jp

1 Trans-Pacific Partnership, signed on 4 February 2016. Chapter 9 is available at   www.mfat.govt.nz/assets/_securedfiles/Trans-Pacific-Partnership/Text/9. -Investment-Chapter.pdf; https://ustr.gov/sites/default/files/TPP-Final-Text-Investment.pdf

2 See US Trade Representative Ron Kirk's letters to Speaker of the House Nancy Pelosi and Senate President Pro Tempore Robert Byrd, dated 14 December 2009, as quoted in USTR Press Release, 14 December 2009. Available at https://ustr. gov/about-us/policy-offices/press-office/press-releases/2009/december/ trans-pacific-partnership-announcement

3 See the 2012 US Model Bilateral Investment Treaty, published on 20 April 2012. Available at www.state.gov/documents/organization/188371.pdf

4 ASEAN Comprehensive Investment Agreement, signed on 26 February 2009, entered into force on 29 March 2012.

5 See the subsection on 'Expropriation and compensation'.

6 On ratcheting obligations, see Adlung and Mamdouh (2013).

7 ACIA also has an illustrative list of investments, which is similar but not identical to that of the TPP. See Article 4(c) of ACIA.

8 See Article 5.1 of ACIA, which states that 'Each Member State shall accord to investors of any other Member State treatment no less favourable than it accords, in like circumstances, to its own investors with respect to the admission, establishment, acquisition, expansion, management, conduct, operation and sale or other disposition of investments in its territory'.

9 See Article 6.1 of ACIA, which states that 'Each Member State shall accord to investors of another Member State treatment no less favourable than that it accords, in like circumstances, to investors of any other Member State or a non-Member State with respect to the admission, establishment, acquisition, expansion, management, conduct, operation and sale or other disposition of investments'.

10 This is most likely a bilateral investment treaty (BIT) or an investment chapter of a free trade agreement.

11 This is clearly stipulated in footnote 4(b) of ACIA, which states that '(A)ny preferential treatment granted by a Member State to investors of any other Member State or a non-Member State and to their investments, under any existing or future agreements or arrangements to which a Member State is a party shall be extended on a most-favoured-nation basis to all Member States'.

12 See footnote 4(a) in ACIA, which states that '(t)his Article shall not apply to investor-State dispute settlement procedures that are available in other agreements to which Member States are party'.

13 See Bonnitcha (2014, p. 143).

14 See Abs and Shawcross (1960, p. 115), Article 1.

15 See OECD (1967, pp. 7–9), Article 1(a).

16 See Bonnitcha (2014, pp. 143–144).

17 Ibid., p. 144.

18 The second sentence of Article 9.6.2 states that '(t)he concepts of "fair and equitable treatment" and "full protection and security" do not require treatment in addition to or beyond that which is required by that standard, and do not create additional substantive rights'.

19 See, for instance, Japan-Australia Economic Partnership Agreement, Article 14.5, Note 2.

20 On the doctrine of legitimate expectations, see Bonnitcha (2014, pp. 167–194).

21 See, for instance, Tirado (2015).

22 Article 11.1 of the ACIA states that '(e)ach Member State shall accord to covered investments of investors of any other Member State, fair and equitable treatment and full protection and security'.

23 It states that '(a) fair and equitable treatment requires each Member State not to deny justice in any legal or administrative proceedings in accordance with the principle of due process; and (b) full protection and security requires each Member State to take such measures as may be reasonably necessary to ensure the protection and security of the covered investments'.

24 It states that '(a) determination that there has been a breach of another provision of this Agreement, or of a separate international agreement, does not establish that there has been a breach of this Article'.

25 See Dolzer and Schreuer (2012, p. 183).

26 See the International Law Commission (ILC), 'Draft Articles on State Responsibility', in ILC, *Report on the Work of Its Fifty-Third Session* (23 April – 1 June and 2 July – 10 August 2001), *UN General Assembly Official Records, Fifty-fifth Session*, Supplement No.10 (A/56/10), Article 23.1.

27 See Dolzer and Schreuer (2012, p. 188).

28 Ibid. See pp. 188–189 for examples of this treaty practice.

29 See Article 12 of ACIA, which states that '(e)ach Member State shall accord to investors of any other Member State, in relation to their covered investments which suffered losses in its territory due to armed conflict or civil strife or state of emergency, non-discriminatory treatment with respect to restitution, compensation or other valuable consideration'.

30 See Dolzer and Schreuer (2012, pp. 99–101) for the classical requirements for expropriation.

31 Ibid., see p. 100.

32 See Article 14.1 of ACIA, which states that '(a) Member State shall not expropriate or nationalise a covered investment . . ., except: (a) for a public purpose; (b) in a non-discriminatory manner; (c) on payment of prompt, adequate, and effective compensation; and (d) in accordance with due process of law'.

33 See Article 14.2 of ACIA, which states that '(t)he compensation . . . shall: (a) be paid without delay; (b) be equivalent to the fair market value of the expropriated investment immediately before or at the time when the expropriation was publicly announced, or when the expropriation occurred, whichever is applicable; (c) not reflect any change in value because the intended expropriation had become known earlier; and (d) be fully realisable and freely transferable . . .'.

34 Instead, Article 14.3 of ACIA requires the payment of 'an appropriate interest'.

35 The 2012 US Model BIT is a typical example. See De Luca (2014, pp. 65–66).

36 Article 14.5 states that '(t)his Article does not apply to the issuance of compulsory licences granted in relation to intellectual property rights in accordance with the TRIPS Agreement'.

37 Article 13.5 provides for the conditions for a member state to resort to the restrictions under Article 13.4(c).

38 Footnote 10 to Chapter 11 explains the meaning of 'prudential reasons' that include the maintenance of the safety, soundness, integrity, or financial responsibility of individual financial institutions or cross-border financial service suppliers, and the safety and financial and operational integrity of payment and clearing systems.

39 This conclusion is supported by Annex 9-E, which states Chile's reservation of the right of its central bank to maintain or adopt measures to ensure currency stability and the normal operation of domestic and foreign payments, because we may conclude from this that no such right is admitted to the other parties to the TPP.

40 See, for instance, Dolzer and Schreuer (2012, pp. 90–92).

41 The WTO TRIMs Agreement prohibits performance requirements relating to trade in goods and does not cover those relating to trade in services.

42 This provision has a proviso that such formalities do not materially impair the protections afforded by the party to investors of another party and covered investments pursuant to Chapter 9.

43 See Sornarajah (2010, p. 222).

44 See Dolzer and Schreuer (2012, p. 55). Also, see US 2012 Model BIT, Article 17.

45 The latter refers to the case where the denying party denies protection to investment by its own nationals, as it is practically not a foreign investment.

46 See Article 17 of ACIA, which allows member states to adopt or maintain measures that are (i) necessary to protect public morals or to maintain public order; (ii) necessary to protect human, animal, or plant life or health; (iii) necessary to secure compliance with ACIA; (iv) aimed at ensuring the equitable or effective imposition or collection of direct taxes of investments or investors of any member state; (v) imposed for the protection of national treasures of artistic, historic, or archaeological value; and (vi) related to the conservation of exhaustible natural resources if such measures are made effective in conjunction with restrictions on domestic production or consumption.

47 This is different from commercial disputes between foreign investors and private firms of host states, which are settled through international commercial arbitration or litigation at local courts of host states.

48 See supra note 3.

49 See Section 4.3.

50 These are non-binding methods of settling disputes involving third parties. Good offices refer to the involvement of a third party with the aim of contributing to the settlement or at least easing relations between the disputing parties. Conciliation and mediation refer to the involvement of a third party to facilitate communication between the parties to help them settle their differences. See *Black's Law Dictionary*, 8th ed.

51 See case (c) of Article 9.19.1(a).

52 A tobacco control measure is a measure of a party on the production or consumption of manufactured tobacco products, their distribution, labelling, packaging, advertising, marketing, promotion, sale, purchase, or use, as well as enforcement measures, such as inspection, record-keeping, and reporting requirements. See footnote 12 to Chapter 29 of the TPP.

53 See, for instance, Lester (2015).

54 See 'Australia Says It Intends to Deny Tobacco ISDS Challenges under TPP', *Inside U.S. Trade*, 19 February 2016.

55 Convention for the Settlement of Disputes between States and Nationals of Other States, signed 18 March 1965, entered into force on 14 October 1966. Available at https://icsid.worldbank.org/apps/ICSIDWEB/icsiddocs/Documents/ICSID%20Convention%20English.pdf. The following ASEAN member states are parties to the ICSID Convention: Brunei Darussalam, Cambodia, Indonesia, Malaysia, Philippines, and Singapore. Thailand signed the ICSID Convention but has not ratified it. The Lao PDR, Myanmar, and Viet Nam have not signed it.

56 ICSID Arbitration Rules, or ICSID Rules of Procedure for Arbitration Proceedings, were adopted on 25 September 1967 and have since been revised three times. The current rules came into effect on 10 April 2006. Available at https://icsid.worldbank.org/apps/ICSIDWEB/resources/Documents/2006%20CRR_English-final.pdf

57 ICSID Additional Facility Rules apply to arbitrations commenced under ICSID Additional Facility, created on 27 September 1978. It offers arbitration, conciliation, and fact-finding services for certain disputes that fall outside the scope of the ICSID Convention. These services include arbitration or conciliation of

investment disputes between a state and a foreign national, one of which is not an ICSID member state or a national of an ICSID member state. ICSID Additional Facility Rules were published in 1978 and have been revised twice. The current rules came into effect on 10 April 2006. Available at https://icsid.worldbank. org/apps/ICSIDWEB/resources/Documents/AFR_2006%20English-final.pdf

58 The UNCITRAL Arbitration Rules provide procedural rules for international commercial arbitrations. Originally adopted in 1976, the current rules have been effective since 15 August 2010. With the adoption of the UNCITRAL Rules on Transparency in Treaty-based Investor-State Arbitration ('Rules on Transparency') in 2013, a new Article 1.4 was added to the text of the 2010 Rules to incorporate the Rules on Transparency for arbitration initiated pursuant to an investment treaty concluded on or after 1 April 2014. In all other respects, the 2013 UNCITRAL Arbitration Rules remain unchanged from the 2010 revised version.

59 As an exception to this rule, Article 9.21.3 provides that the claimant may initiate a claim that seeks interim injunctive relief before a judicial or administrative tribunal of the respondent even after initiating arbitration, provided that the action is brought for the sole purpose of preserving the claimant's rights and interests during the arbitral procedure. The same rule is provided under Article 34.2 of ACIA.

60 See Article 28(a) of ACIA, which provides that an 'Appointing Authority' means (i) the Secretary General of the ICSID in the case of arbitration under the ICSID Arbitration Rules and ICSID Additional Facility Rules, (ii) the Secretary General of the Permanent Court of Arbitration in the case of arbitration under the UNCITRAL Arbitration Rules, or (iii) the Secretary General of that arbitration institution in the case of arbitration under the Regional Centre for Arbitration in the ASEAN and any other arbitration institution that the disputing parties agree.

61 Convention on the Recognition and Enforcement of Foreign Arbitral Awards, done on 10 June 1958, entered into force on 7 June 1959. As of March 2016, ASEAN member states are all parties to the New York Convention.

62 See Potestà and Sobat (2012). Also see Uchkunova and Temnikov (2014).

63 It should be noted, however, that the ultimate power to render an authentic interpretation of the TPP belongs to the TPP Commission, which is composed of government representatives of each party. See Article 27.2.2(f).

64 See, for instance, Nakagawa (2012).

65 See Explanatory Notes to Annex I, Note 1.

66 Provisional central product classification codes refer to codes used in the Provisional Central Product Classification, prepared by the UN Statistical Office in 1991. See Explanatory Notes to Annex I, Note 2 (c).

67 See, for instance, Nurridzki (2015).

68 The reservation lists of each ASEAN member state are available at http://investasean.asean.org/index.php/page/view/acia-reservation-list. For a detailed information on the reservation lists of ACIA, see ASEAN Secretariat (2013). Also, see Nurridzki (2015, pp. 9–14).

69 See, for instance, Losari (2014, pp. 17–18).

70 Done at Bangkok, 15 December 1995 and entered into force on 19 September 1998. The text of AFAS is available at http://investasean.asean.org/files/upload/Doc%2008%20-%20AFAS.pdf. For the liberalisation of trade in services under AFAS, see ASEAN Secretariat (2015).

Bibliography

Abs, H. and H. Shawcross (1960), 'Draft Conventions on Investments Abroad', *Journal of Public Law*, (1), pp. 115–118. Available at https://international-arbitration-attorney.com/wp-content/uploads/137-volume-5.pdf

Adlung, R. and H. Mamdouh (2013), 'How to Design Trade Agreement in Services: Top Down or Bottom up?', *WTO Staff Working Paper* ERST-2013–08. Available at www.wto.org/english/res_e/reser_e/ersd201308_e.pdf

ASEAN Secretariat (2013), *ASEAN Comprehensive Investment Agreement: A Guidebook for Businesses & Investors*. Jakarta: The ASEAN Secretariat. Available at www.asean.org/storage/images/2013/news/documents/acia%20guidebook%20final.pdf

ASEAN Secretariat (2015), *ASEAN Integration in Services*. Jakarta: The ASEAN Secretariat. Available at www.asean.org/storage/2015/12/ASEAN-Integration-in-Services-(Dec%202015).pdf

Bonnitcha, J. (2014), *Substantive Protection Under Investment Treaties: A Legal and Economic Analysis*. Cambridge: Cambridge University Press.

De Luca, A. (2014), 'Indirect Expropriations and Regulatory Takings: What Role for the "Legitimate Expectations" of Foreign Investors?', in G. Sacerdoti, P. Acconci, M. Valenti, and A. De Luca (eds.), *General Interest of Host States in International Investment Law*. Cambridge: Cambridge University Press, pp. 58–75.

Dolzer, R. and C. Schreuer (2012), *Principles of International Investment Law*, 2nd ed. Oxford: Oxford University Press.

Ishikawa, K. (2010), 'ASEAN *hokatsuteki toushi kyoutei no gaiyou to igi* (Outline and the Significance of the ASEAN Comprehensive Investment Agreement)', *Kikan Kokusaiboueki to Toushi* (Quarterly International Trade and Investment), (79), pp. 3–20. (in Japanese).

Jouvin-Bret, A. (2008), 'Admission and Establishment in the Context of Investment Protection', in A. Reinisch (ed.), *Standards of Investment Protection*. Oxford: Oxford University Press, pp. 9–28.

Lester, S. (2015), 'The TPP Tobacco Carveout: A Triumph of Politics over Good Policy', *Huffington Post Politics Blog*, posted 30 November. Available at www.huffingtonpost.com/simon-lester/the-tpp-tobacco-carveout_b_8683498.html

Losari, J.J. (2014), 'Searching for an Ideal International Investment Protection Regime for ASEAN+ Dialogue Partners (RCEP): Where Do We Begin?', *ERIA Discussion Paper Series* ERIA-DP-2014–25. Available at www.eria.org/ERIA-DP-2014-25.pdf

Nakagawa, J. (ed.) (2012), *Transparency in International Trade and Investment Dispute Settlement*. London: Routledge.

Nurridzki, N. (2015), 'Learning from the ASEAN+1 Model and the ACIA', *ERIA Discussion Paper Series* ERIA-DP-2015–19. Available at www.eria.org/ERIA-DP-2015-19.pdf

Organisation for Economic Co-operation and Development (OECD) (1967), *Draft Convention on the Protection of Foreign Property: Text with Notes and Comments*. Paris: OECD. Available at www.oecd.org/investment/internationalinvestmentagreements/39286571.pdf

Organisation for Economic Co-operation and Development (OECD) (2011), *OECD Guidelines for Multinational Enterprises*, 2011 ed. Paris: OECD.

Potestà, M. and M. Sobat (2012), 'Frivolous Claims in International Adjudication: A Study of ICSID Rule 41(5) and of Procedures of Other Courts and Tribunals to Dismiss Claims Summarily', *Journal of International Dispute Settlement*, 3(1), pp. 137–168.

Sornarajah, M. (2010), *The International Law on Foreign Investment*, 3rd ed. Cambridge: Cambridge University Press.

Tirado, J.M. (2015), 'Renewable Energy Claims Under the Energy Charter Treaty: An Overview', *Transnational Dispute Management*, 3. Available at www.transnational-dispute-management.com/article.asp?key=2223

Uchkunova, I. and O. Temnikov (2014), 'Rule 41(55) of the ICSID Arbitration Rules: The Sleeping Beauty of the ICSID System', *Kluwer Arbitration Blog*, posted 27 June. Available at http://kluwerarbitrationblog.com/2014/06/27/rule-415-of-the-icsid-arbitration-rules-the-sleeping-beauty-of-the-icsid-system/

2 The investment chapter of the Trans-Pacific Partnership and Indonesia

Riza Noer Arfani

1. Introduction

Indonesia's legal framework on investment follows a basic structure stipulated in and governed by laws and regulations currently enforced in the country.[1]Under such a framework, regulations on investment and other related sectors are formulated in reference to the State Constitution (*Undang-Undang Dasar 1945* or UUD 1945) (particularly as specified in Article 33, which protects certain national economic sectors), the Law (*Undang-Undang* or UU) No. 25 of 2007 concerning investment (hereafter called 'Law No. 25 (2007)'), and other related laws.[2] Rulings that are lower than the laws take the form of government regulations *(peraturan pemerintah)*, presidential regulations *(peraturan presiden* or *perpres)*, and regional regulations *(peraturan daerah* or *perda)*. The provisions – which are often followed by a series of rulings that regulate detailed procedures in the forms of presidential instructions *(instruksi presiden* or *inpres)*, presidential decrees *(keputusan presiden* or *keppres)*, ministerial regulations *(peraturan menteri* or *permen)*, ministerial decrees *(keputusan menteri* or *kepmen)*, and ministerial circulation letters *(surat edaran menteri)* – convey specific sector-based directives and basic guidelines on status, domiciles, and other specific requirements of a legal entity.

Beyond its domestic legal framework, Indonesia's investment sector is one of the primary loci in scores of international trade and investment agreements or treaties. The country's legal framework on investment is hence (and should be) set to be in line with and obliged to the existing treaties it has adopted. To date, apart from its 28 in force and 17 signed (not in force) bilateral investment treaties[3] and 16 treaties with investment provisions (TIPs)[4] (UNCTAD, 2016), Indonesia's legal obligation on international investment-related provisions are mostly reflected in the country's legal obligations/commitments under ACIA reservation lists and AFAS packages. The ACIA reservation list contains existing restrictions on foreign investment in manufacturing, agriculture, fisheries, forestry, mining and quarrying, and the adjacent services to these sectors. The AFAS schedule covers existing restrictions on foreign investment in the services sector (Mode 3).

This chapter aims to elucidate Indonesia's investment legal framework based on the country's general provisions as stipulated in Law No. 25 (2007) and other related laws and regulations within Indonesia's jurisdiction. It also intends to assess the country's legal obligations as provided in its ACIA reservation list and AFAS packages Schedule. The assessment intends to map out overlapping and/or cross-cutting nexuses between the existing restrictions under the country's legal framework and its regional commitments in investment protection.

Law No. 25 (2007) specifies basic rulings and common ground on domestic and foreign investment policies as it offers categorical restrictions on investment. This category of restrictions applies horizontally across different sectors that regulate activities and certain requirements relating to foreign direct investment covering basic provisions, such as scope and definition of investment, investor, domestic and foreign investment/investor, types of business entities and forms, land titles, company licensing and validation, investor–labour relations, and immigration and investment facility services. Categorical restrictions also offer regulations for general purposes that are in line with the spirit of Article 33 of the State Constitution, such as provisions regulating protection of micro, small, and medium-sized enterprises (MSMEs).

Other related laws and regulations additionally offer non-categorical types of restrictions that apply not only within specific individual sectors. Other laws apply across different sectors with certain commonalities in regulating generic provisions, such as laws on forms of business entity and types of land titles or usage. Non-categorical restrictions also cover sectors relating to portfolio and other non-direct investment. Aside from these two categories, the government's investment negative list (regulated under Presidential Regulations on Investment Negative Lists or *Daftar Negatif Investasi* [DNI]) offers regular update on sectors/sub-sectors that are open, open with conditionality, and closed for foreign investment.

This chapter is structured as follows. The first part presents an overview of restrictions on foreign investment (currently enforced in the country) consisting of three sections that (i) elaborate on categorical restrictions as stipulated in Law No. 25 (2007) covering basic provisions on investment, business entity status and domicile, company validation and licensing, business sectors, land titles and immigration services, investor–labour relations, and protection of MSMEs; (ii) elaborate on non-categorical restrictions as provided in other related laws/regulations, that is, to cover sector-specific restrictions that are in line with Article 33 of the State Constitution; and (iii) present the country's investment negative lists. The second part of the chapter assesses restrictions on foreign investment previously elaborated in the first part, that is, by finding nexuses to the country's obligations under ACIA and AFAS. It consists of three sections that (i) summarise essential attributes of Indonesia's ACIA Reservation Lists and AFAS packages; (ii) offer stylised assessment on the nexuses as commitments to obligations to the ACIA reservation lists and AFAS packages; and (iii) are an endeavour to find and outline nexuses between the country's investment reservation lists and Chapter 9 of the Trans-Pacific Partnership agreement.

2. Overview of the restrictions

Based on the currently enforced legal structure regulating investment practices in Indonesia and despite progressive legal reform[5] provided by Law No. 25 (2007), restrictions on foreign investment are generally derived from the mandates, norms, and provisions of Article 33 of the State Constitution.[6] Law No. 25 (2007) translates and conveys the mandates, norms, and provisions of Article 33: Chapter 1, Article 1 (General Provisions); Chapter 4, Article 5 (Forms of Business Entity and Domicile); Chapter 6, Article 10 (Labour); Chapter 7, Article 12 (Business Sector); Chapter 8, Article 13 (MSMEs and Cooperatives); Chapter 10, Articles 21–23 (Investment Facility for Land Titles and Immigration Services); and Chapter 11, Article 25 (Company Validation and Lilicensing). These legal provisions under Law No. 25 (2007) are categorical restrictions on investment or foreign investment where rulings are applied horizontally across different sectors.

2.1. Categorical restrictions

Table 2.1 summarises categorical restrictions in Law No. 25 (2007). Specific provisions on business types, MSMEs and cooperatives, land titles and immigration services, and validation and licensing of foreign businesses are offered in Chapters 7, 8, 10, and 11 of Law No. 25 (2007), respectively.

Chapter 7, Article 12 of the law regulates business types which could be opened or closed to investment. Article 12 provides that all business sectors or business types be open to investment activities except for those that are declared to be closed and open with requirements (Section 1).[7] The government under presidential regulation *(peraturan presiden* or *perpres)* establishes business sectors closed to both foreign and domestic investments based on the following criteria:

Table 2.1 Categorical restrictions: provisions under law no. 25 on investment (2007)

Provisions	Remarks
General provisions	Distinguishing foreign investment from domestic investment, foreign investor from domestic investor, and foreign capital from domestic capital
Forms and domicile of legal business entity	Further regulated under Law No. 40 (2007) on Limited Liability Company *(Perseroan Terbatas)*
Investors and labour relations	(a) Priority shall be given to host country workers. (b) Detailed and further provisions of laws and regulations shall be stipulated for companies engaging foreign-national experts on specified office and expertise. (c) Companies shall improve competency of host country workers and conduct training and technology transfers if employing foreign nationals (detailed/further legal rulings: Law No. 13 (2003) on manpower/labour, governmental regulations *(peraturan pemerintah)*, and ministerial decrees *(keputusan menteri)* regulating visas, entry permits, and immigration permits.
Business sectors or types or fields	Regulations are regularly enacted for fields of business closed and conditionally open for investments as the basis of the country's investment negative list (*Daftar Negatif Investasi* or DNI)
Legal protection of MSMEs and cooperatives	Reservations are made for MSMEs and cooperatives in certain business sectors and where the sectors are open for investors and/or large businesses provided they cooperate and build partnerships with MSMEs and cooperatives[i].

Provisions	Remarks
Investment facility	Investors are regulated in obtaining 'land titles' (of rights to cultivate for a maximum period of 95 years, rights to build for a maximum period of 80 years, and rights to use for a maximum period of 70 years) and immigration services for temporary foreign workers, permanent as well as non-permanent residency.
Company validation and licensing	Investors shall be willing to comply with all requirements regarding the establishment of a legal business entity (in accordance to Law No. 40 (2007) regulating limited liability companies as well as other provisions stipulated in rulings below the law).

Note:
(i) Detailed regulations are stipulated in the Laws No. 3 (2014) on industry, No. 25 (1992) on cooperatives, and No. 20 (2008) on micro, small, and medium-sized enterprises (MSMEs).

Source: Author.

soundness, morals, culture, the environment, national defence and security, as well as other national interests (Section 2).[8]

Chapter 8, Article 13 regulates special provisions on MSMEs and cooperatives. Under Article 13 provision, the government must establish business sectors that are reserved for MSMEs and cooperatives, as well as business sectors that are open to large businesses on condition that they cooperate with MSMEs and cooperatives (Section 1).[9] The government guides and enhances MSMEs and cooperatives through partnership programmes, increase of competitiveness, inducement of innovation and market expansion, as well as wide dissemination of information (Section 2).

Chapter 10, Articles 21–22 regulate land titles.[10] The provision on land titles stipulates that the government provide simplified services and/or permission to investment companies to obtain land titles (i.e. in addition to immigration service facilities and import permission facilities) (Article 21). Simplified services and/or permission of land titles as intended by Article 21 may be granted and extended all at once in advance and is renewable at the investor's request for the following stipulations (Article 22).[11]

Chapter 10, Article 23 regulates immigration services facilities. Simplified services and/or permission in connection with immigration facilities may be granted: (i) for investments that need temporary foreign workers to realise investments; (ii) for investments that need temporary foreign workers to service machines, other production aids, and after-sales service; and (iii) to prospective investors to explore possibilities for investments (Section 1). Investment got granted the simplified services and/or permission in connection with immigration facilities after the Investment Coordinating Board (ICB) or *Badan Koordinasi Penanaman Modal* (BKPM) (Section 2) has recommended investors.[12]

Chapter 11, Article 25 regulates validation and licensing of foreign investment companies. Investors in Indonesia must comply with the provisions of Article 5 of Law No. 5 (Section 1). Validation of establishment of a foreign business entity in the form of a limited liability company shall be made in accordance with provisions of laws and regulations (Section 3).[13]

2.2. Non-categorical restrictions

Aside from Law No. 25 (2007), other laws and regulations also apply restrictions to investment practices. These laws are applied both horizontally (i.e. regulating basic provisions such as on land and business forms) and vertically based on specific sectors. The horizontal ones include Law No. 5 (1960) (*UU Pokok Agraria* [UUPA]) concerning basic regulations on agrarian principles and Law No. 40 (2007) *(UU Perseroan Terbatas)* concerning limited liability companies. The sectoral ones embrace – but are not necessarily limited to – Law No. 22 (2001) on oil and gas, Law No. 4 (2009) on mineral and coal mining, Law No. 39 (2014) on plantation, Law No. 13 (2003) on workforce, Law No. 21 (2011) on the Financial Service Authority, Law No. 19 (2003) on state-owned enterprises (SOEs), Law No. 3 (2014) on industry, Law No. 25 (1992) on cooperatives, and Law No. 20 (2008) on MSMEs.

Non-categorical restrictions also apply to non-direct investment that is regulated by different laws and regulations. Foreign investment in securities, multi-finance and insurance companies, and portfolio investment transacted through the stock exchange are regulated by the Financial Service Authority or *Otoritas Jasa Keuangan* (OJK) by virtue of Law No. 21 (2011). Previously it was under the Capital Market and Financial Institutions Supervisory Agency or *Badan Pengawas Pasar Modal dan Lembaga Keuangan* (Bapepam-LK) before the transfer to OJK on 31 December 2012. Foreign investment in banking is regulated by the Central Bank (Bank Indonesia) and is governed under different laws and regulations, particularly Law No. 3 (2004) amending Law No. 23 (1999) concerning Bank Indonesia.

Other specific industries are also regulated differently, for example, in downstream and upstream oil and gas sectors. Investments in these areas are regulated and governed by other government authorities beyond Law No. 25 (2007), which means beyond the authority of the Investment Coordinating Board. Foreign investment in downstream and upstream oil and gas sector is regulated by the Oil and Gas Downstream Business Regulatory Agency or *Badan Pengatur Hilir Minyak dan Gas Bumi (BPH Migas)*, the Special Task Force for Upstream Oil and Gas Business Activities or *Satuan Kerja Khusus Kegiatan Usaha Hulu Minyak dan Gas Bumi (SKK-Migas)* and is governed by Governmental Regulation No. 36 (2004) and Governmental Regulation No. 30 (2009) for BPH Migas (with specific reference to Chapter 5, Articles 23–30 of Law No. 22 (2001)] on oil and gas), and Presidential Regulation *(Perpres)* No. 9 (2013) for SKK Migas (with specific reference to Chapter 4, Articles 11–21 of Law No. 22 (2001) on oil and gas as amended by Constitutional Courts Rulings No. 21 (2004) and No. 5 (2012).

Several other sectors, such as industry, agriculture, fishery, forestry, mining and quarrying, and services incidental to these sectors (which have been included in Indonesia's ACIA reservation lists) are also subject to non-categorical restrictions due to the existence and enactment of specific laws regulating individual sectors. Table 2.2 assesses areas of non-categorical restrictions and specific provisions stipulated under several selected laws regulating those sectors.

Table 2.2 Non-categorical restrictions: areas/subjects and provisions under selected laws relating to foreign investment

Law	Areas/Subjects	Provisions

Law No. 3 (2014) on Industry	• Application of Indonesian National Standard of Professional Competency (*Standar Kompetensi Kerja Nasional Indonesia/ SKKNI*) and Indonesian National Standard of Product (*Standar Nasional Indonesia/SNI*)
	
	 • Empowerment of small and medium industries (SMIs)
	
	 • Strategic industries and the use of local products (local content provisions)
		• Chapter 6 (industrial resources development), Part 2 (human resources development)
		   • Articles 18, 19, and 25 (on the application of SKKNI, especially in industries relating to manufacture)
		   • Articles 28 and 29 (on the use of foreign workers that shall meet SKKNI provisions as also regulated by various workforce/labour and transmigration ministerial regulations/decrees (*peraturan/keputusan menteri tenaga kerja* and *transmigrasi* or *permenakertrans/kepmenakertrans*) such as No. 136 (2016) on the provision of SKKNI to professional, scientific, and technical services in the manufacturing system at headquarter offices and management consultancy
		 • Chapter 7 (industrial modes and infrastructure development), Part 2 (industrial standardisation), Articles 50–61 (on the application of SNI in the manufacturing industry sectors)
		 • Chapter 8 (industrial empowerment)
		   • Part 1 (SMIs), Articles 72–76 on SMIs' facilitation and protection
		   • Part 3 (strategic industry), Article 84 on state-controlled strategic industries
		   • Part 4 (intensification of the use of local products), Articles 85–90 on promotion of local products and incentives for local products preference

Law No. 39 (2014) on Plantation	• Land use
	 • Business entity
	 • Foreign investment
		• Chapter 4 (land use), Articles 11–18 on rights to cultivate land for industrial plantation under specific land status (state and customary laws) and governmental rulings on land use limitations and plant variety
		 • Chapter 7 (plantation enterprise)
		   • Part 1 (plantation business entity), Articles 39 and 40 regulating foreign investors in the plantation industry
		   • Part 2 (types and licences of business entity), Articles 41–50 regulating the establishment of plantation business entity
		 • Chapter 13 (investment), Article 95 on the limitations of foreign investment

(*Continued*)

Table 2.2 (Continued)

Law	Areas/Subjects	Provisions

Law No. 31 (2004) on Fishery	• Business entity
	• Services in fishery/marine research and development (R&D)
	• Services in fishery education, training, and counselling
		• Chapter 5 (business entity)
		  • Articles 26–28 on licences for fishery business entity (*surat ijin usaha perikanan*), fishing permits (*surat ijin penangkapan ikan*), and fishing boat permits (*surat ijin kapal pengangkut ikan*)
		  • Article 30 on licences or permits for foreign legal business entity enterprising within the Indonesia Economic Exclusive Zone (IEEZ)
		  • Article 38 on registration and provisions for foreign flagships enterprising in the IEEZ
		• Chapter 8 (fishery R&D)
		  • Articles 55 and 56 on permits and provisions for foreign legal entities conducting fishery/marine R&D
		• Chapter 9 (fishery education, training and counselling), Articles 58 and 59 on international cooperation in fishery education, training, and counselling.

Law No. 41 (1999) on Forestry	Use of forest zone for mining and other non-forestry activities
	• Services in forestry R&D, education, training, and counselling
		• Chapter 5 (forest management), Part 3 (forest utilisation and use of forest zone), Articles 38 and 39 on use permits of forest zone for mining and other non-forestry activities
		• Chapter 6 (forestry R&D, education, training, and counselling)
		  • Part 2 (forestry R&D), Article 54 Section 3 on permits for foreign researchers
		  • Part 5 (funding and infrastructure), Article 57 Section 1 on the obligation of business entity to procure investment fund for forestry R&D, education, training, and counselling

Law No. 4 (2009) on Mineral and Coal Mining	• Licences for mining enterprise, processing and purification of mining products, mining services and mining zones	• Chapter 3 (control of minerals and coal), Article 4 on the basic provision that minerals and coal mining are controlled by the state and are regulated under and implemented by central and regional governments
		• Chapter 4 (authority to manage minerals and coal mining), Article 6 on the types of governmental authority over minerals and coal mining in:
		  • delineating the mining zones (*wilayah pertambangan*)
		  • issuing mining licences (Mining Enterprise Licence or Izin Usaha Pertambangan [IUP] and Special Mining Enterprise License or Izin Usaha Pertambangan Khusus [IUPK] for mining exploration and operation)
		• Chapter 5 (mining zones):
		  • Part 1 (general provisions), Article 13 on types of mining zones that consist of mining enterprise zones or *wilayah usaha pertambangan* (WUP), community mining zones or *wilayah pertambangan rakyat*, and state reserves zones or *wilayah pencadangan negara*

- Part 2 (mining business territories/zones), Articles 14–19 on the provisions of WUP, the WUP holders and mining enterprise licensed zone or *wilayah izin usaha pertambangan*
- Part 3 (community mining territories or zones), Articles 20–26 on the provisions of community mining zones
- Part 4 (state reserves territories or zones), Articles 27–33 on the provisions of state reserves zones, special mining enterprise zones (*wilayah usaha pertambangan khusus*) and special mining enterprise licensed zones (*wilayah izin usaha pertambangan khusus*)
- Chapter 6 (mining enterprises), Articles 34 and 35 on the types and legal entities of mining enterprises
- Chapter 7 (licences for mining company), Articles 36–49 on the provisions of IUP for mining exploration and production
- Chapter 8 (conditions for IUP), Articles 64 and 65 regulating authorities of central and regional government and requirements to be met by IUP applicants before the issuance of IUP
- Chapter 13 (rights and obligations of IUP and IUPK holders), Part 2 (obligations)
- Articles 95, Sections 3 and 102 on the IUP/IUPK holders' obligation to increase value added of minerals and coal resources
- Articles 103–105 on obligations of IUP/IUPK production operation holders to undertake processing and purification activities on domestic mining products
- Article 106 on the IUP/IUPK holders' obligation to prioritise the use of local or domestic workers, goods, and services
- Article 107 on the IUP/IUPK holders' obligation to ensure participation of local enterprises
- Chapter 16 (mining services enterprise), Article 124
- Sections 1 on the obligation of IUP/IUPK holders to use local or national mining services companies
- Section 2 on the exemption to use other than local or national mining services
- Section 3 on the types of mining services

Source: Author.

2.3. *Investment negative list*

Currently, Indonesia's version of negative listing on investment – known as Investment Negative Lists (*Daftar Negatif Investasi* or DNI) – classifies types of business that are open or closed to investment into (i) open to investment (including foreign investment) with no conditions; (ii) open to investment with certain requirements, reservations (i.e. reserved for MSMEs and cooperatives), partnership requirements, specific conditionality such as capital ownership, specific location, and licensing; and (iii) closed or prohibited to investment. Regulation on the DNI is widely known by a presidential regulation *(peraturan presiden* or *perpres)*, which is regularly updated. A special coordinating agency called the Investment Coordinating Board (*Badan Koordinasi Penanaman Modal* or BKPM),[14] which is directly under the President's supervision, administers and monitors the DNI.

The latest regulation is *Perpres* No. 44 (2016) on the List of Business Fields Closed for Investments and Business Fields Conditionally Open for Investments (signed on 12 May 2016 and enacted on 18 May 2016) amending *Perpres* No. 39 (2014). It sets out the following categories of business lines (Molina and Nugraha, 2016):

i   Business lines that are open for 100 percent foreign ownership (subject to specified licensing/technical requirements in certain instances);
ii Business lines where 100 percent foreign ownership is not permitted, but where the level of permitted foreign investment has been increased;
iii Business lines that are reserved for investment by, or in partnership with, domestic small and medium-sized enterprises.

Indonesian DNI suggests a positive-list approach in providing information or updates on business types/sectors open or closed to foreign investment subject to the aforementioned categorisations (A, B, and C). Category A (open for 100 percent foreign ownership) covers seven sectors comprising 14 sub-sectors/provisions. Category B (100 percent foreign ownership is not permitted, but levels of permitted foreign investment are increased) includes sectors or sub-sectors open for foreign investment with ownership that are capped at 49 percent (four sectors/sub-sectors), at 67 percent (14 sectors/sub-sectors), and at 67 percent or up to 70 percent (six sectors/sub-sectors). Category C (reserved for investment by, or in partnership with, domestic small and medium-sized enterprises) includes four sectors/sub-sectors.

3. Nexuses to ACIA and AFAS

After a general overview of restrictions on foreign investment (which consist ovf categorical, non-categorical restrictions, and the country's negative list version), this chapter discovers nexuses between those restrictions and the country's exemption to national treatment and senior management and board of directors (SMBD) obligations as specified in ACIA Reservation Lists and the country's commitments as specified in AFAS packages. In addition to intertwining features with other related laws and/or regulations that are domestically enforced, the categorical restrictions in Law No. 25 (2007) indicate in specific exemptions/commitments under both agreements. This part thus presents a summarised assessment on such nexuses. It offers a brief overview of the country's ACIA reservations lists and AFAS packages and assesses links of categorical and non-categorical restrictions to the country's exemption and commitments under both agreements.

3.1. ACIA Reservation Lists

As of 29 March 2012 (i.e. when the agreement took effect) and as of 27 August 2012 (i.e. when a revised version of Reservation List No. 5 was released), Indonesia's ACIA Reservation Lists encompassed 22 schedules (ACIA1–22).[15] The lists refer to schedules of Indonesia's measures that do not conform to the obligations under Article 5 (National Treatment) and Article 8 (SMBD) pursuant to Article 9 (Reservations) of ACIA. These 22 lists are categorised as follows.

The first category contains exemption measures that apply to all sectors in national treatment at the central government. The second category comprises measures that apply to all sectors in both national treatment and SMBD at the central government. Three types fall under the third category, that is, measures that apply to (i) all sectors in national treatment at both central and regional governments, (ii) all sectors in national treatment but only at the regional government, and (iii) all sectors (but with particular reference to the mineral and coal mining sector) in national treatment at the central government. The fourth, fifth, and sixth categories comprise measures that apply to specific sectors and/or subsectors in national treatment at the central government.

Table 2.3 maps out and summarises the overall lists elaborating exemption measures for each list, its sector/sub-sector, type of obligation, and level of government.

Table 2.3 Summary on Indonesia's ACIA reservation lists

Category (number of ACIA lists)	*Reservation lists (exemption measures)*	*Sector/sub-sector*	*Type of obligation*	*Level of government*
Category 1 (7)	ACIA1, ACIA2, ACIA3, ACIA4, ACIA10, ACIA12, ACIA13	All sectors	NT	Central
Category 2 (4)	ACIA6, ACIA8, ACIA15, ACIA16	All sectors	NT and SMBD	Central

(*Continued*)

Table 2.3 (Continued)

Category (number of ACIA lists)	Reservation lists (exemption measures)	Sector/sub-sector	Type of obligation	Level of government
Category 3 (3)	ACIA7	All sectors	NT	Central and Regional
	ACIA14	All sectors	NT	Regional
	ACIA5	All sectors/mineral and coal mining	NT	Central
Category 4 (2)	ACIA9	Agriculture and fishery	NT	Central
	ACIA11	Fishery	NT	Central
Category 5 (5)	ACIA17	Manufacturing and services incidental to manufacturing	NT	Central
	ACIA18	Agriculture and services incidental to agriculture	NT	Central
	ACIA19	Forestry and services incidental to forestry	NT	Central
	ACIA20	Mining and quarrying, services incidental to mining and quarrying	NT	Central
	ACIA21	Fishery	NT	Central
Category 6 (1)	ACIA22	Agriculture, manufacturing, and services incidental to agriculture, manufacturing horticulture	NT & SMBD	Central

Note:
ACIA = ASEAN Comprehensive Investment Agreement
NT = national treatment
SMBD = senior management and board of directors

Source: Author.

3.2. AFAS Packages

Table 2.4 maps out the country's most-favoured-nation (MFN) exemption lists, schedule of horizontal and specific commitments for national treatment, and market access under mode 3 (commercial presence):

Table 2.4 Summary on Indonesia's AFAS packages

Packages	Sector/sub-sectors	Number of services	Type of obligation	Level of government
AFAS1–9	Banking services	Not applicable (n.a.)	MFN treatment	Central
AFAS1–9	Movement of personnel: Semi-skilled workers	n.a.	MFN treatment	Central
AFAS1–9	Construction services: Government-funded projects	n.a.	MFN treatment	Central
AFAS(h)1–9	All sectors (on income tax and land acquisition)	n.a.	NT	Central
AFAS(h)1–9	All sectors (on commercial presence of foreign service provider)	n.a.	Market access	Central
AFAS(s)1 Mode 3	2 sectors/sub-sectors in 5 CPCs	5 CPCs	Market access	Central
AFAS(s)2 Mode 3	5 sectors/sub-sectors in 33 CPCs (for market access) and 17 CPCs (for NT)	50 CPCs	Market access and NT	Central and regional
AFAS(s)3 Mode 3	6 sectors/sub-sectors in 39 CPCs (for market access) and 29 CPCs (for NT)	68 CPCs	Market access and NT	Central and regional
AFAS(s)4 Mode 3	2 sectors/sub-sectors in 5 CPCs	5 CPCs	Market access and NT	Central and regional
AFAS(s)5 Mode 3	17 sectors/sub-sectors in 54 CPCs (for market access and NT), 15 CPCs (for market access) and 3 CPCs (for NT)	82 CPCs	Market Access and NT	Central and Regional
AFAS(s)6 Mode 3	18 sectors/sub-sectors in 77 CPCs (for market access and NT), 16 CPCs (for market access) and 3 CPCs (for NT)	96 CPCs	Market access and NT	Central and regional
AFAS(s)7 Mode 3	23 sectors/sub-sectors in 102 CPCs (for market access and NT), 19 CPCs (for market access) and 3 CPCs (for NT)	124 CPCs	Market access and NT	Central and regional
AFAS(s)8 Mode 3	25 sectors/sub-sectors in 145 CPCs (for market access) and 75 CPCs (for NT)	220 CPCs	Market access and NT	Central and regional
AFAS(s)9 Mode 3	28 sectors/sub-sectors in 99 CPCs (for market access and NT), 37 CPCs (for market access) and 26 CPCs (for NT)	162 CPCs	Market access and NT	Central and regional

Note:
AFAS = ASEAN Framework Agreement on Services
CPC = Central Product Classification
MFN = most-favoured-nation
NT = national treatment

Source: Author.

Measures relating to joint venture bank (banking services), limited exemptions for low-level occupations (movement of personnel, semi-skilled workers), and measures relating to preferential shortlisting in international competitive bidding of ASEAN nationals (construction services, government-funded projects) are committed in terms of MFN. These three commitments in the MFN treatment obligation are conducted at the central government.

Under AFAS 1–9 for MFN treatment obligation, the banking services sector offers measures relating to a joint venture bank of national and foreign origin. Under this, the entry of foreign banks in Indonesia is allowed on a reciprocity basis. The source of such measures is Ministry of Finance Decree No. 220/KMK017/1993 dated 26 February 1993 (Article 14: 3), stipulating that for joint venture banks, licences can be granted only to foreign banks of countries that adopt reciprocal policies with Indonesian banks. Since AFAS 2, however, it was suspended until the end of 60 days beginning on 1 November 1997 as stipulated in the Second Decision on Financial Services adopted on 21 July 1995 by the Council for Trade in Services.

As for the movement of personnel sector, sub-sector of semi-skilled workers, AFAS 1–9 for MFN treatment stipulate that although low-level occupations are reserved for Indonesian citizens, limited exemptions may be granted to citizens of certain countries. Nationals of Australia, Brunei Darussalam, Malaysia, Papua New Guinea, and Singapore have been granted limited access to low-level occupations. The construction services sector, in the sub-sector of government-funded projects, releases measures relating to preferential shortlisting in international competitive bidding where nationals of Brunei Darussalam, Malaysia, the Philippines, Singapore, and Thailand have been granted special treatment.

Horizontally, under AFAS packages, measures are taken in areas of income tax and land acquisition (for national treatment obligation) that are applied to all sectors. The law on income tax stipulates that non-resident taxpayers will be subject to a withholding tax of 20 percent if they derive from Indonesian sources income from interest, royalties, dividend, and fee from services performed in Indonesia. The source of such measure is Law No. 7 (1983) on income tax *(pajak penghasilan)* as amended by Law No. 7 (1991), Law No. 10 (1994), Law No. 17 (2000), and Law No. 36 (2008). Law No. 5 (1960) on land acquisition stipulates that no foreigners (judicial or natural persons) can own land. However, a joint venture enterprise can hold the right for land use and building rights, and they may rent/lease land and property.

Commercial presence of foreign service provider(s) may be in the form of joint venture and/or representative office, unless mentioned otherwise, where the joint venture should be in the form of a limited liability enterprise *(perseroan terbatas)* and not more than 49 percent of the capital share of said enterprise may be owned by foreign partner(s).

Specific commitments for market access and national treatment obligations are offered in nine consecutive packages based on certain AFAS sectors/sub-sectors.

As shown in Table 2.4, sector/sub-sector specific commitments have steadily increased in terms of number and scope, that is, to reach 28 sectors and sub-sectors of 99 categories under the Central Product Classifications (CPC) (for market access and national treatment), 37 CPC categories (for market access) and 26 CPC categories (for national treatment) in the 9th AFAS Package (AFAS 9) for Mode 3 Typical provisions of AFAS 1–9 have generated the following pattern with more sectors and sub-sectors included over time during negotiation/agreement on the succeeding AFAS packages:

a   Increasing number of sectors/sub-sectors be covered in Indonesia's AFAS specific commitments where the numbers for AFAS 8 and AFAS 9 have reached 25–28 sectors/sub-sectors, respectively.

b   Trends of increasing Foreign Equity Participation (FEP) in certain sectors/sub-sectors where, in the last AFAS 9:

   i   Business services (professional services and R&D services) offer up to 51 percent FEP

   ii   Business services (computer and related services) offer up to 70 percent FEP

   iii Business services (rental and leasing services without operator) offer up to 60 percent FEP

   iv   Communication services (telecommunication services) offer up to 70 percent FEP

   v   Construction and related engineering services, distribution services, education services, environmental services offer up to 51 percent FEP

   vi   Healthcare services (expect in certain areas) offer up to 70 percent FEP

   vii Tourism and travel-related services offer up to 100 percent FEP in certain areas, and up to 70 percent FEP in most other areas for certain CPC groups

   viii Transport services (maritime transport services, internal waterways transport) offer up to 60 percent FEP

   ix   Transport services (rail transport services) offer up to 51 percent FEP;

   x   Transport services (road transport services) offer up to 70 percent FEP

c   More varied measures that are based on specificity of sector/sub-sectors or CPC groups and geographical areas/locations of services offered, such as in tourism and travel-related services, education services, healthcare services and transport services where some areas (e.g. the eastern part of Indonesia, major tourism spots, major cities with advanced education and healthcare services) have been the key focus of the measures.

3.3. ACIA and FAS Linkages to Existing Restrictions

Indonesia's ACIA Reservation Lists have links to the existing restrictions in Law No. 25 (2007). The country's ACIA2 and ACIA3 Reservation Lists have generally linked to provisions on definitions, scope, and legal entity status of foreign investment, foreign investors, and foreign capital as provided in Articles 1 and 5 of Law No. 25 (2007). These ACIA2 and ACIA3 Reservation Lists are also linked to the provisions on company validation and business licensing as regulated in Article 25 of Law No. 25 (2007) in terms of requirements and procedures for the establishment of a legal business entity. Measures taken via *Perpres* No. 44 (2016) on negative investment lists have also impacted the changes in conditions, requirements, and implementation of ACIA2 and ACIA3 Reservation Lists.

Other ACIA Reservation Lists (ACIA6, ACIA8, ACIA10, and ACIA14) are linked to Law No. 25 (2007) in several aspects; these are also regulated by other relevant laws. The country's ACIA6 Reservation Lists are related to the provisions on investors (including foreign investors) and labour relations of Article 10 of Law No. 25 (2007). These are regulated further in Law No. 13 (2003) on priority of local workers, authorisation of foreign national expertise, obligation of workers' competency enhancement, and technology transfer and training. The country's ACIA8 Reservation Lists link to the provisions on the protection and empowerment of MSMEs and cooperatives stipulated in Article 13 of Law No. 25 (2007), which are also elaborated in Laws No. 20 (2008) and No. 25 (1992) on MSMEs and cooperatives.

Articles 21 and 22 of Law No. 25 (2007) are unequivocally linked to the country's ACIA10 Reservation Lists on which provisions on investment facility for land titles are based. Reference to other relevant laws and regulations is made on its granting rights of land as regulated in Law No. 5 (1960) on basic regulations of agrarian principles. Investment facility in immigration services, as provided in Article 23 of Law No. 25 (2007), is also part of the country's ACIA6 reservation lists for temporary foreign workers, permanent and nonpermanent residency. Meanwhile, the country's ACIA14 (along with ACIA2 and ACIA3) Reservation Lists are also linked to the provisions on company validation and licensing of Article 25 of Law No. 25 (2007), No. 40 (2007) on limited liability companies, other relevant ministerial regulations and decrees, and regional regulations.

As for Indonesia's AFAS packages, linkages to the provisions of Law No. 25 (2007) are to be found in Articles 5, 10, 12, 13, 21, 22, 23, and 25. The country's horizontal commitments for market access (AFAS[h]1–9) are in line with Article 5 of Law No. 25 (2007) regulating the legal status of business entities, which is also enacted further in Law No. 40 (2007). Such stipulation has also been applied in the country's AFAS specific commitments (AFAS[s]1–9), especially in measures relating to joint ventures, joint operations, contract management, and other business partnerships involving foreign investments/investors, foreign capital, or with an FEP (as stipulated in Article 25 of Law No. 25 (2007) for company validation and licensing). These commitments are also in line with *Perpres* No. 44 (2016) regulating negative investment lists which are also the subjects of Article 12 of Law No. 25 (2007). These commitments are finally in line with the provisions on MSMEs and cooperatives of Article 13 of Law No. 25 (2007) which are further regulated by Laws No. 20 (2008) and 25 (1992).

The country's horizontal commitments (AFAS1–9) on MFN treatment for semi-skilled workers are in line with Article 10 of Law No. 25 (2007) which gives precedence to local workers. These commitments are also in line with the provisions on investment facility regulating immigration services of Article 23 of Law No. 25 (2007). The country's horizontal commitments (AFAS[h]1–9) on national treatment for land acquisition are in line with the provisions on investment facility for land titles stipulated in Articles 21 and 22 of Law No. 25 (2007).

Last, but not least, the country's ACIA investment lists that are linked to several sectors regulated by relevant laws with non-categorical restrictions include ACIA12 and ACIA4 (in non-direct investment sectors); ACIA5 and ACIA7 (in oil and gas sectors); ACIA17 and ACIA2 (in manufacturing sectors); ACIA9, ACIA2, and ACIA3 (in agriculture sectors); ACIA11, ACIA9, ACIA2, and ACIA3 (in fishery sectors); ACIA7 and ACIA15 (in forestry sectors); and ACIA2, ACIA5, ACIA7, and ACIA15 (in mining and quarrying sectors).

The country's AFAS packages that are linked to several sectors regulated by several relevant laws with non-categorical restrictions include AFAS1–9 on MFN treatment for banking services (in non-direct investment sectors); AFAS4 on financial services (in non-direct investment sectors); AFAS9 on transport services for pipeline transport of petroleum and natural gas (in oil and gas sectors); AFAS2–9 on certain business, construction, communication and telecommunication, and transport services (in manufacturing sectors); AFAS6–9 on education services for vocational education services (in agriculture, fishery, and forestry sectors); AFAS 6–9 on business services for R&D services (in forestry sectors); and AFAS6–9 on energy services for coal liquefaction and gasification (in mining and quarrying sectors).

Table 2.5 recaps linkages of non-categorical restrictions currently regulated under relevant laws to the country's ACIA reservation lists and AFAS packages.

4. Concluding remarks

Law No. 25 (2007) on investment stipulates categorical restrictions on foreign investment in Indonesia. These categorical restrictions, along with non-categorical ones (which are stipulated in other relevant laws and rulings regulating business sectors associated with the provision of Article 33 of the State Constitution and other provisions on strategic sectors), entail nexuses with the country's existing obligations under ACIA reservation lists and commitments under AFAS packages. Assessment undertaken by this study locates major sectors and areas (product and services lines) where measures taken by relevant authorities in the country are found to be intricate. Unbundling such complexity, that is, by mapping out and classifying linkages of those restrictions, the study suggests that the categorical and non-categorical features of restrictions imply different approaches to the country's regional obligations and commitments to be implemented: immediateness for the former and measured and gradual for the latter.

Table 2.5 Non-categorical restrictions: linkages to Indonesia's ACIA reservation lists and AFAS packages

Sectors (ACIA and AFAS Nexuses)	Related laws, specific / sample selected areas	Provisions
Non-direct investment (ACIA2, ACIA4) (AFAS1–9 on MFN treatment for banking services, AFAS4 on financial services)	Law No. 21 (2011), Financial Services	Financial Services Authority (Otoritas Jasa Keuangan) regulating on securities company, multi-finance company and insurance company, and portfolio investment transacted through stock exchange Central Bank (Bank Indonesia) regulating foreign investment banking
Oil and gas (ACIA5, ACIA7) (AFAS9 on transport services for pipeline transport of petroleum and natural gas)	Law No. 3 (2004), Foreign Investment Banking Law No. 22 (2001) as amended by Constitutional Courts Rulings No. 21 (2004) and No. 5 (2012), oil and gas downstream and upstream businesses	Oil and Gas Downstream Business Regulatory Agency (Badan Pengatur Hilir Minyak dan Gas Bumi/BPH Migas) regulating oil and gas downstream business as governed by Government Regulations No. 36 (2004) and No. 30 (2009); Special Task Force for Upstream Oil and Gas Business Activities (Satuan Kerja Khusus Kegiatan Usaha Hulu Minyak dan Gas Bumi/SKK-Migas) regulating oil and gas upstream business activities as governed by Presidential Regulation No. 9 (2013)
Manufacturing (ACIA17, ACIA2) (AFAS2–9 on certain business, construction, communication and telecommunication, and transport services)	Law No. 3 (2014), Industry: SKKNI, SNI, empowerment of small and medium industries (SMIs), strategic industries, and the use of local products (local content)	Chapter 6, Part 2, Articles 18, 19, and 25 on the application of SKKNI; Articles 28 and 29 on the use of foreign workers that shall meet SKKNI provisions (as also regulated under various related ministerial regulations/decrees); Chapter 7, Part 2, Articles 50–61 on the application of SNI in the manufacturing industry; Chapter 8, Part 1, Articles 72–76 on SMIs' facilitation and protection; Part 3, Article 84 on state-controlled strategic industries; Part 4, Articles 85–90 on local products promotion and incentives for the local products preference
Agriculture (ACIA9, ACIA3) (AFAS6–9 on education services for vocational education services)	Law No. 39 (2014), Plantation: land use, business entity, and foreign investment	Chapter 4, Articles 11–18 on rights to cultivate land for industrial plantation under specific land status (state and customary laws) and governmental rulings on land use limitations and plant variety; Chapter 7, Part 1, Articles 39 and 40 regulating foreign investors in plantation industry; Part 2, Articles 41–50 regulating the establishment of plantation business entity; Chapter 13 Article 95 on the limitations of foreign investment
Fishery (ACIA11, ACIA9, ACIA2, ACIA3) (AFAS6–9 on education services for vocational education services)	Law No. 31 (2004) as amended by Law No. 45 (2009), Fishery: business entity, services in fishery/marine research and development (R&D), services in fishery education, training, and counselling	Chapter 5, Articles 26–28 on licences for fishery business entities (surat ijin usaha perikanan), fishing permits (surat ijin penangkat ikan), and fishing boat permits (surat ijin kapal pengangkut ikan); Article 30 on licences or permits for foreign legal business entity enterprising within the Indonesia Economic Exclusive Zone (IEEZ); Article 38 on registration and provisions for foreign flagships enterprising within the IEEZ; Chapter 8, Articles 55 and 56 on permits and provisions for foreign legal entity conducting fishery/marine research and development; Chapter 9, Articles 58 and 59 on international cooperation in fishery education, training, and counselling

| Forestry (ACIA7, ACIA15) (*AFAS6–9 on business services for R&D services, inter-disciplinary R&D for industrial activities, AFAS6–9 on education services for vocational education services*) | Law No. 41 (1999), Forestry: use of forest zone for mining and other non-forestry activities, and services in forestry R&D, education, training, and counselling | Chapter 5, Part 3, Articles 38 and 39 on use permits of forest zone for mining and other non-forestry activities; Chapter 6, Part 2, Article 54, Section 3 on permits for foreign researchers; Part 5, Article 57, Section 1 on the obligation of business entities to procure investment fund for forestry R&D, education, training, and counselling |
| Mining and quarrying (ACIA2, ACIA5, ACIA7, ACIA15) (*AFAS1/s16–9 on energy services for coal liquefaction and gasification*) | Law No. 4 (2009), Mineral and coal mining: licences for mining enterprise, processing and purification of mining products, mining services and mining zones | Chapter 3, Article 4 on the basic provision that minerals and coal mining are controlled by the state and are regulated under and implemented by central and regional governments; Chapter 4, Article 6 on the types of governmental authority over minerals and coal mining, that is, in delineating the mining zones (*wilayah pertambangan*), issuing mining licences (Mining Enterprise License/[IUP] and Special Mining Enterprise License or *Izin Usaha Pertambangan Khusus* [IUPK] for mining exploration and operation); Chapter 5, Part 1, Article 13 on types of mining zones that consist of mining enterprise zones or *wilayah usaha pertambangan* (WUP), community mining zones or *wilayah pertambangan rakyat* (WPR), and state reserves zones or *wilayah pencadangan negara* (WPN); Part 2, Articles 14–19 on the provisions of WUP, the WUP holders and mining enterprise licensed zone (*wilayah izin usaha pertambangan* [WIUP]); Part 3, Articles 20–26 on the provisions of WPR; Part 4, Articles 27–33 on the provisions of WPN, special mining enterprise zones (*wilayah usaha pertambangan khusus*), and special mining enterprise licensed zones (*wilayah izin usaha pertambangan khusus*); Chapter 6, Articles 34 and 35 on the types and legal entities of mining enterprises; Chapter 7, Articles 36–49 on the provisions of IUP for mining exploration and production; Chapter 8, Articles 64 and 65 regulating authorities of central and regional government and requirements to be met by IUP applicants before the issuance of IUP; Chapter 13, Part 2, Articles 95, Sections 3 and 102 on the IUP/IUPK holders' obligation to increase the value added of minerals and coal resources; Articles 103, 104, and 105 on the IUP/IUPK production operation holders' obligation to undertake processing and purification activities on domestic mining products; Article 106 on the IUP/IUPK holders' obligation to prioritise the use of local or domestic workers, goods, and services; Article 107 on the IUP/IUPK holders' obligation to ensure participation of local enterprises; Chapter 16, Article 124, Sections 1 on the obligation of IUP/IUPK holders to use local or national mining services companies; Section 2 on the exemption to use other than local or national mining services companies; and Section 3 on the types of mining services |

Source: Author.

Notes

1 Based on Law No. 10 (2004) on the formulation of laws and regulations, the legal framework, in order of hierarchy, is as follows: the State Constitution, the laws and the government regulations in lieu of law, government regulations, presidential regulations, and regional regulations. The following laws and government regulations, additional rulings, and detailed procedures for government regulations take the form of presidential instructions, ministerial regulations and decrees, ministerial circulation letters, and other rulings at the level of regional and central governments.

2 That is, Laws No. 5 (1960) basic regulations on agrarian principles, No. 40 (2007) on limited liability companies, No. 22 (2001) on oil and gas, No. 4 (2009) on mineral and coal mining, No. 39 (2014) concerning plantation, No. 13 (2003) on workforce, No. 21 (2011) concerning the Financial Service Authority, No. 19 (2003) on state-owned enterprises (SOEs), No. 3 (2014) concerning industry, No. 25 (1992) concerning cooperatives, No. 20 (2008) on micro, small, and medium-sized enterprises (MSMEs), No. 3 (2004) amending No. 23 (1999) concerning the Central Bank, No. 41 (1999) on forestry, and No. 45 (2009) amending No. 31 (2004) concerning fishery.

3 Those bilateral investment treaties (BITs) are in addition to 26 BITs that were terminated. Included are 17 BITs that were terminated in past 2 years which comprise treaties with China, India, the Netherlands, Switzerland, France, and several ASEAN countries. Indonesia has never had a BIT with either the United States or Japan, but recent Indonesia–Japan Economic Partnership Agreement does include investment (Magiera, 2017). The full list of Indonesia's BITs partners is available at http://investmentpolicyhub.unctad.org/IIA/CountryBits/97#iiaInnerMenu

4 ASEAN–EU Cooperation Agreement (signed/into force 1980); Organization of the Islamic Conference Investment Agreement (signed 1981, into force 1986); ASEAN Investment Agreement (signed 1987); ASEAN Services (signed 1995, into force 1998); ASEAN–China Framework Agreement (signed 2002, into force 2003); ASEAN–Japan Framework Agreement (signed 2002, into force 2003); ASEAN–India Framework Agreement (signed/into force 2004); ASEAN–Korea Framework Agreement (signed 2005, into force 2006); ASEAN–US Trade and Investment Framework Arrangement (TIFA) (signed/into force 2006); Indonesia–Japan Economic Partnership Agreement (signed 2007, into force 2008); ASEAN–Japan FTA (signed 2008); ASEAN Comprehensive Investment Agreement or ACIA (signed 2009, into force 2012); ASEAN–Australia–New Zealand Free Trade Agreement (signed 2009, into force 2010); ASEAN–Korea Investment Agreement, signed/into force 2009); ASEAN–China Investment Agreement (signed 2009, into force 2010); and ASEAN–India Investment Agreement (signed 2014).

5 The spirit of reform in the formulation and enactment of Law No. 25 (2007) is reflected not only in its acknowledgement of the need to keep pace with the changes in contemporary international economic environment, but also in its content especially as regards affirming investment promotion and legal protection (Chapter 3, Major Investment Policies, Article 4; Chapter 5, Treatment towards Investments, Articles 6–9; Chapter 10, Investment Facility, Articles 18–24; Chapter 12, Coordination and Implementation of Investment Policies, Articles 27–29; Chapter 13, Administration of Investment Affairs, Article 30; and Chapter 14, Special Economic Zones, Article 31).

6 The article contains five sections which state that: (i) The economy shall be organised as a common endeavour based on familial principles; (ii) Sectors of production which are vital for the state and affect the livelihood of the majority of the population shall be under the powers of the state; (iii) The land, the waters, and

the natural resources shall be under the powers of the state and shall be exploited to the greatest benefit of the people; (iv) The national economy shall be organised based on economic democracy, upholding the principles of solidarity, efficiency along with fairness, sustainability, keeping the environment in perspective, self-sufficiency, balanced progress, and unity of the national economy; (v) Further provisions regarding the implementation of this article are to be regulated by the law(s). Sections 4 and 5 were added as a result of the fourth amendment of the State Constitution enacted on 11 August 2002. The original Article 33 consists only of three sections (Sections 1–3).

7 Business sectors or business types that are closed and open with requirements are provided for by presidential regulations in a list based on the standard for classification of business sectors or business types applicable in Indonesia. The classification is based on *Klasifikasi Baku Lapangan Usaha Indonesia (KBLI)* and/or the International Standard for Industrial Classification (ISIC), see: *KBLI* of 2005 issued by the Statistics Central Agency (October 2005).

8 The current regulation on the negative list is Presidential Decree (Keppres) No. 44 of 2016 on list of business fields closed for investments and business fields conditionally open for investments. It replaced the previous regulations Presidential Regulation No. 39 of 2010 on list of business fields closed for investments and business fields conditionally open for investments, President Decree No. 96/ 2000 concerning business sectors that are closed and business sectors that are open to investment with specified requirements (20 July 2000), as amended by President Decree No. 118/2000 (16 August 2000).

9 'Business sectors that are reserved' refer to business sectors that are for the special benefit of micro, small, and medium-sized enterprises (MSMEs).

10 Regulations on land before the law was enacted were (i) Presidential Decree No. 34/1992 concerning the use of HGU and HGB land (see footnote 11 for the meaning of HGU and HGB land) by Joint Ventures Businesses for Foreign Investments (6 July 1992), (ii) Agrarian Ministerial Regulation No. 2/1993 (500–3302.A) concerning procedures for obtaining a location permit and land titles for investment companies (23 October 1993), (iii) Kepmenagr No. 22/ 1993 (400–3972) concerning guidelines to location permits in the implementation of Permenagr No. 2/1993 (4 December 1993), and (iv) Kepmenagr No. 21/1994 (500–3827) concerning procedures for acquiring land for investment companies (7 December 1994). Overall rulings on land are stipulated under Law No. 5 of 1960 *(UU Pokok Agraria)* concerning basic regulations on agrarian principles.

11 The right to cultivate (*Hak Guna Usaha* [HGU]) may be granted for a period of 95 years by being granted and extended all at once in advance for 60 years and renewable for 35 years. The right to build (*Hak Guna Bangunan* [HGB]) may be granted for a period of 80 years by being granted and extended all at once in advance for 50 years and renewable for 30 years. The right to use *(Hak Pakai)* may be granted for a period of 70 years by being granted and extended all at once in advance for 45 years and renewable for 25 years. Elucidation of Article 22, Section (1) Subsection a: HGU is acquired by being granted and extended all at once in advance for a period of 60 years and renewable for 35 years; Subsection b: HGB is acquired by being granted and extended all at once in advance for a period of 50 years and renewable for 30 years; Subsection c: *Hak Pakai* is acquired by being granted and extended all at once in advance for a period of 45 years and renewable for 25 years.

12 Elucidation of Article 23, Section 2: recommendation is given after an investment has complied with the provisions of foreign worker employment in accordance with the provisions of labour laws and regulations (especially with reference to Law No. 13 of 2003). Under such a provision, a foreign investor is granted

the following facilities: A non-permanent residence permit is granted to a foreign investor for a period of 2 years. A change in the status from non-permanent residence to permanent residence is granted to an investor after the investor has resided in Indonesia for a period of 2 consecutive years. A multiple re-entry permit to the holder of non-permanent residence permit is granted with a validity period of 1 year for a period not exceeding 12 months from the time the non-permanent residence permit is granted. The holder of a non-permanent residence permit is granted a multiple re-entry permit with a validity period of 2 years for a period not exceeding 24 months from the time the non-permanent residence permit is granted. The holder of a permanent residence permit is granted a multiple re-entry permit for a period not exceeding 24 months from the time the permanent residence permit is granted (Section 3). A non-permanent residence permit for a foreign investor, as intended by Section 3, items a and b, shall be granted by the Directorate General of Immigration on the recommendation of the Investment Coordinating Board or the *Badan Koordinasi Penanaman Modal* [BKPM]. Regulations on foreign employment and immigration before the law was enacted were (i) Governmental Regulation No. 32/1994 concerning visas, entry permits, and immigration permits (14 October 1994), as amended by *Peraturan Pemerintah* or PP No. 18/2005 (4 May 2005) and PP No. 38/2005 (12 Oct 2005); (ii) Justice Ministerial Decree No. M.02-IZ.01.10/1995 concerning transit visa, visit visas, non-permanent resident visas, entry permits, and immigration permits (14 March 1995), as amended by Ministerial Decree No. M.01-IZ.01.10/2003 (23 May 2003) and Law and Human Rights Ministerial Regulation No. M.01-IZ.01.10/2007 (13 February 2007); (iii) Labour and Transmigration Ministerial Regulation No. 07/Men/IV/2006 concerning simplified procedures for obtaining a foreign worker employment permit (29 March 2006), as amended by Ministerial Decree No. 15/Men/IV/2006 (28 April 2006); and (iv) Ministerial Decree No. M.06-IL.01.10/2006 concerning the provision of special facilities in the field of immigration in special economic zones (31 August 2006).

13 Validation of legal entity and regional authority is further regulated by (i) Ministerial Decree No. 837-KP.04.11/2006 concerning delegation of ministerial authority (Ministry of Law and Human Rights) in granting validation of legal entity of limited liability companies to the head of regional ministerial offices throughout Indonesia (24 March 2006); and (ii) Ministerial Decree No. M.01-HT.01.10/2006 concerning procedures for filing applications for and validation of deeds of establishment, approvals, deliveries of reports and notice of deeds of amendments to the articles of association of limited liability incorporation (19 June 2006).

14 Status, roles, and working scope of the *Badan Koordinasi Penanaman Modal* (BPKM) or the Investment Coordinating Board. The BKPM is regulated in Chapter 12, Articles 27–29 of Law No. 25 (2007) concerning investment.

15 These 22 reservation lists are symbolised and numbered as ACIA1 to ACIA22. Documents of each list comprise information on sector, sub-sector, industry classification, level of government, type of obligation, and description and source of measures to be reserved. The full lists can be downloaded at http://investasean. asean.org/files/upload/Indonesia%20Rsv%20List%20%20(Final%20120411).pdf

Bibliography

ASEAN (2015), *ASEAN Integration in Services*. Jakarta: ASEAN Secretariat.

Butt, S. and L. Tim (2009), 'Economic Reform When the Constitution Matters: Indonesia's Constitutional Court and Article 33 of the Constitution', *Sydney Law School Legal Studies Research Paper* No. 09, 29 May, University of Sydney, Sydney. Available at http://ssrn.com/abstract=1400505

Government Regulation *(Peraturan Pemerintah/Perpres)* No. 44 (2016) on the List of Business Fields Closed for Investments and Business Fields Conditionally Open for Investments (Investment Negative List).

KPMG Indonesia (2015), 'Investing in Indonesia'. Available at www.kpmg.com/ID/en/IssuesAndInsights/ArticlesPublications/Documents/Investing%20in%20Indonesia%202015.pdf

Magiera, S. L. (2017), 'International Investment Agreements and Investor-State Disputes: A Review and Evaluation for Indonesia', ERIA Discussion Paper, No. ERIA-DP-2016-30.

Melli D. (2011), 'Overview on Foreign Investment in Indonesia', *China Go Abroad*. Available at http://transasialawyers.com/publicfiles/N2-MelliDarsa-E.pdf

Ministry of Energy and Mineral Resources (2015), '*Revisi UU Migas: Mendorong Terwujudnya Tata Kelola Migas Nasional Sesuai Konstitusi*', Presentation materials at public discussion of GERINDRA Party, 9 April.

Molina, K. and N. Putra (2016), 'Indonesia's New 2016 Negative List', *Witara Cakra Advocates*. Available at www.whitecase.com/sites/whitecase/files/files/download/publications/indonesias-new-2016-negative-list.pdf

UNCTAD (2016), World Investment Reprot 2016. Geneva: United Nations.

Widyawan and Partners (2014), 'Legal Guide to Investment in Indonesia', July. London: Allens and Linklaters. Available at www.allens.com.au/pubs/pdf/Investing-in-Indonesia.pdf

ASEAN documents:

'Indonesia Final List of MFN Exemptions, AFAS1–9'. Jakarta: ASEAN Secretariat.

'Indonesia Reservation Lists (Schedule of Measures Non-Conforming Obligations to NT and SMBD), ACIA1–12'. Jakarta: ASEAN Secretariat.

'Indonesia Schedule of Horizontal Commitments', AFAS(h)1–9'. Jakarta: ASEAN Secretariat.

'Indonesia Schedule of Specific Commitments, AFAS(s)1–9'. Jakarta: ASEAN Secretariat.

Government of Indonesia documents:

Governmental Regulation (*Peraturan Pemerintah/Perpres*)

Governmental Regulation No. 44 (2016) on the List of Business Fields Closed for Investments and Business Fields Conditionally Open for Investments (Investment Negative List).

Governmental Regulation No. 32 (1994) concerning Visa, Entry Permission, and Immigration Permits.

Government Regulation No. 38 (2005) second amendment to No. 32 (1994) concerning Visa, Entry Permission, and Immigration Permits.

Government Regulation No. 18 (2005) first amendment to No. 32 (1994) concerning Visa, Entry Permission, and Immigration Permits.

Governmental Regulation No. 30 (2009) for BPH Migas

Governmental Regulation No. 36 (2004) on Earth oil and gas business activity

Law No. 1 (1967) on Foreign Investments (amended by UU No. 11 of 1970).

Law No. 3 (2004) amending UU No. 23 (1999) on Bank of Indonesia (Central Bank).

Law No. 3 (2014) on Industry.

Law No. 4 (2009) on Mineral and Coal Mining.

Law No. 5 (1960) (*UU Pokok Agraria*/UUPA) on Basic Regulations of Agrarian Principles.

Law No. 10 (2004) on the Formulation of Laws and Regulations.

Law No. 13 (2003) on Manpower.

Law No. 19 (2003) on State-Owned Enterprises (SOEs).

Law No. 20 (2008) on SMEs.

Law No. 21 (2011) on the Financial Service Authority (OJK).

Law No. 22 (2001) on Oil and Gas.

Law No. 25 (1992) on Cooperatives.

Law No. 25 (2007) on Investment.

Law No. 30 (1999) on Arbitration and Dispute Settlement Alternatives.

Law No. 31 (2004) on Fishery.

Law No. 39 (2014) on Plantation.

Law No. 40 (2007) (UU *Perseroan Terbatas*/PT) on Limited Liability Company.

Law No. 41 (1999) on Forestry Law.

Law No. 45 (2009) amendment to No. 31 (2004) on Fishery.

Law No. 7 (1983) on income tax.

Law No. 7 (1991) first amendment to Law No. 7 (1983) on income tax.

Law No. 10 (1994) second amendment to Law No. 7 (1983) on income tax.

Law No. 17 (2000) third amendment to Law No. 7 (1983) on income tax.

Law No. 36 (2008) fourth amendment to Law No. 7 (1983) on income tax.

Ministerial regulations, decrees *(Peraturan Menteri or Permen, Keputusan Menteri or Kepmen)* (various).

Agrarian Ministerial Regulation (Permenagr) No. 2/1993 concerning procedures for obtaining a location permit and land titles for investment companies.

Kepmenagr No. 22/1993 concerning guidelines to location permits in the implementation of Permenagr No. 2/1993.

Kepmenagr No. 21/1994 concerning procedures for acquiring land for investment companies.

Presidential regulations, decrees *(Peraturan Presiden or Perpres, Keputusan Presiden or Keppres)* (various).

Presidential Decree No. 34 (1992).

Presidential Decree No. 96 (2000).

Presidential Regulation No. 9 (2013) for SKK Migas.

Regional regulations *(Peraturan Daerah or Perda)* (various).State Constitution (*Undang-Undang Dasar*/UUD 1945).

Constitutional Courts Rulings No. 5 (2012).

3 An assessment of the Philippines' readiness to mega new generation agreements

Investment

Glenda T. Reyes

1. Introduction

As countries internationalise and expand their reach in the global value chain, economies are also intensifying their participation in regional integration and free trade agreements (FTAs). The FTAs have become important instruments in increasing the economies' participation and foothold in the global value chain.

With the world economy also entering a new phase and increasingly becoming more interconnected, the FTAs have been reshaped to adapt to these changes and address the concerns in earlier versions. To ensure that the use of the FTAs is optimised and to produce commercially meaningful outcomes for FTA members, the new generation agreements have taken a bolder and more aggressive stance with expanded scope and obligations, and new approaches to liberalisation.

These new generation agreements will serve as model in future FTAs. Thus, it is practical and highly sensible that a country embarking on new negotiations should undertake a review of its regulatory regime in relation to the elements of the new generation agreements to assess their impact, and the country's readiness to meet its obligations. The benchmark for the review and assessment is the Trans-Pacific Partnership (TPP) agreement signed by 12 countries in the Asia-Pacific region on 4 February 2016. The Philippines, along with some ASEAN member states, such as Thailand and Indonesia, has also expressed interest to join the TPP. Four ASEAN member states and three ASEAN dialogue partners are signatories to the TPP.

When the United States withdrew from the agreement, the Comprehensive and Progressive Agreement for Trans-Pacific Partnership (CPTPP) involving the other 11 signatory countries[1] was signed on 8 March 2018. Without prejudging the elements or disciplines of the FTAs under or to be negotiated by the Philippines, it is judicious to look into the implications of the new generation agreements and ascertain the agenda for reform.

This chapter focuses on the investment provisions of new generation agreements. Using the TPP as benchmark, it attempts to assess the conformity of the Philippine investment regime with obligations under Chapter 9 on investment, which embody the principles of non-discrimination, free(r) trade, competition, and predictability. It examines the investment-related measures in the Philippines in relation to compliance to the obligations of the TPP member states from four aspects, as defined and described in Table 3.1: (i) national treatment,

Table 3.1 Investment liberalisation obligations in the TPP agreement

Obligation	Description
National Treatment	Investors from other TPP member states and their investments are to be treated in the same manner or equally as domestic investors and their investments.
MFN Treatment	Investors from a TPP member states are not treated less favourably than investors from other countries, either TPP and non-TPP member states. The same treatment applies to their investments.
Performance Requirements	A TPP member is prohibited from imposing condition(s) to investors from other TPP members prior to approval of their investment.
SMBD	A TPP member is not to impose a nationality or residency requirement or both for SMBD in enterprises.

Note:
CPTPP = Comprehensive and Progressive Agreement for Trans-Pacific Partnership
MFN = most-favoured nation
SMBD = senior management and board of directors

Source: TPP agreement.

(ii) most-favoured-nation (MFN) treatment, (iii) performance requirements, and (iv) senior management and board of directors (SMBD). This entails a mapping and an assessment of the relevant provisions of existing national laws, rules, and regulations affecting foreign investors and their investments in the Philippines, as well as the implications of the TPP investment scheduling approach to liberalisation for the country.

2. Sources of Philippine measures

The legal system regulating foreign investors and investments consists of the Philippine Constitution, national statutes or laws, and departmental rules and regulations.[2] The 1987 Philippine Constitution, which is the fundamental and supreme law of the Philippines, spells out many provisions that may infringe upon the obligations for non-discriminatory treatment of foreign investors and their investments. The relevant measures are found in six articles, but the majority are laid down in the Article on National Economy and Patrimony. Table 3.2 briefly describes the relevant articles of the Constitution.

Investment-related measures are further spelled out in national statutes or laws, which may cover rules of general application or a specific industry, area, or activity. General rules and regulations affecting investors and investments are contained in the (i) Omnibus Investment Code (Executive Order [EO] 226), (ii) Foreign Investment Act (Republic Acts [RAs] 7042 and 8179), (iii) Corporation Code (Batas Pambansa 68), (iv) Civil Code of the Philippines (RA 386), and (v) special laws on economic zones and freeport areas (see Table 3.3).[3]

Table 3.2 Relevant articles of the 1987 Philippine Constitution

Article	Description
Article II	Articulates the State policies, which, amongst others, include the promotion and protection of national interest, pursuit of freedom from nuclear weapons, development of self-reliant and independent economy controlled by Filipinos, promotion of the rights of indigenous cultural communities, and ensuring autonomy of local governments.
Article X	Recognises the role of local governments in addressing and attending to local affairs. For this purpose, the Constitution defines the territorial and political subdivisions of the Philippines and grants autonomy to local governments to help them develop their full potentials. The political subdivision refers to provinces, cities, municipalities, barangays, and the autonomous regions in Muslim Mindanao and the Cordilleras.
Article XII	Enunciates the goals of the Philippine economy, and lays down the guidelines to achieve these, which include limitations on ownerships and conditions to investment. It encompasses policies on land ownership, development and use of natural resources (including marine resources), grant of franchise on public utility, preferential use of Filipino labour, local materials and goods, trade policy based on equality and reciprocity, practice of professions, and use of appropriate technology. Moreover, it defines the rights of former natural-born citizens of the Philippines, and states sanctions on any acts that may circumvent or negate the article's provisions.
Article XIII	Promotes social justice and, thus, addresses the inequities in society and provides for the creation of economic opportunities, especially for the poor. It outlines the rights of and support for farmers, farmworkers, fishermen, and fish workers, amongst others.
Article XIV	Prescribes prohibition on ownership, control, and administration of educational institutions in line with the objective of imbuing a sense of patriotism and nationalism in the Philippine educational system.
Article XVI	General Provisions, includes policies for the protection of public interest and, thus, in this respect, stipulates regulations and ownership and management limitations on mass media and advertising.

Source: The 1987 Constitution of the Republic of the Philippines. Available at www.dotr.gov. ph/images/front/GAD/issuances/1987constitution.pdf

Table 3.3 Investment-related laws of general application

National Statute/Law	Description
Omnibus Investment Code	Sets out the general policies on investment and the incentives scheme, specifically for preferred areas of investments and multinational companies establishing regional operations in the Philippines. Also spells out the regulations and the qualification requirements for enterprise registration and entitlement to incentives granted under the Code.

(*Continued*)

Table 3.3 (Continued)

National Statute/Law	Description
Foreign Investment Act	Lays down the rules regarding foreign investment in the Philippines, particularly with respect to ownership or equity participation.
	Clarifies that foreign ownership of up to 100% is allowed as a general rule except for areas in the Foreign Investment Negative List (FINL), which consists of:
	(i) List A that covers areas of activities reserved to Philippine nationals or where foreign ownership is limited as mandated by the Philippine Constitution and specific laws; and
	(ii) List B that covers areas of activities or enterprises regulated pursuant to laws which have implications to security, defence, public health, and morals, and protection of small and medium-sized enterprises.
	It excludes from its coverage banking and other financial institutions governed under the General Banking Act of the Philippines and other laws and regulated by the Bangko Sentral ng Pilipinas (Central Bank of the Philippines).
Corporation Code of the Philippines and Civil Code of the Philippines	Contain pertinent provisions on the setting up and operation of legal entities in the Philippines:
	The Corporation Code defines the rules and regulations pertaining to the incorporation and organisation of domestic corporations in the Philippines, which includes fulfilment of requirements on ownership, location of office; residency for the board of directors and trustees; and citizenship of the corporate secretary. The Corporation Code also states and clarifies the conditions under which foreign corporations incorporated and organised under the laws of other countries may do business in the Philippines.
	The Civil Code governs partnerships and associations as a juridical personality separate from each of the partners.
Special laws on economic zones (ecozones) and freeport areas	These have been enacted to disperse industries, promote development, and create employment in various parts of the country. Foreign citizens and companies are encouraged to locate their businesses and set up export-oriented enterprises in designated zones/areas in the Philippines with the grant of investment incentives[i].
	Stipulations on investments, including conditions and incentives, vary across special laws on ecozones and/or freeport areas. The list of special laws on ecozones and freeport areas appears as Appendix 3.

Note:
(i) The grant of incentives is subject to the guidelines and requirements stipulated in the specific laws and corresponding implementing rules and regulations.

Source: Author.

3. Review of investment-related measures

3.1. In relation to liberalisation obligations

This section reviews the existing Philippine investment measures against the four core liberalisation obligations under the TPP chapter on investment. Measures that discriminate against foreign investors and their investments are considered non-conforming measures to the obligation(s) concerned, and subject to negotiations and may be listed in either Annex I or Annex II as exemptions to the obligations.

3.1.1. National treatment

The national treatment obligation requires parties to extend equal treatment between foreign and domestic investors and their investments. Discrimination against foreign investors in the Philippines is usually in the form of ownership, whereby participation of foreign capital is limited in terms of the maximum foreign shareholding. In most cases, foreign equity participation is limited to a maximum of 40 percent, which leaves control of the entity to local investors. Notwithstanding this, some areas are totally closed to foreign investors, such as mass media, defence-related construction, and security agency. In some cases, foreign equity participation is more restricted or set at a lower percentage, for example, in advertising, and placement and recruitment.

The Philippine Constitution has set a minimum level of Filipino participation in investments and shareholding to be 'at least 60% owned by Philippine citizens'. The Constitution further broadens the 'Filipino-first' policy by allowing Congress to increase Filipino ownership beyond 60 percent in line with national interest. Consistent with this, some measures require divestment of foreign equity after a period to increase Filipino ownership in such industry as iron and steel, rice and corn, educational institutions, and authorised activity in forestlands.

Some measures also prescribe limits on the type of legal entity but mostly in professional services. Of the 41 regulated professions, only seven allow 'corporate practice' as explicitly provided in their specific laws. Participation of foreign professionals or ownership, if allowed, is subject to reciprocity arrangement.

In areas where the state maintains ownership and control specifically as regards natural resources, rights or concessions to explore, develop, lease, or use may be granted exclusively to Filipino citizens or may be granted to associations or corporations with limited participation by foreign investors. Such is the case for:

i   large-scale exploration, development, and utilisation of mineral resources, petroleum, and other mineral oils;
ii exploration, tapping, or use of geothermal energy, natural gas, or methane gas;
iii utilisation, exploitation, occupation, possession, and conduct of any activity in forestlands, including the establishment and operation of wood-processing plant, may be authorised under a licence agreement, lease, licence, or permit;
iv use and enjoyment of marine wealth, that is, fishery and aquatic resources; and
v   commercial fishing vessels.

Subsistence activities in farming and fishing, small-scale utilisation of natural resources, as well as cooperative activities are not open to foreign engagement. Similarly, investment in small- and medium-scale enterprises is exclusive to Filipino citizens. Foreign investors can participate only when the investment meets a certain capitalisation amount, involves advanced technology, or directly employs 50 employees.

3.1.2. Most-favoured-nation treatment

The MFN treatment obligation ensures that investors from TPP member economies are not treated any less favourably than those from the other TPP members
and other countries. Any violation of this obligation must be scheduled or listed
as non-conforming. In the case of the Philippines, such non-conforming measures would stem from international treaties and agreements it is a party to, and
international conventions it supports.

The MFN non-conforming measures would include the FTAs the Philippine
has negotiated and entered into, which give differential treatment to other countries party to these agreements, and measures being undertaken by the Philippines
as part of regional economic integration such as the ASEAN Economic Community, and as member of sub-regional arrangements amongst ASEAN member states. Regarding ASEAN, it is noted that under the Omnibus Investment
Code, the President, upon the recommendation of the Board of Investments,
can suspend the nationality requirement 'for ASEAN projects, or investments by
ASEAN nationals, regional ASEAN or multinational financial institutions including their subsidiaries in preferred projects and/or projects allowed through either
financial or technical assistance agreements entered into by the President, and in
the case of regional complementation for the manufacture of a particular product
which seeks to take advantage of economies of scale projects' (Article VII, paragraph [13]).

The Philippines' MFN Exemption List in the ASEAN Framework Agreement
on Services (AFAS), which is the same as the MFN Exemption List submitted for
the General Agreement on Trade in Services (GATS), will have to be part of the
measures in Annex II. This contains measures that do not conform to the MFN
treatment obligation in AFAS and GATS.

Economic provisions in the Philippine Constitution and national statutes could
also be considered bearing upon the MFN treatment obligation, such as the

i   mandate for the state to pursue a trade policy based on equality and
     reciprocity;
ii   reciprocity required for the practice of profession by foreign professionals;
iii reciprocal arrangement in allowing foreign corporations not incorporated in
     the Philippines to do business in the country; and
iv   grant of rights to former natural-born citizens of the Philippines or those
     who maintain dual citizenship to own lands and to have same investment
     rights as citizens of the Philippines.

3.1.3. Performance requirements

The obligation on performance requirements prohibits the attachment of conditions to the establishment, acquisition, expansion, management, conduct,
operation, or sale or other disposition of an investment. In the context of the
'Filipino-first' policy, the Constitution declares to promote the preferential use of

Filipino labour, local materials, and products and to encourage the use of appropriate technology. National statutes also prescribe the following requirements:

i   use of advanced technology or employment of specific number of workers allowed to engage in small and medium-sized domestic enterprises (RA 7042 as amended by RA 8179);
ii export of certain percentage of total production under the Foreign Investment Act, Omnibus Investment Code, and laws pertaining to economic zones and free ports;
iii use of iron and steel products manufactured in the country in infrastructure, industrial, and construction projects (RA 7103);
iv employment of Filipino labour in every phase of construction activities under the build-operate-transfer scheme (RA 6957 as amended by RA 7188) in the exploration, development, and utilisation of geothermal energy and natural and methane gas (RA 5092); and
v   local sourcing of certain percentage of inventory in retail trade (RA 8762).

3.1.4. Senior management and board of directors

The SMBD obligation warrants that TPP parties or members will not impose nationality or residency requirement for holding SMBD position in a company. The Corporation Code of the Philippines provides the rules for companies incorporated and registered under Philippine laws. In some cases, rules pertaining to SMBD are also found in specific provisions of other Philippine national laws.

The review of the Philippine measures reveals the following:

a   In general, the participation of foreign investors in the governing board of a company is proportionate to their shares in the company's capital.
b   For companies incorporated and registered under Philippine laws:

   i   Majority of incorporators and board of directors or trustees must be residents of the country.
   ii   The corporate secretary must be a Filipino citizen and resident of the country.
   iii The corporate treasurer shall be a resident of the country.

c   In most cases, the executive and management positions are reserved also to Filipino citizens as in the case of public utility, educational institutions, and mass media.

3.2. In relation to scheduling approach

While the two-annex negative list approach adopted in the TPP allows flexibility to its members to maintain existing measures and/or make future measures by scheduling, it imposes additional obligations to them in terms of the level of commitment and future liberalisation. In Annex I, measures are scheduled on a standstill basis, that is at the level of current regulatory practice, with further obligation of no backtracking of commitments, and automatic extension of future unilateral liberalisation to the other members without need for further negotiations ('ratchet obligation'). Annex II allows members to reserve their right to take on future measures for any sector listed therein even if these are more restrictive than the current regulatory practice (i.e. before the proposed change or amendment).

The 1987 Philippine Constitution explicitly provides that Congress can adopt discriminatory or more restrictive measures to foreign investors[4] upon the recommendation of the National Economic and Development Authority, the central planning body of the Philippines. This should be noted in relation to the scheduling of reservations, particularly in Annex I as Congress can (i) reserve certain investment to Filipino citizens or association or corporations at least 60 percent owned by Filipino citizens or higher; or (ii) enact measures for the formation and operation of enterprises wholly owned by Filipinos as national interest dictates; and (iii) require an increase in Filipino participation in educational institutions. These provisions may bear upon the additional obligation attached to Annex I of no backtracking, and vice versa.

Other constitutional provisions also specify that the State or Congress can take future action in relation to national development objectives including promotion of inclusive growth, which therefore requires flexibility for members to reserve their right to take on future measures for any sector. Such measures, including those to be adopted in the future, may be more restrictive than the current regulatory practice, and can be listed in Annex II. In the case of the Philippines, measures pertaining to the following tend to be scheduled: (i) protection of the indigenous cultural communities or indigenous peoples; (ii) provision of livelihood and promotion of self-reliance of vulnerable segments, such as small farmers, subsistence fishermen, and fish workers; (iii) development of small and medium-sized enterprises; and (iv) granting of autonomy to local government units and autonomous regions. In addition, measures relating to national interest, security, and defence as specified in the Constitution and national laws (e.g. Foreign Investment Act) can also be scheduled in Annex II, such as those which limit foreign participation for reasons of security, defence, public health, and morals.

3.2.1. Measures of horizontal application

Several measures reviewed earlier are horizontal in nature, which means that the application cuts across all sectors. Most of them are state policies and economic provisions found in the 1987 Philippine Constitution which, in most cases, have been enunciated and further clarified in national laws. The measures cover the following categories: (i) land, in terms of ownership, lease, transfer, and conveyance; (ii) natural resources, in terms of exploration, development, and use; (iii) indigenous cultural communities and indigenous people; (iv) local governments and autonomous regions; (v) cooperatives as vehicle for social justice; (vi) small and medium-sized enterprises; (vii) Filipino-first policy which encourages preferential treatment to Filipinos; (viii) protection of national interest instructing Congress to reserve certain areas for Filipinos; (ix) domestic and export market enterprises; (x) corporations incorporated and organised in the Philippines; (xi) foreign corporations incorporated and organised under the laws of other countries; (xii) activities related to security and defence; (xiii) activities that may pose risks to public health and morals; (xix) special economic zones and freeport areas; (xx) foreign and domestic loans; (xxi) rights of former natural-born citizens of the Philippines; and (xxii) circumvention or negation of laws on nationalisation.

3.2.2. *Measures of sectoral application*

The review revealed that discriminatory measures exist in generally all services sectors.[5] The scope of application of national statutes, however, does not necessarily correspond to international classification standards[6] because these laws were enacted for particular purposes and under specific circumstances. Thus, the coverage may refer to a specific or multiple activities or areas that straddle between sectors or industries.

Following are some discriminatory measures that apply to specific services sectors or sub-sectors:

i   Construction services (Central Product Classification [CPC] 54). The limitations to participation of foreign investors in construction services pertain mainly to public works, construction of civil works, and infrastructure development projects. The national statutes that is, Letter of Instructions 630, Commonwealth Act 456, and RA 6957 as amended by RA 7188, stipulate rules on who may be contracted by government instrumentalities to provide such construction services. The rules on ownership, including limitations of equity participation, differentiate between those that are publicly funded, financed by international lending institutions, and undertaken under a build-operate-transfer scheme or other similar schemes. Clearly, in the latter laws relating to infrastructure development projects, the rules on ownership have been relaxed by allowing the engagement of services of either foreign or Filipino contractors or both in the construction stage of such projects. As set out in RA 6957 and RA 7188, different rules apply to the management and operation of construction facilities, especially where the facilities are considered public utility.

ii Distributive trade services (CPC 61 and CPC 62). The participation of foreign investors in wholesale or retail trade activities or both is contained in various laws promulgated for different objectives, that is, for the protection of small and medium-sized enterprises, to ensure food security, for reasons of national security or risks posed to public health and morals, and international treaties or conventions that the Philippines signed or supports. The Retail Trade Act (RA 8762) sets out the paid-out capital requirement for retail trade activities that foreign companies may engage into as well as the activities excluded from the scope of the act. RA 7183 and EO 184 limit ownership or foreign equity participation in the wholesale or retail sale of firecrackers and pyrotechnics devices. RA 3018, as amended by PD 194, governs who may engage in the rice and corn industry, which covers trade distribution of rice and corn and their by-products. RA 3018 specifies that non-Philippine nationals, associations, partnerships, or corporations not wholly owned by Filipino citizens may engage in the handling or distribution of rice and corn and the by-products but subject to certain conditions. RA 7042, as amended by RA 8179, meanwhile restricts foreign equity participation in nightclubs, beer houses, and dance halls to 40 percent for the risks these may pose on public morals.[7]

iii   Professional services. The Constitution limits the practice of profession in the Philippines to Filipino citizens, except in cases prescribed by law. As provided for in specific laws, more than 40 professions in the Philippines are regulated by the Philippine Regulation Commission. The specific laws, which cover practice of profession (CPC 84) in the field and related fields of medicine, architecture, engineering, science, teaching, agriculture and fisheries, business services, and other technical services, lay down the rules and regulations on (i) the practice of these professions including by individuals or otherwise, (ii) the requirement for licensure for Philippine nationals and/or non-Philippine nationals, and (iii) the requirement for reciprocal arrangement with other countries for professionals from other countries to be allowed to practice in the Philippines. The practice of legal profession (CPC 83), on the other hand, is under the Supreme Court of the Philippines. As prescribed in the Philippine Constitution and further defined in Rule 138 of the Rules of Court, only Filipino citizens can be admitted to the bar. On the other types of legal entities, the Civil Code of the Philippines allows individual professionals to form partnerships. Corporate practice is allowed but only to a limited number of regulated professions, as specifically prescribed in their respective governing laws. Real estate service, landscape architecture, forestry, metallurgical engineering, sanitary engineering, sugar technology, and naval architecture and marine engineering are the seven professions that allow corporate practice, subject to certain conditions and requirements, which may include limitations on equity ownership, citizenship of the board of directors, or a requirement for all executives to be licensed professionals. As allowed in the governing law of the profession, the reciprocity principle also applies to corporate practice.

iv   Support services under business and production services (CPC 85). Limitations on ownership and foreign equity participation apply to support services involving (i) placement and recruitment of workers, domestic or international (Presidential Decree [PD] 442 and EO184, Annex on Regular FINL), and (ii) organisation and operation of business activities of private detectives, security watchmen, or security guard agencies (RA 5487).

v   Education services (CPC 92). The 1987 Constitution limits investment in education institutions to Filipino citizens or corporations at least 60 percent owned by Filipino citizens. Control and administration of educational institutions shall be by Filipino citizens. Exceptions are those institutions established by religious groups and mission boards and schools for diplomats and their dependents, and temporary foreign residents, unless otherwise specified by law.

vi Recreational, cultural, and sporting services (CPC 96). The Constitution and the special laws for indigenous cultural communities and the autonomous regions specifically mandate the protection and promotion of the rights of indigenous cultural communities or peoples, which include the protection and preservation of their culture, tradition, and institutions. The law on cockfighting (PD 449) also limits the establishment, operation, and management of cockpits to Filipino citizens.

vii Other services (97) and beauty and physical well-being services (CPC 973). The 1991 Foreign Investment Act, as amended, and as specified in the 10th FINL, included sauna and steam bathhouses, massage clinics, and other activities as regulated sectors for the risks these may pose to public health and morals. Thus, foreign equity participation is limited to 40 percent.

In several cases, the application of discriminatory measures encompasses a number of different sectors or sub-sectors. This multi-sector coverage is aimed to address specific issues relating to certain products or services that possess generally the same characteristics. In the Philippines, these include the following measures:

i RA 3018 and PD 194 on the rice and corn industry – pertain to such activities as (i) acquiring by barter and purchase rice and corn and the by-products as inputs; and (ii) engaging in the culture, production, milling, processing, and trading of rice and corn.

ii The 1987 Constitution and CA 146 on the operation of a public utility – require a franchise, certificate, or authorisation that may be secured only by Filipino citizens or associations, partnerships, and corporations with at least 60 percent Filipino equity participation. CA 146 defines public utility as the provision of public service that includes any common carrier:

  a railroad, street railway, traction railway, subway motor vehicle, either for freight or passenger or both with or without fixed route and whether its classification may be freight or carrier service of any class;

  b express service, steam boat or steamship line, pontines, ferries, and water craft engaged in the transport of passengers or freight or both;

  c shipyard, marine railways, marine repair shop, wharf, or dock;

  d ice plant, ice-refrigeration plant;

  e canal, irrigation system;

  f gas, electric light, heat and power, water supply and power, petroleum;

  g sewerage system;

  h wire or wireless communications system, wire or wireless broadcasting stations; and

  i other similar public services.

Exceptions, inclusions,[8] and clarifications to the scope of CA 146, were made through the subsequent legal enactments resulting in the exclusions of the following from the original list: (i) warehouses; (ii) vehicles drawn by animals; (iii) *bancas* (boats) drawn by oars or sail, tugboats, airships within the Philippines; (iv) radio companies; and (v) public services owned by government instrumentality. The latest progressive move on the redefinition of scope of public utility was the Electricity Reform Act of 2001 (RA 9316). This unbundled the electricity sector and clarified that only transmission of electric power and distribution of electricity are considered as regulated common carrier business requiring franchise. It further stated that generation and supply of electric power are not public utility operations.

iii   1987 Constitution on mass media – limits ownership and management to Filipino citizens and corporations wholly owned by Filipino citizens. PD 1018 defines mass media to cover print medium of communication; billboards, neon signs and the like; and broadcast medium of communication, including all other cinematographic and radio promotions, and advertising.[9] Presidential Memorandum dated 5 May 1994 further clarified that the recording business is not part of the scope of mass media.

iv   RA 9165 on dangerous drugs – considers the following as unlawful acts: (i) manufacture, importation, cultivation, delivery, and sale of dangerous drugs; and (ii) manufacture and delivery of equipment, instrument, apparatus, and other paraphernalia for dangerous drugs, unless authorised by law. Where legally permitted, RA 7042 as amended by RA 8179 and EO 184, Annex on Regular FINL, limits the ownership of such to Filipino citizens or corporations with at least 60 percent Filipino equity participation for the risks these may pose to public health and morals.

v   For security and defence reasons, RA 7042 as amended by RA 8179 and EO 184 limit foreign equity participation to 40 percent in defence-related activities and security-related activities, which refer to the manufacture, repair, storage, and distribution of products that require clearance from the Secretary of National Defense and the Chief of the Philippine National Police, respectively;

vi   RA 7042 as amended by RA 8179 also limits foreign equity participation of up to 40 percent to activities that may pose risk to public health and morals, which include sauna and steam bathhouses, and massage clinics[10] as specified in EO 184. To protect public morals and health, RA 7042 as amended by RA 8179 and as listed in the 10th FINL promulgated by EO 184, prescribes the following activities with limited foreign equity participation of up to 40 percent only: all forms of gambling, except those under the Philippine Amusement and Gaming Corporation, and under specific laws on economic zones and free ports, for example, Cagayan Economic Zone.

vii   Activities within the forestlands, which include utilisation, exploitation, occupation, possession, and conduct of any activity, and establishment and operation of wood-processing plants require a licence agreement, lease, or permit. The Revised Forestry Code of the Philippines (PD 705), while encouraging diffusion to as many qualified applicants, also encourages increased Filipino participation beyond the 60 percent equity ownership and prioritises applicants with more Filipino equity. It also requires corporations to submit a programme for divestment of 20 percent of their capital stock to employees.

viii RA 9175 regulates the manufacture, importation, distribution, and sale of chainsaws to conserve, develop, and protect forest resources. The act specifies that selling and importation of chainsaws may be done only by manufacturers, dealers, and private persons authorised by the Department of Environment and Natural Resources, while permit for possession and use of chainsaws may be granted only to those with subsisting timber licence agreement, production-sharing agreement, or similar agreements; a licensed wood processor; an industrial tree farmer; and an orchard and fruit tree farmer.

ix RA 7188 limits the manufacture and wholesale and retail distribution of firecrackers and pyrotechnic devices to Filipino citizens or entities with 100 percent capital owned by Filipinos. The law also limits the importation of chemicals or explosive ingredients only to licensed manufacturers.

x RA 7103 entitles enterprises engaged in the iron and steel industry to incentives if these are owned by Filipino citizens or associations or corporations with at least 35 percent of the capital owned and controlled by Filipino citizens. Those with foreign equity are also encouraged to further increase Filipino participation in the business.

3.2.3. Measure for health and environmental protection

The Philippines also adopted measures prohibiting certain products or areas of activities in the country that are contrary to national interest or deemed inimical to the country. These measures include those that aim to protect the environment and public health, such as the Toxic Substances and Hazardous and Nuclear Wastes Control Act of 1990 (RA 6969), Ecological Solid Waste Management Act of 2000 (RA 9003), and Philippine Clean Air Act of 1999 (RA 8749). Based on these national statutes, services and activities relating to the following are prohibited:

i chemical substances and mixtures that may present unreasonable risk or injury or both to health or the environment (RA 6969);

ii hazardous and nuclear wastes (RA 6969);

iii manufacture, testing, storage, and transit of nuclear weapons, devices, and parts thereof (1987 Constitution, EO 184);

iv incineration and open burning of waste (RA 9003);

v establishment or operation of open dumps (RA 9003);

vi manufacture, distribution, or use of non-environmentally acceptable packaging materials (RA 9003);

vii manufacture, import, and sale of leaded gasoline and engines or components or both requiring leaded gasoline (RA 8749); and

viii incineration or the burning of municipal, biomedical, and hazardous wastes, which process emits poisonous and toxic fumes (RA 8749).

While these measures are consistent with the core liberalisation obligations, for transparency and clarity, these measures should be noted to avoid any future confusion and unintended consequence of possibly non-listing in the annexes. These measures do qualify as exemptions under the general and security exceptions (Chapter 20) and are consistent with the TPP chapter on environment (Chapter 20).

4. Assessment of non-conforming measures

New generation trade agreements have set a higher bar than their predecessors, and thus, have taken a more aggressive and bolder approach to achieve more commercially meaningful outcomes. Countries that have expressed interest or intent to accede to the TPP, therefore, are bound to accept the obligations already set out in the agreement and must be prepared to negotiate the conditions of their accession that would involve market access negotiations with its members.

From the previous FTA experiences, the Philippines will have to make a major shift in its position and policies if it pursues TPP accession or participates in other new generation agreements. This would involve, amongst others:

i   Agreeing to the new structure and treatment of investment and services. The chapter on investment covers all sectors, that is, no separate treatment for services investment as is the case in ASEAN FTAs. The chapter on services focuses on cross-border trade in services. There will also be separate chapters on financial services, telecommunication services, and movement of business persons.

ii   Adopting the negative list approach would entail the listing of all the non-conforming measures. Attached to this approach and part of the mechanism are the standstill and ratchet obligations for non-conforming measures in Annex I. This will be a major adjustment for the Philippines, which has been too accustomed to the GATS-style positive list approach in most of its FTAs where countries are not obliged to commit to the level of applied regulatory practice.

iii   Accepting the automatic MFN provision and the performance requirements provision as part of the core liberalisation obligations of the chapter on investment. In the case of performance requirements, it is also detailing and specifying any performance requirement measures (e.g. local content requirements, export requirements, and technology transfer requirements) that countries maintain, which are prohibited under the TPP.

iv   Agreeing to reduce or eliminate some of the discriminatory barriers to trade and investment as part of the accession condition and negotiating which measure shall be listed in Annexes I and II.

The Philippines must prepare for a thorough review of sectors for regulatory reforms, including liberalisation. As the FTAs aim to create a more liberal trade and investment environment, other countries would inevitably demand further opening up of markets with specific requests for improved market access in various sectors at the start of negotiations.

For the Philippines, the major challenge would be the economic policies embodied in the 1987 Constitution, which specifically gives preferential treatment to Philippine nationals in several areas/activities/sectors. Unlike in national statutes, any change to the Constitution requires ratification through a plebiscite. Some provisions of the Constitution though that provide a general language or a broad terminology, for example, 'public utility' or 'mass media', could be addressed by an act of Congress clarifying the extent and scope of application, that is, through a legislation defining or redefining coverage or application.

Country analysis of the Philippines based on the ASEAN Integration Report 2015 (ASEAN Secretariat 2015b) and the ASEAN Services Integration Report 2015 (ASEAN Secretariat and the World Bank 2015)[11] revealed that:

i   The Philippines had the second most restrictive services regime amongst the ASEAN member states with an overall services trade restrictiveness index (STRI) of 50.7 in 2012. This index is considerably way above the STRI of the country with the least restrictive regime, and the newer ASEAN member states.[12]

ii   On foreign direct investment (FDI), the Philippines had an FDI restrictiveness index of 0.425 in 2013, which again is the highest in ASEAN and ASEAN Plus 1 FTAs. The average FDI restrictiveness index for ASEAN is 0.243, while that for ASEAN FTA partners is 0.206.

Beyond the FTAs and trade negotiations, the Philippines should seriously consider the implications of a restrictive regime. The Organisation for Economic Co-operation and Development (OECD), in its *Investment Policy Reviews for the Philippines* (2016), reported that despite the potential of the Philippines, its investment performance is lower than that of its neighbouring countries. The share of foreign and domestic investment to gross domestic product is also, by standard, amongst the lowest. One observation in the OECD policy reviews was the apparent locational shift of investors to other destinations, particularly in ASEAN, especially when the other ASEAN member states intensified their liberalisation efforts. The report noted that the sectoral improvements to the business climate in the Philippines in the 1990s were not enough to alter the locational preference of foreign investors. The main stumbling block remains to be the statutory restrictions, particularly the constitutional restrictions limiting participation of foreign investors to up to 40 percent equity. As the OECD cites, countries with lower FDI stock were observed to have the highest level of restrictions, which is the case for the Philippines. It is thus expected that the Philippines ranked 56th amongst 144 countries and seventh amongst its ASEAN peers in terms competitiveness performance (WEF, 2016).

The country's restrictiveness and performance indicate areas needing improvement. Notwithstanding the FTAs, these draw great concern and the Philippines should see this as an opportune time to pursue reforms for its development interest.

5. Conclusion

New generation agreements present a new challenge to countries as they set out to participate in new rounds of free trade negotiations. With a higher level of ambition, the new generation agreements thrust more stringent obligations amongst its parties to establish a freer, more transparent, and competitive environment amongst them. Thus, the decision to join a new generation agreement would prompt an evaluation of stance as regards the FTAs, especially for countries used to the World Trade Organization/GATS-style approach. Inevitably, this will demand countries to revisit their regulatory practice and consider certain policy reforms.

In the case of the Philippines, the assessment reveals that a significant number of its regulatory measures are inconsistent with the obligations of new generation agreements. Explicit provisions in the Constitution and national statutes close or limit the participation of foreign investors in certain areas, industries, or activities. In the context of new generation FTAs, the Philippines should seriously consider improving market access and levelling the playing field for investors from the other FTA parties. This would require removal or reduction of restrictions and regulations imposed on foreign investors at the border and across the border pre- and post-establishment. While the FTAs may serve as impetus for review, the undertaking for reforms should be grounded on the gains that would accrue to the economy in the long run as well as the costs, including opportunity cost, to the economy if the existing regulatory measures are maintained.

As any other country that have been so used to the approach of the World Trade Organization and GATS, the Philippines will need to revisit its approach to the FTAs, particularly with respect to obligations that apply to investments in non-services and services sectors and the level of commitments in the FTAs. Unlike its experience in existing ASEAN FTAs, new generation agreements have set out a different framework, structure, and obligations for investment and trade in services. And this would significantly alter the way the Philippines would make its commitments on market access and for future liberalisation. In this context, the country would have to seriously consider accepting the additional standstill and ratchet obligations, which are integral elements of the investment chapter of new generation agreements. Understandably, this would entail a deep reorientation and revamp of perspective, approach, and position.

While the new generation agreements present a big challenge for the Philippines, they also present a great opportunity for the country to embark on a comprehensive and thorough review of its existing policies. The review and needed reforms are long overdue with or without the new generation agreement; as noted, several measures have been framed and issued many decades ago under different circumstances. These bring to forth the question on the effectiveness and efficiency of these policies in the light of significant advancement in technology and the changing landscape of the global and regional economies.

Notes

1 The other 11 signatories to the Trans-Pacific Partnership agreements are Australia, Brunei, Canada, Chile, Japan, Malaysia, Mexico, New Zealand, Peru, Singapore, and Viet Nam.
2 In this chapter, the author has limited its scope and referred only to the Constitution and national laws.

3 In accord with international treaties and agreements, the Philippines also enacted laws to implement its obligations under these agreements. These laws, regardless of ownership, prohibit economic activities or restrict investments in certain activities.

4 This is barring the benefit of any ruling by the Supreme Court as final arbiter in cases involving questions of constitutionality of an act concerning these provisions.

5 Based on the WTO Services Sectoral Classification, these refer to services on construction, business, education, distributive trade, recreational, cultural and sporting, transport, communication, environmental, financial, and other services.

6 These refer to the International Standard for Industrial Classification (ISIC) and the Central Product Classification (CPC).

7 Based on the CPC classification, these can be considered part of the beverage serving services of alcoholic or non-alcoholic beverages or both (CPC 63).

8 In some cases, re-inclusions of areas were made as what happened in Commonwealth Act 454 s.1939 and Republic Act 2677 s.1960 concerning ice and refrigeration plants.

9 The 1987 Constitution, while also limiting foreign equity participation, separates the provisions for the advertising industry and mass media.

10 It is noteworthy that Central Product Classification (CPC) Version 2 classifies these activities under physical well-being services (CPC 97230).

11 The reports measure the level of restrictiveness of member states based on the World Bank and the foreign direct investment (FDI) regulatory restrictiveness index of the Organisation for Economic Co-operation and Development (OECD).

12 The newer ASEAN member states refer to Cambodia, Lao PDR, Myanmar, and Viet Nam.

Bibliography

ASEAN Secretariat (2007), *AEC Blueprint*. Jakarta, Indonesia: ASEAN Secretariat.

ASEAN Secretariat (2015a), 'A Blueprint for Growth', in *ASEAN Economic Community 2015: Progress and Achievements*. Jakarta, Indonesia: ASEAN Secretariat.

ASEAN Secretariat (2015b), *ASEAN Integration Report*. Jakarta, Indonesia: ASEAN Secretariat.

ASEAN Secretariat and the World Bank (2015), *ASEAN Services Integration Report*. Jakarta, Indonesia: ASEAN Secretariat.

De Leon, H.S. and H.M. De Leon Jr. (2014), *Textbook on the Philippine Constitution*. Manila, Philippines: Rex Book Store.

Nolledo, J.N. and M.S. Nolledo (2009), *The Constitution of the Republic of the Philippines Explained*. Mandaluyong, Philippines: National Book Store.

Organisation for Economic Co-operation and Development (OECD) (2016), *OECD Investment Policy Reviews: Philippines 2016*. Paris, France: OECD Publishing.

Serafica, R.B. (2015), 'A Comprehensive Philippine Government Strategy on the Competitiveness of the Services Sector', in *Philippine Institute for Development Studies (PIDS) Discussion Series* 2015–05. Makati: PIDS.

World Economic Forum (WEF) (2016), *Global Competitiveness Report 2016–2017*. Geneva: WEF.

Part II

Rules and regulations on intellectual property rights

4 Understanding the IP-related contents of the Trans-Pacific Partnership agreement

Akiko Kato

1. Introduction

The Trans-Pacific Partnership (TPP, or TPP12) is a free trade framework, having been negotiated and signed amongst 12 trans-Pacific countries on 4 February 2016. In response to the Trump administration's statement of withdrawal from the TPP12 on 23 January 2017, 11 countries without the United States (US) started the reconstruction of the TPP and finally signed the texts of the Comprehensive and Progressive Agreement for Trans-Pacific Partnership (CPTPP) on 8 March 2018. In adapting to the withdrawal of the US, the CPTPP parties suspended the application of certain provisions of the TPP12, listed in the annex of the CPTPP, until the parties agree to end the suspension of one or more of these provisions (Article 2 of CPTPP).

The protection of intellectual property (IP), especially of patent rights and data for the pharmaceutical products, has been one of severe contestations of the TPP, which jeopardised the completion of the whole negotiation. After all the discussions, IP-related contents of the TPP12 – contained in several chapters, with 83 articles in Chapter 18 focusing IP alone – aim to regulate in a more expansive and detailed manner areas and issues covered in existing international treaties on IP. Therefore, although the parties of the CPTPP decided to suspend the obligations of Chapter 18, reflecting the severe contestations in the making process of the TPP12, the agreement is the expression of US interests and of the power relations amongst negotiating countries on IP. And we know of one approach to strengthen protection of IP. For example, the Japanese government announced the TPP as a model of future trade negotiation on 20 January 2017. On the same day, it notified the Government of New Zealand, the designated depositary, of the completion of its domestic procedures to ratify the TPP.

This chapter aims to clarify the structure and implication of IP-related contents of the TPP, completed through twists and turns. First, it points out the characteristics of IP-related contents of the TPP. Second, it analyses selected IP-related contents of the TPP and their subject matters, specifically the sections on general principles, cooperation, patent rights, copyright and related rights, enforcement, and final provisions of Chapter 18 on IP (2.1), Chapter 9 on investment (2.2). Finally, the third part presents the conclusion.

2. General comments on the characteristics of the TPP and its IP-related chapters

The TPP's regulative approach has several characteristics, which are also shared by its IP-related chapters. First, it takes a 'plus-approach' to the rules of the World Trade Organization (WTO) by framing free trade area in compliance with Article 24 of the General Agreement on Tariffs and Trade (GATT) and Article 5 of the General Agreement on Trade in Services.[1] Simultaneously, the TPP parties repeatedly and ubiquitously declare their intention to comply with existing international trade agreements. Furthermore, the TPP clearly specifies that the interpretation of WTO agreements, for example, GATT Article 20, will be applied in TPP articles. If a party believes that a provision of the TPP is inconsistent with that of another agreement to which it and at least one other party are signatories, the relevant parties to the TPP shall, upon request, consult with a view to reaching a mutually satisfactory solution (Article 1.2).

This policy is also adopted in IP-related chapters of the TPP. Chapter 18 on IP obliges parties to comply with many existing IP agreements through ratification. Table 4.1 shows the situation of ratification by the TPP parties to existing IP agreements as of 24 January 2017. Moreover, IP-related chapters add further obligations to existing obligations imposed by many treaties. The TPP especially takes a 'plus-approach' to the Agreement on Trade-Related Aspects of Intellectual Property Rights, or TRIPS Agreement of the WTO,[2] the so-called TRIPS-plus (see Table 4.2). Historically, IP is one of the most 'active' areas on which countries and trade areas have concluded many treaties to establish both user-friendly and administratively efficient system of IP protection. The TRIPS Agreement itself takes a 'plus-approach' to four universal treaties: (i) Paris Convention for the Protection of Industrial Property, (ii) Berne Convention for the Protection of Literary and Artistic Works, (iii) Washington Treaty on Intellectual Property in Respect of Integrated Circuits, and (iv) Rome Convention on Related Rights.[3] Consequently, TPP parties will be obliged to provide unprecedentedly comprehensive IP protection.

At the same time, however, drafters of the TPP struggled to balance enhancement of IP protection and permission of an appropriate setting of exemptions and limitations of IP protection. Therefore, like the TRIPS Agreement, it is an agenda for us to clarify the exemptions and limitations of IP protection recognised by the TPP.

Second, like the WTO, the TPP takes a single-undertaking approach, which asks parties to accept wholly the chapters and their annexes, appendices, and footnotes when they ratify the TPP (Article 30.1). Although the TPP prepares Chapter 29 on exceptions and general provisions, it establishes all the exemptions to the parties' obligations until its effectivity and does not permit request of reservations by a party after effectuation. Therefore, the TPP is stricter than the WTO on compliance of implementation by parties.

Third, no least-developed country is a party to the TPP, whose parties are exempt from most obligations of the TRIPS Agreement until 2032, according

Table 4.1 Participation of TPP parties in existing international agreements on intellectual property[a]

Abbreviated name	Madrid agreement and its protocol[b]	Budapest Treaty[b]	Singapore Treaty on the Law of Trademarks[b]	UPOV[b]	WCT: WIPO Copyright Treaty[b]	WPPT: WIPO Related Rights Treaty[b]	Protocol Amending TRIPS[b]	PLT: Patent Law Treaty[f]	Hague Agreement[f]	Brussels Convention[d, e]
Related Article of the TPP	18.7.2	18.7.2	18.7.2	18.7.2	18.7.2	18.7.2	18.7.2	18.14.4	18.56	(18.79)
Australia	11 July 2001	7 July 1987	16 Mar. 2009	1 Mar. 1989	26 July 2007	26 July 2007	12 Sept. 2007	16 Mar. 2009	–	26 Oct. 1990
Brunei	6 Jan. 2017	24 July 2012	–	–	–	–	10 Apr. 2015	–	24 Dec. 2013	–
Canada	–	21 Sept. 1996	–	4 Mar. 1991	13 Aug. 2014	13 Aug. 2014	16 June 2009	–	–	–
Chile	–	5 Aug. 2011	–	5 Jan. 1996	6 Mar. 2002	20 May 2002	26 July 2013	–	–	8 June 2011
Japan	14 Mar. 2000	19 Aug. 1980	11 June 2016	3 Sept. 1982	6 Mar. 2002	9 Oct. 2002	31 Aug. 2007	11 June 2016	13 May 2015	–
Malaysia	–	–	–	–	27 Dec. 2012	27 Dec. 2012	10 Dec. 2015	–	–	–
Mexico	19 Feb. 2013	21 Mar. 2001	–	8 Aug. 1997	6 Mar. 2002	20 May 2002	23 May 2008	–	–	25 Aug. 1979
New Zealand	10 Dec. 2012	–	8 Jan. 2014	8 Nov. 1981	–	–	21 Oct. 2011	–	–	–
Peru	–	20 Jan. 2009	–	8 Aug. 2011	6 Mar. 2002	18 July 2002	13 Sept. 2016	–	–	7 Aug. 1985
Singapore	31 Oct. 2000	23 Feb. 1995	16 Mar. 2009	30 Jul. 2004	17 Apr. 2005	17 Apr. 2005	28 Sep. 2007	–	17 Apr. 2005	27 Apr., 2005
United States of America	2 Nov. 2003	19 Aug. 1980	16 Mar. 2009	8 Nov. 1981	6 Mar. 2002	20 May 2002	17 Dec. 2005	18 Dec. 2013	13 May 2015	7 Mar. 1985
Viet Nam	11 July 2006	–	–	24 Dec. 2006	–	–	23 Jan. 2017	–	–	12 Jan. 2006

Note:

a. As of 24 January 2017. *Agreements to which all the Parties have already participated (Article 18.7.1): Patent Cooperation Treaty, Paris Convention, Berne Convention.

b. The TPP also mentions 'the Joint Recommendation Concerning Provisions on the Protection of Well-Known Marks' adopted in 1999. The recommendation is accessible at WIPO's site, available at www.wipo.int/edocs/pubdocs/en/marks/833/pub833.pdf (Article 18.22).

c. Agreements to which the TPP obliges parties to accede.

d. Agreements in which the TPP recognises the importance of parties' participation.

e. Brussels Convention: Brussels Convention Relating to the Distribution of Programme-Carrying Signals Transmitted by Satellite. Entered into force in 1979, with 37 contracting parties.

Source: Author.

Table 4.2 Relationship between TPP obligations and existing international agreements on intellectual property rights

Chapter	Section	Subsection	Obligation	Related Article of TPP	Suspended by the CPTPP P: Partially C: Completely	Relationship between TPP obligations and Existing International Agreements
Chapter 18: Intellectual Property	A: General Provisions	1	Objectives and principles	18.1.2 and 3		TRIPS 7 and 8
		2	Understanding in respect of this Chapter	18.4		(TRIPS-plus)
		3	Understanding regarding certain public health measures	18.6		(TRIPS-plus)
		4	(Acceptance of protocol amending TRIPS →Table 1)	18.6		–
		5	(Acceptance of existing international agreements (Table 1)	18.7		–
		6	National treatment	18.8	P	TRIPS 3
		7	Transparency by using the Internet	18.9		(TRIPS-plus)
		8	Temporal subject matter to be protected	18.10		–
		9	Exhaustion of IPRs	18.11		TRIPS 6
	B: Cooperation	1	Contact points for cooperation	18.12		(TRIPS plus)
		2	Cooperation activities and initiatives	18.13		(TRIPS plus)
		3	Improvement of the quality and efficiency of patent system, simplification of patent procedure	18.14.1		(TRIPS plus)
		4	Work sharing of patent search and examination results, exchange of information	18.14.2		(TRIPS plus)
		5	Reduction of differences in procedures and processes of patent offices	18.14.3		(TRIPS plus)
		6	Incorporation of PLT standards into national system	18.14.4		PLT
		7	Recognition of importance of public domain	18.15		(TRIPS plus)
		8	Recognition of relevance of IP system and traditional knowledge with genetic resources	18.16		(TRIPS plus)
		9	Cooperation on request	18.17		(Established principle)

C: Trademarks

1	Protection of new-typed trademarks	18.18	(TRIPS-plus)
2	Protection of collective marks	18.19	(TRIPS-plus)
3	Protection of certification marks	18.19	(TRIPS-plus)
4	Exclusive rights conferred to the owner of registered trademarks	18.2	(TRIPS-plus on 'including subsequent GI': See TRIPS 16.1)
5	Exceptions	18.21	TRIPS 17
6	Ban to require registration, listing, or prior recognition for condition of protection of well-known marks	18.22.1	(TRIPS-plus: See TRIPS 16.2, second sentence)
7	Application of same measure to holders of well-known marks by Paris Convention Art.6bis	18.22.2	(TRIPS-plus: Application of the condition of TRIPS 16.3 to well-known marks) Paris Convention 6bis
8	Recognition of importance of WIPO Joint Recommendation Concerning Provisions on the Protection of Well-Known Marks	18.22.3	(TRIPS-plus) WIPO Joint Recommendation Concerning Provisions on the Protection of Well-Known Marks
9	Provision of appropriate measures to refuse application or cancel the registration and prohibit use of a trademark that is identical or similar to a well-known mark	18.22.4	(TRIPS-plus): See WIPO Joint Recommendation Concerning Provisions on the Protection of Well-Known Marks, Arts.4 and 5
10	Provision of communication between applicant of trademark registration	18.23(a) and (b)	(TRIPS-plus: See TLT 14)
11	Provision of opportunity to oppose registration/seek cancellation of trademark and to require administrative decisions in their procedures	18.23(c) and (d)	(TRIPS-plus: See TRIPS 15.5)
12	Electrically available trademarks system	18.24	(TRIPS-plus)

(*Continued*)

Table 4.2 (Continued)

Chapter	Section	Subsection	Obligation	Related Article of TPP	Suspended by the CPTPP P: Partially C: Completely	Relationship between TPP obligations and Existing International Agreements
		13	Adoption of Nice International Classification	18.25		(TRIPS-plus)
		14	Term of trademarks protection	18.26		(TRIPS-plus: See TRIPS 18)
		15	Ban to require recordal of trademark licence	18.27		(TRIPS-plus)
		16	Provision of appropriate procedure for dispute settlement on domain name in line with Uniform Domain-Name Dispute-Resolution policy	18.28(a)		(TRIPS-plus)
		17	Provision of online public access to database on domain name	18.28(b)		(TRIPS-plus)
		18	Provision of appropriate remedies at least registered or held with a bad faith intent on profit by identical or confusingly similar trademark	18.28(c)		(TRIPS-plus)
	D: Country Names	1	Protection of parties' country names from commercial use misleading as to the origin of the good	18.29		Paris Convention 10
	E: Geographical Indications	1	Exercise of protection of GI through any legal means	18.30		TRIPS 22
		2	Provision of transparent, user-friendly, and applicant-driven procedure *Specific requirements are listed at clause (a) to (f)	18.31		(TRIPS-plus)
		3	Grounds of opposition and cancellation of GI protection	18.32		TRIPS 22 (TRIPS-plus: more specific)
		4	Guidelines for term customary in common language	18.33		(TRIPS-plus)
		5	Guidelines for multi-component terms	18.34		(TRIPS-plus)

		#	Description	Article	C	Notes
		6	Commencing date of GI protection	18.35		(TRIPS-plus) –
		7	Adjustment of applied rule on GI protection between TPP and other international agreements	18.36		(TRIPS-plus)
F: Patents and Undisclosed Test or Other Data	General patent	1	Patentable subject matter: protection for new uses of a known product, new methods of using a known product and new processes of using a known product	18.37.2	C	(TRIPS-plus)
		2	Definition of grace period: based on the intention of patent applicant and occurred within 12 months before the date of application	18.38		(TRIPS-plus)
		3	Grounds of patent revocation	18.39		(TRIPS-plus) Paris Convention 5A *1st condition 'only on grounds that would have justified a refusal to grant the patent' relates to PLT 10.1.
		4	Condition of limitation and exception to the exclusive rights of patent	18.40 and 41		TRIPS 30, 31 and exemption derived from them
		5	Adoption of first-to-file principle	18.42		(TRIPS-plus)
		6	Provision giving patent applicant opportunity to amend, etc. on application	18.43		(TRIPS-plus) PLT 5 and 6
		7	Publication of applications 18 months after filing date or earliest priority date	18.44.1 and 2		(TRIPS-plus)
		8	Introduction of earlier publication system	18.44.3		(TRIPS-plus)
		9	Publication of information relating patent application and granted patents	18.45		(TRIPS-plus)
		10	Introduction of patent term adjustment for unreasonable delays by granting authority	18.46	C	(TRIPS-plus)

(Continued)

Table 4.2 (Continued)

Chapter	Section	Subsection	Obligation		Related Article of TPP	Suspended by the CPTPP P: Partially C: Completely	Relationship between TPP obligations and Existing International Agreements
		Measures relating to agricultural chemical products	11	At least 10-year data protection for granting marketing approval of new agricultural chemical products	18.47		(TRIPS-plus)
		Measures relating to pharmaceutical products	12	Patent term adjustment for pharmaceuticals	18.48	C	(TRIPS-plus)
			13	Introduction of regulatory review exception	18.49		(TRIPS-plus)
			14	At least 5-year data protection for granting marketing approval of new pharmaceuticals	18.50.1	C	(TRIPS-plus) *See also exemption of taking measures to protect public health (18.50.3)
			15	At least 3-year data protection for new clinical information of previously approved pharmaceutical product	18.50.2	C	(TRIPS-plus) *See also exemption of taking measures to protect public health (18.50.3)
			16	Data protection for granting marketing approval of new pharmaceuticals that is or contains 'biologics'	18.51	C	(TRIPS-plus)
	G: Industrial Designs		17	Introduction of patent linkage system	18.53		(TRIPS-plus)
			1	Protection of design of a part of an article	18.55		(TRIPS-plus)
			2	(Due consideration to ratifying or acceding Geneva Act of Hague Agreement (Table 1)	18.56		–
	H: Copyright and Related Rights	Copyright protection	1	Right of reproduction	18.58		WCT 9

#		Description	Section		Treaty references
2		Right of communication to the public	18.59		WCT 8
3		Right of distribution	18.60		WCT 6
4		Limitation and exception to protection of copyright	18.65, 66		TRIPS 13 WCT 10
5		Term of protection; based 70-year	18.63, 64	P	(TRIPS-plus) TRIPS 12 and 14.6
6	Related rights:	Right of reproduction	18.58		TRIPS 14.1 and 2 WPPT 7 and 11
7		Right of communication to the public of unfixed performance, for performers	18.62.2(a)		Rome 7(a) WPPT 6(i)
8		Right of fixation, for performers	18.62.2(b)		Rome 7.1(b)and(c) WPPT 6(ii)
9		Right of communication to the public of already fixed performance, for performers/producers of phonograms	18.62.3(a)		Rome 7.1(c) and 10 WPPT 10 and 14
10		Right of distribution	18.60		WPPT 8 and 12
11		Limitation and exception to protection of related rights	18.65, 66		(TRIPS-plus, WPPT-plus) Rome 15 TRIPS 14.6 WPPT 16
12		Term of protection; based 70-year	18.63, 64		(TRIPS-plus, WPPT-plus), TRIPS 14.6, WPPT 17
13	Retroactive effects of protection		18.64		TRIPS 9.1 and 14.6
14	Contractual transfers		18.67		(TRIPS-plus)
15	Technological Protection Measures (TPMs)	Protection of TPMs through providing civil, administrative, and criminal procedures and remedies	18.68	C	(WCT-plus, WPPT-plus), WCT 11, WPPT 18
16	Rights management information (RMI)	Protection of RMI through providing civil and administrative procedures and remedies	18.69	C	(WCT-plus, WPPT-plus), WCT 12, WPPT 19

(Continued)

Table 4.2 (Continued)

Chapter	Section	Subsection	Obligation		Related Article of TPP	Suspended by the CPTPP P: Partially C: Completely	Relationship between TPP obligations and Existing International Agreements
			17	Protection of RMI through providing criminal procedures and remedies	18.69	C	(WCT-plus, WPPT-plus), WCT 12, WPPT 19
		Collective Management	18	Importance of collective management societies	18.70		(TRIPS-plus)
I: Enforcement		General provisions	1	Making domestic enforcement system in line with this section, in the spirit of fairness and equity	18.71		TRIPS 41.1 and 41.2
			2	Presumption of validity of copyright and related rights, trademark, and patent rights	18.72		(TRIPS-plus)
			3	User-friendly and electronically adapted practice on the civil, administrative, and criminal procedure on IP enforcement	18.73		(TRIPS-plus) TRIPS 41.3 and 41.4
		Civil, administrative procedure and relief	4	Availability of civil judicial procedure	18.74.1		TRIPS 42 and below
			5	Authorisation to judicial authority to order injunctive relief	18.74.2		TRIPS 44
			6	Authorisation to judicial authority to order wilful infringer to pay right holder damages adequate as compensation	18.74.3		TRIPS 45
			7	In determining amount of damages, authorisation to judicial authority to consider legitimate measure of designated values	18.74.4		(TRIPS-plus) TRIPS 45
			8	In determining amount of damages by copyright and related rights/trademark infringement, authorisation to judicial authority to order the infringer to pay infringer's profit by infringement	18.74.5		(TRIPS-plus) TRIPS 45

9	In determining amount of damages by copyright and related rights/trademark infringement, selectable introduction of pre-established/additional damages	18.74.6 to 9	(TRIPS-plus) TRIPS 45
10	Authorisation to judicial authority to order losing party to pay court costs, etc. at copyright and related rights, trademark, or patent right infringement case	18.74.10	(TRIPS-plus) TRIPS 45.2
11	Ban to set burdensome costs to appoint technical or other expert in civil proceeding	18.74.11	(TRIPS-plus) TRIPS 41.2
12	Authorisation to judicial authority to order designated disposal of pirated copyright goods and counterfeit trademark goods	18.74.12	(TRIPS-plus) TRIPS 46
13	Authorisation to judicial authority to order parties to submit information relating to civil judicial proceedings	18.74.13	(TRIPS-plus) TRIPS 43.1
14	Authorisation to judicial authority to impose sanction on a party for violation of judicial order within the civil judicial proceeding	18.74.14	(TRIPS-plus)
15	Authorisation to judicial authority to order adequate compensation to abused enforcement procedures	18.74.15	TRIPS 48
16	Fulfilment of same conditions as provided in this article on administrative procedures on IP enforcement	18.74.16	TRIPS 49
17	Authorisation to judicial authority to impose provisional measures, to order damages, order court costs, etc., destruction of devices, etc. in civil judicial proceedings on TPMs and RMI	18.74.17	(TRIPS-plus, WCT-plus, WPPT-plus) WCT 11 and 12 WPPT 18 and 19
Provisional measures 18	Authorisation to authority to act on request for relief *inaudita altera parte* expeditiously	18.75.1	(TRIPS-plus) TRIPS 50.2 and 50.4

(Continued)

Table 4.2 (Continued)

Chapter	Section	Subsection		Obligation	Related Article of TPP	Suspended by the CPTPP P: Partially C: Completely	Relationship between TPP obligations and Existing International Agreements
			19	Authorisation to judicial authority to require applicant for a provisional measure to provide reasonably available evidence	18.75.2		TRIPS 50.3 and 50.5
			20	Authorisation to judicial authority to order applicant for a provisional measure to provide security or equivalent assurance	18.75.2		TRIPS 50.3
			21	In civil judicial proceedings on copyright or related rights infringement and trademark counterfeiting, authorisation to judicial authority to order seizure suspected infringing goods, materials, and implements	18.75.3		(TRIPS-plus) TRIPS 50.1
			22	In civil judicial proceedings on trademark counterfeiting, authorisation to judicial authority to order seizure documentary evidence	18.75.3		(TRIPS-plus) TRIPS 50.1
		Special requirement related to border measures	23[a]	Provision to suspend the release of or to detain such goods	18.76.1		TRIPS 51
			24[a]	Authorisation to competent authorities to require right holder initiating procedures to suspend release of suspected goods, to provide adequate evidence and sufficient information	18.76.2		TRIPS 52
			25[a]	Authorisation to competent authorities to provide reasonable security	18.76.3		TRIPS 53.1
			26[a]	Provision of information to right holder detail on related parties, goods, country of origin	18.76.4		(TRIPS-plus) TRIPS 57

	27[b]	Goods subject to *ex officio* border measures: imported	18.76.5(a)	TRIPS 51
	28[b]	Goods subject to *ex officio* border measures: destined for export	18.76.5(b)	TRIPS 51
	29[b]	Goods subject to *ex officio* border measures: in transit	18.76.5(c)	(TRIPS-plus) TRIPS 51 footnote 13
		*Attached two footnotes		
	30[b]	Adoption or maintenance of procedure within a reasonable period	18.76.6	(TRIPS-plus) (Part III, Section 4)
	31[b]	Authorisation to competent authorities to order destruction or dispose of outside channels of commerce, of goods determined as infringed	18.76.5	TRIPS 59
	32[b]	Ban to impose unreasonable deterrent fee of application, storage, destruction	18.76.8	(TRIPS-plus) TRIPS 51 and 57
	33[b]	Application of conditions of this article to goods of a commercial nature sent in small consignments	18.76.9	(TRIPS-plus) TRIPS 60
		*Exclusion of travellers' personal luggage is permitted.		
Criminal procedures and penalties	34[c]	Provision for criminal procedures and penalties	18.77.1	TRIPS Art.61
	35[c]	Treatment of wilful importation/exportation as unlawful activities subject to criminal penalties	18.77.2	(TRIPS-plus) TRIPS 61
	36[c]	Provision for criminal procedures and penalties in case of wilful importation and domestic use, in the course of trade, of designated label/packaging	18.77.3	(TRIPS-plus) TRIPS 61
	37[c]	Recognition of the need to address unauthorised copying of cinematographic work from a performance in a movie theatre	18.77.4	(TRIPS-plus) TRIPS 61

(Continued)

Table 4.2 (Continued)

Chapter	Section	Subsection	Obligation	Related Article of TPP	Suspended by the CPTPP P: Partially C: Completely	Relationship between TPP obligations and Existing International Agreements
			38[c] Recognition of the need to provide appropriate criminal procedures and penalties addressed to unauthorised copying of cinematographic work from a performance in a movie theatre	18.77.4		(TRIPS-plus) TRIPS 61
			37[d] Making criminal liability for aiding and abetting available	18.77.5		(TRIPS-plus)
			38[c] Provision of penalties including sentences of imprisonment and monetary fines	18.77.6(a)		TRIPS 61
			39[e] Authorisation to judicial authorities, in determining penalties, to account for seriousness of circumstances	18.77.6(b)		TRIPS 61
			40[e] Authorisation to judicial or other competent authorities to order seizure of suspected goods, etc.	18.77.6(c)		TRIPS 61
			41[e] Authorisation to judicial authorities to order forfeiture of any assets	18.77.6(d)		TRIPS 61
			42[e] Authorisation to judicial authorities to order forfeiture/destruction of designated goods	18.77.6(e)		TRIPS 61
			43[e] Authorisation to judicial or other competent authorities to release/provide access to designated goods	18.77.6(f)		(TRIPS-plus) TRIPS 61
			44[e] Authorisation to judicial authorities to order seizure/forfeiture of assets or fines/the value corresponding to assets by infringing activity	18.77.7		(TRIPS-plus) TRIPS 61
		Trade Secrets	45 Protection of trade secrets defined here	18.78.1		TRIPS 39

	46	Provision of criminal procedures and penalties for unauthorised and wilful access/misappropriation/fraudulent disclosure of trade secret *Certain limitation of criminalisation is permitted by clause (3)	18.78.2 and 3		(TRIPS-plus)
Protection of encrypted programme-carrying satellite and cable signals	47	Provision of criminal offence to acts decoding encrypted programme-carrying satellite signal without authorisation of lawful distributor	18.79.1(a)	C	(TRIPS-plus) (BC-plus) BC 2 to 7
	48	Provision of criminal offence to wilfully receive/further distribute such signal	18.79.1(b)	C	(TRIPS-plus) (BC-plus) BC 2 to 7
	49	Provision of civil remedies for interested persons of such signals **infered** by activity described in (1)	18.79.2	C	(TRIPS-plus) (BC-plus) BC 2 to 7
	50	Provision of criminal penalties/civil remedies for manufacturing/distributing equipment used for unauthorised reception of such signals	18.79.3(a)	C	(TRIPS-plus) (BC-plus) BC 2 to 7
	51	Provision of criminal penalties/civil remedies for receiving/assisting another to receive such signals without authorisation of lawful distributor	18.79.3(b)	C	(TRIPS-plus) (BC-plus) BC 2 to 7
Government use of software	52	Recognition of importance of government awareness on protection of IPRs	18.80.1		(TRIPS-plus)
	53	Adoption/maintenance of appropriate measures to provide appropriate use of computer by central government	18.80.2		(TRIPS-plus)

(*Continued*)

Table 4.2 (Continued)

Chapter	Section	Subsection	Obligation	Related Article of TPP	Suspended by the CPTPP P: Partially C: Completely	Relationship between TPP obligations and Existing International Agreements
	J: Internet Service Providers (ISP) *See also Annexes 18-E and F		1 Definition of 'ISP'	18.81		(TRIPS-plus)
			2 Compliance of TRIPS Article 41	18.82	C	TRIPS 41
			3 Provision of legal incentives for ISP to cooperate with copyright owners to deter unauthorised storage and transmission of copyrighted materials	18.82.1(a)	C	(TRIPS-plus)
			4f Provision of such limitation *See also Article 18.82.6 and 8.	18.82.1(b) and 6, 8	C	(TRIPS-plus)
			5f Provision of limitation especially transmitting, routing/providing connections for material without modification of its content, etc.	18.82.2(a)	C	(TRIPS-plus)
			6f Provision of limitation especially caching carried out through automated process	18.82.2(b)	C	(TRIPS-plus)
			7f Provision of limitation especially storage, at direction of user, of material residing on system/network *See also Article 18.82.3.	18.82.2(c) and 3	C	(TRIPS-plus)
			8f Provision of limitation especially referring/ linking users to online location by using information on location tools *See also Article 18.82.3.	18.82.2(d) and 3	C	(TRIPS-plus)

	9[f]	Requirement to ISP to restore material subject to counter-notice in certain circumstances	18.82.4	C	(TRIPS-plus)
	10[f]	Provision of monetary remedies available against any person making knowing material misrepresentation in a notice/counter-notice that causes injury to any interested party	18.82.5	C	(TRIPS-plus)
	11[f]	Provision in judicial/administrative procedures with due process and privacy that enable copyright owner sufficiently claiming copyright infringement to obtain expeditiously information from ISP	18.82.7	C	(TRIPS-plus)
K: Final Provisions	1	Giving effect to provisions of this chapter on the date of entry into force	18.83.1		(TRIPS 70)
	2	Transition period permitted to designated party regarding certain obligations * See also Article 18.83.2 on ban to amend/adopt domestic measure less consistent with obligations under transition period	18.83.2 to 4		TRIPS 65 and 66
Chapter 9: Investment	A				
	1	Inclusion of IPRs and their licences as investment	9.1(f) and (g)		—
	2	Exclusion from application to issuance of compulsory licences in accordance with TRIPS/revocation, limitation, or creation consistent with Chapter 18 and TRIPS	9.8.5		—

(Continued)

Table 4.2 (Continued)

Chapter	Section	Subsection	Obligation	Related Article of TPP	Suspended by the CPTPP P: Partially C: Completely	Relationship between TPP obligations and Existing International Agreements
		3	Ban to impose or enforce any requirement, or enforce any commitment/ undertaking, to adopt a given rate/ amount of royalty or given duration of the term, of licence contract * See also the exceptions on authorised use of IP in accordance with TRIPS Article 31, requirement, etc. enforced by tribunal as equitable remuneration under copyright laws, government procurement and measures to protect legitimate public welfare objectives (Article 9.10.3[b], [c], [f] and [h])	9.10.1(i), 9.10.3(b), (c), (f) and (h)	—	
Chapter 29: Exceptions and General Provisions	A: Exceptions	1	Incorporation of interpretation of GATT Article 20 to each TPP chapter *Note: Chapters 9 and 18 are not listed as subject chapter of such incorporation.	29.1	—	
		2	Permission of measures of parties to exclude objection to national tobacco control measure from subject matter of ISDS system provided at Chapter 9, Section B	29.5 (Chapter 9, Section B)	—	

| 3 | ('may' – not mandatory – clause) Establishment of appropriate measures to respect, preserve, and promote traditional knowledge and traditional cultural expressions | 29.8 | – |

Note:

GI = geographical indication

IP = intellectual property

IPR = intellectual property rights

ISDS = Investor–State Dispute Settlement

PLT = Patent Law Treaty

TPP = Trans-Pacific Partnership

TRIPS = Agreement on Trade-Related Aspects of Intellectual Property Rights

WIPO = World Intellectual Property Organization

a. For suspected counterfeit or confusingly similar trademark/pirated copyright goods that are imported into the territory.

b. For suspected goods infringing IPRs in general that are imported into the territory.

c. For wilful trademark counterfeiting/copyright or related rights piracy on a commercial scale, 'on a commercial scale' are defined at 1(a) and (b).

d. With respect to the offences relating to this article.

e. With respect to the offences relating to (1) to (5) of this article.

f. For limitation having effect of precluding monetary relief against ISP for copyright infringements that they do not control, etc.

Source: Author.

to the transitional arrangement of TRIPS (Article 66). On the other hand, all ASEAN countries – including Cambodia, the Lao PDR, and Myanmar, which are categorised as least-developed countries – are already members of the WTO. Article 1.3 of the TPP places a footnote on the definition of TRIPS, stating that TRIPS 'includes any waiver in force between the Parties of any provision of the TRIPS Agreement granted by WTO Members in accordance with the WTO Agreement'. Therefore, the status of TRIPS exemptions enjoyed by Cambodia, the Lao PDR, and Myanmar will remain unchanged by their ratification of the TPP, and details of conditions for exemptions on each country will be a matter of negotiation.

On the other hand, in December 1995, ASEAN countries adopted the Framework Agreement on IP Cooperation (ASEAN, 1995), which is still ineffective. Under this agreement, ASEAN countries agree to (i) implement their international obligations of TRIPS; (ii) strengthen cooperation amongst them for more strengthened administrative ability and enforcement of IP, that is, copyright and related rights, patents, trademarks, industrial designs, geographical indications (GI), layout designs (topographies) of integrated circuits, protection of undisclosed information, and control of anticompetitive practices in contractual licences; and (iii) pursue the possibility of establishing an inter-ASEAN patent and trademark system. However, the agreement includes no substantive obligation to protect each IP. For the reasons stated earlier this report compares substantive obligations between the TPP and TRIPS, not the ASEAN Framework Agreement.

Fourth, the dispute settlement system of the TPP, established by Chapter 28, follows the WTO system, on understanding dispute settlement. Parties can choose the forum for settling disputes on the TPP. If a complaining party requests the establishment of a panel or other tribunal based on another international trade agreement, the use of any forum other than the chosen forum will be prohibited (Article 28.4.2). Like the WTO system, dispute settlement procedure comprises consultation between parties, good offices, conciliation and mediation, panel trial, adoption of panel report including recommendation and, in case of noncompliance of adopted recommendation, a possibility of retaliation including cross-retaliation. This system applies also to IP-related disputes.

These four characteristics will affect the construction of a subsystem on IP protection in the trans-Pacific region, and they will gradually spill over into other regions based on the most-favoured-nation principle in Article 4 of TRIPS.

3. IP-related provisions of the TPP and their subject matter

The TPP has a special chapter on IP, Chapter 18, which the next section analyses article by article. To fully understand the regulation of IP under the TPP, it is also important to realise that other chapters, including Chapters 9 and 29, and some bilateral agreements between individual parties, which are attached to the TPP text and also have a certain relationship with the regulation of IP.

3.1. *Chapter 18, intellectual property*

Chapter 18 is the main part of the TPP regulating the IP system of the parties, and it has 83 articles. Eleven sections of this chapter can be divided into three groups: (i) Sections A and B on general principles and on cooperation, (ii) Sections C to J on reference to each IP category, and (iii) Section K on final provisions. Most articles have footnotes, totalling 169, and Annexes A to F stipulate various conditions for the application of Chapter 18. The categories mentioned earlier will be analysed here.

3.1.1. *Section A: general provisions*

The definition of IP in this section is identical with that of TRIPS: 'all categories of intellectual property that are the subject of Sections 1 through 7 of Part II of the TRIPS Agreement' (Article 18.1).

The articles stating the objectives and principles of IP protection in the TPP (Articles 18.2 and 18.3) are the same as Articles 7 and 8 of TRIPS. Moreover, the TPP, in Article 18.4 on 'Understandings in Respect of this Chapter', states that '*the Parties recognise the need to (i) promote innovation and creativity; (ii) facilitate the diffusion of information, knowledge, technology, culture and the arts; and (iii) foster competition and open and efficient markets, through their respective intellectual property systems . . .*' This is a TRIPS-plus clause and it shows an updated, detailed understanding of the modern IP system. It is, therefore, important to clarify its meaning in its practice, including dispute settlement.

The TPP obliges the parties to implement TPP articles within their national legal system and practice. However, it gives the parties freedom on how to implement such articles. It also permits a TPP-plus agreement between the parties (Article 18.5). This means that the TPP provisions are a minimum standard, mandating parties to set the minimum level of IP protection according to them.

Article 18.6, 'Understandings Regarding Certain Public Health Measures', indicates 'TRIPS' flexibility' that aims at reserving each party's sovereign right to take appropriate measures, including compulsory licensing, to protect national public health and promote universal access to medicines. It confirms that the obligations cited in this chapter do not and should not prevent a party from taking measures cited earlier, and from effectively utilising paragraph 6 of the Doha Declaration,[4] by which international trade of generic medicines produced or exported and imported under compulsory licensing of both exporting and importing countries without permission by the patent holder is allowed, to the exclusion of the application of Article 31(f) of TRIPS. This system was initially introduced by the Decision of the WTO General Council on 30 August 2003 and was later made into a permanent system by the Protocol Amending the TRIPS Agreement of 2005, that became effective on 23 January 2017, with the ratification by two-thirds of WTO members (WTO, 2017). All TPP parties ratified the protocol.

While the parties, especially the US, aim to strengthen IP protection, they have also transformed the aforementioned measures into a sacred cow. More details can be seen in 3.1.3 of this chapter, Section F: Patents and Undisclosed Test or Other Data.

Including the protocol cited, the TPP obliges its parties to ratify many existing international agreements on IP (Article 18.7). The parties affirm that they have already ratified the Patent Cooperation Treaty, Paris Convention, and Berne Convention (Article 18.7.1). They are also obliged to ratify the (i) Madrid Protocol for the international application and registration of trademarks, (ii) Budapest Treaty for the international deposit of microorganisms, (iii) Singapore Treaty for the harmonisation of national trademark laws, (iv) International Convention for the Protection of New Varieties of Plants 1991, (v) World Intellectual Property Organization Copyright Treaty (WCT); and (vi) WIPO Performances and Phonograms Treaty (WPPT) (Article 18.7.2). Table 4.1 shows the parties' ratification status of these treaties.

In principle, the TPP requires parties to accord to nationals of another party the same treatment it accords to its nationals regarding the protection of IP (Article 18.8.1), with a few exceptions, including certain copyright and related rights (Article 18.8.2). The TPP does not adopt a most-favoured-nation principle stated in Article 4 of TRIPS.

The TPP obliges parties to achieve a high level of transparency in IP protection, especially by using the Internet (Article 18.9). A TPP party should make accessible on the Internet its applicable laws and regulations and administrative decisions relating to the protection and enforcement of IP (Article 18.9.1) and information on application and registration of trademarks, GI, industrial designs, patents, and new plant variety rights (Article 18.9, paras. 2 and 3). However, it must be noted that these obligations are best effort requirements rather than strictly legally binding obligations.

As for the timeframe of IP protection, Article 18.10.1 provides that a party shall protect any IP subject matter existing at the date of entry into force of the TPP for the party and those which will come subsequently to meet the criteria for protection under the TPP.

Like Article 6 of TRIPS, the TPP does not treat exhaustion of IP (Article 18.11). Today, the harmonisation of IP exhaustion is a vital issue for both business and private users. However, the parties decided not to address it.

3.1.2. Section B: cooperation

This section would have great implication on developing and least-developed countries because the TPP asks its parties for a high-level IP protection. For members to understand and implement the IP protection system, their respective domestic authorities need to cooperate.

The parties are asked to notify each other of their general administrative contact points (Articles 21.3 and 27.5.2). Especially for the utilisation of this section, parties could do so on additional contact points on IP (Article 18.12).

The TPP requires parties to implement cooperation activities and initiatives on, but not limited to, broad subject matters listed in subparagraphs (a) to (g) of Article 18.13.

Within IP, patent is the most progressive area of administrative cooperation.[5] Article 18.14 asks parties to cooperate on improving the quality and efficiency of their national patent system, simplifying patent procedure (Article 18.14.1), sharing patent search and examination results, exchanging information (Article 18.14.2), and reducing the differences in the procedures and processes of patent offices (Article 18.14.3). Moreover, the TPP recognises the importance of the Patent Law Treaty (PLT) and asks the parties to incorporate PLT standards in their patent procedures (Article 18.14.4).

TPP's statement on the recognition of public domain is unique amongst international agreements on IP (Article 18.15). The parties recognise the importance of a rich and accessible public domain and intend to establish publicly accessible databases of registered IPs to assist in identifying public domain (Article 18.15.2). This kind of 'fact-based approach' works closely with Article 18.16 on cooperation in traditional knowledge.

The TPP clearly states the parties' recognition of 'the relevance of intellectual property systems and traditional knowledge associated with genetic resources to each other, when that traditional knowledge is related to those intellectual property systems' (Article 18.16.1). This recognition is the same in intent as the affirmation of parties' appropriate measures to respect, preserve, and enhance their traditional knowledge and traditional cultural expression, subject to compliance with their international obligations as stated in Article 29.8 on exceptions and general provisions.

The following subparagraphs 2 and 3 adhere to this recognition, with aforementioned 'fact-based approach'. The parties will cooperate '*to enhance the understanding of issues connected with traditional knowledge associated with genetic resources, and genetic resources*' (Article 18.16.2). They will also '*pursue quality patent examination, which may include, . . . relevant publicly available documented information related to traditional knowledge associated with genetic resources . . . the use of databases or digital libraries containing traditional knowledge associated with genetic resources*' (Article 18.16.3).

The TPP follows established principles of international cooperation based on mutual respect of each sovereignty with its employment of phrases like '*shall be subject to the availability of resources*', 'on request', and '*on terms and conditions mutually agreed upon between the Parties involved*' (Article 18.17).

3.1.3. *Section F: patents and undisclosed test or other data*

The TPP places many TRIPS-plus obligations either on substantive and procedural aspects of patent protection and related undisclosed test or other data, from patentable subject matter to complete disclosure of information on each aspect of patent procedure (Subsection A). Therefore, it is understandable that many provisions in this section are the subject to be suspended by the CPTPP.

For agricultural chemical products (Subsection B) and pharmaceutical products (Subsection C), a cluster of obligations strengthening protection have introduced harsh controversy in and out of the parties.

For agricultural chemical products and pharmaceutical products, the TPP approves (i) protection of undisclosed test or other data ('data protection' (Articles 18.47, 18.50, and 18.51)); and (ii) patent term adjustment for unreasonable curtailment derived from acquiring marketing approval for them ('patent term adjustment on pharmaceuticals' (Article18.48)). Pharmaceutical products are divided further into (i) biologics, as defined in Article 18.51.2; (ii) new pharmaceutical products, as defined in Article 18.52; and (iii) others. For each category, the TPP places different obligations on data protection and patent term adjustment. Furthermore, the TPP aims to introduce linkages between patent procedure and marketing approval procedure of pharmaceutical products to prevent confusion with the enforcement of pharmaceutical patents to marketed generic pharmaceuticals ('patent-linkage' (Article 18.53)).

Articles 18.53.1(a) to (c) are the packages introduced first in the US in 1984 by the Hatch–Waxman Act and recently included in many trade agreements between the US and other countries (Valdés and Tavengwa, 2012). For the assessment of these obligations, it is useful to watch closely Annexes 18-B to 18-D concerning attached conditions on the obligations of Chile, Malaysia, and Peru.

a   Subsection A: general patent

Patentable subject matter (Article 18.37) is almost the same as the TRIPS scheme. However, there are two sources of difference between them. First, the TPP asks for the establishment of patent protection for at least one of the following: '*new uses of a known product, new methods of using a known product, and new processes of using a known product*' (paragraph 2). This has raised concerns on whether it would have 'ever-greening' effect, meaning that an invention would be permanently and abusively protected by switching amongst various types of patent right. In Japan, these inventions are protected by 'new use invention' patent, covering an unknown and non-obvious use. They would be either product or process patent. However, the CPTPP has stated to suspend the related obligations.

Second, the TPP clearly permits the exclusion of '*diagnostic, therapeutic and surgical methods for the treatment of humans or animals*' from patentable inventions (paragraph 3[a]). This is made for consideration of existing exclusion built in the patent system of Japan, Malaysia, and so forth, although there is strong criticism for such exclusion in Japan. In practice, most of them are substantially protected as industrially applicable inventions.

Grace period is defined as public disclosure based on the intention of the patent applicant and occurred within 12 months before the date of filing of the application in the territory of the party (Article 18.38). This is a TRIPS-plus clause. To fulfil the latter condition, Japan amended Article 30 of its Patent Law, and extended the period from 6 to 12 months (still unenforced).

Conditions of patent cancellation, revocation, or nullification are set in Article 18.39.1,[6] such as fraud, misrepresentation, or inequitable conduct, provided cancellation or revocation is done in a manner consistent with Article 5A of the Paris Convention and TRIPS (Article 18.39.2).

The condition of limitation and exception to the exclusive rights conferred by patent right is a subject of keen contestation[7] worldwide. The TPP places Article 18.40 (following TRIPS Article 30) and Article 18.41 (following TRIPS Article 31) and exemptions therefrom. The TPP, therefore, follows the TRIPS scheme. One should also notice the obligation to introduce experimental use exception within the parties' system (Article 18.49).

The TPP mandates first-to-file principle (Article 18.42), which is a TRIPS-plus clause. A user-friendly system is pursued by asking for the admission of at least one opportunity for amendment, correction, and observation for patent applicants (Article 18.43) (WIPO, 2000a), transparency of patent system, publication of pending patent applications after the expiration of 18 months from the filing date or from the earliest priority date, and introduction of earlier publication system (Article 18.44). In addition, a list of the types of information to be published is provided (Article 18.45). These are TRIPS-plus provisions and would impose considerable administrative burden on developing countries. Strengthening international cooperation in this area is crucial to realise the vision of these clauses.

Systematically, one difficult provision of the TPP to implement, especially for parties that are developing countries, is the obligation to introduce patent term adjustment for unreasonable delays by granting authority (Article 18.46). The CPTPP will suspend the application of this obligation. Delays over 5 years from the date of filing or 3 years after the request for examination of the application will extend patent term. For example, Japan is incorporating this system in Article 67 of its Patent Law (which is still not yet enforced though).

A high level of administrative ability is obviously needed in processing patent examination. This could, therefore, be an obstacle, especially for developing countries, to join the TPP. This would require deepening international cooperation on patent procedures between parties.

b   Subsection B: measures relating to agricultural chemical products

For new agricultural chemical products, if a party requires, as a condition of granting marketing approval, the submission of undisclosed test or other data concerning the safety and efficacy of the product or permits the submission of evidence of prior marketing approval of the product in another territory, at least 10 years should be given for data protection (Article 18.47). '*New agricultural chemical product*' is defined as '*one that contains a chemical entity that has not been previously approved in the territory of the Party for use in an agricultural chemical product*' (Article 18.47.3).

Moreover, this data protection should not be altered when patent protection ends on a date earlier than the end of the period for data protection (Article 18.54). This data protection is not provided in TRIPS.

c   Subsection C: measures relating to pharmaceutical products

Patent term adjustment for pharmaceuticals (Article 18.48) is distinguished from the provision on general patents mentioned previously. This is a TRIPS-plus clause and its application will be suspended in accordance with the CPTPP.

Some developed countries have already introduced such system. However, they are different in the details of the system. For example, Japan's Patent Law has a patent term adjustment system for agricultural chemical products and pharmaceutical products as provided in its Articles 67(2), 67bis, 67bis-bis, and 67ter. As to the interpretation of these articles, the provision of the Patent Examination Guidelines on the exclusive rights conferred by extended patent rights has been amended (Japan Patent Office, 2018a) based on the case law and cumulative discussion. Furthermore, in 2015, patent rights on pharmaceutical products using or introducing iPS or induced pluripotent stem cell were added to be extended patent term.

The TPP obligates to '*adopt or maintain a regulatory review exception for pharmaceutical products*' (Article 18.49). In 2000, the WTO panel, on the dispute between Canada and the European Union regarding TRIPS-compatibility of Canadian regulatory review or stockpile exceptions, concluded in a panel report (WTO, 2000) that the former exception did not infringe Canada's obligations, but the latter did. After the adoption of this report, several countries introduced the regulatory review exception into their patent law. However, setting this obligation in a multilateral international agreement is a new movement.

Data protection required by the TPP is a TRIPS-plus provision because for TRIPS Article 39, the conditions of protection does not matter.

In parallel with Article 18.47, Article 18.50 on new pharmaceutical products states that if a party requires, as a condition of granting marketing approval, the submission of undisclosed test or other data concerning the safety and efficacy of the product or permits the submission of evidence of a prior marketing approval of the product in another territory, at least 5 years should be given as data protection (Article 18.50.1). Moreover, previously approved pharmaceutical products requiring new clinical information results should be given at least 3 years' data protection (Article 18.50.2[a]), and new pharmaceutical products containing a chemical entity that has not been previously approved in that party and fulfilling conditions, with at least 5 years' data protection (Article 18.50.2[b]). A party that provides at least 8 years' protection pursuant to Article 18.50.1 will not be obliged to apply Article 18.50.2 (footnote 55). Furthermore, in applying Article 18.50.2(b), a party may choose to protect only the data on safety and efficacy (footnote 57).

Article 18.51 states further that, for a new pharmaceutical product that is or contains 'biologics', parties are obliged to provide effective market protection for about 5 or 8 years through the implementation of Article 18.50.1.

'Biologics' is defined in Article 18.51.2 as '*a product that is, or alternatively contains, a protein produced using biotechnology processes, for use in human beings for the prevention, treatment, or cure of a disease or condition*'. Like in other agricultural chemical products, this data protection should not be altered if the patent protection terminates on a date earlier than the end of the period of data protection (Article 18.54).

The aforementioned obligations have raised controversy on their possible impact on the domestic pharmaceutical and industrial policies of TPP parties and non-parties and the CPTPP includes suspension of these two articles.

To reach agreement, these articles provide many footnotes for clarification. For example, footnote 59 clarifies that Article 18.51 does not require extending the protection of Article 18.51.1 to any second or subsequent marketing approval of such a product, or a pharmaceutical product that is or contains a previously approved biologic. Also, footnote 60 clarifies that a party may allow an applicant to request approval of a pharmaceutical product that is or contains a biologic under the procedures set forth in Articles 18.50.1(a) and (b) within 5 years from the date of entry into force of the agreement for that party, provided that the party has approved other pharmaceutical products in the same class of products under the procedures set forth in clauses cited above before the effectivity date of the agreement for that party.

The impact of these obligations can be seen from footnote 58, Annexes 18-B to 18-D regarding exemptions on Chile, Malaysia, and Peru. Furthermore, the TPP schedules consultation to review the impact of these obligations after 10 years from date of entry into force of the TPP (Article 18.51.3).

Last, notwithstanding such obligations, the TPP permits parties to take measures to protect public health in accordance with existing and future TRIPS schemes (Article 18.50.3). The measures to be permitted are ambiguous from the text; therefore, further clarification is needed.

The TPP provides for the introduction of the patent linkage system (Article 18.53). In general, the system contains the obligation, imposed at the procedure for marketing approval regarding both new and generic pharmaceutical products, to submit information on the status of a related patent. Under the system, when the patent holder of a new pharmaceutical product files a patent infringement suit against generic producers, then the procedure for marketing approval of the generic pharmaceutical product is automatically resumed. This system is not provided under TRIPS.

3.1.4. Section H: copyright and related rights

On the protection of copyright and related rights, the TPP obliges parties to ratify or accede to the WIPO Copyright Treaty (WCT) and the WIPO Performances and Phonograms Treaty (WPPT) (Article 18.7.2), which raises the level of protection of these rights up from the Berne Convention, Rome Conventions, and TRIPS, and even places the norms of the WCT and the WPPT-plus protection in this section. The correspondent relationship amongst them is shown in the Annex.

The area covered by this section is wide and deep, from traditional copyright works to technological protection measures (TPMs) (Article 18.68) or rights management information (RMI) (Article 18.69). Furthermore, protection of encrypted programme-carrying satellite and cable signals (Article 18.79) and government use of software (Article 80), both included in Section I on enforcement, are also aspects of copyright protection.

i   Definition (Article 18.57)

On rights conferred to performers and producers of phonograms provided in Articles18.58–18.70, which define 'broadcasting', 'communication to the public', 'fixation', 'performers', 'phonogram', 'producer of a phonogram', and 'publication'.

ii   Contents of copyright and related rights (Articles 18.58–18.62)

On copyright, the TPP obliges parties to provide authors the following rights: reproduction (Article 18.58), communication to the public (Article 18.59), and distribution (Article 18.60).

On the right of communication to the public, like WCT Article 8, the TPP does not preclude the application of related articles of the Berne Convention (Article 18.59).

On related rights, the TPP obliges parties to provide performers and producers of phonograms the right of reproduction (Article 18.58) and the right of distribution (Article 18.60). The TPP does not provide for the rights of broadcasters.

Furthermore, parties shall grant performers the exclusive right to authorise or prohibit the broadcasting, communication to the public of their unfixed performances, and fixation of their unfixed performances. Performers and producers of phonograms are also provided the right to authorise or prohibit broadcasting or any communication to the public of their performances or phonograms by wire or wireless means and making available to the public those performances or phonograms (Article 18.62). On analogue transmissions and non-interactive free over-the-air broadcasts, the TPP leaves to parties the discretion to apply the provision (Article 18.62.3[b]).

The TPP prohibits parties from putting a hierarchy between the copyright holder (author) and the holder of related rights (performer or producer) when authorisation is needed from both (Article 18.61). Therefore, authorisation by one holder will not substitute for the other. This obligation will cause controversy because the difficulty and complication to handle many authorisations to use one copyright work may create barriers to creative activities.

iii   Term of protection of copyright and related rights (Article 18.63)

The TPP changes the basic term of protection of copyright and related rights from 50 years to 70 years. This is of TRIPS-, Berne-, and WPPT-plus, however, the CPTPP decides to not apply this obligation. In fact, this had been debated for many years in Japan, but agreement was reached only in 2016. The Copyright Law was finally amended in December 2016 through the passage of the implementing law on TPP obligations; it is not yet enforced.[8] Even after its passage, controversy continues not only amongst scholars and business entities but also amongst citizens. For example, many Japanese adolescents enjoy making and exhibiting derivative works of popular works created by others. The Japanese government encourages such activities as one branch of the 'Cool Japan' policy.[9] That means, the scale of these activities should be broad and active. Some Japanese comic artists or publishers adopt a new business strategy. Instead of focusing on sales of comic books, they make their works copy-free on the website and gain income through other means, such as the sale of tangible goods using their works.

The extension of the term of protection of copyright and related rights makes these adolescents feel threatened by copyright infringement. Its impact on creative activities, together with the issue of orphan works, facilitation of registration for copyright works, and so forth, is to be discussed widely, with Japan included in the discussion. In short, reconstruction of the modern copyright system may need to be considered.

iv Retroactive effects of protection (Article 18.64)

On the retroactive effects of protection of copyright and related rights, the TPP adopts the principle in Article 18 of the Berne Convention and Article 14(6) of TRIPS.

v Limitations and exceptions to the exclusive rights of copyright and related rights, and appropriate balancing of the protection system of copyrights and related rights (Articles 18.65 and 18.66)

The TPP requires parties to set the limitations and exceptions to the exclusive rights of copyright and related rights according to the conditions of Article 9 of the Berne Convention and its successor, Article 13 of TRIPS. The TPP also does not affect the scope of the limitations and exceptions provided by the Berne Convention, TRIPS, and the WCT or the WPPT (Article 18.65).

Moreover, the TPP will likely take another step further by placing an article mentioning an appropriate balance in parties' copyright and related rights system, apart from the article on limitations and exceptions cited earlier. Especially, the phrases '*by means of limitations or exceptions . . ., including those for the digital environment*' and '*giving due consideration to legitimate purposes*' are worth paying attention to.

In this regard, it must also be noted that footnote 79 says '*a use that has commercial aspects may in appropriate circumstances be considered to have a legitimate purpose under Article 18.65 (Limitations and Exceptions)*'. The scope of this footnote is not limited to facilitating access to published works for persons who are blind, visually impaired, or otherwise print disabled, as explained in footnote 78, that it is in line with the Marrakesh

Treaty of 2013. However, it leaves a room to consider the reconstruction of copyright scheme as aforementioned suggested item (c).

vi   Contractual transfers (Article 18.67)

Parties are obliged to protect the economic aspects of copyright and related rights as a property right. See also footnote 80 which states that '*this provision does not affect the exercise of moral rights*'.

vii   Technological protection measures (Article 18.68)

The TPP requires regulating various actions circumventing TPMs by making them the subject of civil, administrative, and criminal procedures and remedies. These are WCT or WPPT-plus provisions which are more inclusive and detailed. However, this obligation is to be suspended in reply to the CPTPP.

Implementing these obligations takes much attention because of the many conditions on the scope of application, such as 'knowingly, or having reasonable grounds to know' (Article 18.68.1[a]), '*have only a limited commercially significant purpose*' (Article 18.68.1[b][ii]), and so on. Articles 18.68.2 to 18.68.4 permit parties to make certain limitations and exceptions to their application and set conditions towards such limitations and exceptions. Article 18.68.5 defines 'effective technological measure', which is equal to the TPM.

viii   Rights management information (Article 18.69)

The TPP also requires making civil, administrative, and criminal remedies available to persons using the RMI, with many conditions on the scope of application. This is also a WCT or a WPPT-plus provision and will be suspended in accordance with the CPTPP.

It is worth knowing that footnote 96 says, '*A Party may comply with the obligations in this Article by providing legal protection only to electronic RMI*'. Moreover, the last sentence of paragraphs 1 and 2, which states that '*A Party may provide . . .*', permits parties to limit the scope of application. Paragraph 3 bans parties to require the right holder to provide the RMI copies of work or communications. Paragraph 4 defines the RMI and it resembles WPPT Article 19(2).

ix   Collective management (Article 18.70)

This article states the importance of well-constructed collective management societies for copyright and related rights.

3.1.5. Section I: enforcement

This section contains many TRIPS-plus provisions. For example, mention is made on (a) 'damage' in civil proceedings (Article 18.74), (ii) obligation to apply border measures to transit goods (Article 18.76), and (iii) criminal sanction to certain infringement action of protected trade secret (Article 18.78). The focus, common with TRIPS, is the enforcement in case of infringement of copyright and related rights and trademarks, amongst many IP rights. Moreover, deterrent to future infringement is stressed here.

On 'Protection of encrypted programme-carrying satellite and cable signals' (Article 18.79), the precedent treaty is the Brussels Convention of 1974,[10] and 'Government use of software' provisions (Article 18.80) are new regulations amongst multilateral IP agreements.

i   General provisions (Articles 18.71 to 18.73)

Parties are obliged to make their enforcement system in line with this section in the spirit of fairness and equity (Articles 18.71.1 and 18.71.3). These words follow those of TRIPS Article 41.

The obligations set by this section apply to the acts of trademark, copyright, or related rights infringement also in the digital environment (Article 18.71.2).

The TPP confers parties' discretion to choose the manner of implementing their obligations (Article 18.5). Reflecting this principle, the parties are permitted to choose the judicial formality and the manner of distribution of legal resources in implementing the obligations imposed by this section (Article 18.71.4). This is the same as TRIPS Article 41(5).

The TPP requires parties to '*take into account the need for proportionality between the seriousness of the infringement of intellectual property (IP) rights and the applicable remedies and penalties, as well as the interests of third parties*' (Article 18.71.5).

It is a unique provision of the TPP, not contained in TRIPS, to presuppose the validity of copyright and related rights, trademarks, and patent rights (Article 18.72).

On the civil, administrative, and criminal procedures regarding IP enforcement, the TPP asks for user-friendly and electronically adapted practices, including '*collecting and analyzing statistical data and other information concerning IP infringements, as well as collecting information on best practice to prevent and combat infringements*' and providing such information to the public (Article 18.73). This is a TRIPS-plus provision (Article 41.3), demanding parties' administrative effort and ability.

ii Civil, administrative procedure, and relief (Article 18.74)

This article is voluminous, with 17 paragraphs, which authorise the right holder and judicial authority of various abilities in civil and administrative procedures and relief.[11]

Paragraphs 4 to 9 mention the manner of calculating damages from infringement of IP, including selective introduction of pre-established or additional damages plus exemplary or punitive damages (footnotes 112 and 113), and for the infringement of trademarks, copyright, and related rights. Japan established the principle of overall actual damage, and therefore tries to introduce a kind of pre-established damages by amending the Copyright and Trademark Law in December 2016 (still unenforced). It is said that the principle would not be changed by this amendment.

iii　Provisional measures (Article 18.75)

The TPP agreement requires the provisional measures to be taken with no involvement of suspected IP infringer. At the same time, parties are required to check the likelihood of abuse for application and to control related materials through seizure or other custody. These obligations are TRIPS-plus (Articles 51 to 60).

iv　Border measures (Article 18.76)

The TPP places conditions of border measures more precisely than TRIPS Articles 51 to 60. 'Counterfeit trademark goods' and 'pirated copyright goods' to be regulated in this article are defined in footnote 116.

Paragraph 5 states that parties' competent authorities may initiate border measures *ex officio* with respect to 'in transit', 'imported', and 'destined for export' counterfeit trademarks or pirated copyright goods. At the same time, it allows flexibility in that a party could provide available information on suspected goods to another party, instead of regulating goods in transit (footnote 123).

Regulated goods include goods of commercial nature sent in small consignments. This is a TRIPS-plus provision; however, each party is permitted to exclude small quantities of goods of non-commercial nature sent in small consignments (footnote 125). Moreover, paragraph 9 excludes small quantities of goods of non-commercial nature contained in travellers' personal luggage, as provided in TRIPS Article 60.

v　Criminal procedures and penalties (Article 18.77)

On the application of criminal procedures and penalties towards counterfeit trademarks or pirated copyright goods, this article provides for the subject matter under paragraphs 1 to 5, including labelling or packaging to be considered trademark infringement and unauthorised copy by secretly filming movies in theatres. It also sets procedural requirements in paragraphs 6 and 7, including disposal of goods, seizure or forfeiture of assets, or imposing fines corresponding to the value of infringing activity. The bulk of these requirements are TRIPS-plus provisions. Furthermore, in implementing these requirements, the power and functions of judicial authority would be in the agenda.

The term 'on a commercial scale' is defined in paragraph 1 and in its footnotes 126 and 127.

As mentioned in the section on copyright, Japanese adolescents feel threatened to be penalised by creating derivative works, infringing others' copyright works. The TPP draws their attention because they concern the possibility of giving authorities power to initiate legal action without a formal complaint by the right holder. Under Article 18.77.6(g), the sentence on the obligation to confer such power to party's authorities uses 'may'. Specifically, on piracy of copyright and related rights, a party is permitted to limit the power '*to the cases in which there is an impact on the right holder's ability to exploit the work, performance or phonogram in the market*' (footnote 135).

vi   Trade secrets (Article 18.78)

TRIPS is ambiguous on the scope of protection of trade secrets. While it incorporates Article 10bis of the Paris Convention, requiring regulation of unfair competitive action in general, in its Part II on containing substantive articles, Article 39 refers only to protection of undisclosed information. As a result, the national legal system to protect trade secrets is diverse amongst WTO members. The TPP includes undisclosed information in its definition of 'trade secrets' and sets a purpose of protection as '*ensuring effective protection against unfair competition as provided in Article 10bis of the Paris Convention*' (Article 18.78.1).

Unauthorised wilful access, and misappropriation and fraudulent or unauthorised and wilful disclosure of trade secrets shall be criminalised. A party, however, may make exceptions or limit the level of penalties (Articles 18.78.2 and 18.78.3).

vii Protection of encrypted programme-carrying satellite and cable signals (Article 18.79)

This is a TRIPS-plus and Brussels Convention-plus clause but would not be applied until the decision of the parties of the CPTPP. The TPP obliges parties to protect encrypted programme-carrying satellite and cable signals to criminalise certain acts disturbing them, or to add such acts to the subject of civil remedies.

viii Government use of software (Article 18.80)

The title of this article is mistakable. The phrase 'government use' is used in patent law or other IP laws as the use of IP by government, with no authorisation by the right holder, for some sort of national purpose, such as preservation of natural environment and improvement of access to medicines. Rather, this article states parties' resolution not to infringe IP rights.

3.1.6. Section K: final provisions (Article 18.83)

This article defines parties' obligation to implement the provisions of Chapter 18 (Article 18.83.1), with many subparagraphs permitting a transitional period for each party, including both developing and developed countries, to extend the deadline of complying with their obligations (Articles 18.83.2 and 18.83.4, Annexes A to D), and to prohibit measures to make the level of IP protection lower than the level in effect on the date of signing of the agreement during the transitional period (Article 18.83.2). This approach resembles TRIPS Articles 65, 66, and 70 in its structure.

Paragraph 3 refers to the transitional period for Japan and Mexico on the term of protection of copyright and related rights. Paragraph 4 provides for a transitional period for Brunei Darussalam, Malaysia, Mexico, New Zealand, Peru, and Viet Nam.

3.2. Chapter 9, investment, especially its subsection A

In the TPP, 'investment' includes IP and '*licences, authorisations, permits and similar rights conferred pursuant to the Party's law*' (Articles 9.1[f] and 9.1[g]). The IP-related articles of this chapter will not be affected by the CPTPP.

Regarding expropriation and compensation, the TPP provides that this article shall not apply to the issuance of compulsory licences granted in relation to intellectual property rights in accordance with the TRIPS Agreement, or to the revocation, limitation, or creation of intellectual property rights to the extent that the issuance, revocation, limitation, or creation is consistent with Chapter 18 and the TRIPS Article 9.8.5.

Parties are prohibited to impose or enforce any requirement or enforce any commitment or undertaking 'to adopt a given rate or amount of royalty under a licence contract or a given duration of the term of a licence contract' (Article 9.10.1[i]). However, it is permitted to do so '*if a Party authorizes use of an intellectual property right in accordance with Article 31 of TRIPS or to measures requiring the disclosure of proprietary information that fall within the scope of, and are consistent with, Article 39 of TRIPS*' (Article 9.10.3[b]). Furthermore, it is also permitted to do so '*if the requirement is imposed or the commitment or undertaking is enforced by a tribunal as equitable remuneration under the Party's copyright laws*' (Article 9.10.3[c]). '*Adopting or maintaining measures to protect legitimate public welfare objectives*' is also permitted '*provided that such measures are not applied in an arbitrary or unjustifiable manner, or in a manner that constitutes a disguised restriction on international trade or investment*' (Article 9.10.3[h]).

4. Conclusion

With the US government's withdrawal, the future of the TPP is difficult to predict. It looks like the US government will not hesitate to take bilateral pressure and even enforce 'Super 301' or 'Special 301' measures, which have long been blamed as unilateral measure.[12] However, as pointed out in the introduction of this chapter, the chapters relating to IP are the expression of US interests and of power relations amongst negotiating countries on IP, and therefore they are a model for the IP chapter of subsequent free trade agreements. It is worth analysing their structure and content, and assessing their repercussions on the IP system, with the perspective of revisiting one's own IP strategy and reconstructing the IP system to respond appropriately and timely to new technology and new stakeholders.

Notes

1 Article 1.1, included in Chapter 1, Section A of the Trans-Pacific Partnership (TPP) agreement. Hereinafter, the article number is of the TPP, in the absence of another citation.

2 Appendix 1C of the Marrakesh Agreement establishing the World Trade Organization, which took effect on 1 January 1995.

3 Articles 1, 2, 9, 14, 35, and 39 of the Agreement on Trade-Related Aspects of Intellectual Property Rights.

4 The Doha Declaration is the 'Declaration on the TRIPS Agreement and Public Health', adopted at the 4th WTO Ministerial Conference held at Doha, Qatar, 14 November 2001. With the progress of the application of the TRIPS Agreement by 1995 and appearance of the IP chapter in many bilateral and regional agreements, the protection of IP has been improved more than ever. Simultaneously, the room of the national discretion for the domestic IP system in accordance with each countries' socio-economic situation has been limited. Especially, the WTO members face legal uncertainty that the trade of generic medicine produced under compulsory licence would infringe their obligations under Article 31(f) of the TRIPS Agreement, which states that the product produced under compulsory licence must be predominantly supplied for the domestic market of the member authorising the compulsory licence. In the 1990s, countries have faced pandemics such as HIV/AIDS, malaria, and tuberculosis, in some instances, severe as to constitute national emergency. The ministers discussed the issue and adopted the aforementioned declaration, which places the principle that the interpretation of the TRIPS Agreement can and should be in a manner supportive of the members' rights to protect public health. The principle is called the 'TRIPS flexibility'. Paragraph 6 of the declaration also instruct the Council for TRIPS to find an expeditious solution to the issue. For more details, visit the gateway site 'TRIPS and public health' of the WTO homepage, available at www.wto.org/english/tratop_e/trips_e/pharmpatent_e.htm

5 For example, the Patent Prosecution Highway is 'a framework in which an application whose claims have been determined to be patentable in the Office of First Filing is eligible to go through an accelerated examination in the Office of Second Filing with a simple procedure upon an applicant's request'. See PPH portal site, available at www.jpo.go.jp/ppph-portal/globalpph.htm (accessed 24 January 2017).

6 See WIPO (2000b), Patent Law Treaty, Article 10(1).

7 One example is the dispute of the complaint by EC to the WTO DSU procedure (WT/DS114), whether the exception clause of the Canadian patent law on the experimental use of pre-expired pharmaceutical patents – to acquire the clinical test data for submitting them to the authority to get marketing approval and to stockpile the products by that use – is consistent with Article 30 of the TRIPS Agreement. The report of the panel provided that the former exception was consistent, and the latter was inconsistent. Although this report has been the subject of much critics, Canada abolished the latter exception clause, and several countries introduced the same clause as the former into their patent laws. Another example is the public health issue, mentioned in Section A: General Provisions.

8 Law No. 2016–102, implemented on 16 December 2016. English translation is not yet published at the website of the Government of Japan, available at www.japaneselawtranslation.go.jp/?re=02

9 See METI site 'Cool Japan/Creative Industries Policy', available at www.meti.go.jp/english/policy/mono_info_service/creative_industries/creative_industries.html

10 See Table 4.1 on the explanation of this treaty.

11 See obligations listed in the Annex.
12 For example, since August 2017, the Trump administration of the US has investigated China's IP protection. In March 2018, the administration decided to enforce both countermeasures based on 'Super 301' and complained on this issue to the WTO DSU (WT/DS542). For 'Super 301', meaning the Chapter 1 of Title III of the Trade Act of 1974 (codified as amended in 19 U.S.C. §§ 2411–2417), see USTR, 'Section 301 Report into China's Acts, Policies, and Practices Related to Technology Transfer, Intellectual Property, and Innovation', available at https://ustr.gov/about-us/policy-offices/press-office/press-releases/2018/march/section-301-report-chinas-acts. For 'Special 301', meaning Section 182 of the Trade Act of 1974, as amended by the Omnibus Trade and Competitiveness Act of 1988, the Uruguay Round Agreements Act, and the Trade Facilitation and Trade Enforcement Act of 2015 (19 U.S.C. § 2242), specifically focusing on the IP protection of US trade partners, see USTR, '2017 Special 301 Report', available at https://ustr.gov/issue-areas/intellectual-property/special-301/2017-special-301-review

Bibliography

ASEAN (1995), 'ASEAN Framework Agreement on Intellectual Property Cooperation'. Available at www.aseanip.org/About (accessed 24 January 2017).

Australian Government Attorney-General's Department (2011), 'Tobacco Plain Packaging – Investor – State Arbitration'. Available at www.ag.gov.au/tobacco plainpackaging

Japan Patent Office (2018a), 'Examination Guidelines for Patent and Utility Model in Japan, Part III Chapter 1 (Eligibility for Patent and Industrial Applicability), 3.1.1'. Available at www.jpo.go.jp/tetuzuki_e/t_tokkyo_e/files_guidelines_e/03_0100_e.pdf

Japan Patent Office (2018b), 'Examination Guidelines for Patent and Utility Model in Japan, Part IX Extension of Patent Term'. Available at www.jpo.go.jp/tetuzuki_e/t_tokkyo_e/files_guidelines_e/09_0100_e.pdf

Law No. 2016–102, implemented on 16 December 2016. Available at www.japaneselawtranslation.go.jp/?re=02

Ministry of Economy, Trade and Industry (METI) (2014), 'Cool Japan /Creative Industries Policy'. Available at www.meti.go.jp/english/policy/mono_info_service/creative_industries/creative_industries.html

Ministry of Foreign Affairs of Japan (2017), 'Notification of Completion of Domestic Procedures for the Patent Prosecution Highway Portal'. Available at www.jpo.go.jp/ppph-portal/globalpph.htm (accessed 24 January 2017).

'Trans-Pacific Partnership (TPP) Agreement', 20 January 2017. Available at www.mofa.go.jp/press/release/press4e_001443.html (accessed 23 January 2017).

USTR (2017), '2017 Special 301 Report'. Available at https://ustr.gov/issue-areas/intellectual-property/special-301/2017-special-301-review

USTR (2018), 'Section 301 Report into China's Acts, Policies, and Practices Related to Technology Transfer, Intellectual Property, and Innovation'. Available at https://ustr.gov/about-us/policy-offices/press-office/press-releases/2018/march/section-301-report-chinas-acts

Valdés, R. and R. Tavengwa (2012), 'Intellectual Property Provisions in Regional Trade Agreements', WTO Economic Research and Statistics Division, *Staff Working Paper* ERSD-2012–21, 31 October, paras. 107–121. Available at www.wto.org/english/tratop_e/region_e/region_e.htm (accessed 2 February 2017).

WIPO (2000a), *Joint Recommendation Concerning Provisions on the Protection of Well-Known Marks*. Geneva: WIPO.

WIPO (2000b), *Patent Law Treaty*. Geneva: WIPO. Available at www.wipo.int/wipolex/en/details.jsp?id=12642

WTO (1994), 'Disputes by Agreements: Intellectual Property (TRIPS)'. Available at www.wto.org/english/tratop_e/dispu_e/dispu_agreements_index_e.htm?id=A26#

WTO (1995), *Agreement on Trade-Related Aspects of Intellectual Property Rights*. Geneva: WTO.

WTO (2000), *Canada – Patent Protection of Pharmaceutical Products – Complaint by the European Communities and their Member States – Report of the Panel*. Geneva: WTO.

WTO (2001), 'TRIPS and Public Health'. Available at www.wto.org/english/tratop_e/trips_e/pharmpatent_e.htm

WTO (2017), 'WTO IP Rules Amended to Ease Poor Countries' Access to Affordable Medicines', 23 January. Available at www.wto.org/english/news_e/news17_e/trip_23jan17_e.htm (accessed 24 January 2017).

5 Intellectual property rights in TPP agreement

Commitments and implications for Viet Nam

Nguyen Anh Duong[1]

1. Introduction

After three decades of continuous economic reforms, Viet Nam has achieved high economic growth. Since 2015, Viet Nam has been promoting productivity[2] as the key pillar for sustainable growth and avoidance of the middle-income trap.[3] Accordingly, Viet Nam seeks to strengthen its competition policy, aiming for a more robust innovative capacity and sustainable development of its private sector. Meanwhile, despite the pledge to improve its science and technology policies, not much has been seen out of these policies. This is partly due to the weak enforcement of existing regulations on intellectual properties (IPs) for years (American Chamber of Commerce in Vietnam, 2013).

This chapter attempts to discuss the implication of the IP Chapter under the Trans-Pacific Partnership (TPP) Agreement – which was transformed into the Comprehensive and Progressive Trans-Pacific Partnership agreement (CPTPP) after the United States withdrew from TPP – on Viet Nam's economy. In doing so, the chapter mainly employs a qualitative approach, seeking to explain Viet Nam's major commitments under the Chapter and briefly assesses their associated impact on the nation's different sectors. Some policy measures to realise the opportunities and alleviate the adverse impacts of enforced IP protection under the TPP will be recommended.

The rest of the chapter is structured as follows: Section 2 introduces the IP system in Viet Nam. Section 3 summarises the key commitments of Viet Nam under the IP Chapter of the TPP. Section 4 discusses several potential impacts of the IP Chapter on Viet Nam's economy. Section 5 makes some recommendations on how Viet Nam can adapt to and benefit from the IP commitments under the TPP.

2. Intellectual property system in Viet Nam

Viet Nam's aim to improve its intellectual property (IP) system was closely associated with the attempt to integrate itself with the world economy. The first major push was from the Bilateral Trade Agreement (BTA) with the United States, which incorporates comprehensive provisions on IP protection in various areas such as trademarks, copyrights and related rights, and encrypted programme-carrying satellite signal. The second push was from Viet Nam's negotiation to become a World Trade Organization (WTO) member since 2007. To prepare for WTO accession, Viet Nam had to establish and enforce IP laws that meet the standards accepted by WTO members.

2.1. Categories of IP

Viet Nam's IP system is divided into three areas, namely: (i) copyrights and related rights; (ii) industrial property rights; and (iii) rights to plant varieties.

Viet Nam joined the Berne Convention on copyrights in 2004. Per the agreement, copyright protection should be enforced for at least 50 years from publication for cinematographic works, photographic works, dramatic works, works of applied art and anonymous works, and at least 50 years after the death of the author for other works. Registration of copyright is recommended and can be made with the National Copyright Office. Computer programmes are included within Viet Nam's copyright legislation, although computer programmes as such cannot be patented.

Viet Nam differentiates patents (or invention patents) from utility solution patents (also known as 'utility models' or 'minor patents'). Although most rules adopted by other nations treat utility solution patents and invention patents alike, utility solution patents require no demonstration of an 'inventive step' in the concerned products/items, whereas invention patents do. In addition, invention patents protect for a maximum of 20 years, whereas utility solution patents are valid for 10 years.

Other regulations on patents deserve attention. Viet Nam's patent law operates under the first-to-file principle. If two people submit applications for a patent on an identical invention, the first one to file the application will be awarded the patent. In another aspect, the law gives protection to industrial designs for a maximum of 5 years, which can then be renewed for two consecutive periods of 5 years.

In terms of trademarks, Viet Nam's system covers protection of symbols, colours, and other visual devices used to identify a business' products or services, including three-dimensional objects. Meanwhile, trade names constitute a form of industrial property in Viet Nam, with rights established through their use rather than under a formal registration system. Domain names are again allocated based on the first-to-file principle. If registered (within 13 months from filing), trademarks are valid for 10 years, after which they may be renewed indefinitely for further 10-year periods.

Registration of industrial property rights (patents, utility solutions, industrial designs, trademarks, etc.) can be made with the National Office of Intellectual Property (NOIP) under the Ministry of Science and Technology. The NOIP usually refuses newly filed marks that are confusingly similar to famous ones, even if goods or services bearing such marks are neither identical nor similar. More recently, nonetheless, this view seems to be changing on the basis of the examination of the presumption that no famous trademark exists in the absence of official recognition through a decision or judgement of an authority or court (Bross and Partners, 2017).

2.2. Enforcers of IP regulations

Different categories of IPs are administered by different agencies in Viet Nam. The copyright and related rights are administered by the Copyright Office of Viet Nam (under the Ministry of Culture, Sport and Tourism, formerly the Ministry of Culture and Information). Meanwhile, industrial property rights are under the authority of the NOIP. The rights to plant varieties are under the purview of the Plant Variety Protection Office. For IP issues in general, however, the NOIP holds the chief coordinator role.

Enforcing IP regulations require the participation of other agencies. In particular, the Law on IP in 2005 identifies different kinds of civil and criminal penalties on violations of IP. Such violations are mainly in the trade and distribution of products. In such a case, the General Department of Customs (under the Ministry of Finance), the Department for Market Management (under the Ministry of Industry and Trade) and their subsidiaries in Viet Nam are the relevant authorities on IP enforcement. These departments' scope of actions also extends to imported and exported goods. Customs agencies have their own recordal system that IP rights owners can refer to when registering their marks with Customs. This presents a need for information to be shared between Vietnamese agencies, specifically the NOIP and Customs agency.

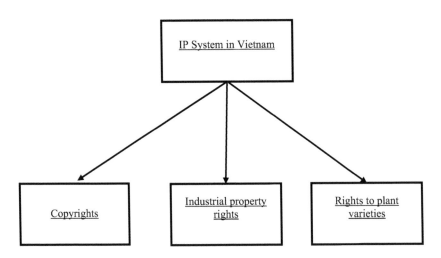

Figure 5.1 IP system in Viet Nam

Source: Author's compilations.

By 2016, foreign investors seeking to operate in Viet Nam can have various legitimate options to register and enforce intellectual property rights in Viet Nam. Patents (including inventions, utility models, and industrial designs) may be individually registered in Viet Nam. For rights other than industrial designs, investors can also refer to the terms of the Patent Cooperation Treaty, which usually provide for easier and quicker processing. For trademarks, foreign investors may opt to either register within Viet Nam or get entitled to unitary rights under national or Community Trademark registration systems (as per the Madrid Protocol). For copyrights, registration is not obligated, but advised to be made with the copyright authorities. 'Priority rights' under the Paris Convention enables local registration of trademarks, designs, and patents by allowing rights previously registered elsewhere to become recognised and thus effective in Viet Nam, if filed within a required period.

Enforcing IP rights in Viet Nam is more problematic than scoping IPs under legal protection. Intellectual property rights may be enforced at three levels: first, administrative actions; second, civil court action; and third, criminal prosecution.

Intellectual property holders may resort to administrative actions for settling IP disputes. Sanctions may take the forms of warnings, fines, the seizure or destruction of the counterfeit goods, business license suspension, and re-exportation of infringed imported or transit goods out of Viet Nam.

Meanwhile, civil court actions are a higher and more serious approach to resolving IP disputes. Such actions may be in the form of preliminary injunctions or compensation for damages.

Criminal prosecution by government authorities or IP holders, the third option, may carry penalties ranging from fines, imprisonment, to even death penalty in serious, organised or business-related cases.

In practice, a major portion of IP rights enforcement may be in the form of administrative actions. During 2012–2015, 25,543 cases ended up with administrative actions, whereas 55 cases were brought to courts (criminal courts) (Nguyen, 2016). Administrative actions are generally considered fast and comparatively straightforward. Civil court actions, meanwhile, are rare in Viet Nam because of the poor standard of training of the judiciary in IP matters. Criminal prosecution against IP violations is even less popular.

From regulatory and procedural perspectives, IP holders are exposed to several potential problems in Viet Nam. On the one hand, even enforcement agencies have difficulty keeping up with recent rapid changes in the law. Administrative enforcement often involves a large number of bodies that, without appropriate and timely coordination, may be complicated. While acknowledging the acts of counterfeiting, particularly of foodstuff and medicines, as a crime, Vietnamese people tend to take more easily other types of IP infringement – unless they involve a product that could cause injury or damage. Therefore, while producing quick outcome by nature, administrative action has only produced limited deterrent effect, if any, because of the low level of penalties and lack of compensation. Accordingly, Viet Nam still ranked low in terms of IP protection by 2016.

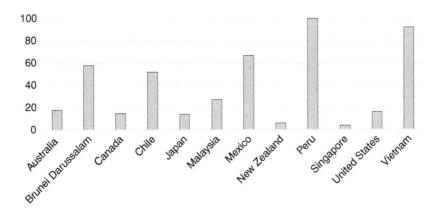

Figure 5.2 Global rankings in terms of intellectual property protection among original TPP countries, 2016

Note: Lower rank (i.e. higher column) reflects lower quality of IP protection.

Source: World Economic Forum (2016).

3. Viet Nam's commitments under the IP chapter

Compared with Viet Nam's existing laws and regulations on IP protection, various commitments under the IP Chapter of the TPP agreement (and that of the CPTPP agreement as well) are quite consistent and applicable. Some of these commitments may actually lead to substantial additions and/or changes in the prevailing laws and regulations of the country.

3.1. Protection of trademarks, country name, and geographical indications

While well-known trademarks are already recognised, Viet Nam is committed – together with other TPP parties – to refrain from using visually perceptible signs as a necessary condition for protection. That is, protection must be extended to sound as well. Viet Nam is also exerting efforts to protect scent marks. It should be noted that sound and scent marks are non-traditional types of trademarks, which Viet Nam had no formal regulations until the end of 2016.

Viet Nam is likewise committed to establish an electronic information system that features an online database of registered trademarks and applications for trademarks.

When it comes to licensing of trademark, Viet Nam automatically recognises the licence without imposing a requirement for registration or proof of its validity. Should an Internet address be coincident with or misleadingly similar to an existing trademark, Viet Nam relies on a dispute settlement mechanism that replicates the policy of the Internet Corporation for Assigned Names and Numbers

(ICANN). Alternatively, the government can adopt a dispute settlement mechanism that is neutral, low cost, and sufficiently simple and fast. Finally, its online database of registrants of Internet addresses is expected to be reliable, accurate, and publicly available.

Third parties are prevented from commercial use of a country name (i.e. of Viet Nam or other TPP partners) in relation to a good so as not to cause confusion over the good's origin.

Geographical indications are protected via a trademark or a *sui genesis* system. Viet Nam is committed to simplify the procedures to register geographical indications. That is, the procedures must not be overly burdensome, and the governing laws and regulations must be disseminated to the public. Should there be disputes, the settlement process must include (i) the procedure on how to oppose applications to register geographical indications, and (ii) procedures to cease or cancel the registration of geographical indications.

Grounds for opposing an application to register indications are specified. First, the geographical indication or individual component of geographical indication will not be protected in Viet Nam if it is a term customary in common language in the country. Guidelines for determining a customary term are also specified in Article 18.33 of the IP Chapter, to wit:

i   whether competent sources such as dictionaries, newspapers, and relevant websites use the term to refer to the type of good in question; and
ii how the good referenced by the term is marketed and used in trade within Viet Nam.

Second, if a geographical indication is coincident with or similar to a pre-existing trademark, the protection and use of such geographical indication is restricted by the rights of the owners of the trademark. In that case, trademark owners may opt to forbid the use of that geographical indication if the use may cause some confusion of the commercial origin of the product.

Third, if the protected or recognised terms no longer meet the conditions upon which the protection or recognition was originally granted, Viet Nam may allow such protection or recognition to be cancelled.

By signing an international agreement for the protection of geographical indications, Viet Nam will have to publicise (i) procedures for protecting or recognising geographical indications, and (ii) details regarding the terms that it may consider protecting or recognising, for example, restrict the protection of new geographical indication that might conflict with pre-established trademarks, or customary terms (Article 18.36.1 of the IP Chapter). In addition, Viet Nam will have to establish information on the subjects under consideration within a required period so that the stakeholders may have an opportunity to oppose or seek cancellation before the signing of the international agreement. It is also obliged to inform other TPP parties of the opportunity for opposition, no later than the commencement of the opposition period.

3.2. Patents and undisclosed or other data

In the original TPP text (i.e. prior to the suspension of Article 18.37.2 in the TPP agreement), patents can be granted to a known product if it satisfies either of the following conditions: (i) new use of a known product, (ii) new method to use a known product, and (iii) a new process for using a known product. These conditions are different from Viet Nam's IP law, which specifies that patents are granted only if the product demonstrates (i) new aspects, (ii) level of innovation, and (iii) potential for industrial applications. It is not clear in Viet Nam's IP law whether a new process of using a known product can be considered a new aspect. The suspension of Article 18.37.2 in the TPP agreement, however, may offer some flexibility in implementation for Viet Nam.

To determine whether an invention has an inventive step, Viet Nam shall disregard information contained in the public disclosure if the public disclosure originates directly or indirectly from the patent applicant and is made within 12 months prior to the date of application in the country (Article 18.38). Viet Nam is committed to provide at least one opportunity for the patent applicant to amend, correct, or observe in connection with its application. Management of patents has to be more consistent, in the sense that the ground for cancelling, revoking, or nullifying the patents must justify the refusal to grant a patent.

Viet Nam is also committed to make information on patents transparent. Such information must at least cover search and examination results, non-confidential information provided by the applicant, and citations of patent and non-patent documents by the applicants and related stakeholders (Article 18.45). This commitment should be in line with Viet Nam's reform of the IP system, although enforcement of this information provision is a concern.

Under the original TPP agreement, Viet Nam was required to comply with the period for the granting of patents. Specifically, if an authority unreasonably fails to grant the patent after 5 years from the date of application or after 3 years from the date of request for content appraisal, a compensatory adjustment of the patent term shall be made (Article 18.46). As Article 18.46 is now suspended in the TPP, this clause has no major implications for Viet Nam.

Protection of test data for pharmaceutical products (Articles 18.50 and 18.51) is another new area of commitment for Viet Nam. Under the original TPP, data exclusivity is granted to the test data and other confidential data on the safety or effectiveness of new pharmaceutical products submitted before their registration date.

A minimum period for data exclusivity (from the date of licence) is 5 years for pharmaceutical products with new content, 5 years for completely new pharmaceutical products, and 3 years for added data for old pharmaceutical products without new content (i.e. only new indication, new use). The granting authority is obliged to provide compensation if there is a delay in the awarding of licence for the pharmaceutical products. However, both Articles 18.50 and 18.51 in the TPP have been suspended in the CPTPP agreement.

Test data for agricultural chemical products with new chemical contents are also granted a period of exclusivity (Article 18.47) of 10 years from the date of certification. Viet Nam is committed to protect such test data and other confidential data on these products' safety or effectiveness that are submitted at the time of application for certification.

There is, however, some flexibility in Viet Nam's compliance with the commitments towards IP of pharmaceutical products. In particular, Viet Nam can exercise its sovereign rights to protect public health and nutrition, which is consistent with the Declaration on the Trade-Related Aspects of Intellectual Property Rights (TRIPS).

3.3. Industrial designs

Viet Nam is obligated to protect industrial designs that are either (i) a part of a (separate) article or (ii) 'have a particular regard, where appropriate, to a part of an article in the context of the article as a whole' (Article 18.55). The country is likewise committed to duly consider the accession to the Geneva Act of the Hague Agreement Concerning the International Registration of Industrial Designs, which aims to facilitate the international registration of such designs.[4]

3.4. Copyrights and related rights

Activities that form the pre-conditions for the violation of copyrights and related rights need to be prohibited. Emphasis is also made on those rights in the digital environment – that is, using technology to protect rights and information on management of rights. Viet Nam also seeks to balance the benefits between owners of rights and the societal use of rights via restrictions and exceptions.

The period for protection of copyrights and related rights under the original TPP are (i) life of the author(s) plus 70 years on the basis of life of natural person or (ii) 70 years from the end of calendar year of first authorised publication (if announced within 25 years), or 70 years from the end of calendar year of creation/record/demonstration (if not announced within 25 years) (Article 18.63). Viet Nam is also required to protect cable signals and satellite signals. However, all these commitments under TPP will be suspended, leaving Viet Nam with no direct obligation.

3.5. Enforcement of IP rights

The TPP stipulates clear and strict regulations and requirements on the enforcement of IP rights. Of particular emphasis are the measures to address such IP infringements as piracy of trademarks and violations of copyrights and related rights. In principle, enforcement should be fair and equitable and should not discriminate against foreign IP holders. Moreover, the process in IP rights enforcement should not be unreasonably complicated, costly, or time consuming. These principles are not entirely new to Viet Nam, given its participation in

WTO/TRIPS and other IP conventions. Because there are already existing IP rights regulations in place (e.g. TRIPS, TPP), there is no need for Viet Nam to create new systems or regulations regarding IP rights enforcement.

Enforcement and sanctions are divided into two levels, namely: (i) civil and administrative procedures and remedies, and (ii) criminal court action.

Through civil and administrative procedures and remedies, compensation for IP infringement may be imposed. Damages or losses are based on any legitimate values submitted by IP holders such as lost profits, value of infringed good measured by actual price, or suggested retail price (Article 18.74.4). Judicial authorities can order the products that have infringed trademarks or copyrights or related rights to be destroyed without compensation, except in exceptional circumstances. They can also order materials and equipment used for producing the infringing goods to be destroyed or removed from commercial channels (Article 18.74.12).

Viet Nam is committed to impose a similar sanction on online violation of trademarks, copyrights, and related rights by Internet users. In the digital space, Viet Nam must clearly stipulate the responsibility, conditions, and obligations of Internet service providers (ISPs) so that these ISPs can be legally exempted from IP disputes.

In terms of criminal court actions, Viet Nam's commitments under the TPP are more restrictive compared with its national rules on infringement of IP rights. It should be noted that the current regulations are already in line with the standards set under the TRIPS/WTO and Bilateral Trade Agreement with the United States. Should the TPP enter into force, an array of violations previously falling under the category of administrative actions will trigger criminal court actions. In particular, the TPP requires criminalisation of various behaviours related to copyrights and related rights, trademarks, and business secrets. Even acts that are yet to be considered as actual infringement of rights and do not seek to exploit the markets where such rights are protected – as long as they are on a commercial scale and have a substantial prejudicial impact on the interest of IP holders – must be subject to criminalisation (Article 18.77.1).

In addition, TPP lowers the specific conditions for considering infringements of copyrights and related rights as a criminal act. Under Viet Nam's IP laws, wilful importation or exportation of counterfeit trademark goods may be subject to administrative actions.[5] Article 18.77.1 of the IP Chapter in the TPP agreement, on the other hand, requires that such wilful acts be subject to criminal penalties.

3.6. Transition period

Viet Nam is granted a transition period (from the date the TPP enters into force), which varies according to the type of commitments. On the IP Chapter alone, Viet Nam has the largest number of commitments subject to a transition period (Table 5.1).

Specifically, Viet Nam has up to 2 years to join and implement the Budapest Treaty, and up to 3 years for the WIPO Copyright Treaty and WIPO Performances

Table 5.1 Summary of commitments subject to a transition period in IP chapter

	Brunei	*Malaysia*	*Mexico*	*Peru*	*Viet Nam*
Number of commitments subject to a transition period	7	12	6	2	26
Longest transition period (years)	4	4.5	5	10	10*

Note: * without one-off justified request for extension.

Source: Author's compilations.

and Phonograms Treaty. It has a 3-year transition period for almost all obligations that trigger regulatory impacts (i.e. to amend existing laws and regulations) with respect to sound marks, patent term adjustment for unreasonable granting authority delays,[6] technological protection measures, criminal procedures and penalties, and so forth. For some commitments that have potential social impacts (such as IP over agricultural and chemical products), the transition period is 5 years. Viet Nam may have 10 years of transition regarding its obligation on data exclusivity for pharmaceutical products, presumably the area with the largest social implication.

4. Potential impacts of the IP chapter on Viet Nam's economy

Notwithstanding the IP Law and various regulations since 2005, their enforcement in Viet Nam fails to improve continuously. The score of Viet Nam's IP protection, as measured by the World Economic Forum, depicts no continuous progress in 2007–2016 (Figure 5.3). As of 2016, Viet Nam ranked above only Peru in terms of IP protection in the TPP region.

Counterfeit and pirated goods, whether produced locally or imported, are not difficult to find even in rural or urban markets in Viet Nam. As reported by the Department for Market Management under the Ministry of Industry and Trade, over 8,000 cases of IP infringement were detected in 2012, representing an increase of 14 percent over the number in 2011. In more recent years (i.e. 2015–2016), the number of cases rose to about 12,000 per year.[7] The volume of pirated software products in Viet Nam remained high, despite decreasing by 7 percentage points between 2009 and 2016 (from 85 percent in 2009 to 78 percent in 2016).

Online piracy has been a prolonged but still growing problem in Viet Nam. The proportion of its pirated digital contents provided to users on the Internet is even estimated at up to 90 percent. The American Chamber of Commerce in Vietnam (2013) noted the case in 2012 of Zing.vn, the sixth most visited website in Viet Nam with more than 30 million Internet users, where music downloading does not respect the copyright of artists. Due to pressures from an Associated

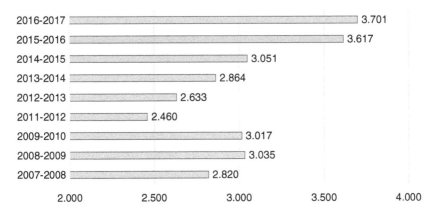

Figure 5.3 Score of Viet Nam's intellectual property protection, 2007–2017

Note: Score is from 1 *(worst)* to 7 *(best)*.

Source: World Economic Forum (2016).

Press journalist, several major international companies withdrew their advertisements from Zing.vn.

As the quality and originality of products sold online are known only upon delivery or consumption, controlling IP infringement is no easy task. In fact, some of the questionable products indicate counterfeit or piracy of trademarks held by Japanese or US owners. This renders Viet Nam and its companies at risk of being penalised/fined and/or subjected to other actions under the TPP. Yet, the cost of enforcement – in terms of time and money – reduces the incentive for IP holders and government agencies to seek appropriate enforcement actions. The American Chamber of Commerce in Vietnam (2013) believes that enforcement efforts should be strengthened. In this scenario, the TPP commitments may be binding and useful towards IP enforcement in Viet Nam.

As Viet Nam works to improve its technological innovations and attract foreign direct investments, it should pay parallel attention to the enforcement of IP rights, *among others*. To begin with, infringements of IP must be handled boldly, fairly, and transparently to deter similar acts in the future. Activities such as information dissemination campaigns and capacity building will help increase public awareness on IPRs and the implication.

Finally, meeting the TPP's IP standards is neither simple nor easily fulfilled. Nonetheless, its demand for long-term credible commitment can enhance investors' confidence in the implementing country and reduce the risk of inconsistency in IP management. In Viet Nam, this can translate favourably in terms of the impact on the economy's performance.

The implementation of IP Chapter under TPP also presents several challenges to Viet Nam. First, Viet Nam may find it difficult to ensure transparency when disclosing IP information. Le (2016) identifies requirements on transparency in

Article 18.9, Article 18.45, and Article 18.73 of the IP Chapter. In practice, online publication of laws and regulations in Viet Nam has been satisfactory, with a range of websites[8] offering access to full-text laws and regulations on either a free or subscription basis. Even draft regulations, following the Law on the Promulgation of Legal Normative Documents (2008 and 2015 versions), have to be published online to solicit stakeholders' comments.

However, the website for searching registered and copyrighted works is available only in Vietnamese.[9] Online access to the website of the New Plant Variety Protection Office (under the Ministry of Agriculture and Rural Development)[10] is hardly seamless. Coordination is an ongoing issue, as search queries on copyrights or plant variety cannot be made via the NOIP website, even though this agency is the national coordinator on IP issues. In addition, the information systems of the NOIP and the Copyright Office of Viet Nam frequently encounter problems of overloading and/or suspension from operations (Le, 2016).

Second, adapting the scope of protected IP objects under Vietnamese law and harmonising such with the TPP is no easy task. For example, the IP Chapter of the TPP allows for the protection of a range of non-traditional marks where Viet Nam had not done any prior in-depth investigation or public disclosure. Registration of scent marks is also encouraged, although Viet Nam is obliged to do so only on best effort basis.

Such scoping fails to be completely consistent with the current IP law of Viet Nam, which requires a trademark's composition to be a visible sign in the form of letter, wording, drawing, or image as a condition for protection. Moreover, implementation of the TPP will require Viet Nam's IP law to extend its protection to sound and scent trademarks as well. In turn, Viet Nam will have to upgrade its related regulations and build human and technical capacities for the smooth implementation of these regulations.

Another area of difference in regulations is in the patents for new uses of a known product. The IP Chapter under the original TPP allows for patents to be granted for at least one of the following: (i) new uses of a known product, (ii) new methods of using a known product, and (iii) new processes of using a known product. As previously discussed, Viet Nam's IP law has yet to recognise new use of a known product as an invention as such provisions are currently suspended in the TPP. Should Viet Nam perceive the need to prepare in advance for such new patentable objects, its regulatory framework needs to be amended.

Third, if Viet Nam has the ambition to unilaterally adopt the IP Chapter under the TPP (moving beyond the commitment under the CPTPP), it needs its domestic regulations to follow the adjustment in the terms of patents found in the TPP. Compensatory patent term adjustment should still be made should there be unreasonable delays on the part of Viet Nam's granting authorities.

This provision requires that the Vietnamese law on IP be revised, and its granting authorities conform to the time limit set for examining and granting patents.

Realistically, as Viet Nam's IP system is not deeply in sync with the international system, the eventual implementation of the TPP is expected to see a spike in the number of requests for registration or recognition from foreign IP owners within a short period of time. As such, Viet Nam's granting authorities may run the risk of (i) causing delays in granting or recognising patents without reasonable justification, and (ii) granting or recognising patents without thorough deliberation, which may lead to disputes, amendment, or cancellation later.

Fourth, harmonising the protection of geographical indications across various integration tracks may present another challenge to Viet Nam. The TPP does require Viet Nam to provide advance and detailed information on new geographical indications (including those of Viet Nam and non-TPP members) under new international agreements.

In addition, Viet Nam must allow for sufficient time so that the general public can oppose the protection of new geographical indications. This requirement presented significant pressures during the finalisation of the TPP and the EU-Viet Nam free trade agreements, because both the United States and the European Union want to have their own geographical indications protected to the fullest extent. Such pressures are not the last of their types, because Viet Nam may still consider to negotiate/implement new free trade agreements, which may lead to more geographical indications being included for protection.

5. Recommendations

From the analysis and considerations presented earlier, one sees that IP protection has both benefits and challenges for Viet Nam. The enforcement of IP protection plays an essential role in promoting technological advances and innovative growth. The higher the standard of IP protection, the larger the net benefits for Viet Nam.

As IP constitutes an area in behind-the-border reforms, adopting higher IP standards should be meaningful even if the concerned agreement/provisions are yet to take effect (or remain suspended). Given this perspective, Viet Nam should dedicate efforts in the following areas.

5.1. Regulatory preparations

To implement the TPP, Viet Nam has to join a number of international agreements related to IP protection and cooperation. As documented in Table 5.2, Viet Nam will have to seek membership in international agreements such as Budapest Treaty, Singapore Treaty on the Law of Trademarks, WCT, and WPPT. Viet Nam has to endeavour to join the Patent Law Treaty, and the Hague Agreement, though these are by no means an obligation under TPP, as well as accept the protocol amending the TRIPS.

Viet Nam must simultaneously amend existing regulations on IP protection (i.e. its IP Law) and the related guidance on these regulations. Both must incorporate and/or be compatible with Viet Nam's new commitments under the IP Chapter of the TPP. For instance, the period of protection for copyrights and related rights, non-traditional marks, and data exclusivity are major areas where regulatory adjustments are needed.

Table 5.2 Status of Viet Nam's participation in existing international agreements on IP

Agreements	Related Article(s) of TPP	Participation: Yes/No	Detailed Status Information
WTO TRIPS Agreements that all TPP Parties already joined	(whole)	Yes	
Patent Cooperation Treaty (PCT)	18.7.1	Yes	Implemented 10 March 1993
Paris Convention	18.7.1	Yes	Stockholm Act (1967): Effective date is the date of unification of the Democratic Republic of Viet Nam and the Republic of South Viet Nam to form the Socialist Republic of Viet Nam. Declaration of continued application: 7 April 1981. Republic of Viet Nam: Acceded 30 January 1975; Effective date 30 April 1975.
Berne Convention	18.7.1	Yes	Acceded 26 July 2004; Implemented since 26 October 2004
Agreements to which TPP obliges Parties to accede			
Madrid Agreement and Its Protocol	18.7.2	Yes	Acceded 8 March 1949; Amendment on 11 July 2006
Budapest Treaty	18.7.2	No	
Singapore Treaty on the Law of Trademarks	18.7.2	No	
International Union for the Protection of New Varieties of Plants (UPOV)	18.7.2	Yes	Acceded 24 December 2006
The WIPO Copyright Treaty (WCT)	18.7.2	No	

(*Continued*)

Table 5.2 (Continued)

Agreements	Related Article(s) of TPP	Participation: Yes/No	Detailed Status Information
The WIPO Related Rights Treaty (WPPT)	18.7.2	No	
Protocol Amending TRIPS	18.7.2	No	
Agreements where TPP recognises the importance of Parties' participation			
Patent Law Treaty (PLT)	18.14.4	No	
Hague Agreement	18.56	No	
Brussel Convention	18.79	Yes	Acceded 12 October 2005; Implemented 12 January 2006

Source: Author.

More important, Viet Nam has to improve the enforcement structure for IP protection. Civil and administrative court actions may no longer be dominant resorts. Criminalising IP infringements is also compulsory. IP protection is essential, but the practices over such protection must also be considered and/or regulated to ensure sound competition in the market. Fundamentally, the revisions of law and improved enforcement should be the foundation for building a culture of respect and compensation for IP.

5.2. Capacity development

Capacity development is necessary if Viet Nam aims to make its IP protection efforts effective. First, the nation needs to extend training programmes to domestic enterprises. For instance, training can be on the technical-legal aspects of the IP Chapter under the TPP and their implications. Domestic enterprises may benefit from training on how to register and protect their IP under the amended TPP-consistent regulations. Those that have patents registered under the existing IP regime may need to be advised on how to adapt to the new IP regime, if required.

Of equivalent importance is the training for domestic enterprises so that they can have their patents, trademarks, copyrights, and related rights protected under TPP-supportive international agreements that Viet Nam plans to accede to. More important, domestic enterprises need guidance and support to promptly change their views towards IP and compliance with IP regulations.

Second, Viet Nam needs to improve the IP-related capacities of management authorities. On the one hand, such authorities need to adapt to the IP protection approach under the TPP and other new-generation free trade agreements. They will have to get ready to resort more court actions to address IP infringements. On the other hand, such authorities and their staffs need capacity improvement to retain reasonable balance between IP enforcement and protection of market competition.

Intellectual property management authorities in Viet Nam also need to understand the various types of IPs (i.e. copyrights and related rights, trademarks, geographical indications, patents, industrial designs) and their ramifications, to provide relevant technical support to local enterprises. In addition, local authorities may need to work with their foreign counterparts to help domestic enterprises register their IPs overseas and/or file IP infringement complaints in overseas markets.

Third, Viet Nam should pay attention to improving the capacity of enforcement agencies to undertake criminal actions against IP infringement cases. This should, on the one hand, focus on formulating a process enforcement agency should follow when handling IP infringement issues. On the other hand, Viet Nam should review and amend the enforcement process so that less time and smaller (procedural and financial) costs would be involved.

Finally, Viet Nam also needs to upgrade its information and communication technology capacity to enhance the effectiveness of its IP protection. This requires investing in the required facilities, regulations, and human capability to manage the facility.

Notes

1 Nguyen Anh Duong is Director, Department for Macroeconomic Policy and Integration Studies, Central Institute for Economic Management (CIEM) of Viet Nam. The views and opinions expressed in this chapter are solely of the author and may not necessarily reflect those of the CIEM.
2 Resolution No. 24/2016/QH13 of the National Assembly dated 30 November 2016 set out the TFP target at 30 percent to 35 percent of GDP growth during 2016–2020.
3 For instance, Ohno (2014) argues that Viet Nam finds itself stuck in the middle-income trap, due to limited creation of value and low productivity growth via human capital upgrade (i.e. skills, technology, innovation, knowledge).
4 Done at Geneva, 2 July 1999.
5 Article 211 of the Law on IP in 2005.
6 Viet Nam may provide its justification for a one-off extension in its transition period by an additional year for patent term adjustment where there are unreasonable delays on the granting authority's side.
7 Available at http://cafef.vn/nam-nao-cung-xu-ly-khoang-12000-vu-hang-gia-hang-nhai-20160714214233485.chn (accessed 21 January 2017).
8 For instance, full-text regulations can be accessed for free at the Ministry of Justice website, available at www.moj.gov.vn. Alternatively, users can pay for access at Viet Nam Law, available at www.luatvietnam.vn.
9 Available at http://cov.gov.vn/cbq/index.php?option=com_mfit&view=mlookup&Itemid=90 (accessed 1 June 2017).
10 Available at www.pvpo.mard.gov.vn/ (accessed 1 June 2017).

Bibliography

American Chamber of Commerce in Vietnam (2013), 'Intellectual Property Rights in the Socialist Republic of Viet Nam'. Submitted to the Office of the United States Trade Representative, 8 February.

Bross and Partners (2017), 'Trends of Divide over Famous Trademark Protection in Viet Nam'. Online. Available at http://bross.vn/newsletter/ip-news-update/Trend-of-divide-over-famous-trademark-protection-in-Vietnam-1245 (accessed 6 April 2017).

Le, T.N.G. (2016), 'Vietnam's Challenges in Protecting IP Under TPP'. Online. Available at www.vir.com.vn/vietnams-challenge-in-protecting-ip-under-tpp.html (accessed 1 October 2016).

Nguyen, H. (2016), 'Handling IP Cases: Only Criminal Prosecutions Produce Sufficient Deterrent Effect' [Xử lý vi phạm quyền sở hữu trí tuệ: Truy cứu hình sự mới đủ sức răn đe]. Online. Available at http://dantri.com.vn/suc-manh-so/xu-ly-vi-pham-quyen-so-huu-tri-tue-truy-cuu-hinh-su-moi-du-suc-ran-de-20160429074703176.htm (accessed 29 October 2016).

Ohno, K. (2014), 'An Approaching Middle Income Trap: How Vietnam Can Escape It?', Presentation to GRIPS and VDF, December.

World Economic Forum (2016), *Global Competitiveness Report 2016–2017*. Online. Available at www.weforum.org/reports/the-global-competitiveness-report-2016-2017-1 (accessed 15 December 2016).

6 Regulatory framework on IPR in Indonesia

Overview and preliminary assessment on the TPP's IP chapter

Poppy S. Winanti

1. Introduction

The Trans-Pacific Partnership (TPP), which was signed on 4 February 2016, was regarded as the most advanced free trade agreement in history. Despite sharp differences, the 12 signatories (Australia, Brunei Darussalam, Canada, Chile, Japan, Malaysia, Mexico, New Zealand, Peru, Singapore, United States, and Viet Nam) finally agreed to conclude the negotiations in October 2015. The conclusion of a trade deal, which covers around 40 percent of the global GDP and two-thirds of world trade, is regarded as 'beyond World Trade Organization (WTO) trade deals'. It should be noted, however, the withdrawal of the US from the initiative after the election of Donald Trump has transformed the TPP into the Comprehensive and Progressive Agreement for Trans-Pacific Partnership (CPTPP). This chapter, however, will focus the discussion on the original text of the TPP but not say much about the CPTPP.

The TPP is not merely about greater market access and trade liberalisation; after all, trade liberalisation is perceived to be already covered by existing trade agreements, including the North American Free Trade Agreement (NAFTA) and ASEAN Economic Community. The TPP, in this regard, has trade agendas that are of a higher standard than those covered by the current Doha Round trade negotiations. In addition, some controversial WTO trade agendas that were postponed for an indefinite period – such as on labour and environmental standards, government procurement, and competition policy – managed to find their way into the TPP deals. The TPP also integrates non-WTO trade agendas such as provisions on small and medium-sized enterprises, state-owned enterprises, and Investor–State Dispute Settlement (ISDS).

This chapter investigates Chapter 18 of the TPP agreement, which deals with intellectual property (IP) and its compatibility with the regulatory framework on intellectual property rights (IPR) of Indonesia, which is an indication of the nation's intent to join the club.

It is composed of two parts. The first part is an overview and evaluation of Indonesia's domestic situation on IPRs. The discussion focuses on the existing state of IPR protection in Indonesia and essentially argues that IPR protection in Indonesia is still unsatisfactory. The second part evaluates the domestic IPR situation in the context of each TPP obligation. It first compares the TPP's IP with the Trade-Related Aspects of Intellectual Property Rights (TRIPS) Agreement under the WTO and then analyses the compatibility of the Indonesian legal framework on IPR issues with the TPP's IP chapter and the TRIPS Agreement.

2. Overview and evaluation of Indonesia's domestic situation on IPRs

Before the TRIPS Agreement, IPR protection was an alien concept in Indonesia's national laws due to its conflicting nature with Indonesia's traditions and norms (Winanti, 2011). Despite the fact that IP legislation existed in Indonesia as early as 1844, these laws, which were introduced by the Dutch, did not apply to native Indonesians. Under the Dutch colonial rule, the legal system for indigenous Indonesians was *adat* (an extensive system of Indonesian customary norms), which did not recognise IPR protection.

Under the unwritten *adat* law, individual ownership in intellectual works or inventions is not recognised because knowledge is regarded as public property, and its main function is to serve the public benefit (Winanti, 2011). Thus, it is not a surprise that IPR protection has no strong roots in Indonesian society and that there is no robust Indonesian legal tradition of protecting IPR. A meaningful IP policy reform was pursued by the Indonesian government only after the country became a WTO member and was obliged to implement the TRIPS Agreement.[1]

Unfortunately, despite the more-than-a-decade of IP policy reforms, the Indonesian society has not fully accepted the benefits of IPR protection. The number of residents' patent applications in Indonesia remains considerably low compared with non-residents' patent application. Figure 6.1 shows that more than 92 percent of patent applications in Indonesia are from non-residents.

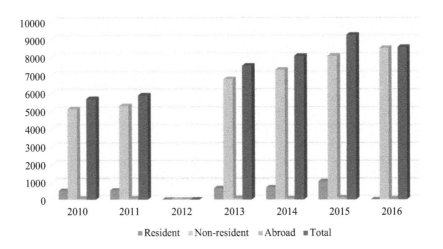

Figure 6.1 Total patent applications in Indonesia 2010–2016

Note: No data available for 2012.

Source: World Intellectual Property Organization statistics database (2017).

It should be noted, though, that a different situation is seen on trademark applications in Indonesia. Unlike the case with patent applications, trademark applications in Indonesia are mostly from residents (Figure 6.2). Winanti (2011) argued that when compared with other forms of IPRs, trademark protection is culturally and historically more acceptable in the Indonesian society. The difference lies in the purpose of the type of IPR. Trademark protection benefits Indonesians as customers because trademarks' main purpose is to differentiate products, which in turn ensures the quality of these products. In contrast, other forms of IPR protection are intended solely to protect the rights of the IPR owners. As will be discussed in the next sections, a relatively high degree of acceptance for trademarks protection also reflects a more robust Indonesian law on trademarks as compared with the laws on other forms of IPR.

With average score only around 5.01 (Figure 6.3), compared with other TPP developing country members, Indonesia ranked poorly in the Property Rights Index from 2010 to 2016 (Table 6.1). Indonesia trails behind Malaysia but has performed slightly better than Mexico, Peru, and Viet Nam during the period.

Indonesia's relatively poor performance in the Property Rights Index is supported by the fact that it has, along with Chile, always been on the United States Trade Representative's (USTR) Priority Watch List between 2010 and 2017. This indicates that Indonesia has been regarded as one with serious IPR inadequacies. According to the USTR Special 301 Report 2017, one of the main reasons Indonesia remained in the USTR's Priority Watch List is the widespread piracy and counterfeiting of dangerous products in the country. Indonesia also lacks an effective protection against the unfair commercial use of pharmaceutical and agricultural chemical products. There are also concerns regarding market barriers on the importation of motion pictures and medicines, particularly those

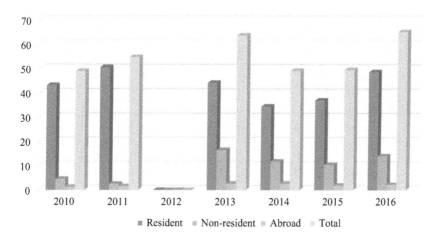

Figure 6.2 Total trademarks applications in Indonesia 2010–2016
Note: No data available for 2012.
Source: World Intellectual Property Organization statistics database (2017).

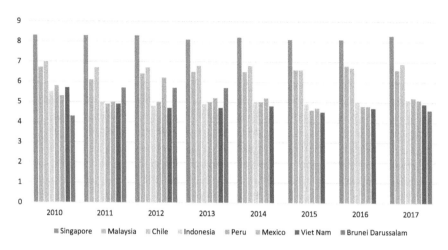

Figure 6.3 Property rights index: Indonesia and ASEAN-Developing Countries TPP Members 2010–2017

Source: Property Rights Alliance (2017).

Table 6.1 Property rights index: the rank of Indonesia and ASEAN/TPP developing countries members (2010–2017)

	2010	2011	2012	2013	2014	2015	2016	2017
Singapore	6	3	4	7	5	5	6	7
Chile	30	30	28	26	74	26	28	28
Malaysia	42	45	38	33	27	28	26	32
Indonesia	**80**	**79**	**86**	**85**	**59**	**70**	**67**	**68**
Peru	66	82	78	78	59	79	76	65
Viet Nam	74	81	91	95	66	85	85	77
Mexico	85	78	40	69	54	75	78	67
Brunei Darussalam	93	54	53	55	–	–	–	92

Source: Property Rights Alliance (2017).

pertaining to technology transfer requirements (USTR, 2017). IPR protection in Indonesia, which still has to be improved, has clearly become the concern of the US government as one of Indonesia's leading trading partners. This existing condition also shows that if Indonesia intends to join the TPP, it will have to work on various areas of its IPR protection laws.

3. Indonesia's IPR national laws and TPP's IPR obligations

This section evaluates Indonesia's domestic IPR situation in the context of each TPP obligation. The first part of this section explains the obligations under the

TPP by comparing the TPP's IP chapter with the TRIPS Agreement under the WTO. This part also analyses the compatibility of the Indonesian legal framework on IPR issues vis-à-vis the TPP's IP chapter and the TRIPS Agreement.

3.1. *Understanding the TPP's IPR protection*

The TPP's IP chapter features the provisions on the protection of patents, trademarks, copyrights, industrial designs, geographical indications, trade secrets, other forms of intellectual property, and enforcement of intellectual property rights. It consists of 11 sections, 83 articles, and six annexes. It is regarded as 'beyond the TRIPS Agreement' – ergo, the term 'TRIPS Plus'. It does not only adopt the basic principles of the TRIPS Agreement on National Treatment (Article 18.8) but also provides more stringent IPR protection. Interestingly, the TPP's IP excludes the other non-discrimination principle under the TRIPS – that is, the most-favoured-nation (MFN) treatment.

Some additional clauses related to IPR protection not available under the TRIPS Agreement are included in the TPP. For instance, the TPP has a specific clause on transparency, which requires each member-nation to make available its laws, regulations, procedures, and administrative rulings of general application on the protection and enforcement of IPR. More specifically, the TPP requires its member-nations to make available on the Internet any information on applied for, registered, and granted trademarks; geographical indications; designs; patents; and plant variety rights (Article 18.9).

Unlike the TRIPS Agreement, the TPP includes a clause on cooperation in the area of traditional knowledge:

> [R]ecognize(s) the relevance of intellectual property systems and traditional knowledge associated with genetic resources to each other, when that traditional knowledge is related to those intellectual property systems.
>
> (Article 18.16.1)

In this regard, the TPP also emphasises the importance of documented information and the use of databases or digital libraries, which are related to traditional knowledge associated with genetic resources.

As mentioned earlier in this report, the TPP has a higher protection for trademarks as compared with the TRIPS Agreement. The TPP protects sound and scent marks (Article 18.19). It requires its member-nations to provide terms of protection for trademarks for no less than 10 years, whereas the TRIPS Agreement requires the protection for trademarks for no less than 7 years. The TPP's IP chapter also introduces a new mechanism called electronic trademark system, which features an electronic application for and maintenance of trademarks (Article 18.24). The TPP goes beyond the TRIPS Agreement regarding well-known trademarks, as the former specifies the exclusive rights of well-known trademark owners and the obligations of each member-nation to provide appropriate measures to protect such rights (Article 18.22).

The TPP specifically addresses the inappropriate use of country names (Section D of Chapter 18). Article 18.29 states that 'each party shall provide the legal means for interested persons to prevent commercial use of the country name of a Party in relation to a good in a manner that misleads consumers as to the origin of that good'. Such clause on the prevention of commercial use of the country name, meanwhile, is missing in the TRIPS Agreement.

Under the TPP, several clauses help prevent the excessive use of geographical indications (GI), especially on grounds of opposition and cancellation (Article 18.32). These provisions ensure that the protection of GIs will prevent any confusion with pre-existing trademarks. Furthermore, a GI will not be considered as legitimate if it uses a common name for relevant goods, thus benefiting countries that usually use common names to export their products as well as nations, such as the United States, that do not protect the generic terms of their products. In addition, Article 18.35 of TPP also rules that the date of protection of a GI should not be earlier than the filing date or registration date. Again, these provisions on GIs are beyond the TRIPS Agreement.

The TPP also adds some clauses and more detailed explanations on patents, which are not available under the TRIPS Agreement. Article 18.37, for example, defines inventions in detail as one that meets any of the following conditions: (i) new uses of a known product, (ii) new methods of using a known product, or (iii) new process of using a known product. The TPP also recognises the first-to-file principle as an international best practice (Article 18.42), whereas the TRIPS Agreement allows members to choose their own patent filing principle – that is, either the first-to-file or first-to-invent. In addition, the TPP's IP also has a provision where the patent term may be adjusted to compensate for unreasonable delays on the part of the granting authority (Article 18.46). Such a provision is missing in the TRIPS Agreement.

Furthermore, the TPP specifically addresses the protection of the test data of new pharmaceutical products that are biologics or contain biologics and provides a minimum protection term of 8 years (Article 18.51). This has made the TPP the first trade agreement to include such a provision.

Interestingly, provisions under the TRIPS Agreement that are designed to protect the needs of developing countries are not specifically addressed in the TPP, such as parallel importation and compulsory licensing. Under the TPP, there is no specific clause on compulsory licensing other than those permitted under the TRIPS Agreement (Article 18.6), which recognises the adoption of the Doha Declaration.

New clauses in the TPP include those on the protection of undisclosed test data submitted for marketing approvals. The TPP provides data exclusivity in agricultural chemicals and pharmaceuticals for at least 10 years; and 5 to 8 years, respectively (Article 18.50). The TRIPS Agreement does not have such a requirement.

In industrial design, the TPP has a specific clause on improving the industrial design systems, particularly to facilitate the cross-border acquisition of rights (Article 18.56). In contrast, the TRIPS Agreement does not specify the cross-border acquisition of rights in the member-nations' respective industrial design systems.

In terms of copyrights, the TPP extends the duration of protection. Under the TRIPS Agreement, the duration of copyrights protection is the life of the author and 50 years after the author's death. In contrast, the TPP extends the protection to a minimum of 70 years after the author's death (Article 18.63).

The TPP also incorporates new provisions on Technological Protection Measures, Rights Management Information, and Collective Management (Articles 18.68–18.70). Under the Collective Management clause, the TPP recognises the role of collective management societies in collecting and distributing royalties on copyrighted (and related rights) materials.

This section has just explained why the TPP's IP chapter can be regarded as beyond the TRIPS Agreement (or 'TRIPS Plus'). According to Braga (2016), the TPP's IP chapter provides higher standards for IPR protection that are in line with US laws and reflect the existing free trade agreements signed and negotiated earlier by the United States.

3.2. Compatibility of the Indonesian legal framework on IPR

This section looks at the compatibility of the Indonesian legal framework on IPR issues with the TPP's IP chapter and the TRIPS Agreement. While Indonesia's trademarks legislation, in general, is compatible with the TPP's IP chapter (Table 6.2), there are some aspects that still need to be adjusted for Indonesia to be fully TPP's IP compliant.

As discussed in earlier sections, there are several clauses under the TPP that prevent excessive use of geographical indications (Article 18.32), especially on grounds for opposition and cancellation. Under these provisions, the safeguards are meant to ensure that the protection of GI will not cause confusion with pre-existing trademarks. Furthermore, the GI is considered illegitimate if it appropriates common names for relevant goods. The TPP's IP also requires parties to ensure transparency, publicly available information, and mechanisms for cancellation (Articles 18.31 and 18.32). In this regard, Indonesia needs to improve its administration and cancellation procedures and to make these publicly available. Improving its administration procedure for GI protection will be beneficial for Indonesia as this may encourage the utilisation of GI to protect Indonesia's rich cultural heritage (Table 6.3).

Compared with the TRIPS Agreement, the TPP's IP provides additional clauses and more detailed explanations on patents protection (Table 6.4). Article 18.37, for example, details the definition of an invention as one that meets any of the following conditions: (i) new uses of a known product, (ii) new methods of using a known product, (iii) or new process of using a known product. In contrast, the TRIPS Agreement grants a patent to a new invention if it can be proven as new, involves an inventive step, and is capable of industrial application.

On the topic of industrial design, the TPP has a specific clause on improving its system, particularly on facilitating the cross-border acquisition of rights (Article 18.56). In contrast, the TRIPS Agreement does not specify such clause in the member-nations' respective industrial design systems. Neither does Indonesia's

Table 6.2 Compatibility of the Indonesian trademark law with the TPP's IP chapter and the TRIPS agreement

Aspects	TPP	The TRIPS Agreement	Law No. 15/2001 on Trademarks	Author's assessment
Scope	Extending the scope by protecting sound and scent marks (Article 18.18).	Any sign, or any combination of signs, capable of distinguishing the goods or services that are visually perceptible (Article 15.1)	Adopting all categories of trademarks protection under the TRIPS Agreement.	Indonesia's existing law on trademarks does not recognise non-traditional visible and non-visible marks such as sounds and scent marks. Indonesia needs to amend these aspects. The question is whether the protection of these types of marks is benefiting the Indonesian consumers in general or whether this will serve only the interest of foreign trademarks owners. No action required. Indonesia is TPP's IP compliant.
	Expanding the scope by protecting collective and certification marks (which can also be protected under the geographical indications) (Article 18.19)	No specific clause	Collective marks are protected (Article 50)	No action required. Indonesia is TPP's IP compliant.
Well-known Trademarks	Exclusive rights of well-known trademark owners and the obligations of each party to provide appropriate measures to protect them (Article 18.22)	No specific clause	Providing exclusive rights of well-known trademark owners and the obligations of each party to provide appropriate measures to protect them (Article 6)	

	TPP's IP	TRIPS	Indonesian Law	Recommendation
Mechanism of Electronic Application	Introducing the electronic trademark system, as system for the electronic application for and maintenance of trademarks (Article 18.24)	No specific clause	No specific clause	Indonesia does not have online trademark registration. The infrastructure for this purpose needs to be established. This will benefit trademark owners in Indonesia in the end because the system will make the process more efficient and cost effective.
Duration of Protection	Minimum 10 years	Minimum 7 years	Minimum 10 years (Article 28)	No action required. Indonesia is TPP's IP compliant.
Country Name	Providing legal means to protect inappropriate use of country names (Article 18.29)	No specific clause on the prevention of commercial use of the country name	Providing legal means to protect inappropriate use of country names	No action required. Indonesia is TPP's IP compliant.

Note:
TPP's IP – Trans-Pacific Partnership Agreement's intellectual property
TRIPS – Trade-Related Aspects of Intellectual Property Rights

Source: Author.

Table 6.3 Compatibility of the Indonesian law on geographical indications with the TPP's IP chapter and the TRIPS agreement

Aspects	TPP	The TRIPS Agreement	Law No. 15/2001 on Geographical Indications	Author's assessment
Common Names	Providing safeguard to prevent excessive use of GI (Article 18.29); 'benefiting countries that do not protect generic terms'	No specific clause	No specific clause	Under the trademark law of the TPP agreement, the use of common names cannot be registered as a trademark. However, this clause is not intended necessarily for preventing the excessive use of GI.
Administrative Procedure and Cancellation	Ensuring transparency, publicly available information, and mechanisms for cancellation (Articles 18.31 and 18.32)	No specific clause	No specific clause	Indonesia needs to improve its administration and cancellation procedures. Improving its administration procedure for GI protection will benefit Indonesia as this may encourage the use of GIs to protect Indonesia's rich cultural heritage.

Note:
TPP's IP – Trans-Pacific Partnership Agreement's intellectual property
TRIPS – Trade-Related Aspects of Intellectual Property Rights
GI – geographical indication

Source: Author.

Table 6.4 Compatibility of the Indonesian patent law with TPP's IP chapter and the TRIPS agreement

Aspects	TPP	The TRIPS Agreement	Law No. 13/2016 on Patents	Author's assessment
Scope	Adopting all categories of patents under the TRIPS Agreement (Article 18.37)	Any inventions, whether products or processes, in all fields of technology, provided that they are new, involve an inventive step, and are capable of industrial application	Adopting all categories of patents under the TRIPS Agreement	No action required. Indonesia is TPP's IP compliant.
Definition of Inventions	New uses of a known product, new methods of using a known product, or new process of using a known product; 'evergreening' (Article 18.37.2)	New, involves an inventive step and is capable of industrial application	No specific clause other than specified under the TRIPS Agreement	Not all patents can be granted under the Indonesian patent law. The obligation under Article 18.37.2 is in conflict with the interest of the Indonesian government especially to provide more affordable medicines for its people. The Indonesian government does not recognise the new definition of inventions under the TPP's IP. Recognising these aspects to be patentable will only expand pharmaceutical companies' opportunity to protect their privileges. (This point is closely related to Article 18.52's definition of new pharmaceutical product).
Patent Filing	Adopting the first-to-file principle (Article 18.42)	Allowing members to choose their own patent filling principle	Adopting the first-to-file principle	No action required. Indonesia is TPP's IP compliant.
Parallel Importation	No specific clause	Permitted	Permitted	No action required. Indonesia is TPP's IP compliant.

(Continued)

Table 6.4 (Continued)

Aspects	TPP	The TRIPS Agreement	Law No. 13/2016 on Patents	Author's assessment
Compulsory Licensing	No specific clause other than what is permitted under the TRIPS Agreement (per Article 18.6), which recognises the adoption of Doha Declaration	Permitted	Permitted; includes provisions dealing with the grant of compulsory licences regarding export of patented pharmaceutical products to developing or under-developed, disease-afflicted countries in need of certain pharmaceutical products (Article 93.3)	No action required. Indonesia is TPP's IP compliant.
Patent Term Adjustment	Adjusting of patent term to compensate for unreasonable delays from the granting authority (Article 18.46) as well as of patent term for pharmaceuticals (Article 18.48)	No specific clause	No specific clause	Indonesia's patent legislation does not have any procedure to expedite the examination of patent applications. In addition, there is no clause regarding compensation for unreasonable delays on the part of granting authority. The procedure to expedite the examination process can be beneficial because it can encourage more patent applications. On the other hand, the compensation mechanism for delays committed by the granting authority may be seen as a way to extend the protection of patented products, which benefits existing patents owners.
Protection of Undisclosed Test Data Submitted for Marketing Approvals	Protecting undisclosed test data for agricultural chemicals for at least 10 years; and pharmaceuticals for 5 to 8 years (Article 18.50)	No specific clause	No specific clause	This will harm society's interests because even after the patent protection ends, other companies cannot use 'the undisclosed test or other data' that are supposed to be freely available and used to produce generic medicine. Under the TPP's IP, one has to wait for at least 5–8 years after a patent protection ends before the undisclosed test or other data can be freely used. Thus, this may be regarded as a way to prolong the monopoly of pharmaceutical industries.

Protection for New Pharmaceutical Products that Are Biologics or Contain a Biologic Agent	Minimum 8 years (Article 18.51)	No specific clause	Indonesia's law on patent needs to be adjusted to accommodate this new clause. Stakeholders, however, must consider how granting of such protection will benefit the Indonesian society. How far can domestic pharmaceutical industries utilise this provision? Will this clause benefit only more the foreign pharmaceutical firms?
Definition of New Pharmaceutical Product	Defining new pharmaceutical product as one that does not contain a chemical entity that has been previously approved for that party (Article 18.52)	No specific clause	Indonesia's legal law on patent acknowledges that a new pharmaceutical product must be an invention that is novel. The clause under the TPP's IP amends and expands the definition of new pharmaceutical product into as long as does not contain a chemical entity that has been previously approved which does not reflect any novelty. This can provide pharmaceutical industries a greater chance of prolonging their monopoly.

Note:
TPP's IP – Trans-Pacific Partnership Agreement's intellectual property
TRIPS – Trade-Related Aspects of Intellectual Property Rights

Source: Author.

industrial design law have specific provisions on this issue. Thus, Indonesia needs to improve the infrastructure and enhance its human resource to facilitate the cross-border acquisition of rights (Table 6.5).

In terms of copyrights, the TPP extends the duration of protection beyond that provided under the TRIPS Agreement (i.e. the life of the author and 50 years after the author's death). Under the TPP, the protection is a minimum of 70 years after the author's death (Article 18.63). In addition, the TPP incorporates new provisions on Technological Protection Measures (Article 18.68), Rights Management Information (Article 18.69), and Collective Management (Article 18.70). Under the Collective Management clause, the TPP recognises the important role of collective management societies in collecting and distributing royalties from copyright (and related rights) materials. Indonesia's current copyright law in all those aspects conforms to the TPP's IP chapter (Table 6.6).

The Indonesian law, to some extent, has met the minimum TPP IP requirements on trade secret protection (Table 6.7). The law on trade secret provides specific criminal provisions to prevent misappropriation of trade secrets. However, the Indonesian national legislation does not have a specific clause governing misappropriation of trade secrets by state-owned enterprises.

On the basis of what had been discussed here, the Indonesian laws can fall under three categories of compatibility with the TPP's IP chapter. The first category is one that fully complies with the TPP's IP chapter (e.g. copyrights). The second is the 'TPP Minus with Minor Revision Required', where the proposed revision will be beneficial to Indonesia. The third category is 'TPP Minus with

Table 6.5 Compatibility of the Indonesian industrial design law with the TPP's IP chapter and the TRIPS agreement

Aspects	TPP	The TRIPS Agreement	Law No. 31/2000 on Industrial Design	Author's assessment
Industrial Design System	Providing specific clause on improving industrial designs (Article 18.55)	No specific clause	Providing specific clause in defining industrial designs	No action required. Indonesia is TPP's IP compliant.
Cross-border Acquisition	Facilitating the process of cross-border acquisition of rights (Article 18.56)	No specific clause	No specific clause	Indonesia needs to improve the infrastructure and human resources to facilitate the process.

Note:
TPP's IP – Trans-Pacific Partnership Agreement's intellectual property
TRIPS – Trade-Related Aspects of Intellectual Property Rights

Source: Author.

Table 6.6 Compatibility of the Indonesian copyrights law with the TPP's IP chapter and the TRIPS agreement

Aspects	TPP	The TRIPS Agreement	Law No. 28/2014 on Copyrights	Author's assessment
Duration of Protection	Life of author +70 years	Life of author +50 years; +20 years for broadcasting organisations	Life of author +70 years; +20 to 50 years for performers, producers, and broadcasting organisations	No action required. Indonesia is TPP's IP compliant.
Traditional Knowledge	Including a clause on the cooperation in the area of traditional knowledge (Article 18.16)	No specific clause	Copyright on traditional cultural expressions are held by the state (Article 38)	No action required. Indonesia is TPP's IP compliant.
TPM, RMI, and Collective Management	TPMs in Article 18.68; RMI in Article 18.69; and Collective Management in Article 18.70.	No specific clause	Included (Means of control technology Chapter VII; RMI Chapter II; Collective Management (Chapter II and XII)	No action required. Indonesia is TPP's IP compliant

Note:
TPM – Technological Protection Measures
RMI – Rights Management Information
TPP's IP – Trans-Pacific Partnership Agreement's intellectual property
TRIPS – Trade-Related Aspects of Intellectual Property Rights

Source: Author.

Table 6.7 Compatibility of the Indonesian trade secret law with the TPP's IP chapter and the TRIPS agreement

Aspects	TPP	The TRIPS Agreement	Law No. 30/2000 on Trade Secret	Author's assessment
Legal Enforcement	Requiring enforceable legal means to prevent misappropriation of trade secrets, including those committed by state-owned enterprises (Article 18.78)	No specific clause	Providing specific criminal provisions but no specific clause on state-owned enterprises	Need to make adjustments to meet the minimum TPP IP standard. However, the domestic situation still requires that state-owned enterprises be protected to achieve social objectives.

Note:
TPP's IP – Trans-Pacific Partnership Agreement's intellectual property
TRIPS – Trade-Related Aspects of Intellectual Property Rights

Source: Author.

Major Revision Required', where it is not clear yet if any adjustments taken (e.g. on trade secrets, patents, and trademarks) will be beneficial or not beneficial to Indonesia. This third category requires a more comprehensive assessment, which is beyond the main objective of this report (Table 6.8).

To ensure the compatibility of national laws on IPRs, the TPP members are also required to ratify international agreements on IPR other than the TRIPS Agreement. These include the Patent Cooperation Treaty, Paris Convention, Berne Convention, Madrid Protocol, Budapest Treaty, Singapore Treaty, International Union for the Protection of New Varieties of Plants (UPOV) Convention, World Intellectual Property Organization (WIPO) Copyright Treaty, and WIPO Performance and Phonogram Treaty. Of these agreements, Indonesia has ratified only the Paris Convention, WIPO Copyright Treaty, and WIPO Performance and Phonogram Treaty, and accedes to the Patent Cooperation Treaty and Berne Convention. Indonesia has not yet ratified or acceded to four main international IP agreements: the Madrid Protocol, Budapest Treaty, Singapore Treaty, and UPOV. If it intends to join the TPP, Indonesia must ratify or accede to the rest of international IP agreements (Table 6.9).

Table 6.8 Indonesian IP laws and the TPP's IP chapter

TPP's IP Compatibility	*Indonesian Law on IP*	*Author's assessment*
TPP's IP minimum	Law No. 28 of 2014 on Copyrights and Related Rights (No. 6/1982; No. 7/1987; No. 12/1997; No. 19/2002)	No action required. Indonesia is TPP's IP compliant.
TPP minus with minor revision required	Law No. 31 of 2000 on Industrial Design	Adjustment needed for cross-border acquisition
TPP minus with major revision required	Law No. 30 of 2000 on Trade Secrets	Adjustment needed on the role of state-owned enterprises
	Law No. 13 of 2016 on Patent (No. 6/1989; No. 13/1997; No. 14/2001)	Massive adjustments, but where the benefits to the Indonesian society remains unclear
	Law No. 15 of 2001 on Trademark (including GI) (No. 21/1961; No. 19/1992; No. 14/1997)	Adjustments needed on the scope of trademarks, although benefits to the Indonesian society remains unclear Adjustments needed for electronic registration, which will benefit Indonesia
Provisions not covered by TPP's IP	Law No. 32 of 2000 on Integrated Circuit Design	No action required. Indonesia is TPP's IP compliant.

Note: TPP's IP – Trans-Pacific Partnership Agreement's intellectual property

Source: Author.

Table 6.9 Indonesia and international IPR agreements

TPP Obligations	Ratified	Acceded	Not Ratified or Acceded	Author's assessment
Patent Cooperation Treaty	✓			TPP compliant
Paris Convention		✓		TPP compliant
Berne Convention		✓		TPP compliant
Madrid Protocol (The International Trademark System)			✓	This system will simplify the international registration although the national government still has the right to acknowledge or ignore the registered trademark. This system will allow domestic trademark owners to be recognised and gain international protection. However, it takes time for international agreements to be ratified under the Indonesian legislation system.
Budapest Treaty (the International Microorganism Deposit System)			✓	This system offers an efficient and cost-effective means for applicants to meet the disclosure requirements for patenting microorganisms. However, national government will not have the authority to examine the inventions involving microorganisms. Ratification of this treaty will be difficult because this is politically unacceptable in Indonesia.
Singapore Treaty (Singapore Treaty on the Law of Trademarks, 2006)			✓	Indonesia's national law on trademark does not recognise non-traditional visible marks and non-visible marks. There needs a comprehensive assessment to evaluate whether expanding the scope of trademarks will be beneficial to Indonesia's economic players.
International Union for the Protection of New Varieties of Plants (UPOV)			✓	Although Indonesia has neither ratified nor acceded to the UPOV, the issue on new plant varieties is governed by Indonesia's UU No. 29/2000 (Protection of Plant Varieties). This law protects Indonesia's interest as an agricultural country and ensures the availability of plant varieties for agricultural development. This law is not designed to grant patent protection for new plant varieties.
World Intellectual Property Organization Copyright Treaty	✓			TPP compliant
World Intellectual Property Organization Performance and Phonogram Treaty	✓			TPP compliant

Source: Author.

The Madrid Protocol governs the international trademark system. It provides a one-stop mechanism for registering and managing marks worldwide. This means that any trademark, once registered at the national or regional IP office, can also be submitted for international application through the same IP office, which will then certify and forward the application to WIPO. After WIPO has formally examined and given its approval, the trademark will be recorded in the international register and published in the *WIPO Gazette of International Marks.*

However, on top of the WIPO approval, the national or regional IP offices still need to conduct substantive examination and issue a decision on the protection of the trademark according to their legislation. This system will simplify the mechanism for international registration although the national government still has the right to acknowledge or ignore the registered trademark. Eventually, domestic trademark owners will benefit from the recognition and international protection.

The Budapest Treaty of 1980 concerns international patent processes related to inventions involving microorganisms. Under the Budapest system, all states party to the treaty are obliged to recognise microorganisms deposited as part of the patent disclosure procedure with an international Depositary Authority. In this regard, there is no requirement for the patent applicants to submit microorganisms to the national authority (WIPO, n.d.). This system offers an efficient and cost-effective means for applicants to meet the disclosure requirements for patenting microorganisms. However, the national government will not have the authority to examine the inventions involving microorganisms.

The Singapore Treaty on the Law of Trademarks was adopted in 2006. Its main objective is to create a modern and dynamic international framework for the harmonisation of administrative trademark registration procedures. The treaty has a wider scope of application, especially in accommodating recent developments in communication technologies (WIPO, n.d.). It is, in this regard, the first international instrument that recognises non-traditional visible marks such as holograms, three-dimensional marks, colour, position, and movement marks as well as non-visible marks such as sound, olfactory or taste, and feel marks (WIPO, n.d.). Indonesia's current national law on trademark does not recognise non-traditional visible marks and non-visible marks. Thus, there should be a comprehensive assessment on whether expanding the scope of trademarks will benefit Indonesia's economic actors or simply protect and further the intentions of foreign trademarks owners.

The International Union for the Protection of New Varieties of Plants (UPOV) Convention was initially adopted in Paris in 1961 and then revised several times in 1972, 1978, and 1991. The main purpose of this convention is to provide and promote an effective system of plant variety protection with the aim of encouraging the development of new varieties. Furthermore, the UPOV convention also encourages plant breeding by granting breeders of new plant varieties an intellectual property right (UPOV, n.d.).

Meanwhile, in Indonesia, its national law UU No. 29/2000 (on Protection of Plant Varieties) protects Indonesia's interest as an agricultural country and ensures the availability of plant varieties for agricultural development. Interestingly, this law is not designed to grant patent protection for new plant varieties. Thus, acceding the UPOV convention will change the nature of plant varieties' protection in Indonesia as the convention grants IPR on new plant varieties to breeders.

4. Conclusion

The TPP's IP chapter can be regarded as beyond the TRIPS Agreement or commonly labelled as the 'TRIPS Plus'. As argued by Braga (2016), the TPP's IP chapter provides higher standards for IPRs protection in line with the US law and reflects the existing free trade agreements signed and negotiated by the United States. Although Indonesia's existing IP legislation is TRIPS compliant, some aspects under the Indonesia's existing legal framework, however, are incompatible with the TPP's IP chapter.

As discussed earlier, the assessment on Indonesia's exiting IP legislation reveals that the compatibility of its laws with the TPP's IP chapter fall under three categories. The first category consists of those that are fully compliant with the TPP's IP chapter (e.g. copyrights). The second is the TPP Minus with Minor Revisions category, whose revisions will be beneficial for Indonesia (e.g. industrial designs). The third is the TPP Minus with Major Revisions category, where there is uncertainty on whether the adjustments in the national laws could benefit the nation. The IP aspects included in the third category concern trade secrets, patents, and trademarks.

Aside from ensuring the compatibility of national IPRs laws with the TPP's IP guidelines, the TPP members are required to ratify other international agreements on IPR aside from the TRIPS Agreement. Thus, if Indonesia intends to join the TPP, it will have to ensure that the national legal framework becomes compatible with the provisions in the TPP's IP chapter. Also, Indonesia needs to ratify or accede to other international agreements on IP. This may not be easy in Indonesia. After all, given its current legislation process, the act of amending national laws and ratifying international agreements cannot be done within a short time.

Note

1 For a more detailed discussion regarding Indonesia's domestic norms and IPR protection, see Winanti (2011).

Bibliography

Braga, C. (2016), 'Innovation, Trade and IPRs: Implications for Trade Negotiations', March, Working Paper, East – West Center Workshop on Mega-Regionalism – New Challenges for Trade and Innovation. Available at SSRN: https://ssrn.com/abstract=2745500 (accessed 29 November 2016).

International Union for the Protection of New Varieties of Plants (UPOV) (n.d.), 'UPOV Lex'. Available at www.upov.int/upovlex/en/upov_convention.html (accessed 1 August 2016).

Property Rights Alliance (2017), '2017 International Property Rights Index'. Available at https://ipri2017.herokuapp.com/admin/elfinder/connector?_token=&cmd=file&target=fls2_SVBSSTIwMTdGdWxsUmVwb3J0SS5wZGY (accessed 15 March 2018).

United States Trade Representatives (USTR) (2017), '2017 Special 301 Report'. Available at https://ustr.gov/sites/default/files/301/2017%20Special%20301%20Report%20final.pdf (accessed 15 March 2018).

Winanti, P.S. (2011), 'External Pressures or Domestic Politics: Explaining Change in Developing Countries' Intellectual Property Legislation', Ph.D. Thesis, University of Glasgow. Available at http://theses.gla.ac.uk/2794/ (accessed 15 August 2016).

World Intellectual Property Organization (WIPO) (n.d.), 'Budapest – The International Microorganism Deposit System'. Available at www.wipo.int/budapest/en/ (accessed 1 August 2016).

World Intellectual Property Organization (WIPO) (n.d.), 'Summary of the Singapore Treaty on the Law of Trademarks (2006)'. Available at www.wipo.int/treaties/en/ip/singapore/summary_singapore.html (accessed 1 August 2016).

World Intellectual Property Organization (WIPO) (2016), *The Madrid System for the International Registration of Marks*. Geneva: WIPO.

World Intellectual Property Organization (WIPO) (2017), 'Statistical Country Profile Indonesia'. Available at www.wipo.int/ipstats/en/statistics/country_profile/profile.jsp?code=ID (accessed 15 March 2018).

7 Access to medicines and plant seeds

The challenges the Philippines faces with the TPP's intellectual property rights rule

Ramon L. Clarete

1. Introduction

This chapter takes up two implications of the intellectual property rights (IPR) rules on medicine prices and farmers' access to seeds of the Trans-Pacific Partnership (TPP). Both are likely among the important indicators of public acceptability of the TPP in the Philippines. The agreement's IPR rules can potentially keep medicine prices up, eroding access to medicines (Correa, 2015).[1] Moreover, its rules on patentability may restrict access of farmers to planting materials. The following sections (i) sum up the legal gaps in aligning the current intellectual property (IP) laws of the country with those of the TPP, (ii) analyse the possible impacts of the TPP on medicine prices and farmers' access to propagating materials of plant varieties, and (iii) discuss key ideas towards making the TPP reflect more closely the goals of universal healthcare and inclusive agriculture growth.

2. Alignment steps towards the TPP's IPR rules

The country's IPR system covers copyright and related rights; patents and utility models; industrial designs; layout designs of integrated circuits; trademarks, service marks, collective marks; geographical indications; and undisclosed information. It has gradually evolved through the years, adopting into its legal system international standards and rules with respect to various IPRs as negotiated in the World Intellectual Property Organization.

The relatively major whole-scale upgrading of the IPR regime in the Philippines occurred in the second half of the 1990s. It was done to comply with the Trade Related Intellectual Property Rights (TRIPS) of the World Trade Organization (WTO) in 1995. The TPP IP rules are at least as substantive as those of the WTO TRIPS Agreement. The following section notes the salient differences between the current TRIPS-compliant IP system and the TPP IP rules.

2.1. Patents and related inventions

Table 7.1 lays down the gaps between the country's IPR system and the TPP[2] with respect to patents and related inventions. In patents, the key reforms are on patentable material, term of protection, undisclosed data protection, and patent linkage.[3]

Table 7.1 Selected TRIPS-plus provisions in the TPP agreement: patents, agricultural chemicals, medicines, and biologics

TPP Provision	Description	Legal gap
Patentable inventions (Article 18.37.2)	The TPP requires patentable inventions to meet as at least one of the following criteria: new uses of a known product, new methods of using a known product, or new processes of using a known product.	Until 2008, the IP Code does not meet this requirement. However, in 2008, the Cheaper Medicines Act was enacted to provide, among other purposes, for so-called secondary patents and safeguards for abuse. This may be encoded into the IP Code.
Patentable inventions (Article 18.37.4)	A party may exclude from patentability plants other than microorganisms. However, each party confirms that patents are available at least for inventions that are derived from plants.	The IP Code does not grant patents to plant varieties nor animal breeds, and biological processes to produce plants or animals. This does not apply to microorganisms or microbiological processes. Whether the TPP requires more than just patenting biologics remains to be seen.
Patent term adjustment (Article 18.46.3)	If there are unreasonable delays in a party's issuance of patents, that Party shall provide the means to, and at the request of the patent owner shall, adjust the term of the patent to compensate for such delays.	No such provision is in the IP Code. However, this may not be an issue because the delays in the Philippines are less than 5 years, which the TPP considers reasonable. Nonetheless, it may have to be legally enabled.
Protection of undisclosed data on new agricultural chemicals (Article 18.47)	The TPP protects the exclusive right of an inventor of a new agricultural chemical product to the undisclosed data on safety and efficacy tests and data with respect to it for a period of 10 years from the grant of the marketing approval.	There is no such provision for new agricultural chemicals in the IP Code.
Patent term adjustment of a new pharmaceutical product (Article 18.48.2)	With respect to a pharmaceutical product that is subject to a patent, each party shall make available an adjustment of the patent term to compensate the patent owner for unreasonable curtailment of the effective patent term as a result of the marketing approval process.	No such provision is in the IP Code. However, this may not be an issue because the marketing approval process for pharmaceutical products is less than a year. Nonetheless, it may have to be legally enabled.

TPP Provision	Description	Legal gap
Data exclusivity for pharmaceutical products (Article 18.50)	A party must hold for 5 years from marketing approval of a new pharmaceutical if the applicant to comply with the requirement of the party for approval submits undisclosed data on safety and efficacy tests and related data without the consent of the person who owns the data and obtained an earlier approval of a similar product. The prescriptive period is 5 years in the case where the product was earlier approved in another territory, and the same required data are undisclosed and submitted without consent of the owner.	There is no such provision for new agricultural chemicals in the IP Code.
Protection of biologics (Article 18.51)	A party is required to implement data exclusivity provisions (Article 18.50) in the case of a pharmaceutical product containing or is a biologic for a period of 5 to 8 years. If 5 years, added measures to arrive a comparable outcome are required.	There is no such provision in the IP Code.
Patent linkage (Article 18.53.2)	A party may preclude the granting of marketing approval to an applicant of a marketing approval if, based on information from the applicant, the patent holder, or the patent office itself of the party, said product is still under a patent and the patent holder had not consented that the applicant markets a similar product.	The IP Code does not have this provision. However, the country's Food and Drug Administration (FDAP) practised patent linkage until 2008. To simplify the work of the marketing regulator for medicines, the Department of Health from which the FDAP gets administrative supervision no longer required the regulator to find out from the Bureau of Patents of the Intellectual Property Office if the pharmaceutical product is still subject to a patent.

Note:
IP = intellectual property
TPP = Trans-Pacific Partnership
TRIPS = Trade-Related Aspects of Intellectual Property Rights

Source: Author's compilation.

2.1.1. Secondary patents

The TPP requires parties to allow secondary patents, that is, those available for inventions of new uses of a known product, new methods of using a known product, or new processes of using a known product. The rule is designed to encourage pharmaceutical firms to further improve a known drug or discover new therapeutic uses of a known substance. The approval is conditioned on the invention meeting the standards of patentable inventions.

Section 22.1 of the IP Code allows secondary patents, if the new use (e.g. second medical use of the substance) is not inherent in the prior art and meets the other tests of patentability (e.g. inventive step, industrial applicability, and novelty).

2.1.2. Plant variety patents

The IP Code does not allow plant patents or, in general, patents on living things, except microorganisms or microbiological processes used in the production of plants. The TPP respects this right of parties, following the flexibility in the TRIPS Agreement. However, it requires that parties provide at least a *sui generis* protection for the rights of plant breeders, and the minimum protection is what the International Union for the Protection of New Varieties of Plants (UPOV) 1991 prescribes, to which the Philippines acceded. [4] Plant variety may be protected using UPOV or plant patents. Plant-based patents are those granted to companies producing genetically modified plant varieties.

2.1.3. Term of protection

The TPP provides for extending the term of protection to compensate for delays in securing approval for patents. The present term of patent protection under the TRIPS Agreement and in the country's IP Code is 20 years from the time of filing without any extension. In the TPP, the patent owner may request for added patent term to compensate for unreasonable delays[5] in getting the patent approved. Similarly, unreasonable delay in securing marketing approval is a ground for the patentee to claim additional term of protection. This may not be an issue in the Philippines because in both processing of the application for the patent and that of marketing approval of the pharmaceutical product are not delayed unreasonably. Even then the IP Code has to be amended to reflect this requirement.

2.1.4. Patent linkage

The TPP requires its parties to practice patent linkage in the case of pharmaceutical products.[6] The countries currently implementing this practice are the United States, Australia, China, and Singapore. Several ASEAN member states do not have this mechanism except Malaysia, Brunei Darussalam, and Viet Nam

(Mirandah, 2012). The Philippines practised patent linkage. However, in 2006, a Department of Health order removed it from the responsibilities of the Food and Drug Administration of the Philippines (FDAP).[7] Generally, patent rights are recognised in the Philippines, and legally enabling patent linkage may not be a large burden on stakeholders.

2.1.5. Protection of undisclosed data

This provision requires a party, in the event its regulator requires for the marketing approval of a new generic pharmaceutical product[8] the use of the undisclosed data on safety and efficacy tests, and related data on the active ingredient in a medicine whose patent expired, to not allow third parties to market for a period of at least 5 years[9] without the consent of the owner to use such undisclosed data. The prescriptive period is reckoned from the date of the marketing approval of the new product before permitting the applicant to market the new product.

Data exclusivity or the protection of undisclosed data for a given period applies as well to new biologics[10] and new agricultural chemical products,[11] which are respectively like the product whose patent had expired. The definition of similarity (see footnote 46) applies as well. The difference, however, is in the length of the protection period. The prescriptive period is at least 10 years in the case of agricultural chemicals, and at least 8 years for biologics. Parties, however, can limit the prescriptive periods to 10 or 8 years, respectively.[12]

This provision potentially delays the entry of legitimate generic products, which may lower the prices of medicines in the country. In 2008, the Cheaper Medicines Act was enacted to allow, before a drug patent expires, the testing, production, and registration of generic versions so that these could be sold immediately upon the expiration of the patents. Nothing in the agreement prevents the implementation of this provision in the country's law. However, data exclusivity deprives generic companies from marketing their new pharmaceuticals for at least 5 years. Table 7.2 summarises the prescriptive terms of protection of undisclosed test and related data.

2.2. Trademarks and geographical indications

2.2.1. Non-visible signs

The TPP broadens the set of signs that can be registered as trade or service marks (Table 7.3). The current IP Code of the country allows only visible signs, which as earlier mentioned include three-dimensional marks, colour marks, holograms, slogans, titles of films and books, motion or multimedia signs, position marks, and gesture marks. The TPP requires parties to not limit to visible signs the collection of indicators that can be used to distinguish goods (trademarks) or services (services marks). Non-visible signs include sound marks, olfactory or scent marks, taste marks, and texture or feel marks. The TPP recognises that non-visible signs can be used to mark goods or services but registering them so may be

Table 7.2 Prescriptive terms of protection of undisclosed data, by type of data

Type of data	Agricultural chemicals	Pharmaceuticals: active ingredient is a	
		Chemical entity	Biologic
Previously submitted data in party's territory	At least 10 years[i]	At least 5 years[iii]	At least 8 years or at least 5 years if implemented in conjunction with other measures[vii]
Previously submitted data in another territory	At least 10 years[ii]	At least 5 years[iv]	At least 8 years or at least 5 years if implemented in conjunction with other measures[viii]
New test and related data required to be submitted in party's territory on new indication, formulation, or method of administration, involving an active ingredient previously approved by the party	Not applicable	At least 3 years[v]	Not applicable
New test and related data required to be submitted in party's territory on new indication, formulation, or method of administration, involving an active ingredient previously approved in another territory	Not applicable	At least 5 years[vi]	Not applicable

Note:
(i)   See Article 18.47.1(a) in the TPP
(ii)   See Article 18.47.1(b) in the TPP
(iii)   See Article 18.50.1(a) in the TPP
(iv)   See Article 18.50.1(b) in the TPP
(v)   See Article 18.50.2(a) in the TPP
(vi)   See Article 18.50.2(b) in the TPP
(vii)   See Article 18.51.1(a) in the TPP
(viii) See Article 18.51.1(b) in the TPP

Source: Author's compilation of relevant provisions in TPP Chapter 18 and the IP Code.

Table 7.3 Selected TRIPS-plus provisions in the TPP: trademarks and geographic indications

TPP provision	Description	Legal gap
Registrable marks (Article 18.18)	This requires not limiting registrable marks to visible signs. 'Best effort' is encouraged for the registration of non-visible signs, e.g. olfactory signs.	Sections 121.1 and 121.2 limit registrable marks to visibly perceptible signs.
Protection of well-known marks (Article 18.22.2)	This requires protection of well-known mark regardless of whether it is registered.	Section 123.1(f) provides for denying registration of marks if such involves products that are dissimilar to those protected by the well-known mark, provided that the latter is registered. This may have to be amended to include well-known marks that are not registered in the Philippines. Related to this is Section 147.2 on the exclusive right of the owner of a well-known mark. This provision needs amending to enable, where the products are dissimilar/not identical, the obligation even if the well-known mark is not registered in the country.
Certification marks (Article 18.19)	The TPP provides for the protection of certification marks.	Sections 121.1 and 121.2 of the IP Code are silent about certification marks. TPP Article 18.19, however, assigns no obligation to set up a separate registration system for certification mark.
Geographical indications (GIs) (Article 18.19)	GIs may now be protected under a trademark regime and can be used to extend protection in other TPP parties.	The IP Code recognises that one function of the IP office is to accept applications for GIs. This must be amended to conform to TPP Article 18.19 and related provisions such as protecting trademark owners from later-in time registry of a GI.
Registration of GIs (Articles 18.3 and 18.32)	These provide for administrative procedures for the registration of GIs, under either the trademark or *sui generis* system.	The IP Code must be amended to enable this obligation.
Destruction of trademark-infringing products (Article 18.74.12)	The TPP requires the destruction of the trademark-infringing products at the request of the owner.	A stronger provision is required for Section 157.1 of the IP Code which says that the 'court may order . . .'. Should the owner so request, the TPP authorises the court to order the destruction of these infringing goods without delay and compensation. This applies as well to copyright-infringing goods.

(Continued)

Table 7.3 (Continued)

TPP provision	Description	Legal gap
Special border measures (Article 18.76)	These provide authorities at the border to take action to protect the rights of the trademark owner against possible entry, exit, or in-transit goods suspected to be violating the country's trademark law.	No such provision is in the IP Code. However, customs authorities had created an anti-piracy unit, which exercises a similar function. Such may be improved and institutionalised in the country's IP code.
Trade in counterfeit products (Article 18.77.2)	The wilful importation or exportation of counterfeit trademark goods is to be declared an unlawful activity subject to criminal penalties.	Section 155.1 of the IP Code must be amended to subject this unlawful act to criminal penalties. Presently if such infringement is wilful, the civil penalties are merely doubled.
Unauthorised commercial use of marks (Article 18.77.3)	The wilful unauthorised use in commerce, importation, or exportation of trademark-infringing labels or packaging materials is to be declared an unlawful activity subject to criminal penalties.	Similarly, Section 155.2 of the IP Code must be amended to subject this unlawful act to criminal penalties. Presently if such infringement is wilful, the civil penalties are merely doubled.
Trade in counterfeit products (Article 18.77.5)	This requires each party to ensure that criminal liability for aiding and abetting the unlawful trade of counterfeit trademark goods or pirated copyright goods on a commercial scale is available under its law.	No such provision is in the IP Code.

Note:
GI = geographical indication
IP = intellectual property
TPP = Trans-Pacific Partnership
TRIPS = Trade-Related Aspects of Intellectual Property Rights

Source: Author's compilation of relevant provisions in TPP Chapter 18 and the IP Code.

more difficult to do compared with visible signs. Thus, registration of non-visible signs, particularly scents, are encouraged on a 'best effort' basis.[13]

2.2.2. Well-known and certification marks

The TPP requires parties to accord protection to well-known marks even if these had not been registered with their respective authorities. These rights are accorded to the owner under the country's IP Code, if the well-known mark it owns is registered in the country. Under the TPP, such protection shall be extended as well even if the well-known mark is not locally registered.

The IP Code does not explicitly provide for the registration of certification marks or signs that a given product, whose container is marked with a certification sign, meets a certain set of characteristics, standards in producing them, and the like as certified by a competent authority. It is implied, however, in the IP Code, which allows the registration of collective marks, the difference being that the product of the organisation, which the collective mark is affixed to, is distinguished from other goods in that it meets a certain set of quality, comes from a given place where the producers come from, or meets certain set of standards in producing it. In certification marks, a single enterprise, which produces goods that likewise meet certain standards such as labour standards, environmental standards, and the like, is certified by the owner of the certification mark.

2.2.3. Geographical indications

The IP Code does not protect GIs that will also be protected with trademark, although this may be implied with collective marks. The TPP recognises that GIs may be protected through trademarks, *sui generis* forms of protection, or through international agreements. In turn, this menu of protection forms of GIs has the promise of a conflict between an earlier collective mark and a GI. The TPP requires protecting the former from a latter conferment of a GI.

The TPP has devoted the entire Section E of Chapter 18 for its rules on GIs. But this and those in other preferential trade agreements can potentially make GI rules emulate the spaghetti problem in preferential rules of origin, except one may refer to it as the rules of destination. The TRIPS Agreement is not specific on how GIs are to be recognised, registered, or cancelled for a valid reason. The guidance is that these have to be protected. Thus, presently, WTO members have different ways of protecting GIs; in particular, the European Union has been active in promoting its rules in its various free trade agreements with its trading partners. According to Vilchez (2016), the proliferation of mechanisms to protect GIs may be an issue in the Philippines if it joins the TPP. The difference of their GI rules may prevent or curtail market access of the Philippines in the European Union market. But that is precisely the spaghetti problem in rules of origin: one just has to know whose rules apply.

2.3. Copyrights and related rights

The TPP extends the term of protection of copyrights to 70 years, or an added 20 years from the current term in the IP Code (Table 7.4). As in the IP Code,

Table 7.4 Selected TRIPS-plus provisions in the TPP: copyright and related rights

TPP Provision	Description	Legal gap
Term of protection (Article 18.63)	(a) Life of author plus 70 years after author's death; or (b) if basis of term is not life of a natural person: (i) not less than 70 years from the end of the calendar year of the first authorised publication of the work, performance, or phonogram; or (ii) failing such authorised publication within 25 years from the creation of the work, performance, or phonogram, not less than 70 years from the end of the calendar year of the creation of the work, performance, or phonogram.	The TPP requires extending the term of protection by 20 years than what the IP Code provides.
TPM circumvention (Article 18.68 in conjunction with 18.74)	The TPP requires parties to provide civil and criminal remedies (if act is wilful) in the circumvention of TPMs, and to regard the act as separate from copyright infringement.	The TPP requires separate civil and criminal remedies for the circumvention of TPMs. Criminal remedy of it is pursued if the act is wilful. Presently the IP Code does not require this. The circumvention is considered part of copyright infringement for which civil damages are imposed, except that where it is done authorities double the civil damages meted to remedy copyright infringement.
RMI circumvention (Article 18.69 in conjunction with 18.74)	The TPP requires parties to provide civil and criminal remedies (if act is wilful) in the circumvention of RMI. The treatment of RMI circumvention as a separate offence is implied unlike that of the TPM.	The TPP requires separate civil and criminal remedies for RMI circumvention. The circumvention is considered part of copyright infringement for which civil damages are imposed, except that where the circumvention is done authorities double the civil damages meted to remedy copyright infringement. Also, the E-Commerce Act imposes added damages if infringement is done using information and communications technology.

TPP Provision	*Description*	*Legal gap*
Special border measures (Article 18.76)	These provide authorities at the border to take actions to protect the rights of the copyright owner against possible entry, exit, or in-transit goods suspected to be violating the copyrights of the owner.	No such provision is in the IP Code. However, customs authorities had created an anti-piracy unit, which exercises this function. Such may be institutionalised in the country's IP code.
Piracy of copyrighted materials (Article 18.77.2)	The TPP requires each party to regard the wilful importation or exportation of counterfeit trademark goods or pirated copyright goods on a commercial scale as unlawful activities subject to criminal penalties.	The IP Code does not consider as unlawful acts subject to criminal liabilities trade on a commercial scale in counterfeit trademark goods or pirated copyright goods.
Piracy of copyrighted materials (Article 18.77.2)	The TPP requires each party to ensure that criminal liability for aiding and abetting the unlawful trade of counterfeit trademark goods or pirated copyright goods on a commercial scale is available under its law.	No such provision is in the IP Code.
Legal remedies and safe harbours for Internet service providers in fighting online copyright infringement (Section J)	The TPP recognises the importance 'of facilitating the continued development of legitimate online services operating as intermediaries and, in a manner consistent with Article 41 of the TRIPS Agreement, providing enforcement procedures that permit effective action by right holders against online copyright infringement'.	No such provision is in the IP Code.

Note:
IP = intellectual property
RMI = rights management information
TPM = technological protection measure
TPP = Trans-Pacific Partnership
TRIPS = Trade-Related Aspects of Intellectual Property Rights

Source: Author's compilation.

this is reckoned from the death of the copyright owner, from date of the first publication of the work and performance or recording of the phonogram.

Several enforcement provisions are introduced in the TPP; two of these relate to the use of information technology. The first discourages the circumvention of technological protection measures (TPMs), which control access to a protected work. To better enforce copyrights, stiffer penalties are provided against circumventing TPMs or in the selling of devices, products, or services intended to circumvent such measures. Civil remedies may continue to apply for circumventions that are done in good faith, not wilful, and certainly without full knowledge of the commercial implications of the circumvention. Otherwise, the TPP requires the application of criminal penalties to such unlawful acts, separate from the civil penalties, and any fines associated with the violation of the copyright law that may apply. Similarly, the same applies in the case of circumvention of risk management information (RMI) measures.

Special border measures are likewise introduced to make more effective the enforcement of copyright. No such provisions can be found in the IP Code. However, customs authorities created an anti-piracy unit, which has similar functions.[14] This can be improved and aligned to TPP obligations in Article 18.47 and institutionalised in the IP Code.

3. Possible impact on medicine prices

The TPP lengthens the term of protection of drug patents through three channels. These are patent term adjustments to compensate for unreasonable delays in patent or marketing approvals; patent linkage, which links marketing approval to information on the patent status of a new similar pharmaceutical; and data exclusivity. Of the three, the third channel has the strongest potential of lengthening the drug monopoly. The drug market regulator would, following TPP rules, not allow the marketing of a new generic drug within 5 to 8 years to protect undisclosed test data belonging to the innovator drug firm.

A study (Danzon and Furukawa, 2011) involving 12 developed countries, except Brazil and Mexico, statistically tested the influence of the number of generic drugs on drug prices using data from 1998 to 2009. It found that the prices of generic drugs are negatively related to the number of unbranded generics in most countries. Moreover, originator drug prices fall as the number of unbranded generics increase, contradicting earlier results from studies based on segmentation theory (Frank and Salkever, 1997; Regan, 2008) that prices of originator drugs increase with the number of unbranded generics.

Generic medicines play an important role in bringing medicine prices down in the Philippines, as illustrated by a 2009 survey of medicine prices in the country. Using as indicator the medicine price ratio (MPR) computed as percentage change of local medicine prices to corresponding international price ratio (Figure 7.1), HAIN (2009) observed that the lowest-price generics sold in private pharmacies are closest to their respective international counterparts. For example, the median MPR of these medicines was 7.95 percent, which is low compared with the median MPR for originator brand (29.32 percent) and highest-priced generics (14.94 percent). Lowest-price generics were even more affordable in government pharmacies (Figure 7.2) where only lowest-priced generics were available for sale.

Using the survey data, the savings per treatment of selected diseases from the use of generic drugs were estimated. Six diseases were cited in the survey (Table 7.5)

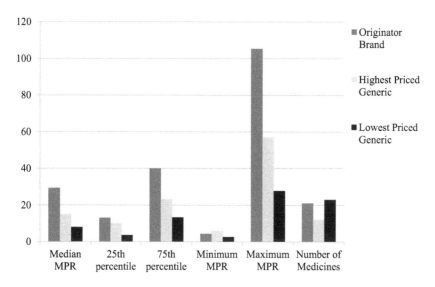

Figure 7.1 Number of times more expensive: prices in Philippine private pharmacies (27 outlets) vs. international reference prices

Source: HAIN (2009).

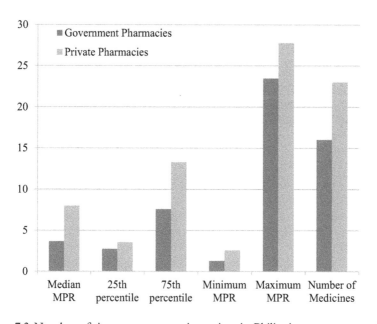

Figure 7.2 Number of times more expensive: prices in Philippine government pharmacies (17 outlets) vs. international reference prices

Source: HAIN (2009).

Table 7.5 Estimated savings per treatment from the use of generic drugs (₱)

Disease	Number of medicines in sample	Private retail			Public patient
		Originator brand	Highest-priced generic (HPG_PRI)	Lowest-priced generic (LPG_PRI)	Lowest-priced generic (LPG_PUB)
Diabetes	2	64,845.00	46,260.00	26,618.00	15,649.00
Savings			18,585.00	38,227.50	49,196.25
Hypertension	1	125,100.00		31,194.00	18,000.00
Savings				93,906.00	107,100.00
Hypercholesterolemia	1	28,350.00	28,535.00	17,325.00	11,088.00
Savings			−184.50	11,025.00	17,262.00
Arthritis	1	80,820.00	43,740.00	18,000.00	18,000.00
Savings			37,080.00	62,820.00	62,820.00
Ulcer	2	128,205.00	44,397.00	31,185.00	11,345.00
Savings			83,808.00	97,020.00	116,860.50
Infectious Disease	1	15,091.00	7,595.00	4,900.00	1,014.00
Savings			7,496.02	10,191.02	14,076.72
Average Saving in % of Originator Medicine Treatment Cost			61.46	70.79	83.03

Source: Author. Based on HAIN (2009), Table 10.

(HAIN, 2009). The number of medicine units was determined per treatment. Altogether, there were two types of treatment: one where the patient was in a private hospital or purchases the medicine from private pharmacies (_PRI), and the other was where the patient is treated in a public hospital or health facility and has access to medicine through the facility or public pharmacies (_PUB). In each, three categories of medicines were considered: (i) originator brand, (ii) highest-priced generic drugs, and (iii) lowest-priced generic drugs. However, for the public patient, only the lowest-priced generic was available.

As expected, the originator medicine treatment had the highest cost. For example, treating diabetes using this type of medicine costs 64,845 pesos (₱), and such type of treatment was available only in a private retail setting. Generic treatment costs varied. The highest of these is treatment with medicine obtained from private pharmacies or private health facilities. These were the branded generic drugs. Following them were the lowest-priced generics in private pharmacies or health facilities. Lowest was the cost of treatment in public facilities using the lowest-priced generics, but the medicines used may possibly get subsidies from the government.

Savings from the use of generic drugs in treating diseases are significant. From the samples in Figure 7.3, they range from as low as 28.66 percent to as high as 93.28 percent of treatment cost using originator medicines.

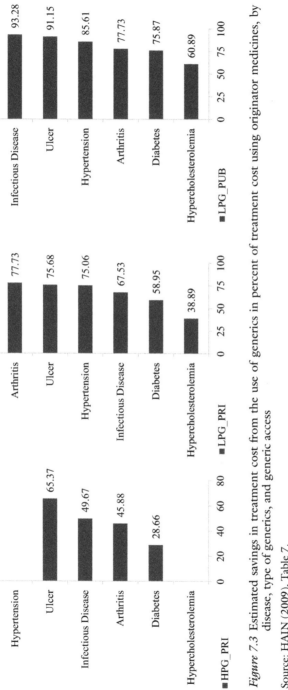

Figure 7.3 Estimated savings in treatment cost from the use of generics in percent of treatment cost using originator medicines, by disease, type of generics, and generic access

Source: HAIN (2009), Table 7.

The lowest saving rate was in the treatment of diabetes using highly priced generic drug (HPG_PRI). HPG treatments of the other diseases likewise tended to have the lowest savings rates. For example, ulcer treatment had 65.37 percent savings rate, compared with 75.68 percent and 91.15 percent for LPG_PRI and LPG_PUB, respectively. The highest saving rate of lowest-priced generic in a private treatment setting (LPG_PRI) was in the treatment of arthritis, whereas it is in infectious disease treatment for LPG treatment in public hospitals or with medicines accessed at public pharmacies.

By delaying the entry of generic drugs in the territories of its parties, the TPP is leaning more to the interests of innovator drug companies. Most of its rules on pharmaceuticals are copied from practices in the US. In particular, market exclusivity was granted to innovator drug companies in consideration of their effort in developing the medicine. At the same time, measures aimed at facilitating the entry of new generic drugs in the market were also introduced. The balance of interests, provided for in the 1984 Hatch-Waxman Act, had provided the growth of the industry in the US. While the TPP copies the market exclusivity for branded manufacturers, it did not have a countervailing measure to encourage the entry of generic drugs, advance competition, and lower drug prices in TPP territories (Luo and Kesselheim, 2016).

Data exclusivity, on the other hand, is needed to encourage the development of new medicines. According to the pharmaceutical industry association in the US, developing a new medicine is high risk. The R&D effort is estimated at $1.2 billion[15] and involves examining 10,000–15,000 compounds, out of which only one chemical substance may succeed to become a drug, get a patent, and be marketed. The expected return on investment, even with patent protection for 20 years, is relatively very low. Market exclusivity is, therefore, seen as giving the innovator drug maker added time to recover development costs (IFPMA, 2011).

Wright (1983) argued that extending *ex post* the patent term introduces a serious moral hazard problem. The R&D costs of companies are not transparent, and ensuring that these are at socially necessary level is a challenge. The TPP, with market exclusivity, can potentially induce more waste by giving more time to companies to recover their costs without parties ascertaining if such R&D investments are reasonable.

Hollis (2004) agrees that some measures, but not market exclusivity, need to be introduced to make the patent system effectively stimulate drug R&D investment, and align it better to social objectives. The inducement of the current patent system to direct R&D efforts towards research areas that have the strong potential for producing drugs with high therapeutic value is weak. Moreover, the idea of giving a monopoly to an innovator company simply raises medicine prices and erodes access to users of life-saving therapies.

Instead, the author proposes a reward system, from public funds, for pharmaceutical innovation based on the incremental therapeutic benefits of their innovation. Compulsory licensing to enable competitive pricing may be part of the reforms, which assure drug innovators a good return on their investments.

4. Implications of the TPP on plant patents

The TPP framers did not push the rules on plant patents beyond what they are under the WTO's TRIPS Agreement in 1995. Parties are allowed to choose the modality how they would protect the intellectual property in plant technologies. If, however, a party opts to use *sui generis* system, the TPP requires the party to use UPOV.[16] If the Philippines decides to accede to the TPP and it decides to use UPOV instead of patents to protect the rights of plant variety owners, then it has to become a member of the UPOV 1991 treaty.[17]

The treaty, however, recognises exceptions to the right of plant breeders. The rights do not apply to the use of protected varieties for private and non-commercial purposes. Persons are free to use protected varieties in experiments or for breeding other varieties. The practice of farmers saving and using their own seeds is also an exception. However, unlike the other exceptions, which are compulsory, the latter is optional.[18]

The Plant Variety Protection Act of 2002 in the Philippines respects 'the traditional right of small farmers to . . . exchange, share or sell their farm produce of a variety protected under this Act, except when a sale is for the purpose of reproduction under a commercial marketing agreement'.[19] But even in the use by Filipino corn farmers of genetically modified yellow corn varieties, which are currently protected by patents of multinational seed companies, farmers can save the seeds. This is not an issue because the genetically modified corn that these companies market in the Philippines are hybrids, which render seed saving not viable.[20] However, in other plant innovations involving open pollinated varieties, the potential conflict between farmers and seed companies remains.

5. Concluding remarks

Just as the Philippines revamped its IPR Code in 1997 to comply with its TRIPS obligations as a WTO founding member country, it may have to amend once again the code to align it with the provisions of the TPP in the event it decides to join the TPP group. Foremost of the steps to take is the extension of the term of patent protection for either of the following: (i) to compensate for the delays in approving patents or marketing approval particularly of medicines, (ii) patent linkage and, most important, (iii) data exclusivity.

The concerns about the impact of the TPP on medicine prices are clarified in this chapter. That the TPP will not oblige the Philippines to buy only branded products is inaccurate. Nothing in the TPP can prevent the continued access of Filipinos to cheaper generic medicines that are locally available. These are off-patent, and the FDAP had already approved these medicines to be marketed locally. Even imported medicines through parallel importation would continue to be accessible to users, if they are already approved by the FDAP to be sold locally as medicines.

The TPP, however, would make users wait from 5 to 8 years before new generic medicines can become available in pharmacies and health facilities. Extending the term of market exclusivity to protect undisclosed test data on safety and efficacy of new medicines translates to longer monopoly of innovator companies without the public getting assured that the R&D costs to be recovered in the first place were socially necessary. Approving waivers or, even better, taking away data exclusivity from its trade rules is a welcome move by the founding members of the TPP.

Several concerns are raised as well with respect to TPP's provisions on plant variety protection. This chapter took up only that on farmers' access to propagating materials of protected plant varieties. Seed saving for use in one's own farm holding is an optional exception to plant breeders' rights. Allowing or prohibiting the practice is consistent with UPOV 1991. If seed saving is prohibited, that is neither a UPOV 1991 rule nor that of the TPP. Rather, it is the decision of the TPP party itself. Exchanging or sharing seeds is not among the acts in Article 14.1 in respect to propagating materials of a protected variety that require prior authorisation of the breeder.

The concern extends to the farmers' not able to sell the harvested plants from their farms or certain products derived from such harvested material. Article 14 in UPOV 1991 assigns the right of breeders to authorise the sale of harvested material of farmers in the condition that such harvest was 'obtained through the unauthorized use of propagating material of the protected variety'. The provision is inapplicable in the case where the propagating materials were legitimately acquired.

But even in the use by Filipino corn farmers of genetically modified yellow corn varieties, which are currently protected by patents of the multinational seed companies, farmers can save the seeds if they want. This is not an issue because the genetically modified corn that these companies market in the Philippines are hybrids, which render seed saving not viable. The difference remains between a patent and the UPOV 1991 – compliant plant variety act or RA No. 9168, with respect to seed saving, using, sharing, exchanging, and even selling. Hybrid corn technology has effectively toned down the conflict. However, the potential clash may surface if genetically modified plant varieties are open pollinated.

Notes

1 Philippine President Duterte said, 'We will no longer have access to generic (medicines). We have a law governing generic so that we can buy cheaper medicines . . .'. See Romero (2016).
2 The discussion in this section benefited from a legal audit of Chapter 18 of the Trans-Pacific Partnership (TPP) agreement. See Vilchez (2016).
3 The analysis is not intended to be a comprehensive legal audit of the TPP.
4 The country should still formally accede to the 1991 accord to comply with this TPP provision.
5 Unreasonable delay, according to the TPP, may be 5 years or more from the date of application of patent or of marketing approval.
6 See Article 18.53 of the TPP.
7 This is Administrative Order (A.O. No. 2005–0001) of the Department of Health. Apparently, the purpose is to address the difficulties in getting information on on-patent pharmaceutical products.

8 The TPP refers to generic drugs as drugs 'similar' to those whose patents had expired. The word 'similar' is defined in a footnote of the agreement as a drug whose marketing approval requires, or in the application of marketing approval of it uses, the undisclosed data on safety and efficacy tests of the drug whose patent had expired (see footnote 52 in 18.50.1 of the TPP).

9 In a footnote, the TPP allows parties to limit the prescriptive period to 5 years (see footnote 53 in 18.50.1 of the agreement).

10 See Article 18.50 of the TPP.

11 See Article 18.48 of the TPP.

12 See footnote 42 in Article 18.47.1 of the TPP for agricultural chemicals and see footnote 53 in Article 18.50.1 of the TPP for biologics.

13 See Article 18.18 of the TPP.

14 In September 2002, the Secretary of Finance approved CAO 6–2002. The enforcement procedures in this order are in line with international standards on border control based on the TRIPS Agreement. Then, in 2003, the Bureau of Customs (BOC) issued Customs Special Order 19–2003 on 12 September creating the Permanent Intellectual Property Unit in the BOC.

15 The figure is quoted by the International Federation of Pharmaceutical Manufacturers Association and is attributed to DiMasi and Grabowski (2007).

16 UPOV was established in 1961 as an independent organisation; it now has 70 members with 15 countries and one organisation initiating application for membership.

17 The Philippines had applied but has yet to deposit its instrument of accession with UPOV. Of the 12 TPP members, five – Brunei Darussalam, Chile, Malaysia, Mexico, and New Zealand – are non-members (Lilliston, 2015).

18 See Article 15.1 in UPOV 1991.

19 See Section 42(d) of RA No. 9168 which is the Plant Variety Protection Act of 2002.

20 The conflict of a patent and the UPOV 1991 compliant RA No. 9168 with respect to seed saving, using, sharing, exchanging, and even selling remains. Hybrid corn technology has effectively held it down. It can surface if genetically modified plants are open pollinated, but the legal farm size limit in the Philippines, which is 5 hectares, may dampen the potential dispute.

Bibliography

Bansal, I.S., D. Sahu, G. Bakshi and S. Singh (2009), 'Evergreening – A Controversial Issue in Pharma Milieu', *Journal of Intellectual Property Rights*, 14 July, pp. 299–306.

Correa, C. (2015), 'Intellectual Property in the Trans-Pacific Partnership: Increasing the Barriers for the Access to Affordable Medicines', *South Centre Research Paper* No. 62, September.

Danzon, P. and M. Furukawa (2011), 'Cross-National Evidence on Generic Pharmaceuticals: Pharmacy vs. Physician-Driven Markets', *NBER Working Paper* No. 17226, July. Available at www.nber.org/papers/w17226

DiMasi, J.A. and H.G. Grabowski (2007), 'The Cost of Biopharmaceutical R&D: Is Biotech Different?', *Managerial and Decision Economics*, 28, pp. 469–479.

Frank, R.G. and D.S. Salkever (1997), 'Generic Entry and the Pricing of Pharmaceuticals', *Journal of Economics & Management Strategy*, 6, pp. 75–90.

Gonzales, L. (2012), *Socio-economic and Environmental Impacts of Bacillus Thuringiensis Corn After a Decade of Commercialization*. Manila: Sikap/Strive Foundation.

Health Action Information Network (HAIN) (2009), *A Survey on Medicine Prices and Availability in the Philippines*. Quezon City, Philippines: HAIN.

Hollis, A. (2004), *An Efficient Reward System for Pharmaceutical Innovation*. Alberta: University of Calgary, Department of Economics.

International Federation of Pharmaceutical Manufacturers Association (IFPMA) (2011), *Data Exclusivity: Encouraging Development of New Medicines*. Geneva: IFPMA.

International Union for the Protection of New Varieties of Plants (UPOV) (1991), *Act of 1991 International Convention for the Protection of New Plant Varieties*. Geneva: UPOV.

Lilliston, B. (2015), *TPP Fine Print: Biotech Seed Companies Win Again*. Washington, DC: Institute for Agriculture Trade Policy. Available at http://iatp.org/blog

Luo, J. and A. Kesselheim (2016), 'Protecting Pharmaceutical Patents and Test Data: How the Trans-Pacific Partnership Agreement Could Affect Access to Medicines in the US and Abroad', *AMA Journal of Ethics*, July, 18(7), pp. 727735.

Regan, T. (2008), 'Generic Entry, Price Competition, and Market Segmentation in the Prescription Drug Market', *International Journal of Industrial Organization*, 4, pp. 930–948.

Republic of the Philippines (2002), 'RA No. 9168 or the Plant Variety Protection Act of 2002', Manila.

Romero, A. (2016), 'Duterte Rejects Trans-Pacific Partnership Deal', *Philippine Star*, 16 December.

United States Trade Representative (USTR) (2015), 'Chapter 18: Intellectual Property'. Available at https://ustr.gov/sites/default/files/TPP-Final-Text-Intellectual-Property.pdf

Vilchez, G. (2016), 'A Study on the Philippine Readiness for the Trans-Pacific Partnership: Focus on Intellectual Property', Report commissioned by the Deloitte Consulting LLP for the United States Agency for International Development (USAID), Manila.

Wright, B.D. (1983), 'The Economics of Invention Incentives: Patents, Prizes, and Research Contracts', *American Economic Review*, 73, pp. 691–707.

World Trade Organization (WTO) (1994), 'Agreement on Trade-Related Aspects of Intellectual Property Rights, Marrakesh Agreement Establishing the World Trade Organization', Annex 1C, Art. 8(1), 33 I.L.M.81.1994.

8 Intellectual property protection under the Trans-Pacific Partnership agreement

From Thailand's perspective

*Jakkrit Kuanpoth**

1. Intellectual property law of Thailand

Currently, there are 10 statutes protecting intellectual property rights in Thailand: the Patent Act B.E.2522 (1979), the Copyright Act B.E.2537 (1994), the Trademarks Act B.E.2534 (A.D.1991), the Plant Varieties Protection Act B.E.2542 (1999), the Protection and Promotion of Traditional Thai Medicine Wisdom Act, B.E.2542 (1999), the Protection of Layout-Designs of Integrated Circuits Act B.E.2543 (2000), the Trade Secret Act B.E.2545 (2002), the Geographical Indications Act B.E.2546 (2003), the Optical Disc Production Act B.E.2548 (2005), and the Film and Video Act B.E.2551 (2008).

The Copyright Act 1994, which is Thailand's current law, came into force on 21 March 1995. It was adopted during a period of intense external pressure demanding a complete overhaul of the country's intellectual property laws. The 1994 Act was considerably influenced by the rules and principles enshrined under the Agreement on Trade-Related Aspects of Intellectual Property Rights (TRIPS Agreement). The new law also clarifies some ambiguous parts of the 1978 Act, especially the question of whether a computer program was protected as a literary work. The Copyright Act 1994 was amended on 5 February 1995, providing tools to tackle copyright infringement in the new digital age, including protection of technological protection measures and rights management information, injunctive relief for copyright infringement on the Internet, and rules on temporary reproduction.

Trademark law was established in Thailand in the 1900s. The first law protecting trademarks was the Trademarks and Brand Names Act 1914. The law for the first time sets up a system for the registration of trademarks. In 1931, a new trademarks law was adopted to replace the 1914 Act. The Trademarks Act 1931 was in effect for 60 years before it was replaced by a new law, the Trademarks Act B.E.2534 (A.D.1991). The new trademark law, which remains in force, was amended in 2000. The amendment was done to facilitate the trademarks registration process and to bring Thai law into compliance with TRIPS standards.

As for patents, there was no legal protection for inventions in Thailand until 1979. In February 1992, Thailand, under pressure from the Government of the United States (US), decided to revise the Patent Act to avoid trade sanctions. The new law amended the previous law in several areas, including an expansion of the scope of patentable subject matters, an extension of the term of patent rights, the establishment of a drug price review committee, and the modification of the process for the grant of compulsory licences.

The Plant Variety Protection Act 1999 was enacted to comply with Art. 27.3(b) of the TRIPS Agreement. It has certain features in common with patents for industrial inventions. Plant variety protection is a *sui generis* (of its own kind or unique) of protection tailored to protect new and traditional plant varieties. The Act recognises the important role played by farmers and local communities as custodians of traditional crop cultivars. The Act acknowledges and compensates those communities for their contribution by allowing local communities to register traditional plant varieties exclusively found within the community. The Act also enables the establishment of a Plant Variety Protection Fund, which would tap a portion of the royalties paid by those who use plant genetic resources for commercial purposes.

Thailand is currently party to five international agreements in the field of intellectual property: the Patent Cooperation Treaty (24 December 2009), the Paris Convention for the Protection of Industrial Property (2 August 2008), the Convention Establishing the World Intellectual Property Organization (25 December 1989), the Berne Convention for the Protection of Literary and Artistic Works (17 July 1931), and the Protocol Relating to the Madrid Agreement Concerning the International Registration of Marks (Madrid Protocol) (7 August 2017).

2. Trans-Pacific Partnership provisions affecting access to medicines

The development of intellectual property law has become the subject of growing concern amongst citizen groups, environmentalists, academics, and the general public in developing countries. They believe that a higher level of patent protection and enforcement will increase the public burden (Drahos and Mayne, 2002). The WTO TRIPS Agreement sets minimum standards of intellectual property protection that all members of the WTO must implement. Despite international concerns about the impact of the TRIPS Agreement on development, intellectual property standards continue to increase. These strict standards, known as 'TRIPS-plus', are often used in bilateral and regional trade agreements and in treaties developed by the WIPO (Roffe, 2004). Some of the TRIPS-plus rules are now examined.

2.1. Second or further medical use of known pharmaceutical products

Claims of nonmedical uses are generally patentable in most countries, provided that the use of the known compound has not been known to the public (e.g. a new use of known cosmetics). By contrast, national law and practices on the patenting of second and further medical uses of known products vary from one country to another. Under European patent law, for example, the method of diagnosis, treatment, and therapy applied on human or animal bodies is not patentable.

However, second and further uses of an existing medical product could be patentable when they are in the form of Swiss-type claims (i.e. claims referring to 'manufacture of a medicament'), provided that the claimed inventions meet the requirements of patentability, such as 'The use of [known compound/substance X] for the manufacturing of a medicament for the treatment of [disease]'.

There are two issues relating to the patenting of a known pharmaceutical: new uses and new methods. When a pharmaceutical substance is already known to the public, claims to the product as such are no longer patentable. Alternative solutions for the pharmaceutical company are to claim new pharmaceutical compositions or to claim a new use of the product that is already known. It is common for a research-based pharmaceutical company to broadly claim pharmaceutical compositions containing the active ingredient (i.e. a formulated product containing a known active ingredient and appropriate additives). Such a claim is advantageous as it is not limited to any specific pharmaceutical indication. The commercial use of the claimed compound for any use whatsoever would constitute a patent infringement. Yet, an invention used in one area may have applications in other areas. For example, a biochemical substance may be used as a pharmaceutical product, or a well-known drug can have a new therapeutic application. Such second use may then be claimed either by the company that holds the patent over the substance or by another company that has discovered such a second use (Kuanpoth, 2010).

The TRIPS Agreement does not require WTO members to patent second use inventions. Some developed countries (e.g. European Union [EU] members, Japan, and the US) have permitted patenting of the second use inventions.[1] If the second use of known drugs is patented, it would limit the freedom of countries to determine what should be protected under product and process patents as provided by the TRIPS Agreement. Medicines that are no longer patented as products can be patented as a second use, new indications, new dosages of existing drugs, or new combinations of existing drugs. Patents for the subsequent uses of a known drug would thereby unnecessarily prolong the monopoly and deprive consumers of affordable access to essential medicines.

The TPP intellectual property chapter confirms the exclusion of patentability of medical practices such as diagnosis, therapy, and surgery on the human or animal body (Article 18.37.3 (a)). The exclusion of methods of treatment is based on the ground of ethical and social policy to protect medical practitioners from the restrictions of monopoly privileges, and at the same time allow for healthy competition to enhance the well-being of the public.[2] From the consumers' perspective, it is fortunate that the TPP provision has extended this exclusion to claims relating to second or further medical use of known pharmaceutical products, as Article 18.37.2 states:

> Subject to paragraphs 3 and 4 and consistent with paragraph 1, each Party confirms that patents are available for inventions claimed as at least one of the following: new uses of a known product, new methods of using a known product, or new processes of using a known product. A Party may limit those new processes to those that do not claim the use of the product as such.

2.2. Exclusivity protection over test or other data

The law of most nations requires pharmaceutical and agrochemical products to be registered with the competent authority before they can be put on the market. The company that seeks registration must submit data relating to the product's quality, safety, and efficacy – the 'test data' – with the relevant regulatory authority. Although Article 39.3 of the TRIPS Agreement stipulates that all member parties must protect the undisclosed data submitted for marketing approval, this legal protection is relatively limited as it is required only for new chemical entities. The protection must be available only to protect against 'unfair commercial use' and 'disclosure' of the data. No TRIPS provisions require WTO members to provide exclusivity protection to the first person who submits the marketing approval data, who are generally the company that developed a new product (Correa, 2002). This has left the WTO members with considerable room to determine rules for the protection of undisclosed test data. For example, a country's legislation may not prevent third parties from using the test data if that use does not constitute 'unfair commercial use' or does not breach the 'nondisclosure' obligation in the framework of unfair competition law. In addition, the regulatory authorities may rely on the data submitted by the originator company or on the evidence of a registration made in a foreign country to grant marketing approval for subsequent applications concerning a similar product.

Some developed countries, including EU members, Japan, and the US, grant TRIPS-plus protection on the basis of data exclusivity.[3] The TPP follows the developed-country approach by requiring the parties to grant exclusivity over those data for at least (i) 10 years for data required for marketing approval of agricultural chemical products; (ii) 5 years for data for a new pharmaceutical product; (iii) 3 years for data for approving a new indication, new formulation, or new method of administration of an existing medicine; and (iv) 8 years for data relating to a new pharmaceutical product that is or contains a biologic. The requirement for data exclusivity seems absolute because the TPP contains no exceptions to the data exclusivity obligation. It is also doubtful if the compulsory licensing can be issued against the data exclusivity protection to meet a country's public health needs.

According to the TPP, the exclusivity over test data must be granted along these lines. A country that joins the TPP must prohibit anyone from marketing the same or a similar product for the specified period, unless that person has obtained consent from the originator of the marketing approval test data. The country must also prohibit anyone who does not have the consent of the originator company from submitting evidence of foreign government marketing approval in support of an application to market in the contracting country for that period from the date of marketing approval in the contracting country or the date of approval in the other country, whichever is later. This comprehensive data protection regime provides exclusivity to all kinds of data submitted for marketing approval, including pharmaceutical data with respect to formulations, dosage forms, new uses, and second indications. This commitment will limit the country's ability to flexibly implement Article 39.3 of the TRIPS Agreement.

This TRIPS-plus obligation on data exclusivity will generate several negative effects. First, it will reduce competition in the private sector and thus limit access to essential products, because the generic medicine manufacturers, most of which are small companies in developing countries, will have to enter into a long and costly testing process before the marketing approval of a generic drug can be obtained. Second, it will limit the effectiveness of the compulsory licence system, as the essential data are not available due to the exclusivity protection. Third, it will prohibit the regulatory authorities of the TPP party from relying on marketing approvals in other countries, despite the fact that most developing countries currently do not have the capacity to review data for purposes of granting marketing approval.

2.3. *Compulsory licences*

Health benefits are measured in terms of gains in life expectancy and quality of life, and economic benefits in terms of the reduction of treatment costs. This calculation is one of the criteria for setting a maximum price for medicines that are to be financed by the public health system (Singham, 2000). Under Article 31 of the TRIPS Agreement, WTO members are permitted to use compulsory licence of patents with certain conditions. The compulsory licensing refers to the issuance of a non-voluntary licence by the state to a third party, without the consent of the patent holder, on the condition that the licensee pays reasonable remuneration to the patent holder in return. The grant of licence by state authorises the licensee to perform acts covered by the patent-exclusive rights (e.g. manufacturing, selling, or importing the patented product). The system can help to curb the monopolistic power of the holder of pharmaceutical patents and keeps the prices of essential products at a reasonable level, as has been successfully used in many countries (Correa, 1999).

FTAs signed by the US and its trade partners generally impose restrictions on the use of compulsory licensing by states. For example, the FTA between Australia and the US limits the grounds for use without the authorisation of the patent holder to three situations only: cases involving anti-competitive conduct, public non-commercial use, and situations of national emergency or other circumstances of extreme urgency (AUSFTA, Article 17.9.7[b][i]). From the consumers' point of view, it is fortunate that the restraints on the use of the compulsory licensing and price control mechanisms do not appear in the TPP text. A TPP provision, Article 18.6, confirms the parties' commitment to the declaration on TRIPS and public health and the 'TRIPS/health solution', which refers to the 2003 and 2005 WTO decisions.[4] The same provision reiterates that the obligations of the TPP intellectual property chapter 'do not and should not prevent a Party from taking measures to protect public health'. Further, Article 18.41, confirms that '[t]he Parties understand that nothing in this Chapter limits a Party's rights and obligations under Article 31 of the TRIPS Agreement, any waiver or any amendment to that Article that the Parties accept'.

However, with the rigid system of data protection under the TPP mentioned earlier, it remains to be seen how the compulsory licensing mechanisms as enshrined under national patent systems will continue to play a significant role to pressurise patent holders to work the patent to maximise public interest. Considering the potential legal scope of data exclusivity under the TPP, the TPP data protection provisions could prevent the registration of generic medicines, and thus have negative consequences for access to life-saving medicines. It is, therefore, recommended that countries considering joining the TPP weigh the socioeconomic costs of rigidities and constraints on policy space against other benefits.

3. Trans-Pacific Partnership provisions affecting agriculture and biodiversity

3.1. Protection of genes and living organisms

The patentability of biotechnological inventions has become the subject of growing controversy around the world. While the biotechnology industry is demanding a high degree of protection, citizen groups, environmentalists, scientists, farmers' organisations, and religious leaders are running a worldwide campaign against the patenting of life forms. To those people, animals, plants, humans, microorganisms, and their parts such as genes and cells, even if they are genetically modified, are not inventions because these life forms are creation of God and nature (Sterckx, 1998).

On the issue of patentable subject matter, TPP Article 18.37 states that 'a product or a process, in all fields of technology, provided that the invention is new, involves an inventive step and is capable of industrial application'. Similar to provisions of the TRIPS Agreement, the TPP permits the signatories to exclude from patentability plants, animals, essentially biological processes for the production of plants or animals, and methods of medical treatment (Article 18.37.3). However, it mandates parties to protect 'inventions that are derived from plants' (Article 18.37.4). It may be noted that the TRIPS Agreement does not mandate the patentability of genetic information, in the forms of genes, parts of genes, DNA molecules, gene sequences, cell lines, and so forth, although a country may choose to extend such protection under its domestic law. This can be seen from several countries' stance on the patentability of biotechnological inventions, which does not treat biomedical inventions as a separate category of potentially patentable inventions (Sherman, Bently, and Hubicki, 2009).

It was decided in a recent US decision in *Association for Molecular Pathology v US PTO*, which received huge publicity, that there would be no patent in isolated DNA in BRCA1 and BRCA2 genes.[5] In *D'Arcy v Myriad Genetics Inc.*, [2015] HCA 35, the High Court of Australia ruled that the isolated nucleic acid sequences encoding the BRCA1 mutant polypeptide and related methods were not eligible subject matter (i.e. a manner of manufacture) for patentability. The decisions of the highest court of the two countries extensively canvassed the scope of the patenting of biotechnology of genes in general and would have enhanced the thoroughness of biological research. It would be interesting to see how great an impact Article 18.37.4 of the TPP, which requires state parties to provide patent protection for inventions that are derived from plants, will have on national patent systems.

As to plant breeding, many countries have adopted a *sui generis* protection for plant varieties in the form of plant variety protection law. The International Union for the Protection of New Varieties of Plants (UPOV) system is recognised to be one such *sui generis* system. The ambiguity of the term 'effective *sui generis* system' under the TRIPS Agreement allows developing countries to avoid having to develop full intellectual property law covering plant varieties. Some developing countries, such as India and Thailand, have flexibly implemented the TRIPS provision by incorporating the concept of farmers' rights and the access and benefit-sharing system under the Convention on Biological Diversity into their national legislation.[6] Article 18.7.2 of the TPP limits this flexibility by requiring participating countries to join the UPOV 1991 Act. According to the Act, protection must cover vegetative or reproductive propagating material and extends to essentially derived varieties and harvested materials. The rights of farmers to save, use, exchange, or sell farm-saved seeds are restricted. This will prevent TPP parties from taking the necessary steps to assure a sufficient supply of seed and food for their populations. Given that ensuring farmers' and breeders' access to seeds is crucial for agriculture-based countries, such full-scale monopoly rights will adversely affect the food and agriculture sectors and poor farmers, in particular when their right to save seeds is removed (Tansey, 2002).

3.2. Protecting geographical indications and biodiversity

As in many other developing countries, the risk of poverty remains high in the remote and rural parts of Asia. The roots of poverty often lie in the loss of control over resources and the loss of sustainable livelihoods as a result of dependence on a market economy. For example, modern agricultural policy that encourages commercial and monoculture crops for export has plunged many Asian farmers into debt. Various government policies, lending practices, and farming contracts have heavily indebted and bankrupted poor farmers. Several Asian farming communities have lost their livelihoods and land. To alleviate poverty, it may be necessary to shift the way natural resources are managed from state-based management to a more community-based model in which local communities are free to control their environment and economic opportunities.

In developing agricultural countries in Asia, such as Indonesia, Malaysia, the Philippines, Thailand, and Viet Nam, the system for the protection of geographical indications (GIs), which provides a collective exclusive right to indigenous and local communities and small farmers, could serve as an important tool for poverty alleviation in the remote areas (Van Caenegem, 2003). The GI protection system can help maintain agricultural profitability and hence activity in marginal areas. It also creates economic rewards through granting premium prices for marginal or small-scale farmers who use traditional methods in regions where the product has been traditionally produced. Moreover, systems to protect and increase the profits small farmers gain from plant-based production would help strengthen bonds between farmers and the species that they have improved and domesticated.

The protection and promotion of GIs can be understood as responding to changing consumer tastes, in particular an interest in the place of origin and production conditions. Appropriate GI protection policies could help transform farming away from quantity-driven indicators towards quality-based factors. Also, by re-embedding production into local contexts, such as organic farming or fair trade, GIs can be seen as part of a broader movement towards alternative agriculture in opposition to the globalisation of trade and standardisation of food and taste (Robinson, 2007).

GIs, which tend to be land-based and strongly linked to agriculture, stand in opposition to production-oriented and subsidy-dependent farming that produces standardised and homogenised products. By maintaining certain long-standing practices and the use of particular raw materials, GI-related products are linked into alternative production networks. Thus, protection and promotion of GIs is, to a great extent, directed at resisting the pressures to delocalise products through a process of standardisation and homogenisation that would allow their production at other, less costly locations. An effective and appropriate GI protection system must be developed with the aim of helping small and medium-sized enterprises promote their products by guaranteeing exclusivity over the use of GIs and helping companies overcome marketing constraints, such as obtaining consumer recognition and customer loyalty. Emerging enterprises, many of which are community-based, would be well advised to shift their strategy from supplying raw materials to producing and selling products under their own brand with the goal of becoming a global brand.

Given the socio-economic benefits of GIs to rural communities, it is unfortunate that the TPP does not consider them a separate class of intellectual property regime. It demands that parties protect GIs through specific categories of trademarks, including certification marks, collective marks, and ordinary trademarks. The TPP provision reflects the US legislative model, which recognises and protects as trademarks. For example, 'Florida' has been registered as a trademark for oranges, 'Idaho' for potatoes, and 'Washington' for apples. This practice differs from the EU approach (Gangjee, 2007). GIs have been protected in a separate regime of protection under the European law, and the EU has sought to extend the higher level of protection to products other than wines and spirits during the WTO Doha Round of multilateral trade negotiations. This attempt has met strong resistance from the US and some other members such as Australia, Canada, Chile, and New Zealand.

The TPP provision mandates the protection of GIs. However, it provides the option for participating countries to adopt a *sui generis* system or to protect GIs through trademarks (Article 18.30). While flexibilities are provided, the TPP contains a number of specific obligations on administrative procedures for the protection or recognition of GIs, including requiring parties to make available to the general public information relating to procedure for filing application, and opposition to and cancellation of geographic indications (Article 18.31). This flexible option might be beneficial for some Asian countries, such as Thailand, which has enacted comprehensive legislation on the protection of GIs, to use GIs as a tool for the promotion of their quality products (Kuanpoth and Robinson, 2009).

It may be noted that GIs have a much wider application than trademarks and the prevention of unfair competitive practices. For developing countries with different production structures and natural endowments, a broader protection of GIs may constitute one of the most important categories of intellectual property. The *sui generis* GI system seems more suitable to countries with an abundance of producers of all kinds of natural and agricultural products and of handicrafts. Such a protection system can be a significant factor in the economic development and the promotion of the country's exports. The protection and recognition of GIs under a *sui generis* regime should therefore be maintained and promoted in any international legal frameworks, as enshrined in the TPP provision.

4. Trans-Pacific Partnership provisions relating to digital technologies

The TRIPS Agreement does not incorporate minimum standards on specific intellectual property issues in cyberspace. In 1996, the WIPO adopted two 'Internet treaties': the WIPO Copyright Treaty and the WIPO Performances and Phonograms Treaty. These treaties create an entirely new body of intellectual property law involved with the Internet. The TPP provisions provide that all TPP partners must envisage the very dynamic digital agenda of the WIPO.

The TPP provisions on copyright and related rights can be summarised as follows:

i   TPP members must adopt the essential provisions of the World Intellectual Property Organization (1996a), WIPO Copyright Treaty, and the World Intellectual Property Organization (1996b), WIPO Performances and Phonograms Treaty.

ii TPP members must provide a longer term of protection than the TRIPS standard, that is, the term of protection shall not be less than the life of the author and 70 years after the author's death.

iii While the TRIPS Agreement is absent on obligations concerning technological protection measures, TPP provisions stipulate that parties must provide adequate legal protection and effective legal remedies against circumvention of effective technological measures that are used by the right holders to protect their works from unauthorised use. This means in effect that the TPP has created a new concept of copyright protection by extending the conventional economic rights of the author to the right to use and distribute circumventing devices.

iv The TRIPS-plus commitment of 'right management information' is imposed on the contracting parties. All TPP parties must impose criminal and civil liability on anyone who provides false information, or removes or alters right management information, and anyone who unlawfully deals with the materials knowing that such information has been removed or altered without authority.

This new area of intellectual property rights will no doubt allow content owners to enjoy greater protection than conventional copyright rules would afford. The provisions on technological protection measures will enable the owners to extend control over access to and distribution of digital works even after the expiration of the copyright term. These rules and those relating to right management information will enable the owners to control access to works that copyright law expressly leaves unprotected to stimulate further creativity (i.e. works that have fallen into the public domain). The scope of fair use online will be narrowed, as the content owners can require payment for any use or for excerpting a digital work, regardless of the user's purpose. The use of the Internet and digital works for educational or private non-commercial purposes or by educational and library organisations will not be possible because of this prohibition (Cohen, 1998).

5. Other provisions enhancing intellectual property protection

5.1. Treaties linked to intellectual property

The TPP demands that each party seek accession to a number of key intellectual property treaties, such as the International Union for the Protection of New Varieties of Plants Agreement 1991, the Madrid Protocol, the Patent Cooperation Treaty, the Budapest Treaty, and the Singapore Treaty on the Law of Trademarks. The treaties that TPP parties are required to ratify or accede to provide for a system of international filing of applications for patents or trademarks in different countries. Applicants who seek to secure their protection in several countries can obtain a single, simplified examination procedure, which reduces the costs and time taken. Some treaties also provide for the use of standardised forms for obtaining and maintaining a patent or trademark. Some, such as the Singapore Treaty on the Law of Trademarks, establish safeguards against loss of rights on procedural grounds that minimise the risk of error.

No doubt the requirement that countries seek accession to those treaties is an attempt to facilitate an international protection system for intellectual property rights. Intellectual property owners will benefit greatly from using the existing mechanisms available under those procedural treaties for international registration of their rights. The treaties will provide a means of international protection in countries that is faster and more effective than the current national system. However, currently, the benefits from effective registration of intellectual property rights are not clearly understood. If a developing country decides to become a member of the TPP and must seek accession to those intellectual property treaties, it is more likely that foreigners from the developed countries will remove technology from the public domain.

5.2. Patent terms and extension

The period of patent granting from filing to approval remains unpredictable. It can take longer than 10 years in some countries. The delay is usually due to a lack of human resources – particularly chemical and pharmaceutical patent examiners – at the national patent office. The problem of patent backlog for developing countries has become even more acute due to the weak institutional capacity in patent administration authorities. The patent application bottlenecks give rise to uncertainty of investment protection for right holders and increase the possibility of infringement from domestic companies during the period when approval is pending. This damages both local businesses and innovators. Under such unpredictable circumstances, patent term restoration or adjustment is envisaged to remedy the patent holders for the patent office delays. TPP Article 18.46.3 provides that '[i]f there are unreasonable delays in a Party's issuance of patents, that Party shall provide the means to, and at the request of the patent owner shall, adjust the term of the patent to compensate for such delays'.

The 20-year patent term under the TRIPS Agreement is supposed to reward inventors for their innovative efforts. The TPP now provides for the so-called patent term adjustment for patent office delays, to provide compensation for the loss of patent term due to the delay in approval process. On the basis of Article 18.46.4, the TPP demands that the parties provide a means to adjust the term of the patent in case of delays of more than 5 years from the filing date or 3 years from the date the applicant has requested the examination of the application, whichever is later. This compensation is not available under the TRIPS Agreement or the Paris Convention. No doubt, the developing countries participating in the TPP, some of which have already experienced hardship from patents on pharmaceuticals, will find the extension of a period of patent protection for the essential products like pharmaceuticals risky to the well-being of their people.

5.3. International cooperation

The TPP comprises both developed and developing economies. The TPP calls for international cooperation activities amongst participating countries. Article 18.13 states

> [t]he Parties shall endeavour to cooperate on the subject matter covered by this Chapter, such as through appropriate coordination, training and exchange of information between the respective intellectual property offices of the Parties, or other institutions, as determined by each Party.

While the TPP provision provides a statement of the principle that international cooperation on intellectual property is crucial, it does not elaborate as to how this principle can be implemented. Technical assistance and capacity building programmes relating to intellectual property protection have been carried out by international organisations, particularly the WIPO. However, developing countries contend that such programmes should be tailored to the development needs of the countries rather than the usual practice of blindly promoting the enforcement of intellectual property in those countries. Related to this is the use of 'model laws', which are given to nations to help them formulate laws and implement their intellectual property legal frameworks. It is important to note that many of these model laws are written according to a TRIPS-plus standard of protection, which – unknown to the recipient country – generally ties them to higher obligations than would be necessarily had they adhered only to the basic TRIPS Agreement.

In this regard, technical assistance training should be multi-sectoral in the sense that the training opinions and curricula offered should be done by a diverse range of people rather than only WIPO or sanctioned individuals (Kuanpoth, 2013). For example, representatives from the medical care sector and non-governmental organisations should also be able to offer their insights into the impact that intellectual property law can have. Similarly, countries needing technical assistance should send a broader representative group of people to receive training instead of only government bureaucrats from the national intellectual property office. This is due to the increased need for capacity to deal with these new laws that are being introduced. This cuts across many areas, such as patent examiners and officers, the courts, the knowledge and understanding of the judges, and training of police and prosecutors. It is in the interests of the governments and the public to take an integrated approach to intellectual property, rather than just a business-oriented approach, to deal with the other related issues as well, such as healthcare, education, and agriculture. In general, technical assistance should be tailored to the individual needs of the country, and it should help countries prioritise intellectual property in their overall development agenda.

6. Conclusion

The debate on intellectual property protection consistently touches upon the socio-economic problems faced by developing countries and the impact that the implementation of intellectual property protection has on these countries. In particular, the impact on local industries and their ability to use and produce new products are particularly felt in emerging economies as their growth is being slowed because of patent protection. The TPP provisions will increase the monopoly rights of patent holders and increase the prices of medicinal products, agricultural chemical products, and seeds. It will lead to the increased use of agricultural chemicals such as fertiliser and pesticides that have some direct harmful effects on plants, lives, and ecosystems. The TPP provisions will also generate severe effects on societal, cultural, and educational development, particularly when the new copyright rules are introduced.

Notes

* Research Director for Economic Laws, Thailand Development Research Institute; Visiting Professorial Fellow, Faculty of Law, Humanities and the Arts, University of Wollongong
1 In Europe, the issue was widely discussed in the first decisions of the European Patent Office's Enlarged Board of Appeal, G 1/83, G 5/83, and G6/83. The board affirmed the patentability of a second medical use, yet it is relatively clear that this is based not strictly on a legal interpretation of the relevant provisions, but on the assumption that such protection is useful to advance technological progress in the

field of pharmaceuticals, and not contrary to the provisions in the European Patent Convention. Refusing protection for second medical uses is compatible with the obligation to grant absolute protection to pharmaceutical products and not contrary to the TRIPS Agreement. The decision is rather one of economic policy, and the answer may well differ between developed and developing countries.

2 The issue is a complicated one that involves ethical as well as practical issues. An overview over the issue from a European perspective is provided by Thomas (2003).

3 US laws adopt an absolute exclusivity regime for pharmaceuticals and a limited exclusivity regime for pesticides.

4 The Decision of the General Council of 30 August 2003 on the Implementation of Paragraph Six of the Doha Declaration on the TRIPS Agreement and Public Health, WT/L/540. The Decision of the WTO General Council of 6 December 2005 on the Amendment of the TRIPS Agreement, WT/L/641.

5 2010 US Dist Lexis 30629, available at www.lexology.com/library/detail.aspx?g=a4750517-f5e1-4366-875a-37592c0449f9

6 The concept of farmers' rights adopted by the Food and Agriculture Organization of the United Nations has the aim of compensating farmers who have been conserving plant genetic resources for centuries and thereby have contributed to the development of plant varieties.

Bibliography

Cohen, J.E. (1998), 'Lochner in Cyberspace: The New Economic Orthodoxy of "Right Management"', *Michigan Law Review*, 97, pp. 462–562.

Correa, C.M. (1999), *Intellectual Property Rights and the Use of Compulsory Licences: Options for Developing Countries*. Available at www.iatp.org/files/Intellectual_Property_Rights_and_the_Use_of_Co.pdf (accessed 28 September 2016).

Correa, C.M. (2002), *Protection of Data Submitted for the Registration of Pharmaceuticals: Implementing the Standards of the TRIPS Agreement*. Geneva: South Centre.

Drahos, P. and R. Mayne (eds.) (2002), *Global Intellectual Property Rights*. Basingstoke: Palgrave-Macmillan/Oxfam; Commission on Intellectual Property Rights, Innovation and Public Health (2006), *Public Health, Innovation and Intellectual Property Rights*. Geneva: World Health Organization.

Flynn, S. (2012), *Law Professors Call for Trans-Pacific Partnership (TPP) Transparency*. Washington, DC: Infojustice.org. Available at http://infojustice.org/archives/21137 (accessed 4 September 2014).

Gangjee, D. (2007), 'Quibbling Siblings: Conflicts Between Trade Marks and Geographical Indications', *Chicago – -Kent Law Review*, 82(3), pp. 1252–1291.

Gervais, D. (2009), 'Of Clusters and Assumptions: Innovation as Part of a Full TRIPS Implementation', *Fordham Law Review*, 77, pp. 2353–2377.

International Centre on Trade and Sustainable Development (2011), *Bridges Weekly Trade News Digest*, 15(5), p. 2.

Kuanpoth, J. (2010), *Patent Rights in Pharmaceuticals in Developing Countries: Major Challenges for the Future*. Cheltenham: Edward Elgar.

Kuanpoth, J. (2013), 'Patents and the Emerging Markets of Asia: ASEAN and Thailand', in F.M. Abbott, C.M. Correa and P. Drahos (eds.), *Emerging Markets and the World Patent Order*. Cheltenham: Edward Elgar.

Kuanpoth, J. and D. Robinson (2009), 'Geographical Indications Protection: The Case of Thailand and Jasmine Rice', *Intellectual Property Quarterly*, 3, pp. 288–310.

Matsushita, M. (2010), 'Proliferation of Free Trade Agreements and Development Perspectives', Paper presented at the Law and Development Institute Inaugural

Conference. Sydney, Australia, October. Available at www.lawanddevelopment. net/img/matsushita.pdf (accessed 14 September 2016).

Merges, R.P. (1988), 'Intellectual Property in Higher Life Forms: The Patent System and Controversial Technologies', *Maryland Law Review*, 47, p. 1051.

Morin, J. (2009), 'Multilateralising TRIPS-Plus Agreements: Is the U.S. Strategy a Failure?' *Journal of World Intellectual Property*, 12(3), pp. 175–197.

Rimmer, M. (2008), *Intellectual Property and Biotechnology*. Cheltenham: Edward Elgar.

Robinson, D. (2007), 'Exploring Components and Elements of Sui Generis Systems for Plant Variety Protection and Traditional Knowledge in Asia', *ICTSD – -UNCTAD and IDRC, Geneva*, pp. 41–43.

Roffe, P. (2004), *Bilateral Agreements and a TRIPS- plus World: The Chile – -US Free Trade Agreement*. Available at www.geneva.quno.info/pdf/Chile(US)final.pdf (accessed 16 September 2016).

Sherman, B. (2009), 'Reference; We Have Never Been Modern: The High Court's Decision in National Research Development Corporation v Commissioner of Patents' in A. Kenyon, M. Richardson and S. Ricketson (eds.), *Landmarks in Australian Intellectual Property Law*. Melbourne: Cambridge University Press.

Sherman, B., L. Bently and S. Hubicki (2009), 'Patent Issues in Biotechnology', in S. Hubicki and B. Sherman (eds.), *The Encyclopaedia of the Human Genome*. London: Macmillan.

Singham, S.A. (2000), 'Competition Policy and the Stimulation of Innovation: TRIPS and the Interface between Competition and Patent Protection in the Pharmaceutical Industry', *Brooklyn Journal of International Law*, 26(2), pp. 363–415.

Sterckx, S. (1998), 'Some Ethically Problematic Aspects of the Proposal for a Directive on the Legal Protection of Biotechnological Inventions', *EIPR*, pp. 123–128; Merges, R.P. (1988), 'Intellectual Property in Higher Life Forms: The Patent System and Controversial Technologies', *Maryland Law Review*, 47, p. 1051.

Thomas, D. (2003), 'Patentability Problems in Medical Technology', *International Review of Intellectual Property and Competition Law*, 34(8), pp. 847–886.

US Department of Commerce and the Office of the United States Trade Representative (2010), *Charter of the United States Trade Advisory Committee on Intellectual Property Rights*. Available at www.trade.gov/itac/committees/itac15.asp (accessed 17 October 2017).

Van Caenegem, W. (2003), 'Registered Geographical Indications: Between Intellectual Property and Rural Policy – Part I', *Journal of World Intellectual Property*, 6(5), pp. 699–719.

Part III
Rules and regulations on state-owned enterprises

9 Disciplines on state-owned enterprises under the Trans-Pacific Partnership agreement

Overview and assessment

Tsuyoshi Kawase and Masahito Ambashi

1. Introduction

Bremmer (2011) assessed the rise of China and other state capitalist countries – those in which governments actively intervene in their economies for the stability of their countries and governments – since the 2000s and how they have come to confront the United States (US) and European countries that embrace traditional economic liberalism. State-owned enterprises (SOEs) are an important policy tool for state capitalist countries, and they have seen remarkable growth in emerging economies. For example, China National Petroleum Corporation, Sinopec Group, and Industrial and Commercial Bank of China have been ranked amongst the top 10 companies in the Fortune Global 500 and the Financial Times Global 500 in recent years (cf. METI, 2016, pp. 445–446).[1]

While subject to state policies, SOEs enjoy various competitive advantages over their private-sector competitors. These include subsidies, soft loans, and credit guarantees backed by an abundance of government funding; preferential tax and regulatory treatment; and less-stringent corporate governance in terms of not being required to make short-term profits because they are state-owned. It has been pointed out, therefore, that SOEs are prone to engage in economically irrational behaviour and anti-competitive business practices that disrupt the order of fair competition in international markets (Capobianco and Christiansen, 2011, pp. 4–10). Since the early 2000s, there has been a series of cases in which such problematic behaviour and practices of SOEs have evolved into an international dispute or issue. Typical examples include a case filed with the World Trade Organization (WTO) over anti-dumping and countervailing duties imposition by the US, growing concerns about irrational investment decisions regarding interests in mineral resources and exploration rights, and investment activities by sovereign wealth funds (Kowalski et al., 2013, pp. 16–17; METI, 2016, pp. 445–453). To sum up, there is concern that SOEs are likely to disturb the fair international competition regime by conducting business activities that go against economic rationality (e.g. dumping and excessive investments) and by their anti-competitive behaviour.

Against this backdrop, it was inevitable that extensive disciplines on SOEs would be introduced during the negotiations on the Trans-Pacific Partnership

(TPP) Agreement, which includes as its signatories a series of emerging econo-mies that embrace state capitalism – Brunei Darussalam, Malaysia, Singapore, and Viet Nam. The application of the SOE disciplines to Viet Nam in particular has been seen as a potential test case for how to deal with China in the future. The US business community hoped strong rules would be introduced for SOEs, and a 2011 joint proposal put forward by the Coalition of Services Industries and the US Chamber of Commerce[2] became the basis for US proposals in the TPP negotiations.[3] Indeed, the US consistently led the SOE negotiations as a 'norm entrepreneur' with a view to pressuring China into meeting basic interna-tional standards (Sylvestre Fleury and Marcoux, 2016). This purpose of creating 'a Western template' for SOE regulation is also shared by the EU in the context of the Transatlantic Trade and Investment Partnership (TTIP) (Griffith et al., 2017, p. 582).

The objective of this chapter is a preliminary analysis of the new SOE rules contained in Chapter 17 of the TPP agreement. We begin our argument by out-lining international economic rules in force governing SOEs such as the WTO Agreement in Section 2. Section 3 provides an overview of the major disciplines of SOEs stipulated in Chapter 17 of the TPP agreement. Section 4 develops an analysis of achievements and remaining issues in the chapter. Section 5 pro-vides guidance for prospective parties on implementing the SOE rules upon their accession to the TPP agreement. Section 6 describes developments after the US withdrawal from the TPP agreement, and the implication of the new accord concluded by 11 countries for the SOE rules. Finally, Section 7 concludes our arguments with an overall estimation of the new TPP SOE disciplines and their implications for future trade negotiations.

2. International economic rules governing SOEs

Several trade agreements provide international rules governing SOEs. Under the WTO framework, the General Agreement on Tariffs and Trade (specifically, Arti-cles III and XVII), the Agreement on Subsidies and Countervailing Measures (SCM Agreement), and the Agreement on Government Procurement impose some discipline on SOEs' discriminatory behaviour and governments' practice of providing unfair competitive advantages (subsidies and preferential regulatory treatment) to SOEs in the area of trade in goods. With respect to trade in ser-vices, the General Agreement on Trade in Services (GATS) (specifically, Articles VIII and XVI, the Annex on Telecommunications, and the Fourth Protocol on Basic Telecommunications) fulfils a similar role (Kowalski et al., 2013).

Obligations under bilateral investment treaties and investment chapters in free trade agreements (FTAs) – such as the principle of fair and equitable treatment and provisions for expropriation – would be applied, through the general inter-national law principle of attribution, to SOEs acting with delegated government authority if they impinge on foreign investment. For instance, Article 9.2, para-graph 2(b) of the TPP agreement has codified such disciplines to some extent. Regarding SOEs as investors, the Organisation for Economic Co-operation and

Development (OECD) Code of Liberalisation of Capital Movements allows host countries to regulate investment by foreign investors for security reasons, while the International Monetary Fund's Santiago Principles and the OECD Declaration on Sovereign Wealth Funds and Recipient Country Policies regulate sovereign wealth funds' strategic investment activities overseas (Kawase, 2014; Li, 2015).

Furthermore, recently concluded FTAs to which the European Union (EU) or the US is a party incorporate the General Agreement on Tariffs and Trade and/or GATS provisions, and their investment chapters regulate SOEs' anti-competitive behaviour (Kawase, 2014). Also, the extraterritorial application of domestic competition law is useful in regulating foreign SOEs' anti-competitive behaviour in the domestic market, as was the case with the European Commission's Statement of Objections sent to Gazprom in 2015, notifying the Russian firm of its alleged breach of EU competition law (European Commission, 2015).

However, this patchwork of existing rules is not enough to address concerns about the competition-distorting effect of SOEs. For instance, ensuring the transparency of corporate information, such as business descriptions and financial information, is a prerequisite for regulating SOEs but is outside the purview of the existing rules. Also, suppose a company has launched operations in a foreign country by making a direct investment there and competes with a SOE from a third country in that market (as in the case where a Japanese company competes with a Chinese SOE in the Association of Southeast Asian Nations market); even if the SOE's investment and operations are subsidised by its home country, it is difficult to determine the existence of and regulate such subsidies. The OECD (2015) called for ensuring a 'level playing field' between public- and private-sector companies as a corporate governance guideline for SOEs, but this is nothing more than a soft-law instrument and its effective enforcement is not necessarily warranted.

Chapter 17 of the TPP agreement is counted on to fill such gaps. Section 3 provides an overview of the chapter's major provisions.

3. Overview of chapter 17 of the TPP agreement

3.1. *Definitions and the scope of application*

A SOE is an enterprise that is engaged in commercial activities in which a TPP party (i) directly owns more than 50 percent of the share capital, (ii) controls more than 50 percent of the voting rights, or (iii) holds the power to appoint a majority of members of the board of directors or any other equivalent management body. Chapter 17 is applicable not only to SOEs but also to designated monopolies, that is, government- or privately owned enterprises designated by the government of a party as the sole provider or purchaser of a good or service. Privately owned monopolies designated as such before the TPP entered into force are excluded (Articles 17.1 and 17.2.1).

Certain types of organisations and their activities are granted a blanket exemption from the application of the chapter. These include the performance of regulatory or supervisory activities and the conduct of monetary and related credit policy and exchange rate policy by a central bank or monetary authority (Article 17.2.2), the exercise of regulatory or supervisory authority by a financial regulatory body (Article 17.2.3), activities for the resolution of a failing or failed financial institution (Article 17.2.4), government procurement (Article 17.2.7), and governmental functions (Article 17.2.8).

Also, a set of core obligations under the chapter (Articles 17.4, 17.6, and 17.10) does not apply to any service supplied in the exercise of governmental authority (Article 17.2.10).[4] Furthermore, sovereign wealth funds (Article 17.2.5) and independent pension funds and enterprises owned or controlled by them (Article 17.2.6) are also excluded from the application of the chapter, except for some provisions for non-commercial assistance (Articles 17.6.1 and 17.6.3).

In addition to the previous exemptions, each party to the TPP can claim party-specific exemptions. First, the activities of SOEs or designated monopolies stated in each country's schedule of non-conforming activities (Annex IV) are exempt from the application of Articles 17.4 and 17.6 (Article 17.9.1, except for Japan and Singapore).[5] Second, subject to the condition that further negotiations will be commenced within 5 years of the date of entry into force of the TPP to narrow the scope of exemptions (Article 17.14 and Annex 17-C[a]), the sub-central SOEs and designated monopolies listed in Annex 17-D are granted a blanket exemption from the application of Articles 17.4–17.6 and 17.10 (Article 17.9, except for Brunei and Singapore). Third, the obligation to ensure non-discriminatory treatment (Articles 17.4.1[b], 17.4.1[c], 17.4.2[b], and 17.4.2[c]) does not apply to purchases and sales by SOEs and designated monopolies pursuant to measures set out in schedules of cross-border trade in services and investment non-conforming measures (Annexes I and II) (Article 17.2.11). Last, Singapore has secured exemption from a set of core obligations under the chapter for SOEs owned or controlled by sovereign wealth funds, such as Temasek Holdings (Annex 17-E), whereas Malaysia has obtained exemption from the entire chapter for some activities of certain SOEs, such as those of a pilgrimage fund (Annex 17-F).

Other exemptions from specific obligations will be explained in the context of their relationships with the respective obligations.

3.2. Commercial considerations and non-discriminatory treatment

A core obligation under Chapter 17 is to ensure that SOEs and designated monopolies act in accordance with commercial considerations in their purchase or sale of goods and services (Articles 17.4.1[a] and 17.4.2[a]). 'Commercial considerations' means the terms and conditions of purchase or sale of goods and services, such as price and quality, and other factors that would normally be taken into account in the commercial decisions of a privately owned enterprise (Article 17.1).

Parties are also obliged to ensure that SOEs and designated monopolies treat the goods, services, and enterprises of another party on a non-discriminatory basis (most-favoured-nation and national treatment). Each party must ensure non-discriminatory treatment by its SOEs (i) between a good or a service imported from another party and a like good or a like service supplied domestically or imported from any other party that is not the one aforementioned (hereinafter referred to as a 'third party') or any non-party, and (ii) between a good or a service supplied by an enterprise established within its territory by investment from another party ('enterprise that is a covered investment') and a like good or a like service supplied in the relevant market in its territory by domestic enterprises or enterprises established by investment from any third party or non-party in purchasing goods and services. Also, each party must guarantee non-discriminatory treatment by its SOEs (i) between an enterprise of another party and its domestic enterprises or enterprises of any third party or of any non-party, and (ii) between an enterprise established within its territory by investment from another party and enterprises established within its territory by domestic investment or investment from any third party or any non-party in the relevant market within its territory in selling goods and services (Articles 17.4.1[b] and 17.4.1[c]).

Parties are also obliged to ensure non-discriminatory treatment by designated monopolies in the same manner, with respect to their purchase and sale of goods and services on which they are allowed to have a monopoly (Articles 17.4.2[b] and 17.4.2[c]). In addition, designated monopolies are prohibited from using their monopoly position to engage in anti-competitive practices in any market in which they are not allowed to have a monopoly (Article 17.4.2[d]). A good example is that of a designated monopoly in telecommunications internally subsidising its own production and sales of cellular phones (Matsushita, 2017, p. 194).

It should be noted that these provisions do not necessarily preclude SOEs and designated monopolies from purchasing or selling goods or services on different terms and conditions, including those relating to prices, or refusing to purchase or sell goods or services, provided that such transactions are in accordance with commercial considerations (Article 17.4.3).

However, the obligations under Article 17.4 are subject not only to the blanket exceptions and exemptions set out in (i) earlier, but also to those specific thereto. No provisions of Article 17.4 apply to any party with respect to temporary measures taken to respond to a national or global economic emergency (Article 17.13.1) or to any SOE or designated monopoly if its annual revenue from commercial activities was less than 200 million Special Drawing Rights (SDR) in any one of the three previous consecutive fiscal years (Article 17.13.5 and Annex 17-A). And as a partial exception or exemption, the obligation to ensure commercial considerations and non-discriminatory treatment (Article 17.4.1) does not apply in the case where a SOE supplies financial services in support of trade or investment pursuant to a government mandate, provided that such services meet certain requirements, such as compliance with the OECD Arrangement on Officially Supported Export Credits (Article 17.13.2). Also, in the case where a SOE provides a public service pursuant to a government mandate (direct or indirect supply of a service to the general public, Article 17.1), the obligation to ensure commercial considerations does not apply (Article 17.4.1[a]), insofar as the SOE does not discriminate against any enterprise established by investment from another party (Article 17.4.1[c][ii]).

3.3. Restrictions on non-commercial assistance

As explained in Section I, the ongoing concerns over SOEs centre on the competition-distorting effect of government assistance that is backed by an abundance of state-owned capital. More specifically, such government assistance is provided mainly in the form of financial assistance to SOEs, such as subsidies, loans, and credit guarantees, and Chapter 17 includes provisions that restrict this 'non-commercial assistance'.

The chapter defines non-commercial assistance as 'assistance to a state-owned enterprise by virtue of that state-owned enterprise's government ownership or control'. Here, 'assistance' means (i) direct transfers of funds or potential direct transfers of funds or liabilities, such as grants or debt forgiveness, loans, loan guarantees, or other types of financing on terms more favourable than those commercially available; or (ii) goods and services other than general infrastructure on terms more favourable than those commercially available. The term 'by virtue of that state-owned enterprise's government ownership or control' refers to a situation where a SOE receives materially favourable treatment as a subject of government assistance or where government assistance is available only to the SOE (Article 17.1).

3.3.1. Prohibition of adverse effects

Non-commercial assistance provided to a SOE directly or indirectly by a party (including cases in which such assistance is provided by a non-SOE entrusted or directed by the government) or by its public enterprises or SOEs must not cause adverse effects to the interests of other parties with respect to the (i) production and sale of a good by the SOE, (ii) supply of a service by the SOE from the territory of the party into the territory of another party, and (iii) supply of a service in the territory of another party through an enterprise established in the territory of that other party or any third party by investment from the party (Articles 17.6.1 and 17.6.2). And adverse effects that the provision of a service by a SOE of a party may cause in the market of a non-party are subject to further negotiations within 5 years of the date of entry into force of the TPP agreement on extending the application of Articles 17.6 and 17.7 (Article 17.14 and Annex 17C[a]).

Although Article 17.7.1 sets out seven types of adverse effects, they can be broadly classified into two categories. Adverse effects in the first category are those that arise by displacing or impeding from its market imports or sales of a like good. Adverse effects are deemed to arise if a good produced or sold by a party's SOE that has received non-commercial assistance (i) displaces or impedes from its market imports of a like good from another party or sales of a like good produced by an enterprise established within its territory by investment from another party (Article 17.7.1[a]), (ii) displaces or impedes from the market of another party sales of a like good produced by an enterprise established within the territory of such other party by investment from any third party or imports of a like good of any third party (Article 17.7.1[b][i]), or (iii) displaces or impedes from the market of a non-party imports of a like good of another party (Article 17.7.1[b][ii]).

Adverse effects are also deemed to arise if a service supplied by a party's SOE that has received non-commercial assistance displaces or impedes from the market of another party a like service supplied by an enterprise of such other party or of any third party (Article 17.7.1[d]). A determination of such displacement or impediment is based on whether there is a significant change in relative shares of the market (Article 17.7.2).

Adverse effects in the second category arise in the form of significant price undercutting, price suppression, price depression, or lost sales. Such adverse effects are deemed to arise if a good produced or sold by a party's SOE that has received non-commercial assistance causes such effects (i) in its market as compared to a like product imported from another party or produced by an enterprise that is a covered investment from another party in its territory (Article 17.7.1[c][i]), or (ii) in the market of any non-party as compared to a like good imported from another party (Article 17.7.1[c][ii]).

Adverse effects are also deemed to arise if a service supplied by a party's SOE that has received non-commercial assistance causes such effects in the market of another party as compared to a like service supplied by an enterprise of such other party or of any third party (Article 17.7.1[e]).

3.3.2. Prohibition of injury

When a party has a SOE that has invested in another party and provides non-commercial assistance to the SOE to help with the production and sale of a good in the market of such other party, the good produced and sold by the SOE may compete with a like good produced and sold by the relevant domestic industry of such other party (host country) in its market. In such a case, the non-commercial assistance provided to the SOE must not cause injury or threat thereof to the host country's domestic industry (Article 17.6.3).

The term 'injury' here means material injury or threat of material injury to a domestic industry or material retardation of the establishment of such an industry (Article 17.8.1; see Article 17.8.5 for the definition of 'threat of material injury'). A determination of injury is based on the examination of various factors, including the volume of production by the SOE that has received non-commercial assistance, the effect of such production on prices for like goods in the host country's market, the impact on the domestic industry of the host country (e.g. decline in output, sales, and market share; negative effects on cash flow and inventories), and the causal relationship between the goods produced by the SOE and the injury to the domestic industry (Articles 17.8.2–17.8.4).

3.3.3. Exceptions and exemptions

Again, there are exceptions specific to Article 17.6 apart from the blanket exemptions explained in Section 1. The economic emergency exception (Article 17.13.1) and exception for SOEs with an annual commercial revenue of less than SDR200 million (Article 17.13.5 and Annex 17-A), discussed in Section 2, are applied to obtain an exemption from all of the obligations under Article 17.6. Also, an enterprise located outside the territory of a party over which a SOE has assumed temporary ownership as a consequence of foreclosure in connection with defaulted debt or payment of an insurance claim by the SOE is outside the scope of application of Article 17.6 (Article 17.13.4).

A partial exemption similar to the one discussed in Section 2 that exempts the supply of trade- or investment-related financial services from the application of Article 17.4 (Article 17.13.2) is provided separately to obtain an exemption from the prohibition of the supply of services causing adverse effects (Articles 17.6.1[b], 17.6.1[c], 17.6.2[b], and 17.6.2[c]) insofar as a party (host country) requires the local presence of another party's SOE that provides trade- or investment-related financial services in its territory (Article 17.13.3). And a service supplied by a SOE of a party within its territory is deemed not to cause adverse effects (Article 17.6.4). Furthermore, non-commercial assistance provided before the signing of the TPP agreement or that provided within 3 years after the signing of the TPP agreement pursuant to a law enacted or contractual obligation undertaken prior to the signing of the TPP agreement are also deemed not to have adverse effects (Article 17.7.5).

3.4. Ensuring transparency

As often pointed out about Chinese SOEs, there is a general lack of transparency regarding the status of activities of SOEs. The US has included a transparency clause as part of SOE provisions under its FTAs, but the disciplines provided for in Chapter 17 are more detailed. Within 6 months after the entry into force of the TPP agreement, each party must make a list of its SOEs and designated monopolies publicly available on its official website or provide it to the other parties (Articles 17.10.1 and 17.10.2). Also, upon request from another party, a party must provide information concerning a specific SOE or designated monopoly (e.g. the percentage of shares owned by the government, the government titles of any government official serving as an officer or member of the board, annual revenue and total assets over the most recent 3-year period), and information regarding any government policy or programme for non-commercial assistance (e.g. the form and amount of the non-commercial assistance and the names of the agencies providing the non-commercial assistance) (Articles 17.10.3–17.10.7).

Obligations under Article 17.10 are subject to the exceptions and exemptions discussed in Section 1 as well as to the exemption for SOEs with an annual revenue of SDR200 million (Article 17.13.5 and Annex 17-A). Measures listed in party-specific schedules (Annex IV) are exempted only from the application of

Articles 17.4 and 17.6, with the exception of Brunei, Malaysia, and Viet Nam for which all or part of the obligations under Article 17.10 do not apply to specific items listed in their respective schedules (Notes 26, 27, and 30 to Chapter 17). Also, these three countries are provided with a grace period of 5 years from the entry into force of the TPP agreement to undertake the obligations under Article 17.10.1, provided that they meet certain requirements (Notes 28 and 29 to Chapter 17).

4. Analysis and assessment

4.1. Expansion of disciplines

Chapter 17 contains detailed disciplines on SOEs. First, regarding the obligation to ensure that SOEs and designated monopolies act in accordance with commercial considerations, similar provisions are set forth, for instance, in Article 12.3 of the US–Singapore FTA. However, the chapter goes further than existing FTAs in that it defines specific types of relevant markets and for each one sets out detailed non-discrimination obligations in trade in goods and services and in the treatment of any enterprise that is a covered investment (Articles 17.4.1[b], 17.4.1[c], 17.4.2[b], and 17.4.2[c]). These provisions partially overlap with, for instance, General Agreement on Tariffs and Trade Articles I and III.4, GATS Articles II and XVII, and the principle of non-discrimination and of fair and equitable treatment under investment treaties, but are expected to be far more effective as they explicitly prohibit discriminatory behaviour by SOEs.[6]

As for disciplines on non-commercial assistance provided by SOEs, the SCM Agreement requires a complainant to prove the characterisation of a SOE as a public body or establish the fact that the SOE has been entrusted or directed by the government with respect to the provision of non-commercial assistance (chapeau and item (iv) of Article 1.1(a)(1) of the SCM Agreement), and it is not easy to provide such proof as required by the Appellate Body of the WTO.[7] In this regard, Chapter 17 can be seen as 'WTO-plus' by virtue of allowing disciplines similar to those under the SCM Agreement to be directly imposed on SOEs that provide injury-causing non-commercial assistance. This reduces costs of 'the threshold matter of whether the rule applied to a certain entity' (Kim, 2017, p. 255).

Most important, the scope of disciplines on non-commercial assistance has been expanded to cover subsidies in trade in services and investment, which have been outside the purview of the WTO. Subsidies for the production, sale, and export of goods by domestic companies have been subject to the rules and disciplines of the WTO's SCM Agreement. However, rules for subsidies in trade in services are under negotiation as part of the WTO Doha Round in accordance with the mandate provided in GATS Article XV, and the talks remain stalled. Rules for home country governments' subsidies to overseas investments have been non-existent in the first place.[8] Chapter 17 is designed to address problems arising from the increasingly globalised business operations by SOEs in particular, in that it expands the scope of disciplines to include assistance to SOEs established by investment in a third party. For these reasons, the non-commercial assistance rules in Chapter 17 merits praise for being 'innovative' (Sylvestre Fleury and Marcoux, 2016).

4.2. Problems and remaining issues

At the same time, however, there is no denying that the disciplines provided in Chapter 17 have problems. The following paragraphs explain several issues that remain unaddressed.

4.2.1. Narrow scope of application and large number of exceptions

First, Chapter 17's definition of a SOE is very narrow and fails to cover enterprises that are effectively government controlled (Willemyns, 2016, p. 666). Even without ownership of, or control over, majority stocks, voting rights, or board-of-director members in an enterprise, there are various means for a party government to exercise its influence over business decisions of the enterprise. These include, interlocking directorates, indirect control through ownership of the enterprise held by another company owned by the government, and even minority share in a situation where the stockholders of the enterprise are widely dispersed (Kim, 2017, pp. 257–258; Matsushita, 2017, pp. 200–201). In China, even formal ownership would not be necessary for the government for this purpose. The Government of China can control its SOEs by Communist Party cells within each of them, and through a dense network of connections and personal relationships between SOEs' managers and political elites ('Networked Hierarchy') (European Commission, 2017, pp. 27–31, 86–87).

In this regard, an approach taken by the US–Singapore FTA has drawn the authors' attention. Under the FTA, an enterprise in which the government has 'effective influence', whose annual revenue is or total assets are greater than 50 million Singapore dollars,[9] and in which the government owns a special voting share with veto rights relating to important matters – such as the appointment of directors and senior officers and the acquisition by any third person of shares therein – are a 'covered entity' and subject to the disclosure requirement (Articles 12.3.2(g) and 12.8.1 of the US – Singapore FTA). A 'government enterprise' subject to the other substantive obligations, including assurance for the SOE's conduct in accordance with commercial consideration, is defined as 'an enterprise in which that party has effective influence' (Articles 12.8.5 and 12.8.6 of the US–Singapore FTA). 'Effective influence' is deemed to exist, not only where the government owns more than 50 percent of the voting rights, but also even where the government owns 50 percent or less of the voting rights if it has the ability to exercise substantial influence over executive appointments or other important management decisions. Regarding the latter case, if the government owns more than 20 percent of the voting rights that constitute the largest block thereof, there is a rebuttable presumption that effective influence exists. Also, for the purpose of applying this

20 percent threshold, voting rights owned by the government are not limited to those directly owned by the government but include those owned by SOEs and enterprises owned by SOEs (Article 12.8.5 and Annex 12A of the US–Singapore FTA). These criteria enable the US–Singapore FTA to cover a far wider scope of enterprises compared with Chapter 17, which defines a SOE as an enterprise in which a government directly owns more than 50 percent of shares or voting rights, or which holds the power to appoint the majority of board of directors members (Article 17.1) and exempts SOEs with an annual revenue from commercial activities of less than SDR200 million (Article 17.13.5 and Annex 17-A).[10]

The draft chapter of the Japan–EU EPA, signed on 17 July 2018, is another good example of a control-based SOE definition. The definition in Article 1 of the draft chapter, disclosed in December 2017, refers to governmental 'power to legally direct the actions of the enterprise or otherwise exercises an equivalent degree of control in accordance with its laws and regulations', in addition to the same three elements as those found in the TPP's SOE definition. It is also notable that some Investor–State Dispute Settlement (ISDS) tribunals have focused on functions and activities of an enterprise in question, rather than its structural aspects including ownership, in considering if the enterprise acts as a state organ.[11] These awards imply that we can explore the possibility of a function/activity-based SOE definition.

In addition to the narrow definition of a SOE, the chapter provides for exceptions and exemptions, and it includes party-specific schedules that allow for a broad range of exceptions. These impose additional limitations on effective control over SOEs by the TPP parties (Willemyns, 2016, pp. 666, 673–674; Kim, 2017, pp. 259–261). On the other hand, one observer argued that they are necessary because the TPP parties have accepted the innovative rules in Chapter 17, compared with much simpler ones in earlier FTAs (Sylvestre Fleury and Marcoux, 2016, pp. 461).

4.2.2. Lack of discipline on government ownership and involvement

Chapter 17 has no provisions that would require parties to reduce government ownership and involvement. In contrast, the US–Singapore FTA prohibits the exercise of government influence over decisions by SOEs (Article 12.3.2[e]). In addition, it includes a unilateral obligation requiring only Singapore to continue to reduce its aggregate ownership in SOEs (Article 12.3.2[f]). A study by the OECD points out that stable ownership by a government (captive equity) absolves SOEs from pressure to pay dividends, which could become a source of anti-competitive activities and unfair competitive advantage (Capobianco and Christiansen, 2011, pp. 6–7).

4.2.3. Insufficient disciplines on preferential regulatory treatment

According to the OECD study, sources of competitive advantage for SOEs are not limited to the non-commercial assistance restricted by Chapter 17, that is, subsidies, but include preferential regulatory treatment (in disclosure requirements, environmental regulations, antimonopoly law enforcement, zoning regulations, etc.) and exemptions from bankruptcy rules (Capobianco and Christiansen, 2011, pp. 6–7). The chapter does not include adequate provisions to address these preferential measures. The principle of non-discrimination applies to SOEs' business activities but not beyond that, and the chapter has no provision regulating preferential regulatory treatment by a party of its SOEs over competing foreign enterprises. Also, while Article 17.5.2 prohibits administrative bodies from providing preferential treatment to SOEs by exercising their regulatory discretion, this does not apply, for instance, in the case where a specific law or regulation explicitly provides for an exemption applicable solely to SOEs.

With respect to covered investment assets, the obligations to ensure national treatment (Article 9.6) and the minimum standard of treatment (Article 9.6) under the Investment Chapter provide some disciplines if there is any regulatory discrimination between enterprises that are covered investments and SOEs of the host country. However, if such obligations are to be enforced through an investor–state dispute-settlement system, the scope of disciplines is confined to cases where such discriminatory regulatory treatment has caused damage for which compensation can be claimed; the regulatory discrimination in question per se is not subject to the dispute-settlement procedure.

Chapter 17 also failed to refer to standard corporate governance in SOEs. Two of the recently concluded EU FTAs – the EU–Viet Nam FTA and the EU–Japan FTA – set out the parties' obligation to respect internationally recognised standards of corporate governance in operation of their SOEs, including the OECD Guidelines on Corporate Governance of State-Owned Enterprises. A similar provision would be useful in Chapter 17 in terms of ensuring regulatory neutrality.

4.2.4. Lack of disciplines for ensuring rational investment behaviour

Chapter 17 exempts sovereign wealth funds entirely from its coverage and has no provisions for ensuring rational investment behaviour by other SOEs. The obligation to act in accordance with commercial considerations is applied only with respect to purchases and sales of goods and services, and not with respect to investment behaviour (Articles 17.4.1(a) and 17.4.2[a]). In its *2015 Report on Compliance by Major Trading Partners with Trade Agreements*, the Ministry of Economy, Trade and Industry (METI) of Japan expressed concerns about the rationality of SOEs' behaviour in securing an interest in or acquiring companies holding an interest in mineral resources and raw materials (METI, 2016, pp. 446–447). How to address such concerns has been left to be dealt with in the future.

4.2.5. Restrictions on non-commercial assistance and policy rationale

In China, the presence of SOEs has been aggravating overcapacity problems in heavy industries such as steel, cement, and chemicals, and structural adjustment of such industries may require a degree of assistance to help them dispose of excess facilities and reduce their workforce (EU Chamber of Commerce in China, 2016; Qi, 2014). Also, when assessed from the perspective of the need to address the problem of natural monopoly in network industries or of externalities in research and development, a degree of rationality is recognised in non-commercial assistance (Chang, 2007, pp. 8–14). However, Chapter 17 assesses the permissibility of non-commercial assistance based solely on its economic impact on the relevant market, giving no consideration to policy goals and the problem of externalities. Prompted by the awareness of such problems, the need to make amendments to the SCM Agreement has been discussed in recent years, but the chapter has failed to respond to those concerns (Horlick and Clarke, 2016).

4.2.6. Challenges in enforcing restrictions on non-commercial assistance

The provisions of Chapter 17 are enforceable through the designated dispute-settlement procedure. In particular, the wording of Articles 17.6 and 17.8 concerning non-commercial assistance is very similar to that of Articles 6 and 15 of the WTO's SCM Agreement. Therefore, a TPP dispute-settlement panel is expected to apply these provisions with reference to relevant precedents in WTO dispute-settlement decisions (Matsushita, 2017, pp. 195–197).

However, the settlement of a dispute over a subsidy involves the determination of facts based on an enormous volume of documentary evidence, including the determination of the existence of the subsidy, the calculation of the benefit to the recipient of the subsidy, and the assessment of injury and causal relationships. For example, extremely complex and voluminous panel reports were issued in two WTO disputes between the US and the EU over subsidies to Airbus and Boeing (about 800 pages from the US report and more than 1,000 pages from the EU report) and in another dispute over US subsidies to upland cotton (more than 2,000 pages including parties' submissions and evidence documents).[12] The TPP dispute-settlement mechanism provides very limited secretariat support for panel members (Article 27.6) and its procedures for collecting evidence for the determination of facts are simple compared with those provided for in Annex V of the SCM Agreement (Article 17.15 and Annex 17-B). It is questionable whether and to what extent the provisions similar to those under the SCM Agreement will be workable under the TPP framework.

4.2.7. Effectiveness of disciplines on transparency

Article 25 of the SCM Agreement requires that members notify the WTO of all subsidies, but this notification system does not function properly. In contrast, Chapter 17 requires parties to provide information on non-commercial assistance upon request from another party affected by the provision of such non-commercial assistance, rather than requiring unilateral notification. In this regard, the chapter has made some improvements on the SCM Agreement. However, because a country making such a request must explicitly show how the activities of the SOE in question and the non-commercial assistance thereto affect trade or investment between the two countries (chapeau of Articles 17.10.4 and 17.10.4), the country on the receiving side may refuse to respond if it finds any defects in the request. In the first place, if the non-commercial assistance in question is provided in secrecy, it would be difficult for other countries to identify which information should be disclosed with respect to the specific assistance measure.

5. Implication for future parties to TPP: to meet the requirements of SOE rules

While this chapter has so far pointed out insufficiencies of the current Chapter 17 of the TPP agreement, it by no means denies that the chapter is a giant step for effective international control over market distortion caused by anti-competitive behaviour of SOEs and has significant implications for future parties to the TPP agreement. Non-TPP ASEAN countries, such as Indonesia, the Philippines, and Thailand, have shown their interest in joining the TPP agreement even before its entry into force. It is obvious that Viet Nam's successful conclusion of the TPP agreement, despite their difficulty in SOE reforms, brought a sense of impending crisis to the aforementioned three countries that they might be left behind the larger global value chain to be available in the Asia-Pacific region. For these countries, Chapter 17 is a vehicle to transform their domestic economies into more efficient and market-oriented economies. Therefore, even after the US pulled out of the agreement, it is worthwhile for the prospective TPP parties to give serious consideration to accepting the set of the rules.

Before joining the TPP agreement, it would be useful for the prospective parties to simulate how to accept the rules in Chapter 17. Figure 9.1 briefly summarises this process. First, it is important to determine whether the enterprise in question meets the criteria of the definition of a SOE as set out in Article 17.1. If the enterprise is not assumed to be a SOE, there is no need for further examination. Second, if the enterprise is assumed to be a SOE, it is necessary to identify a concrete concern that the enterprise has with respect to commercial consideration and non-discriminatory treatment, non-commercial assistance, or transparency. At the same time, we must note that the SOE might be exempted from the disciplines designated in the chapter. Third, it should be clarified whether the SOE can be subject to the disciplines and whether it is difficult to modify conduct, laws, rules, and regulations that pertain to the SOE. Finally, the country-specific annex, or reservation list, is likely to allow the SOE to maintain the concerned behaviour and business practice as critical roles for fulfilling policy objectives. Yet whether the reservation list is available or not depends on negotiations amongst parties.

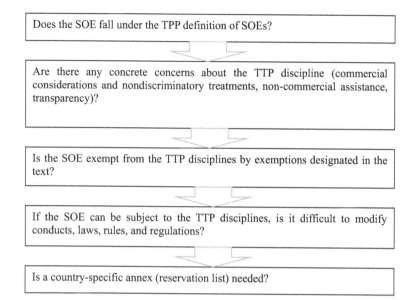

Figure 9.1 Flow chart of the examination of the Trans-Pacific Partnership discipline

Note:
SOE = state-owned enterprise
TPP = Trans-Pacific Partnership
Source: Authors.

6. The Comprehensive and Progressive Agreement for Trans-Pacific Partnership (CPTPP) and its impact on the SOE rule

Despite its leading role in the TPP negotiation, the US officially withdrew from the TPP framework on 23 January 2017 with the presidential order of Donald Trump, then newly elected, who insisted that the TPP would not serve US interests. Since then, and despite the US withdrawal, the other 11 parties have made tremendous efforts to maintain the fundamental framework of the TPP agreement. These efforts resulted in the signing of CPTPP in March 2018 in Santiago, Chile[13] and the scheduled signature of the CPTPP on 8 March 2018 in Chile.[14] The new accord incorporates the text of the original TPP agreement and, once enforced, will suspend 30 clauses in the incorporated agreement, including those in the intellectual properties and investment chapters. The rest of the agreement remains unchanged. The final package does not indicate any major change to Chapter 17.

The only suspension of SOE-related obligations is found in Item 2 of Malaysia's party-specific schedule of non-conforming SOE activities in Annex IV. Malaysia requested to retard the schedule for phasing down preferential purchasing of domestic goods and services by PETRONAS, a national petroleum SOE, which was originally scheduled to start after signature of the CPTPP. This phasing down is now due to start after entry into force of the agreement, which is expected to be in 2019.

7. Conclusion

As we have observed, the TPP's disciplines on SOEs are very limited in their scope of application, with various exceptions, and in some areas, they compare poorly with the US–Singapore FTA – one of the most recently concluded FTAs. Because of these, Chapter 17's direct impact on competitiveness of SOEs in the contracting parties could be limited.

In particular, the SOE provisions, fraught with multiple weakness, fall far short of the initial expectations of the US, which, at the time of negotiations, was hoping to discipline China (Scissors, 2015). It is clear that the TPP disciplines on SOEs failed to reach the level that the US Congress and the US business community behind it had hoped for. In this context, Senator Orrin Hatch, chair of the US Senate Finance Committee since 2015, was concerned about such defects in the SOE chapter immediately after conclusion of the TPP negotiation in the fall of 2015, and called on the administration to take appropriate steps to address the concerns before ratification. Hatch believed that Washington should seek agreement, particularly with Viet Nam, on specific plans for the implementation of Chapter 17. To that end, he proposed that the US negotiate a bilateral consistency plan for the implementation of the SOE provisions, in the same way as it did with Brunei, Malaysia, and Viet Nam with respect to the implementation of the labour chapter of the TPP agreement.[15] Although the anecdote in the US Congress seems irrelevant now that the US has withdrawn, it still shows eloquently the insufficiency of TPP Chapter 17 for the ultimate policy goal of achieving competitive neutrality in the Asia-Pacific region.

Nevertheless, some observers find Chapter 17 ground-breaking[16] and the fact that the TPP includes specific rules for SOEs is appreciated as a first step towards disciplining them (Larson, 2015). Also, given the politically sensitive nature of SOE issues, some believe that it was wise to take such a limited step (Elms, 2015). The SOE chapter will also serve to improve competitive environments in the Asia-Pacific region through other economic forums and trade negotiations.

Notes

1   China National Petroleum Corporation and Sinopec Group were ranked fourth and third, respectively, in the 2017 Fortune Global 500. China National Petroleum and Industrial and Commercial Bank of China were ranked sixth and ninth, respectively, in the latest *Financial Times'* 2015 Global 500.
2   See Coalition of Services Industries and the US Chamber of Commerce (2011). This report proposes that US TPP negotiators address the challenge of SOE issues in the way that the TPP commitments should include a package of addressing the practical market access and market distortion problems caused by government intervention in favour of SOEs and the actions of SOEs in the commercial market in the larger context of competitive neutrality.

3 *Inside U.S. Trade*, 29 September 2011.

4 A 'service supplied in the exercise of governmental authority' is defined as having the same meaning as the identical phrase in GATS Article I, paragraph 3(c) as well as in paragraph 1(b) of the General Agreement on Tariffs and Trade Annex on Financial Services under the framework of the WTO (note 11 to Chapter 17).

5 See Willemyns (2016, p. 674) for an overview of country-specific non-conforming activities.

6 These international agreements regulate only the behaviour of their parties, that is, sovereign states, and are unable to directly regulate any act by SOEs. To apply any provisions under these agreements to a SOE, it must be proven separately that the SOE is an integral part of the government of the party in question or that the government of the party is involved in the discriminatory acts of the SOE.

7 For instance, see Appellate Body Report, *United States – Definitive Anti-Dumping and Countervailing Duties on Certain Products from China*, pp. 282–322, WT/DS379/AB/R (11 March 2011) for the requirement for the proof of the former, and Appellate Body Report, *United States – Countervailing Duty Investigation on Dynamic Random Access Memory Semiconductors (DRAMS) from Korea*, pp. 108–116, WT/DS296/AB/R (27 June 2005) for that of the latter.

8 The coverage of subsidy disciplines under investment treaties is limited to cases where the government of a host country – not of a home country – treats its domestic companies – not a foreign enterprise that is a covered investment – by giving subsidies in a discriminatory manner. Furthermore, investment treaties concluded in recent years tend to exclude subsidies from all or part of disciplines. The Investment Chapter of the TPP agreement is no exception, exempting subsidies or grants from the obligations of most-favoured-nation treatment and national treatment as well as from the prohibition of requiring the appointment of a person of a particular nationality to a senior management position (Article 9.11.6[b]).

9 US$36,800,000 as of 7 July 2018 (S$1.00 = US$0.736).

10 US$151,200,000 as of 7 July 2018 (S$1.00 = US$0.736).

11 *BUCG v. Yemen* (Jurisdiction), pp. 31–47, ICSID Case No. Arb/14/30 (31 May 2017); *CSOB v. Slovak* (Jurisdiction), pp. 16–27, ICSID Case No. Arb/97/4 (24 May 1999).

12 *See* Panel Body Report, *United States – Measures Affecting Trade in Large Civil Aircraft (Second Complaint)*, WT/DS353/R (31 March 2011); Panel Report, *European Communities and Certain Member States – Measures Affecting Trade in Large Civil Aircraft*, WT/DS316/R (30 June 2010); Panel Report, *United States – Subsidies on Upland Cotton*, WT/DS267/ R (8 September 2004).

13 Related documents are available at www.international.gc.ca/trade-commerce/trade-agreements-accords-commerciaux/agr-acc/tpp-ptp/statement-declaration.aspx?lang=eng&_ga=2.239857219.1923031733.1510435660–1966312929.1510435660

14 This information is obtained from official release of the Japanese government (in Japanese). Available at www.cas.go.jp/jp/tpp/naiyou/pdf/tokyo1801/180123_tpp_tokyo_gaiyou.pdf

15 *Inside U.S. Trade*, 20 November 2015.

16 *Inside U.S. Trade*, 6 November 2015.

References

APEC (2016), 'Collective Strategic Study on Issues Related to the Realization of the FTAAP', Appendix 6 of 2016 CTI Report to Ministers, Committee on Trade and Investment, November. Available at www.apec.org/~/media/Files/Groups/CTI/2016/Appendix%2006%20-%20FTAAP%20Study.pdf

APEC (2017), 'FTTAP Capacity Building Workshop on FTA Negotiation Skills on Competition Under the 2nd REI CBNI', Committee on Trade and Investment, Ho Chi Minh City, Viet Nam, 19 August. Available at www.apec.org/Publications/2017/10/FTTAP-Capacity-Building-Workshop-on-FTA-Negotiation-Skills-on--Competition-under-the-2nd-REI-CBNI

Bremmer, I. (2011), *The End of the Free Market: Who Wins the War between States and Corporations?* New York, NY: Portfolio.

Capobianco, A. and H. Christiansen (2011), 'Competitive Neutrality and State-owned Enterprises: Challenges and Policy Options', *OECD Corporate Governance Working Paper Series* No. 1. Paris: OECD. Available at http://dx.doi.org/10.1787/5kg9xfgjdhg6-en

Chang, H. (2007), 'State-Owned Enterprise Reform', in *United Nations Department of Economic and Social Affairs Policy Notes.* New York, NY: United Nations. Available at http://esa.un.org/techcoop/documents/pn_soereformnote.pdf

Coalition of Services Industries and US Chamber of Commerce (2011), 'State-Owned Enterprises: Correcting a 21st Century Market Distortion', Global Services Summit: Engaging the Dynamic Asian Economies. Washington, DC, 20 July. Available at www.esf.be/new/wp-content/uploads/2011/09/Global-Services-Summit-2011-Paper-on-21st-Century-Trade-Issues.pdf

Elms, D. (2015), 'TPP Impressions: Competition and State Owned Enterprises (SOEs)', *Talking Trade Blog* (blog), Asian Trade Center. Available at www.asiantradecentre.org/talkingtrade/2015/11/17/tpp-impressions-competition-and-state-owned-enterprises-soes

European Commission (2015), Press Release, 'Commission sends Statement of Objections to Gazprom for Alleged Abuse of Dominance on Central and Eastern European Gas Supply Markets', IP/15/4828, 22 April. Available at http://europa.eu/rapid/press-release_IP-15-4828_en.htm

European Commission (2017), *Commission Staff Working Document on Significant Distortions in the Economy of the People's Republic of China for the Purposes of Trade Investigations*, SWD (2017) 483 final/2, 20 December. Available at https://ec.europa.eu/transparency/regdoc/rep/other/SWD-2017-483-F2-EN-0-0.pdf

European Union Chamber of Commerce in China (2016), *Overcapacity in China: An Impediment to the Party's Reform Agenda.* Beijing: European Union Chamber of Commerce in China.

Ferguson, V. (2017), 'Why China Won't Save the TPP', *East Asia Forum*, 11 February. Available at www.eastasiaforum.org/2017/02/11/why-china-wont-save-the-tpp/

Griffith, M.K., R.H. Steinberg and J. Zysman (2017), 'From Great Power Politics to a Strategic Vacuum: Origins and Consequences of the TPP and TTIP', *Business and Politics*, 19(4), pp. 573–592.

Horlick, G. and P.A. Clarke (2016), 'Rethinking Subsidy Disciplines for the Future', *E15 Task Force on Rethinking International Subsidies Disciplines – Policy Options Paper: The E15 Initiative.* Geneva: International Centre for Trade and Sustainable Development and World Economic Forum. Available at http://e15initiative.org/wp-content/uploads/2015/09/E15_ICTSD_Rethinking_Subsidy_Disciplines_Future_report_2016_1102.pdf

Kawase, T. (2014), 'Trans-Pacific Partnership Negotiations and Rulemaking to Regulate State-Owned Enterprises', *VoxEU.org*, 29 July. Available at www.voxeu.org/article/trans-pacific-partnership-negotiations-and-rulemaking-regulate-state-owned-enterprises

Kim, M. (2017), 'Regulating the Visible Hands: Development of Rules on State-Owned Enterprises in Trade Agreements', *Harvard International Law Journal*, 58(1).

Kowalski, P., M. Büge, M. Sztajerowska and M. Egeland (2013), 'State-Owned Enterprises: Trade Effects and Policy Implications', *OECD Trade Policy Papers* No. 147. Paris: OECD. Available at http://dx.doi.org/10.1787/5k4869ckqk7l-en

Larson, A. (2015), 'TPP Delivers Only Glancing Blow to State-Owned Enterprises', *Law360*, 17 November. Available at www.law360.com/articles/727904/tpp-delivers-only-glancing-blow-to-state-owned-enterprises

Li, J. (2015), 'State-Owned Enterprises in the Current Regime of Investor-State Arbitration', in S. Lalani and R. Polanco Lazo (eds.), *The Role of the State in Investor-State Arbitration*. Leiden: Brill/Nijhoff.

Matsushita, M. (2017), 'State-Owned Enterprises in the TPP Agreement', in J. Chaisse, H. Gao and C. Lo (eds.), *Paradigm Shift in International Economic Law Rule-Making: TPP as a New Model for Trade Agreements?* Singapore: Springer.

METI (2016), *2016 Report on Compliance by Major Trading Partners with Trade Agreements – WTO, EPA/FTA and IIA*. Tokyo: METI.

OECD (2015), *OECD Guidelines on Corporate Governance of State-owned Enterprises*, 2015 ed. Paris: OECD Publishing.

Qi, L. (2014), 'China to Offer Subsidies to Firms Hit by Overcapacity: Funds Will Help Companies Compensate Workers, Cover Closing Costs', *Wall Street Journal (Online)*, 7 May. Available at www.wsj.com/articles/SB10001424052702303417104579546870229922790

Scissors, D. (2015), 'TPP: A Bronze-standard Free Trade Agreement (Go for Gold)', *AEIdeas* (blog), 12 November. Available at www.aei.org/publication/tpp-a-bronze-standard-free-trade-agreement-go-for-gold/

Sylvestre Fleury, J. and J. Marcoux (2016), 'The US Shaping of State-Owned Enterprise Disciplines in the Trans-Pacific Partnership', *Journal of International Economic Law*, 19(2), pp. 445–465.

USTR (United States Trade Representative) (2017), 'Summary of Objectives for the NAFTA Renegotiation', 17 July. Available at https://ustr.gov/about-us/policy-offices/press-office/press-releases/2017/july/ustr-releases-nafta-negotiating

Willemyns, I. (2016), 'Disciplines on State-Owned Enterprises in International Economic Law: Are We Moving in the Right Direction?', *Journal of International Economic Law*, 19(3), pp. 561–588.

10 TPP and state-owned enterprises in Viet Nam

Vo Tri Thanh

1. Introduction

State-owned enterprises (SOEs) assume important roles in various countries, including developed, emerging, and low-income economies. Despite privatisation (also called equitisation in some countries), SOEs remain a key force in industries such as finance, infrastructure, manufacturing, energy, and mining. Such importance is rooted on their government's long-standing attempts at driving industrial development, correcting market failures, or fulfilling other socio-economic mandates.

In Viet Nam, SOEs have endured even in the midst of the country's transition from a central planning regime. Their presence is reflected in their large number, their major shares in various sectors, as well as their more likely intervention in the policymaking process compared with their counterparts in the private sector. Although SOEs still received preferential treatment, their performance has generally lagged behind that of private companies. Therefore, Viet Nam had to embark on SOE reforms since 1980s using a range of measures such as equitisation, sale, transfer, assignment, or dissolution.

Since 2006, after achieving some concrete progress, SOEs entered an important stage where the target of reforms centred on major corporations and state business groups. By this time, however, the SOE reforms had slowed down and became less meaningful. More important, the linkage between SOEs and the in-charge government ministries weakened the neutrality of policies as well as the momentum of SOE reforms.

In this context, Viet Nam needs an external boost for SOE reforms. The TPP comes in as one of these drivers. In fact, TPP and the EU-Vietnam Free Trade Agreement (EVFTA) are the first major FTAs that incorporate their commitment towards helping SOEs. At the same time, the benefits of reforms to SOEs – such as improved access to most major markets in the Asia Pacific – are enough reasons for SOEs to subject themselves to such reforms.

This chapter attempts to investigate the implications of the SOE Chapter of the TPP Agreement on Viet Nam. Specifically, the chapter seeks to (i) interpret the SOE chapter of the TPP agreement from an economic-legal perspective by comparing the related legal framework and other investment agreements in effect in Viet Nam; (ii) analyse the short-term and long-term (potential) impacts of TPP on the Vietnamese economy, with focus on the SOE issues; (iii) analyse the new rules and regulations set by the TPP agreement that could be *de facto* global standard of international trade and investment; and (iv) make policy recommendations on the promotion of economic integration, trade, and investment in ASEAN and East Asia.

The remainder of this chapter is structured as follows: Section 2 summarises the key commitments of Viet Nam under the SOE chapter of the TPP. Section 3 elaborates on the potential impacts of the TPP on SOE reforms in Viet Nam. Section 4 concludes with some policy recommendations.

2. Commitments under SOE chapter

2.1. Considerations

Prior to the TPP and EVFTA, Viet Nam's international commitments were largely under the framework of the World Trade Organization (WTO), which has not stipulated sufficiently stringent disciplines imposed on SOEs. Thus, Viet Nam was exposed only to fairly weak discipline under the WTO against providing preferential policy treatment for SOEs.

Under the General Agreement on Tariffs and Trade (GATT) 1994, state trading enterprises have been defined as any enterprise, regardless of its ownership, with some exclusive or special privileges in export and/or import trading. The GATT requires that state trading enterprises (i) act in a manner consistent with the general principles of non-discriminatory treatment under the GATT, and (ii) make purchases solely in accordance with commercial considerations relating to factors such as price, quality, availability, and marketability.

Given that SOEs are granted preferential treatment in terms of finance, free input provisions, and/or input provisions at lower prices than the prevailing market price, three groups of articles and commitments tend to challenge SOE practices in Viet Nam.

First, an SOE will be checked against the commercial and non-discriminatory principles in Article XVII of GATT 1994.

Second, Article VI and Article XVI of GATT 1994 and Article 1, 27.13 and 29 of the Agreement on Subsidy and Countervailing Measures do not rule out subsidies for SOEs. Nonetheless, the subsidies for SOEs actionable under GATT and the Subsidy and Countervailing Measures Agreement do not apply to trade in services and investment (Le, 2015). Under WTO, thus, the regulations/commitments related to financial support to SOEs that is linked to trade in service or investment, are absent.

Third, upon calculating the value of Vietnamese subsidies, including but not limited to those available to Vietnamese SOEs, importing members can legitimately use the non-market economy method or the surrogate country technique. As of July 2017, Viet Nam is not yet recognised as a full market economy by major partners such as the United States, European Union, and so forth. Accordingly, the costs of a similar operation in a reference market economy may be used as the basis to calculate the value of subsidies. Because the costs in Viet Nam are generally lower than in other acknowledged market economies, the estimated effort of subsidy could be larger than the actual impact on trade, thereby increasing the probability of Vietnamese enterprises losing international anti-dumping lawsuits.

The SOEs in Viet Nam actually benefit from a range of policy supports. For instance, SOEs are perceived as better engaged in the nation's policymaking process, which puts them at an advantage over the private sector. Also, overdue tax obligations of SOEs may be waived – a practice not available to its private sector counterparts. These treatments weaken the competitiveness of private enterprises. In the absence of relevant reforms and because of the excessive (and poorly justified) support given to SOEs, Viet Nam could, in the process, bring about inadequately developed private enterprises.

The TPP provides a stronger requirement in the area of SOEs and designated monopolies (hereinafter referred to as SOE Chapter). Negotiation of the SOE Chapter is, by no means, a walk in the park. By July 2015, such negotiation was still considered a major challenge, given the wide range of definitions of SOEs (in fact, SOEs, state trading enterprises, government-owned enterprises can be used interchangeably) and the importance of these enterprises in certain economies[1] (such as Viet Nam, Malaysia, Mexico). In that context, the conclusion of TPP cemented the momentum for more concrete SOE reforms in Viet Nam.

2.2. Specific commitments under the SOE chapter

Here are the observed elements of the agreed SOE Chapter:

2.2.1. Scope of agreement (i.e. SOEs that are regulated by the SOE Chapter)

The SOE Chapter refers to enterprises owned or controlled by the Vietnamese government, which has at least 50 percent ownership, or 50 percent voting rights or power to appoint majority of the board of directors or its similar body. These enterprises must have commercial activities, competition with other enterprises, and meaningful scale (based on revenues in the last 3 years).

The chapter excludes (i) operations of the Central Bank (i.e. the State Bank of Vietnam), supervisory and management agencies over monetary and financial aspects, (ii) sovereign wealth funds, (iii) government procurement, (iv) export credit of SOEs, and (v) exemptions that are listed in other chapters (e.g. in investment, cross-border trade in services, financial services).

As exceptions under Article 17.3, Viet Nam and other TPP member states can exercise all necessary measures without violating the obligations in the chapters that dealt with (i) national security, (ii) temporary economic emergency, and (iii) SOEs whose function is purely to provide goods and services to the State.

Finally, Article 17.4 (Non-discriminatory Treatment and Commercial Considerations), Article 17.6 (Non-commercial Assistance), Article 17.10 (Transparency) and Article 17.12 (Committee on State-Owned Enterprises and Designated Monopolies) shall not apply to a SOE or designated monopoly whose annual revenue from commercial activities in any one of three consecutive fiscal years was less than the threshold amount calculated based on Annex 17-A. Five years after TPP's entry into force, the threshold is determined at SDR200 million, equivalent to about 6.323 trillion Vietnamese dong (VND) or US$282.0 million.[2] Within 5 years after TPP's entry into force, the threshold for Viet Nam is SDR500 million, or VND15.8 trillion or US$705 million.

2.2.2. Key obligations of SOEs

First, SOEs must operate on the basis of purely commercial considerations. Unless the SOEs undertake a public service task or are state-designated monopolies in certain markets, their decision should be based on commercial criteria such as price, quality, availability, marketability, and transportation. In such case, SOEs' decision-making process is not much different from that of non-state enterprises. It is worth noting that even in the absence of TPP, Vietnamese SOEs still have to expose to purely commercial considerations under WTO.

Second, SOEs must be non-discriminatory when selling or procuring goods and services. To be more specific, SOEs – particularly designated monopolies – are prohibited from undertaking discriminatory measures when buying from or supplying to enterprises in another TPP member/nation.

Viet Nam made these commitments upon joining the WTO (but restricted only to trade in goods) and under the bilateral trade agreement with the United States (in terms of the most-favoured-nation treatment on service monopolies). Meanwhile, the TPP has expanded such commitment by incorporating the WTO's basic principle of national treatment in service trade and investment. Nonetheless, Viet Nam has indicated its list of non-conforming measures in Annex IV to TPP.

Third, once Viet Nam assigns or authorises SOEs to implement certain tasks such as confiscation, granting, or retrieval of licences, such SOEs must also comply with the Vietnamese government's related commitments to the TPP. Viet Nam has similar commitments in the bilateral trade agreement with the United States (Article 12, Chapter IV).[3]

Fourth, the government's support to SOEs must not adversely affect competition. The government must not provide, either directly or indirectly (i.e. via another SOE), any commercial support to SOEs if such might adversely affect the benefits, including commercial interests, of another TPP member.

This commitment does not apply to (i) support to SOEs that supply services in the domestic market, (ii) general supports that are available to eligible enterprises of all types of ownership, and (iii) support granted before the Agreement was signed.

Viet Nam already promised the WTO (under the Subsidy and Countervailing Measures agreement) that it would not provide specific subsidy to exporters of goods (including SOEs). As such, its commitment under the TPP pertains only to two new aspects, namely: (i) support that may affect competition in the provision of goods in the domestic market, and (ii) support to SOEs that provide services in another TPP country.

These notwithstanding, Viet Nam can still provide the necessary support to SOEs for the implementation of major state policies, namely: (i) equitisation and restructuring of SOEs, which aim to align their activities with market signals; (ii) ensuring macroeconomic stability and major macroeconomic aggregates; (iii) development of remote areas, border and islands, regions of special difficulty, regions with security-defence importance, and so forth; and (iv) programs on social security, hunger eradication and poverty reduction, universal healthcare, education, culture, and so forth.

Fifth, anti-competitive behaviours of designated monopolies are prohibited. Specifically, the designated monopolies must not directly or indirectly make use of its position to restrict competition in another market where it participates and competes with other enterprises, thereby producing adverse impacts on another TPP country.

Viet Nam already has regulations that prohibit the anti-competitive behaviours of enterprises with monopolistic power in a non-monopoly market (Item 3, Article 15 of the Competition Law). This is also a basic obligation incorporated in other FTAs with a chapter on SOEs, and almost all TPP member states have made a commitment regarding this clause. From the viewpoint of Viet Nam, thus, enforcement of regulations against competition-restrictive activities is important.

Sixth, government agencies must ensure neutrality in economic management. That is, agencies must not discriminate between SOEs and other enterprises in their conduct/formulation of policies. From the regulatory perspective, this obligation is already incorporated in Viet Nam's various laws and regulations. In its Enterprise Law and Investment Law in 2005, which were both amended in 2014, Viet Nam aims to avoid discriminating against enterprises of certain ownership types that are engaged in commercial activities and compete with one another.

Seventh, TPP members must allow their domestic courts to receive and make decisions on civil cases against foreign SOEs operating within their border. This provision helps avoid the scenario where a country applies exemptions to its SOEs to avoid compliance with the regulations of another TPP member (where such SOEs operate). This provision is generally regarded as common in international trade laws.

Eighth, TPP members must publicise or announce to fellow members the list of SOEs under the 'scope of adjustment' of this Agreement, or upon designation of a monopoly in a certain market. Should there be a valid concern that activities of an SOE could adversely affect trade and investment between the member states, a member may request for basic information on that SOE (e.g. share of the state, total revenues, total assets, publicised financial reports, legal exemptions) or on non-commercial assistance of the government to such SOE.

In fact, domestic regulations already necessitate SOEs to disclose and make their information transparent. The requirement to provide information on the government's non-commercial assistance to SOEs is similar to the WTO's requisite to notify the body on subsidies from Viet Nam. However, no member is obliged to provide information if there is evidence that sharing of such information could compromise national security or legitimate commercial interest of enterprises. The Agreement also details the rules on the circulation and use of information.

3. Implication of TPP on SOE reforms in Viet Nam

3.1. Evolution of SOEs in Viet Nam

As of 2014, Viet Nam had 796 SOEs[4] with a total asset of almost VND2.87 trillion, and total state equity of almost VND1.15 trillion (Table 10.1). After nearly 30 years of SOE reforms, Viet Nam has gradually revised the legal framework towards establishing a more levelled playing field for SOEs and other enterprises. Prior to 2005, enterprises under different forms of ownership had been governed by separate business laws and regulations.

In 2005, the laws on enterprises were unified into a single Enterprise Law, and the laws governing investment activities were amalgamated into a common Investment Law. Since then, provisions that extended preferential treatment to SOEs were reduced in number. Preferential treatment, if any, had to be institutionalised with common conditions and standards by programs and projects, rather than for a specific enterprise just because of its ownership structure.

Under a centrally planned mechanism before 1988, international trade used to be conducted by SOEs only. Ever since 1989 – with the introduction of the market-oriented reforms – steps were taken to abolish the SOEs' monopoly on trade. The conditions for private sector's entry to international trade were gradually relaxed, though remained very restrictive until 1997. It was only in 1998 that Viet Nam relaxed these conditions by allowing all enterprises to export and import goods registered in their business licence, without requiring additional import/export licences for the products themselves.

Table 10.1 Overview of the SOE sector in Viet Nam

	Value (VND billion)	Structure (%)		
		Business groups	General corporation, holding-subsidiary structured companies	Independent SOEs
Asset	2,869,120	57.9	34.1	8.0
Equity capital	1,145,564	65.6	25.4	9.0
Turnover	1,709,134	57.9	34.4	7.9
Pre-tax income	181,530	75.8	18.7	5.5
Payments of taxes and dividends to State budget	276,063	71.4	20.2	8.4

Source: Government of Viet Nam (2014).

By 2016, SOEs and other enterprises, in principle, have been enjoying full rights to pursue, enter into and implement contracts with business partners, joint ventures, and associates (Le, 2015).

In the area of financial management, SOEs are similarly subjected to state regulations (on taxation, fees and charges, corporate finance, accounting, auditing, and pricing) as other enterprises. Since the *Doi Moi* (Renovation) in 1986, efforts have been made to gradually expose SOEs to market-based decision-making processes. Existing laws and regulations permit prices to be set based on market conditions,[5] with the exception of some essential goods and services whose prices are regulated by the state.[6]

Meanwhile, on wage and industrial relations, the Labour Code in 2012 applies across all types of enterprises (including SOEs), covering issues such as working standards; rights, obligations and responsibilities of employees and employers; representation of employees and employer in industrial relations; and other state administration of labour issues. Like other types of enterprises, SOEs are free to recruit, contract, and negotiate salary and wage rates with employees.

Competition is another area where practical oversight over SOEs differs from what are written in the laws and regulations. In principle, Viet Nam applies the same laws and regulations on competition and antimonopoly over SOEs and other enterprises. Since the promulgation of the Competition Law in 2004, however, the business community appeared to have little faith in the enforcement of this law and/or in the competition authorities. There are several reasons for such inadequacy.

First, the competition authorities, including the Vietnam Competition Council (VCC) and Vietnam Competition Authority (VCA), possess unmatched capacity. VCA, which depended purely on the state budget, arguably lack the necessary resources, staff, and reputation to deal with violations. Meanwhile, both VCA and VCC have no independent legal status. The VCA is a unit of the Ministry of Trade (or Ministry of Industry and Trade – or MOIT – since 2006), while the VCC is also an executive body.

Second, the protection of consumer interests is regulated by the Law on Consumer Protection and rather new in Viet Nam's legal framework.

Finally, the government took only a few attempts to strengthen fair competition and fight monopoly, especially with regard state-owned monopolies. Although the Competition Law has set the legal grounds for combating monopoly, state administration bodies have not fully carried out actions against state enterprise giants.

Viet Nam has also been legally neutral over the dissolution and bankruptcy of SOEs and private enterprises. Since 1995, the law on SOEs has exposed SOEs to dissolution or bankruptcy in accordance with the applicable legislations.

3.2. Preliminary assessment of impact of SOE chapter

Under Viet Nam's amended Enterprise Law of 2014, SOEs are defined as those that are wholly owned by the state. This definition narrows down the list of so-called SOEs, although various enterprises in Viet Nam have majority of shares or voting rights under the authority of the state.

The previous definition, however, fails to work under the TPP. On the basis of the defined scope of adjustment and threshold amount of annual revenues, the implementation of TPP will certainly affect the operations of a major section of Viet Nam's SOEs. This impact, however, may increase over time. In particular, 5 years after the agreement enters into force, the threshold of annual revenue has been reduced from US$ 705 million to US$ 282 million, thereby subjecting a larger number of Viet Nam's SOEs to the obligations set under the TPP.

Subject to the scope of Agreement, the impact on SOEs is defined by the TPP obligations regarding revenues from commercial activities, non-discriminatory treatment, and compliance with tasks assigned and authorised by the government. These commitments are not new, albeit the enforcement based on the WTO and/or bilateral trade agreement with the United States has limited scope.

There still exist signs that SOEs are favoured at the expense of other types of enterprises. For instance, SOEs still enjoy advantages in terms of market entry, especially in important sectors/industries. In particular, private sector enterprises cannot easily enter such sectors as electricity, telecommunication, petroleum and oil, and mining and quarrying in publicly owned assets.

On the other hand, SOEs continue to receive preferential treatment in terms of access to resources such as financing, land, and natural resources.

Major laws in Viet Nam – the Enterprise Law, Securities Law, Law on Credit Institutions, Foreign Exchange Law, Law on the State Bank of Vietnam, Public Debt Management Law – stipulate that borrowers are treated equally, regardless of their ownership forms. However, lenders appeared to prefer SOEs. According to the General Statistics Office's enterprise census, SOEs as of 2014 accounted for 30.3 percent of total liabilities but constituted less than 0.8 percent of the total number of Vietnamese enterprises. Besides, SOEs generally had higher leverage ratios: only 25.5 percent of SOEs' total finance was equity, whereas the corresponding figures of domestic private firms and foreign-invested enterprises were 32.7 percent and 37.9 percent, respectively. The CIEM (2015) also shows large bank loans given to SOEs: at the end of 2013, commercial banks and credit institutions extended loans to state economic groups (SEGs) and general corporations (GCs) amounting to over D489 trillion (or US$22.8 billion).

Lending to SOEs involves two major considerations. First, from banks' view, lending to a few SOEs has its advantages over other smaller private enterprises, including the relatively smaller document-related administrative costs, availability of documented credit profile, and (either explicit or implicit) guarantee by the state underlying SOE borrowings.

It is generally believed that the state may assume responsibility over debt repayment requisites when SOEs encounter problem with their loans. The bailout of Vietnam Shipbuilding Group (Vinashin, then renamed as Shipbuilding Industry Corporation or SBIC, after restructuring) and some other poorly performing SOEs further validates this belief (CIEM, 2015).

Second, only a few SOEs are financially sound and/or perform well to ensure credit worthiness and become trusted customers of commercial banks, especially equitised state-owned commercial banks.

Only a modest number of SOEs chose corporate bonds as a channel for capital mobilisation. Still, the volume of each successful issuance was substantial due to the guarantees given by authorised agencies or organisations. As of 2014, some major SOEs have issued corporate bonds – for example, Vietnam Electricity Corporation (EVN) with VND79 trillion, the Vietnam Coal and Mineral Industry Group (Vinacomin) with VND11 trillion, Becamex Binh Duong with VND6.5 trillion, Song Da Corporation with VND1.5 trillion, Vinalines with VND1 trillion, Lilama with VND1 trillion.

Although from the legal perspective, there is no distinction between SOEs and other enterprises when it comes to their access to external borrowings, projects that actually belonged to major SEGs and GCs such as those engaged in electricity, energy, or mining were prioritised. About 75 percent of these borrowings have been guaranteed or on-lent by the government (CIEM, 2015).

Each year, provincial governments make capital outlay for infrastructure development for public services, a part of which is transferred as assets to public service SOEs. Examples of such infrastructure assets are water supply systems, water drainage systems, public lighting, waste treatment facilities, and waste collection vehicles. Accounting for different financial sources of infrastructure for enterprises then becomes a challenge as the assets, upon formulation, require different sources of financing, including commercial loans.

On access to land, SOEs hold 70 percent of land for production and business purposes. This scenario dates back to the time of the central planning regime, when land was owned and controlled by the state via SOEs, among others. Even in recent years, SEGs or GCs could still enjoy preferential access to land. Such holding was excessive compared with the needs of the SOEs themselves. Consequently, various documentations show that some SOEs rented such land to others or left a substantial part of their land idle.

In addition, SOEs are still considered instrumental in land management. Under the state's system of land ownership, SOEs are delegated to manage land on behalf of the state. For example, Vinacomin is also the mine owner. Various other SOEs are state-owned agricultural farms; state-owned forestry farms; sub-national public corporations, with a substantial pool of land for business and production purposes or for re-assignment to individuals, organisations, and households for investment, farming, exploitation, and use.

Such SOEs' priority access to key production resources (land, finance) undermines the competition-induced efficiency on several areas. First, SOEs have access to excessive production resources but less than full efficiency; these excess resources could have been used instead by the private enterprises for improved market-based payout. Second, because there is no pressure to compete for resources, SOEs lack incentives to improve their management skills or to innovate. Third, implicit preference given to SOEs reduces the transparency in the legal system, which can both restrain legal enforcement and impede participation of private enterprises in the law-making process.

3.2.1. Competition-related aspects

As previously discussed, Viet Nam has no explicit provisions that favour SOEs in any of the major laws governing production and business activities. In actual application, however, such favour exists by means of under-the-radar regulations and assignments at ministerial, agency, and sub-national levels. The following are specific examples of how SOEs continue to enjoy preferential treatment compared with their private counterparts:

First, the accounting regulations do not explicitly require SEOs to do a full and accurate costing. State-owned assets, usually managed and used by SOEs, are recorded at book value, which over time deviates from the market value. For various reasons, several state-invested assets such as land and natural resources are not amortised for inclusion in SOEs' costs and cost of goods sold. As such, these SOEs' actual business performance could turn out to be less impressive if it had amortised the value of assets in its recording of costs (CIEM, 2015).

Second, as the authority in charge of monitoring competition, the VCA was institutionalised as a body under the MOIT. Meanwhile, the MOIT is also in charge of various SOEs. Thus, the relationship between the VCA and other SOEs under the MOIT potentially puts the capacity of VCA to operate independently, objectively, and fairly in question. For instance, the nomination of the VCA chairperson also requires comments from various MOIT members. Relatedly, there is still no specific guidelines or regulations on monopolistic behaviours and market domination under the Competition Law.

It should be noted that the VCA only focuses on investigation of competition complaints. It is the VCC that exclusively handles competition cases. Viet Nam's current regulations, however, permit no actions/decisions from administrative courts, including private ones. In other words, private rights of action are declared null in the current legal settings. Accordingly, VCC is under no pressure to improve its own capacity to handle competition case. For example, although the Competition Law has been in effect for more than a decade, the institutional aspects of the VCC – such as its level of independence, relationship with government agencies, and so forth – have not been defined and clarified.

Third, SOEs are not fully subject to market disciplines. Various SOEs have recorded irrelevant spending, poor performance, and under-achievement of targets, which have had adverse implications on the state budget and public debt. For instance, shipbuilder Vinashin has incurred major losses but then received various support in the form of debt rescheduling, debt transfer and eventually underwent drastic restructure.[7]

Cases of SOEs that were supported or bailed out in various forms are not rare. A popular type of support to SOEs concerns tax treatment, such as tax rescheduling, postponement, and exemption/deduction. In the case of Vinashin, once it was handled by Vinalines (another SOE), tax rescheduling was permitted for the loan of US\$ 600 million, along with other measures such as exemption on maritime fee, tax holidays for cancelled contracts, and freezing of arrears of social insurance, health insurance, and unemployment insurance contributions for subsidiaries (together with Vinalines).

In another example, those in mining and quarrying had sought for exemption and/or reduction of the natural resources' taxes and fees.

Fourth, various means of debt resolution have been made available to SOEs only. These may include debt scheduling, debt transfer, debt freezing, debt rescheduling, and even debt write-off. Measures such as transfer of debt from one SOE to another SOE or state-owned economic entity does not change total debt but can directly lessen the SOE's liabilities and prevent its exposure to default risks.

According to the State Audit Agency's 2016 report, some SEGs and GCs had large overdue debts in 2015. The CIEM (2015) lists two major debt transfer methods in Vinashin's restructuring process. In June 2010, Vinashin directly transferred to Petro Vietnam Corporation (PVN) and Vinalines the amount of VND24.112 trillion worth of debt.

Another way is via indirect debt transfer. For instance, the Debt and Asset Trading Corporation issued debt conversion bonds for Vinashin's creditors, which effectively transferred Vinashin's debt to the domestic banks and credit institutions, foreign banks, to Debt and Asset Trading Corporation. In this way, Vinashin had debt obligations only to Debt and Asset Trading Corporation, and such obligations were eventually rescheduled and lowered.

3.2.2. Implications

Given the aforementioned practices on how SOEs are supported, Viet Nam will encounter several challenges should the TPP come into force. On the one hand, major SOEs will have to change their management, competition, and policy advocacy processes, as these current ways will not work anymore under the TPP. Market-based competition will have to be the core, as the SOEs can no longer rely on such measures as tax incentives, preferential access to finance, and soft budget constraint.

On the other hand, government agencies will have to change their way of working with SOEs. Although SOEs will continue to be instrumental in achieving various socio-economic objectives and priorities, there should be a clear separation of their commercial operations from the non-commercial ones which need State subsidy. Accordingly, the realisation of socio-economic objectives will become more indirect, thereby requiring more appropriate understanding of the policy obstacles, scope, and transmission channels of policies, and so forth.

The challenges to Viet Nam's SOEs can be large in the first 5 years of implementation. To some extent, the direct impact to Viet Nam can be modest given the limited scope of Agreement (i.e. higher threshold set for annual revenues, which reduces the number of SOEs under Agreement).

Indirect impacts, meanwhile, are dependent upon the credibility of the government to adapt to TPP-standard rules. If enterprises still perceive that government agencies will try to find legitimate ways to support them amid slow reforms in the domestic SOE sector, the adjustment will be slower. Alternatively, the possibility of legal disputes involving Viet Nam's SOEs and/or government agencies under TPP may increase the adverse consequences on domestic SOEs in terms of finance, reputation, and so forth.

Private rights of actions under TPP may present another challenge to Viet Nam in undertaking competition policy. The provision for private rights of actions is incorporated in Competition Policy chapter. Such provision allows the private sector to:

> seek redress, including injunctive, monetary or other remedies, from a court or other independent tribunal for injury to that person's business or property caused by a violation of national competition laws, either independently or following a finding of violation by a national competition authority.[8]

Meanwhile, Viet Nam will have to amend its Competition Law to allow for private right of action. Once the private right of action is enforced, private tribunals can conduct such investigation/action even if the VCA and/or VCC are reluctant to investigation or take action against SOEs.

There is the issue with the private sector's perception that the VCA and VCC are incapable and/or unwilling to handle and investigate competition complaints against SOEs. Any loss in reputation because such perception persists will be detrimental to the VCA and VCC's role in the modern competition policy setting.

Provided that the previous challenges are effectively addressed as part of its broad SOE reforms, Viet Nam can enhance its aggregate economic performance in the following two aspects. First, the efficiency of SOEs may increase. Supposing that TPP-induced pressures and domestic reforms could cause the Incremental Capital Output Ratio (ICOR) of SOEs (of 8–9 in 2011–2015) to improve to the corresponding ICOR level of private sector (of around 5), the overall gross domestic product of Viet Nam may rise by 0.39 percent – 0.46 percent as a direct impact from new SOE investment.[9] The benefits could be larger if all existing assets of SOEs are used more efficiently.

Second, improved competitive neutrality between SOEs and the private enterprises may lead to more efficient allocation and utilisation of economic resources. The improvement in efficiency is, again, subject to the degree of change in government agencies' policy approach. If such agencies can quickly create an environment for fair competition between SOEs and other types of enterprises, the net benefit to the economy can be higher, although realisation of such benefit takes time.

4. Policy recommendations

Viet Nam has emphasised that SOEs' reform will be among the key areas for restructuring until 2020. Resolution 24/2016/QH14 of the National Assembly dated 8 November 2016 specifies the prioritised measures as thus:

i   Restructure SOEs, focusing on SEGs and GCs;
ii   Assess and accelerate SOE equitisation process;
iii Divest state capital from SOEs in a public, transparent process;

iv   Further check, inspect, monitor, and audit SOE equitisation to ensure no loss of public capital and assets;

v   Improve SOE governance;

vi   Appropriately control the capital used for merger and acquisition;

vii   List equitised SOEs in the stock market within 1 year of initial public offering;

viii Attract strategic investors;

ix   Prepare and disseminate the annual targets on divestment of state capital from SOEs;

x   Undertake radical market-based measures on SOEs that are making losses;

xi   Consider bankruptcy proceedings for certain SOEs in line with regulations on bankruptcy.

In this respect, SOE reforms have been identified as the means to unilaterally correct the inherent weaknesses in Viet Nam's growth paradigm. Integration commitments related to SOEs, thus, only offer additional push for such reforms to materialise.

The ongoing substantive reforms within SOEs ahead of the TPP-type commitments mean that Viet Nam is on its way to better prepare the domestic economy and increase the long-term benefits to the private sector. Accordingly, SOE reforms in Viet Nam should rest firmly on these enterprises' political will to initiate positive actions at their end.

From that perspective, Viet Nam needs to implement several crucial policies.

4.1. Shorten and publicly announce the list of preferential treatments that are specific or available only to SOEs

Acknowledging the importance of competitive neutrality between SOEs and private enterprises both under TPP and as part of unilateral SOE reforms, Viet Nam should aim towards reducing the scale and scope of preferential treatments for SOEs. It should first review carefully the extent of policy support to SOEs that can exceed those given to other private enterprises.[10]

Then, Viet Nam should define a clear scope for legally ensuring competitive neutrality between SOEs and private enterprises. Such scope for competitive neutrality should at least include access to key traditional financial resources (bank loans, government credit), access to other resources (policy information, land, natural resources, technology), and policy treatment (discipline over debts, credit profile, labour training, and so forth).

Authorised state agencies should strictly avoid granting preferential treatments to SOEs beyond the legal limit. In particular, they must disallow any SOE from borrowing beyond the set credit limit, because this may distort credit activities and produce adverse implications (either explicit or implicit) on the support to SOEs. State agencies must also minimise issuing guarantees on SOEs' enterprise bonds or bank borrowing, either explicit or implicit.

Because of its high public debt and the fact that the National Assembly has kept the debt ceiling unchanged at 65 percent of gross domestic product until

2021, Viet Nam should restrict overall access to foreign loans. Foreign loans (with the state's guarantee) should be made accessible to SOEs only if they have well-evidenced and clear justification that the loans (i) would be essential, (ii) otherwise unavailable from the domestic capital market, and (iii) are neutral to market competition (especially with private enterprises).

4.2. Further improve and enforce regulations on oversight, monitoring, evaluation, information disclosure, and transparency of SOEs

This group of policies should be conditional on state agencies' ability to refrain from giving (explicit and implicit) preferences to SOEs. Viet Nam's mechanism should be able to separate the ownership function of SOEs from the administrative management function. This will help reduce any conflict of interests when government ministries and agencies create policies affecting SOEs on the one hand and represent SOE owners on the other hand. Most of all, such will improve the transparency of policies, which in turn can improve the state ministry/agency's credibility in the eyes of the private sector.

State-owned enterprises must have greater autonomy to undertake their operations. The representative of state owner at SOEs should set out only specific and feasible targets and/or mission for each SOE (or parent company of SEGs and GCs).

Targets should neither be contradictory and/or mutually exclusive. Nor should SOEs be regarded as directly instrumental in fulfilling macroeconomic aggregates. No direct intervention in the SOEs' decision should be permitted. Managers of SOEs should be professionals recruited on a contract basis and assessed in terms of their performance vis-à-vis the assigned targets.

More important, the assignment of targets to SOEs should be sufficiently independent from the policymaking capacity of the government authorities. The effectiveness of SOE governance remains questionable for years in Viet Nam as the representatives of State owner at SOEs are usually the policymaking agencies in the same areas which the SOEs operate. In this regard, Viet Nam decided in 2017 to establish a separate Commission under the government to represent State owner at various selected big SOEs. As of February 2018, the list of SOEs tentatively under the Commission include selected ones formerly under authority of Ministry of Industry and Trade, Ministry of Finance, Ministry of Transport, Ministry of Information and Communication, and Ministry of Agriculture and Rural Development. As an intended effect, the management of these SOEs would be separated from the policymaking capacity in various areas, namely industry and trade, transport, and so forth.

In addition, monitoring and evaluation indicators must be comprehensive, rather than just focused on financial outcomes. There, too, is the need to improve the collection of independent data, so as not to rely wholly on SOEs' own reports, which could be lacking in depth and not exhaustive enough.

Regulations on the way SOEs disclose information should also be improved, covering areas such as the frequency of monitoring and information disclosure systems, including those on business transactions. The information needs to go beyond the usual pre-defined objectives, targets, and plans. Rather, it should also include reports related to policy changes, market forces, and other exogenous factors that may affect the SOEs' operational performance. In this regard, information disclosure should also go beyond the commitment under TPP.

4.3. Re-enforce hard budget constraint

Viet Nam should also produce a meaningful re-application of hard budget constraint on SOEs to eliminate the latter's reliance on policy support. Even in times of difficulties and/or uncertainty, any policy support should be provided across all enterprises, rather than targeting SOEs only. To do this, Viet Nam should first remove all direct support for SOEs in commercial areas. When SOEs are to provide public services, transparency should be set in place via the contracting approach, to ensure market competition or market contestability.

Second, while narrowing the scope of SOEs' preferential access to bank loans, Viet Nam should also lessen the provision of concessionary interest rates to these enterprises, and complement such by removing the tax exemptions, tax reductions, tax postponement, and tax write-offs from SOEs.

Third, regulations must clearly separate the commercial business mandates from the politico-social mandates of SEGs and GCs. Here, Viet Nam must clearly and transparently identify the cost of non-commercial activities. Likewise, any support to SOEs, especially financial ones, for non-commercial mandates should be properly disclosed and justified. Other assessments on opportunity costs of support to SOEs, if any, should be promptly done and publicised. This must be facilitated by an improved management information system, information processing methods, and conduct of risk assessment and management and the national financial burdens caused by SEGs.

4.4. Other policies

Viet Nam should initiate a comprehensive review of its legal framework for its competition policy. It should clearly identify all the legal regulations, rather than just focus on the competition law. This includes looking at ways to improve regulations on property rights, access to resources, market entry, and market exit to ensure that there is no adverse impact on competitive neutrality between SOEs and private enterprises. Thus, the implementation of TPP commitments regarding SOEs should focus not only on the SOE chapter, but also Competition Policy chapter as well.

As discussed in an earlier section, private right of action, too, should be carefully reviewed, considered, and introduced in Viet Nam's competition-related regulations.

Focus should also be directed towards building the institutional and technical capacity of Viet Nam's competition authorities. Specifically, the mandate of the VCA should centre on enforcing measures to protect competition, to avoid dispersion of attention and resources in too many areas (such as trade remedies, etc.).

Making the public aware of VCA's operations by regulating its information dissemination, public monitoring, and feedback processes is more important than maintaining the independence of VCA (if any). Technical skills of VCA in various aspects – use of economic evidence, investigation, and so forth – should also be aligned with international best practices.

Finally, Viet Nam should effectively manage the consensus over how to incorporate TPP standards and SOE reforms. In fact, SOE reforms involve restructuring such enterprises, which in turn leads to (possibly massive) layoff of workers. Overcoming the social pressures in this process is also essential for reforms to be viable and, more important, self-fulfilled.

Notes

1 State-owned enterprises also serve other assigned developmental objectives such as creating employment, building necessary infrastructure for economic development, and pursuing cultural preservation (Le, 2015).
2 Exchange rates of Special Drawing Right (SDR) and US dollar with respect to VND are estimated using data from the IMF (2018) as of November 2017.
3 See Socialist Republic of Viet Nam and United States of America (2000).
4 Eight state-owned business groups, 100 state-owned general corporations, 25 companies under the structure of holding-subsidiary companies, and 663 independent companies, of which there are 309 public corporations as public good and service providers.
5 Although the pricing behaviour is also regulated by the Competition Law.
6 According to the provisions stipulated in the 2012 Pricing Law, the state shall determine prices for the goods and services in the fields, where the state assumes monopolistic production and businesses; important natural resources; public goods and services and state budget-financed public services in the form of specific prices or price ranges, maximum or minimum price limits. The state shall make price intervention through the price stabilisation measures for finished petroleum and oil products, electricity, liquefied and bottled gas products; nitrogen fertilisers, NPK fertilisers, pesticides in accordance with applicable legislations; preventive vaccines for animals and poultries; salt; milk for children under 6 years old; sugar, including white and refined sugar; unpolished rice, normal rice; health preventive and treatment medicines for humans in the list of essential prescriptive drugs used in health examination and treatment facilities in accordance with applicable legislations.
7 See KPMG (2013).
8 Article 16.3, Competition Policy, TPP agreement. VCC
9 The share of SOE investment in total public investment is around 37.7 percent in 2011–2015.
10 The Report by CIEM (2015) can offer a good start.

Bibliography

Central Institute for Economic Management (CIEM) (2015), *State-owned Enterprises and Market Distortions*. Hanoi: Financial Publishing House.

General Statistics Office (2016), 'Enterprise Census for 2014', *Biennial Survey Data*.

Government of Vietnam (2014), *Government Report* No. 512/BC-CP, dated 25 November. (in Vietnamese).

International Monetary Fund (2018), *IMF Data – Exchanges Rates.* Available at http://data.imf.org/regular.aspx?key=61545850 (accessed 30 March 2018).

KPMG (2013), 'Vinashin Stays Afloat – Ground Breaking English Scheme Approved for a Vietnamese Restructuring'. Available at https://home.kpmg.com/content/dam/kpmg/pdf/2013/10/restructuring-newsletter-1309-03-article1.pdf (accessed 10 May 2018).

Le, T.A.N. (2015), 'State-owned Enterprise Reforms in the CPTPP Negotiation: Is It a Win-Win for Vietnam?', *RIETI Discussion Paper Series* No. 15-E-092, July.

Ministry of Industry and Trade (2015), *Full Text of CPTPP Agreement.* Available at http://CPTPP.moit.gov.vn (accessed 3 February 2016).

Organisation for Economic Co-operation and Development (OECD) (2005), 'Guidelines on Corporate Governance of State-Owned Enterprises'. Available at www.oecd.org/daf/ca/oecd-guidelines-corporate-governance-soes-2005.htm (accessed 17 January 2017).

Socialist Republic of Viet Nam, and United States of America (2000), *Bilateral Trade Agreement Between Viet Nam and United States.* Available at www.ustr.gov/sites/default/files/US-VietNam-BilateralTradeAgreement.pdf (accessed 17 January 2017).

11 State trading rules in TPP

Implications for the Philippines

Ramon L. Clarete[1]

1. Introduction

The 11 TPP members launched the Comprehensive and Progressive Agreement for Trans-Pacific Partnership (CPTPP) in March 2018 in Chile. Absent the United States, this trade agreement remains significant economically. This chapter looks at the scenario where CPTPP parties invite the Philippines, which is a significant trading partner of the majority of the parties, to accede to the trade accord. In particular, it looks into how the rules of TPP on SOEs may affect the day-to-day operations of the Philippine State-Owned Enterprises (SOEs).

The following sections note the TPP rules on SOEs in the trading system, discuss the profile of the country's SOEs, and explore the implications of the rules on SOEs. The case study explores how far the TPP agreement can trigger the much-awaited reforms for the National Food Authority (NFA), which has the highest liability to asset ratio amongst the SOEs.

2. TPP rules on SOEs

Preferential trade agreements like the TPP expand and deepen the WTO rules on SOEs. Table 11.1 illustrates the rules of the WTO and the TPP on state-trading enterprises. SOEs engaged in international trade are regarded as non-tariff measures (NTMs) in the international trading rules of the WTO (WTO, 2012). These entities are created to address legitimate public interest issues and are empowered to undertake commercial activities to carry out their mandates. However, like other NTMs, they can become "invisible barriers to trade" (ITC, 2015), if their actions are inconsistent with the State's contractual obligations in the WTO.

As in the WTO, the TPP recognises the right of Parties to create and maintain SOEs or designate monopolies.[2,3] For an SOE of a Party to be covered by TPP's rules on state trading, it must be provided some exclusive or special rights or privileges by the Party. Additionally, it has to be engaged in international trading, or in a business with potential effects on the trade of other Parties.

TPP deepens the SOE rule on non-discrimination in its commercial activities by promoting competition. The observance of commercial considerations in commercial activities is sufficient for promoting competition for SOEs. Designated

Table 11.1 Rules on state-trading enterprises compared: WTO vs. TPP

Subject	WTO	TPP
Definition of a state-trading enterprise (STE)	The term refers to either an instrumentality of government which has the power to buy or sell, or to a non-governmental body, including marketing boards, with such power and to which the government has granted exclusive or special privileges.	It is a state-owned enterprise (SOE) or a designated monopoly that affects trade or investment between parties within the free trade area.
Exclusions: not covered by the rules on STEs	• Public procurement • STEs not engaged in trading	– Central banks and monetary authorities – Financial regulators – Public procurement – Sovereign wealth fund – Independent pension fund – Providing goods/services to other governmental agencies to do their governmental functions – STEs whose activities are for the resolution of a failing or failed financial institution or any other failing or failed enterprise principally engaged in the supply of financial service – SOE operations and of designated monopolies contingent on certain conditions such as in emergency situations
Non-discriminatory treatment	State-owned enterprises (SOEs) to undertake transactions in a manner consistent with the general principles of non-discriminatory treatment	SOEs and designated monopolies to provide non-discriminatory treatment in all its trade transactions
Commercial considerations	SOEs to undertake such transactions in accordance with commercial considerations	SOEs undertake such transactions in accordance with commercial considerations
Pro-competitive practices	*	Designated monopolies not to engage in anti-competitive practices in a non-monopolised market in its territory
Jurisdiction over civil claims	*	Parties to provide jurisdiction on civil claims against SOEs of other parties operating in their respective territories
Impartial regulation	*	Parties to ensure STE regulation be undertaken in an impartial manner

Non-commercial assistance	No specific rule about non-commercial assistance not to cause adverse effects to other parties is in Article XVII. However, the concern that STE operations may adversely affect other parties is accepted as possible, and parties are obliged to provide information to adversely affected parties on the operations of the STE. – No provision on rule about non-commercial assistance not to cause injury to industry is in Article XVII.	Binds parties to ensuring that the non-commercial assistance they provide their SOEs does not cause adverse effects on other parties nor injury to an industry producing a like product of the SOE
Injury to an industry	*	In context of the rule on non-commercial assistance not to cause injury to an industry. Injury is defined.
Transparency	Parties are obliged to notify the other parties through the Council of the Trade in Goods of the products, which are imported into or exported from their territories by their STEs. Parties, who are principal suppliers or perceive or to be adversely affected by the STEs, have the right to request information from parties concerned, 'import mark-ups' or at least domestic prices of covered goods of STEs, and the party concerned is obligated to respond promptly.	All parties are required to provide other parties, or through an official website, a list of its SOEs no later than 6 months after the date of entry into force of this agreement for that party, and thereafter shall update the list annually; designated monopolies; the operations of SOEs and designated monopolies; non-commercial assistance; and how these activities may affect trade and investments.
Body in charge of notifications and review	Council for Trade in Goods designated to receive notifications related to STE operations, to review notifications and counter-notifications, and to make recommendations as regards the adequacy of notifications and the need for further information.	Committee on State-Owned Enterprises and Designated Monopolies is created to, amongst other functions, review, and consider the operation and implementation of the rules on state trading; assist parties consulting on any matter arising from the rules on SOEs; and develop cooperative efforts to promote the principles underlying the disciplines contained in this chapter in the free trade area.
Other provisions	*	Technical cooperation, party-specific annexes, further negotiations, and process for developing information on SOEs and designated monopolies.

Note:
* = No such provision in Article XVII.

Source:
1 Text of Article XVII, World Trade Organization
2 Interpretative Note Ad Article XVII and Uruguay Round
3 Understanding on Interpretation of Article XVII, 1995
4 Chapter 17, Trans-Pacific Partnership agreement

monopolies are further required not to engage in anti-competitive acts in non-monopolised markets.

Moreover, TPP parties are obligated to use of non-commercial assistance, which Parties provide their SOEs by virtue of their ownership, in a way as not to cause any adverse effects to the public interests of any other Parties or injury to their domestic industries.

The difficult part of the rule is to establish causality of the non-commercial assistance and adverse effects or displacement of the industry. '[T]he non-commercial assistance must be examined within the context of other possible causal factors to ensure the appropriate attribution of causality'.[4]

TPP patterned its definition of injury after Article 3 of the WTO Anti-Dumping Agreement. Injury is (a) material, (b) a threat of material injury, or (c) a threat of material retardation of the industry of another Party producing a like product to the product of an SOE of a Party. The definition is borrowed from Article 3 of the WTO Anti-Dumping Agreement.

The TPP rule, however, grandfathered three types of non-commercial assistance: those that were provided before the agreement or in the period of 3 years after the agreement entered into force, the initial investment by a Party to create the SOE or to acquire controlling assets into an existing enterprise, and assistance deemed incapable of causing adverse effects to other Parties or injury to their industries.

3. The SOEs of the Philippines

The government corporate sector in the Philippines is large. In 2014, the sector's revenues accounted for 7.59 percent of the country's GDP in 2014. This financial performance is also a significant improvement compared with about 4 decades ago. According to the Governance Commission,[5] the number of state-owned enterprises had grown from 27 in 1965 to 212 in 1981 and peaked at 303 three years later. The number of SOEs, which the Governance Commission monitors on a regular basis, is 107. There are other SOEs, however, that are regulated or administratively supervised by other agencies. Altogether the current number including those in the process of being dissolved or abolished is 188.

The largest group of these SOEs are inactive corporations, which may be in the process of being dissolved, by the Governance Commission. To date, the Commission had abolished 20 SOEs.

Part of the Commission's work is to identify SOEs with duplicative functions, with functions that the private sector can perform better, that no longer have outlived their *raison d'etre*, or those that are no longer cost-efficient. These SOEs are in the possible list of being dissolved or abolished, and their assets disposed in favour of the national government. The Commission works to get these SOEs perform their mandates at the least cost to the public. For some SOEs, the Commission likewise guides them to become more effective in attaining their mandates, and profitable in order to contribute to the overall income of the government.

But there are SOEs that the Governance Commission do not supervise. In addition to the research institutions and the economic zone authorities, there are

SOEs that remain with the mandate in education, the state-owned universities and colleges (SUCs); and the local SOEs starting with the hundreds of water districts with the mandate from their respective local governments to generate and distribute potable water and provide related services to local communities. The Governance Commission do not supervise the SUCs nor the sub-national SOEs.

3.1. *Financial profile of SOEs*

The Governance Commission in the Philippines classified SOEs in the country into eight sectors (Table 11.2). The sectors with the largest number of SOEs are the government financial institutions; trade, area development, and tourism; and the utilities and communications sector. All three account for two-thirds of the total number of SOEs with complete financial records.

Both the GFIs and the Energy and Materials Sectors account for 84 percent of the total assets of SOEs. Moving on to liabilities and net worth, all of the sectors except agriculture, fisheries, and food had positive average net worth in 2014. The financial and energy sectors account for 82.45 percent of the financial liabilities of all SOEs reporting. The utilities and communications and the trade, area development, and tourism sectors had comparable average net worth. Both with the GFIs and the energy SOEs make up 98 percent of the net worth of all SOEs reporting.

Table 11.2 Average asset, liability, and net worth of GOCCs in the Philippines, 2014 (in million pesos)

Sector	Number	Average value in 2014		
		Assets	Liabilities	Net worth
Government Financial Institutions	29	3,696,201	1,706,125	1,990,078
Trade, Area Development, and Tourism	15	294,787	86,509	208,279
Educational and Cultural	4	16,292	1,752	14,540
Gaming	2	51,695	28,987	22,707
Energy and Materials	10	1,434,574	1,025,800	408,774
Agriculture, Fisheries, and Food	9	49,148	174,739	−125,592
Utilities and Communications	18	534,301	289,406	244,997
Realty Holding Companies	4	216	40	174
All State-Owned Enterprises reporting	91	6,077,214	3,313,358	2,763,957

Note:
GOCC = government-owned and controlled corporation

Source: Governance Commission.

The GFIs, the leading sector in assets, had 46 percent of their assets in liabilities, which may pose to be a potential solvency issue. For all SOEs, the assets to liabilities ratio averaged 54 percent in 2014. The GFIs' had a lower ratio at 46 percent but is a major contributor to the high L/A ratio. The banking subsector had an average L/A ratio of about 90 percent, and this includes the largest banks, the Land Bank of the Philippines (LBP) and the Development Bank of the Philippines (DBP). In the non-banks sector, there are companies with liabilities exceeding their assets, such as the Quedan and Rural Credit Corporation (Quedancor) and the National Home Mortgage Corporation.

Interestingly, the social protection SOEs, led by the GSIS and SSS, had very low average L/A ratio in 2014, at 3 percent.

Above average in L/A ratio are the energy and materials, utilities and communication, gaming and especially the agriculture, fisheries, and food sector, that brought up the SOE sector L/A ratio. The energy SOEs L/A ratio is 71.5 percent in 2014. Two companies contributed significantly to it, namely the PSALM and the National Electrification Administration. Each had at least 86 percent of their assets in liabilities.

It is the agriculture, fisheries, and food sector, which incurred on average liabilities 3.5 times larger than its average assets in 2014. The average L/A ratio for agriculture is high because of these companies, Philippine Fisheries Development Authority (1.25 L/A ratio) and especially the National Food Authority (NFA) with a ratio of nearly 7. The NFA is among the oldest SOE of the country.

Figure 11.1 shows the total comprehensive income (TCI), net of operational subsidies provided by the government, by major sector of SOEs. The government financial institutions dominate the other sectors in TCI. At least 60 percent

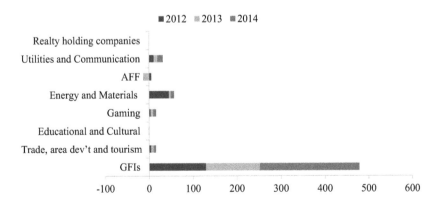

Figure 11.1 Total comprehensive income of SOEs (net of operational subsidies), 2012 to 2014

Note:
AFF = Agriculture, Fisheries, and Food
GFI = government financial institution

Source: Governance Commission.

of the TCI is accounted for by the GFIs. The far second performer is the sector of energy and materials in 2012, although their TCI in 2013 and 2014 were significantly lower. The next largest sector following the GFIs with the largest income is the utilities and communications sector.

Generally speaking, most of sectors had lower incomes in 2013 compared with 2012. But most of them recovered in 2014, except for trade, area development, and tourism and the realty holding sector.

Among the GFIs, 2014 is a good year with most of the large institutions having a higher income compared with 2013 such as the LBP. In the energy sector, PSALM's income in 2014 recovered from a slump a year ago. In the utilities and communications sector, utilities in general had a good 2014 with their incomes higher than in 2013. The Light Rail Transit Authority, which had the largest income in 2012 among the utility SOEs had lower incomes in 2013 and 2014 compared to a year ago.

The SOEs in agriculture, fisheries, and food had a negative income in 2012 and 2013. The sector's income was positive in 2012, and that was about 2.3 percent of total. But in 2012, it fell to nearly –10 percent of total. It recovered in 2014, but the sector remained in the red. The NFA after 2 years with a financial loss emerged in 2014 with a positive income.

3.2. Mandate of the SOEs

The current pool of SOEs serves several public interest purposes. First, the state banks increase the access to credit of farmers; micro-, small, and medium-sized enterprises (MSMEs); infrastructure; and other priority sectors. The Development Bank of the Philippines and the Land Bank of the Philippines, along with its subsidiaries, provided ₱147.87 billion and ₱331.3 billion, respectively, in 2014.

Second, public pension companies, housing-related GFIs, and the Philippine Health Insurance Corp. are into ensuring social protection particularly of vulnerable groups. The Philippine Health Insurance Corp. increased the coverage of the national health insurance to 87 percent of the population in 2014. Indigent patients as identified by the Department of Social Welfare and Development do not have to pay out-of-pocket charges. The Social Security System increased the amount of pension benefits released to members to ₱102.82 billion in 2014.

Third, the housing SOEs are to improve access of marginalised sectors in society to secure shelter. They construct new low-cost shelters, lend to build houses or repair shelters damaged by extreme typhoons or flooding, and move residential units to safer locations.

Other public interest purposes for which SOEs were created include:

i The energy-related SOEs are mandated to ensure total electrification of the country at competitive prices of energy.
ii The SOEs in natural resources are tasked to promote investments in natural resources – based industries by providing financial, technical, and management assistance.

iii   The SOEs in the water utilities sub-sector are mandated to improve access to safe, potable water and water for use in irrigating farms.
iv   The SOEs in the transport sector are created to ensure the population's access to a safe and efficient transport system. The SOEs in this group own and operate airports, seaports, railways, and light rail transits.
v   The SOEs in communications run the government's television network, printing facilities, and intercontinental broadcasting network.
vi   Promoting international trade and access to parallel imports of less expensive medicines are the tasks of the SOEs in the trade.
vii   The government has strategic areas of land that can be developed to generate value added for the public sector's income. Developing these areas is the mandate of the area-development SOEs.
viii   Promoting tourism in local areas that the private sector has not gone into for whatever reason is the business of tourism SOEs.
ix   Ensuring access to education and promoting the country's culture are the tasks of the SOEs in education. The Governance Commission does not supervise many state universities and colleges, but these corporations belong to this group of SOEs with the education mandate.
x   The SOEs in the agriculture, fisheries, and food sector are mandated to promote the livelihood of the country's farmers and fisherfolk, increase the productivity of the agriculture and fisheries sector, and attain food security.

4. TPP and the Philippine SOEs

Not all SOEs of the Philippines are covered by the rules of TPP on SOEs. The agreement requires members, however, to ensure that such SOEs, state enterprises and designated monopolies function in a 'manner that is not inconsistent with that Party's obligations under this Agreement'.[6]

More important, in general, the agreement has no intention to thwart the exercise of regulatory or any governmental functions of a Party's agencies by imposing disciplines on SOEs. The rules do not prevent an SOE 'from providing goods or services exclusively to that Party for the purposes of carrying out that Party's governmental functions'.[7] Accordingly, the agreement exempt SOEs from its rules on SOEs given certain features. Because of this, the majority of the GFIs in the Philippines are likely outside the discipline of TPP Chapter 17.[8]

4.1. Scope of TPP rules on SOEs

The Philippine SOEs are more into regulating economic activities or delivering a public good or is a public utility, and less engaged in trading for trading sake, which generally place them outside the scope of the rules on SOE. The agreement on SOEs "'shall apply with respect to the activities of state-owned enterprises and designated monopolies of a Party that affect trade or investment between Parties within the free trade area".[9]

The concern, however, is that the SOEs may operate in a way that contravenes inadvertently the free trade area benefits of Parties. The agreement requires that in the 'exercise any regulatory, administrative or other governmental authority that the Party has directed or delegated to such entities to carry out, those entities act in a manner that is not inconsistent with that Party's obligations under this Agreement'.[10]

This provision places SOEs in the group like those of non-tariff measures (NTM), which are 'policy measures, other than ordinary customs tariffs, that can potentially have an economic effect on international trade in goods, changing quantities traded, or prices or both'. (UNCTAD, 2010). It should be pointed out that state trading is one of the measures classified as NTMs affecting competition.[11]

To the extent that the functions of the SOEs may not have anything to do with international trade, then these are generally outside TPP's SOE rules. Several provisions in the agreement[12] free several activities of SOEs from TPP's rules on SOEs. These include monetary authorities, financial regulatory bodies including duly authorised self-regulating organisations, sovereign wealth funds, a Party's independent pension fund, enterprises owned and controlled by such pension funds, and government procurement.

SOEs that may have likely impact on international trade in goods and services are covered by TPP's rules on SOEs. Both goods and services are the subject of the existing multilateral agreement. In its SOE rules, the TPP agreement covers investment concerns as well.

4.2. Non-commercial assistance

The SOEs perform governmental functions such as regulating economic activities, promoting desirable activities such as trade, infrastructure investments, and the like, which require the use of public funds. In the agreement, the assistance covers transfer of funds or goods and services by any Party to its SOE, the assistance including the beneficial terms of which largely specific to the receiving SOE itself.[13] The purpose of the assistance is for the Party to help the concerned SOEs to carry out its mandated task.

It is useful to consider two examples. PITC Pharma, Inc., a subsidiary of an SOE supervised by the Department of Trade and Industry, which is Philippine International Trading Corporation (PITC), is tasked to undertake parallel imports of branded medicines and distribute the same to the various public outlets of medicines maintained by the Department of Health and the local government units. In undertaking this work, the DTI had provided the resources to PITC Pharma, Inc. to undertake such imports. Another in the food sector, the NFA, which is supervised by the Department of Agriculture, is tasked to support the incomes of rice farmers by buying high their harvest. The fund used by the NFA for this purpose comes out of the current funds of the corporation, although the national government had given the SOE authority to borrow commercially if it needed funds to undertake the work. There are many such other instances. An alternative option is for a government agency, not an SOE, to undertake the task. However, the agency does not have the flexibilities that business corporations have, which are needed to dispense with the function more effectively.

The assistance may also take the form of increasing the capital holdings of the government in order to improve the financial capability of the SOE. Non-commercial assistance is the blood that ties SOEs with the national government, but does it mean that the TPP rules can render difficult the exercise of the governmental functions of the SOEs?

It is very unlikely for the following reason: if an SOE does not engage in trading or investing for the purpose of selling a good or service, which can compete with a like good or service of another Party, there is not a chance that the rules on SOE can obstruct its normal governmental function. The rule on non-commercial assistance is that the Party does not cause any adverse effects to the interests of another Party with the use of such assistance. This rule is qualified to apply only to (i) the production and sale of a good, (ii) the export of a service to the territory of another Party from its territory, (iii) the export of a service of an SOE of a Party, which represents to be a covered investment[14] operating in the territory of another Party.[15] The Party shall ensure that its SOEs would not be able to abuse the non-commercial assistance to cause adverse effects.[16]

It is further provided that a Party's SOE operating in the territory of another Party to engage in the business of producing a good or service for sale in the territory of the latter and is a covered investment should not cause injury to the domestic industry producing identical or like product produced by it as a result of its receipt of non-commercial assistance from its owner.[17]

From these qualifications, being actually or potentially in the international trading business and receiving non-commercial assistance from the State appear necessary for any SOE in the Philippines to be potentially covered by the rules of TPP on SOEs. The majority of SOEs are not into international trading or investing, or if they are producing and selling a product, the latter is non-traded. It is useful to cite some examples. The Light Rail Transport Inc. is an SOE, which is supervised by the Department of Transportation. It operates the light rail transport service in the National Capital Region, and its product is non-traded. Provision of non-commercial assistance to LRTI could not possibly cause adverse effects to the interests of another Party. Several SOEs in the utilities and energy sector are like LRTI. They produce non-traded products. These are designated monopolies, operating air or seaports, by virtue of the technological specificity to a firm of such facilities.

There are SOEs that are just into regulating economic activities and could not cause any adverse effects to another Party's trading interests.

4.3. *Extent of non-commercial assistance*

The Governance Commission distinguishes between program and operational subsidies, which make no difference insofar as TPP's definition of non-commercial assistance. Program subsidies are 'commercial transactions between the State and the GOCC[18] for vital social services and infrastructure not offered by the private sector'. (GCG, 2014) Table 11.3 shows the extent of these subsidies from 2012 to 2014.

The largest of program subsidies went in 2014 to the GFI group, and the amount is largely explained by the government's support for the premium of enlisted poor families in the Philippine Health Insurance Corporation. The second largest went to the trade group, and the National Housing Authority, which builds low-cost housing for the poor. In energy, the largest recipient of subsidies in 2014 was the National Electrification Administration, while it is the National Food Authority in the agriculture and food sector.

The size of operational subsidy to SOEs in 2014 was only 3 percent of program subsidy. At least half of the PhP 2.1 billion of state support went to the utilities and communications sector. It was the National Irrigation Administration, which received nearly all of program subsidies going to the utilities sector. The Tourism Promotion Board followed as a far second with 27 percent, while the Philippine Coconut Authority came in third with 11 percent.

The state support was 7.6 percent of the total dividend remitted by SOEs to the national treasury in 2014. According to the Governance Commission, total dividend remitted was about 27 billion pesos. This and the program subsidies are considered in TPP as non-commercial assistance. It is important, therefore, to know the likelihood that such non-commercial assistance can cause adverse effects to the interests of other Parties.

In the list of the large recipients of program funds, all of them except the National Food Authority are SOEs, which produce non-traded products: Philippine Health Insurance Corporation, National Housing Authority, and National

Table 11.3 Programme subsidies to SOEs, the Philippines, 2012–2014 (in million pesos)

State-owned enterprises	2012	2013	2014
Programme Subsidy			
Government Financial Institutions	19,949.62	9,886.31	45,642.35
Trade, Area Dev't., and Tourism	10,694.27	31,152.75	11,421.09
Educational and Cultural	169.82	343.33	316.66
Energy and Materials	60,479.46	18,305.15	9,675.80
Agriculture, Fisheries, and Food	9,581.51	7,921.49	6,660.46
Utilities and Communications	5,693.83	5,525.58	1,210.00
Total	106,568.51	73,134.61	74,926.36
Operational Subsidy			
Government Financial Institutions	254.78	28.41	71.96
Trade, Area Dev't., and Tourism	281.29	61.9	573.17
Educational and Cultural	89.12	9	73.04
Agriculture, Fisheries, and Food	184.8	552.59	225.03
Utilities and Communications	301	515.64	1165.68
Total	1,110.99	1,167.54	2,108.88

Source: Governance Commission.

Electrification Administration. The NFA is in the business of selling and buying traded cereals, particularly rice. The NFA commercial operation has a potential issue, which is explored in the following section.

In terms of operational subsidies, the SOEs getting the larger state support, which included the National Irrigation Administration, Tourism Promotion Board, and the Philippine Coconut Authority, are likely not to cause adverse effects to other parties. They either produce a non-traded service or promote exports of a service in the case of the tourism board.

4.4. Non-discrimination and commercial considerations

Philippine SOEs, like the rest of government agencies, are required by its procurement law to abide by the principle that their procurement of 'infrastructure projects, goods and consulting services shall be competitive and transparent, and therefore shall go through public bidding, except as otherwise provided in this IRR'.[19]

TPP rules on non-discrimination and commercial considerations are observed by all Philippine government entities including SOEs by virtue of the country's procurement law. In the evaluation for example of bids on infrastructure and goods, the bid evaluation is done on the basis of the lowest calculated bid.[20] Bidders are further required to make sure that their respective bids would have to be responsive to the technical specifications of the procurement of infrastructure and goods, to be included in the evaluation. In the procurement of consulting services, the bids are evaluated following the principle of 'highest rated bid'. [21]

The Philippine procurement rules, however, have a potential problem on TPP's rules on non-discrimination. The gap is the preference of the country's procurement laws to local products and bidders. On the other hand, the preference may not be exercised if the domestic bid is more than 15 percent in excess of the lowest foreign bid, with both bids found to be responsive to specifications of the procurement. Thus, when the SOEs are importing such as for example the NFA in the case of rice, the preference cannot be exercised on the ground of insufficient supply.

Moreover, the preference is also not exercised in the obvious case where local supplies are not responsive to the specifications, or the procurement is funded by official development assistance funds.

The local preference of the country's procurement law potentially is inconsistent with the non-discrimination rule in TPP. However, the procurement rules[22] waive local preference in the following situations, which cover preferential trade agreements such as TPP:

i   local supplies are not available;
ii   to promote competition;
iii if the country of a foreign supplier grants reciprocal rights or privileges to Philippine suppliers; or
iv   when provided for under any treaty or international or security agreement.

4.5. *Transparency*

The procurement law of the Philippines proceeds from three important principles: non-discrimination, competition, and transparency.[23] Non-discrimination requires parties to treat other parties no less favourably than their respective most-favoured trading partners or nation. The third principle of transparency ensures a level playing field for all potential suppliers. Transparency guarantees accountability in conducting tenders and facilitates competitive bidding by providing all necessary information to bid participants that they may need in preparing their respective responsive bids.

4.6. *Exemptions*

Article 17.13(5) introduced a *de minimis* rule, which excepts any SOE from the rules on SOE, including the obligation of non-discriminatory treatment and commercial considerations,[24] non-commercial assistance,[25] transparency,[26] and supervision by the Committee on State-Owned Enterprises and Designated Monopolies,[27] if in any of the last 3 consecutive fiscal years, the annual revenue of the SOE is less than a threshold amount specified in Annex 17-A of the Chapter. The amount initially agreed by the Parties when they closed their negotiations is 200 million special drawing rights. They agreed that the amount will be reviewed and adjusted in 3-year periods as the agreement is implemented.

Table 11.4 shows the implications of the *de minimis* rule to see how many SOEs may be covered by the TPP's disciplines. The latest data is for 2014, which if the TPP agreement entered into force in 2017, would have been one of the 3 consecutive years. The exchange rate used is the current rate of 71.222 pesos per special drawing right (SDR). Only 13 SOEs, or about 14 percent of the total

Table 11.4 SOEs covered by TPP rules in accordance with Article 17.13(5)

SOE		2014 Revenue
Development Bank of the Philippines	DBP	19,626
Land Bank of the Philippines	LAND BANK	38,250
Philippine Deposit Insurance Corporation	PDIC	24,307
Government Service Insurance System	GSIS	231,541
Home Development Mutual Fund (HDMF)	HDMF	30,680
Philippine Health Insurance Corporation	PHILHEALTH	88,019
Social Security System	SSS	153,334
National Housing Authority	NHA	26,770
Philippine Amusement and Gaming Corporation	PAGCOR	39,989
Philippine Charity Sweepstakes Office	PCSO	33,896
National Electrification Administration	NEA	14,769
Power Sector Assets and Liabilities Management Corporation	PSALM	38,054
National Food Authority	NFA	41,180

Source: Governance Commission.

number of SOEs for which financial data is available, are covered by these rules. The rest of the SOEs regardless of what they do are exempted in accordance with Article 17.13(5).

How the TPP rules may affect the activities of the more than one hundred SOEs in the Philippines was explored in this section. The discussion pointed to low likelihood that these rules might change the normal operations of these SOEs. Some are completely regulatory entities, which the TPP agreement had exempted from its rules. Others produce non-traded products, and this includes the services of area-specific utilities such as ports. More important, Article 17.13(5) introduced a *de minimis* rule, by which SOEs with annual revenues less than 200 million special drawing rights are exempted from TPP's disciplines on SOE. Only about 13 SOEs are included using revenue data in 2014.

5. Concluding remarks

This chapter has taken up the rules on SOEs of TPP on the SOE sector in the Philippines and explored how these rules may affect the operations of Philippine SOEs. While the TPP agreement recognises the right of Parties to establish or maintain SOEs, or even to designate monopolies, most of the SOEs in the Philippines are outside the scope of TPP's rules because these are (i) not into international trading or into investing, or if they are producing and selling a product, the latter is non-traded; and (ii) if they are into international trading, their revenues fall below the *de minimis* rule of the agreement. Of the nearly 100 SOEs with financial data, only 13 SOEs are covered by the rules on SOEs.

Notes

1 Professor of Economics, University of the Philippines.
2 The TPP recognises an enterprise to be an SOE if a Party "(a) directly owns more than 50 per cent of the share capital; (b) controls, through ownership interests, the exercise of more than 50 per cent of the voting rights; or (c) holds the power to appoint a majority of members of the board of directors or any other equivalent management body". See TPP, Chapter 17.2(1).
3 See TPP, Chapter 17.2(9). State ownership of an enterprise is not necessary for it to be covered by the trade agreement's rules on state-owned enterprises. The State may confer monopoly rights to a private firm, which still subjects it to the disciplines of a trade agreement's rules on SOEs.
4 See footnote no.17 in TPP Chapter 17.
5 Republic Act No. 10149 created the Governance Commission in 2011 in order to supervise and raise the quality of the SOEs.
6 See TPP Chapter 17.2(3).
7 See TPP Chapter 17.2(8).
8 For the list, please see TPP Chapter 17.2 (2 through 9).
9 See TPP Chapter 17.2(1).
10 See TPP Chapter 17.3.
11 This is classified as H100 in UNCTAD's NTM classification.
12 See the paragraphs in TPP Chapter 17.2.
13 See TPP Chapter 17.1.

14 It an investment of a Party in the territory of another Party which already existed as of the date of entry into force of the TPP agreement. See TPP Chapter 9.1.
15 See TPP Chapter 17.6(1).
16 See TPP Chapter 17.6(2).
17 See TPP Chapter 17.6(3).
18 GOCCs are government owned and controlled corporations. The term is interchangeably used with state-owned enterprises (SOEs).
19 See Section 3 of the Revised Implementing Rules and Regulations of Republic Act 9184 Otherwise known as the Government Procurement Reform Act.
20 See Section 32 of IRR of the procurement law (see footnote 10).
21 See Section 33 of the IRR of the procurement law.
22 See Section 4.1 of IRR of the procurement law, Appendix 9.
23 See Section 2 of IRR of procurement law.
24 See TPP Chapter 17.4.
25 See TPP Chapter 17.6.
26 See TPP Chapter 17.10.
27 See TPP Chapter 17.12.

Bibliography

Governance Commission for GOCCs (2014), *2014 Annual Report, Defining Strategic Performance and Leadership Accountability*. Makati City, Philippines: GOCCs.

Government Procurement Policy Board (GPPB) (2009), *The Revised Implementing Rules of Republic Act No. 9184, Otherwise Known as the Government Procurement Reform Act, Manila*, 2 September.

International Trade Center (ITC) (2015), *The Invisible Barriers to Trade: How Businesses Experience Non-Tariff Measures*. Geneva: ITC.

UNCTAD (2010), *Non-tariff Measures: Evidence from Selected Developing Countries and Future Research Agenda: Developing Countries in International Trade Studies*. Geneva: UNCTAD.

World Trade Organization (WTO) (2012), *World Trade Report 2012: Trade and Public Policies: A Closer Look at Non-tariff Measures in the 21st Century*. Geneva: WTO.

12 Disciplines on state-owned enterprises in Indonesia vis-à-vis the Trans-Pacific Partnership agreement

Maharani Hapsari[1]

1. Introduction

Indonesia's 118 state-owned enterprises (SOEs) are important pillars of its economy. They operate in almost all sectors/industries, including banking, tourism, agriculture, forestry, mining, construction fishing, energy, and telecommunications (information and communications). On the basis of the State-owned Enterprise Roadmap 2015–2019, the government of Indonesia focuses on 15 economic sectors – that is, energy security, logistics and trade, tourism and education, food security and plantation, health service, maritime economy, connectivity, construction and infrastructure, mining, manufacture, strategic defence, heavy and shipping industry, telecommunication and digital, finance and banking, and people's economy. In the current roadmap, the restructuring of SOEs will form seven sector-based holding companies. These sectors cover logistics and trade, plantation, pharmacy, shipping, construction and infrastructure, mining, and strategic defence. Eventually, the roadmap aims to streamline the number of SOEs down to 85, according to statistics by Ministry of State-owned Enterprise in 2017.

There is a need to develop a comprehensive understanding of the current legal landscape that regulates SOEs in the country and how it possibly responds to the Trans-Pacific Partnership (TPP) agreement. State-owned enterprises in Indonesia have long enjoyed various privileges under a nationalistic economic policy. They take strategic directions from the government on how to align with more competitive and credible international market players.

In the domestic scene, regulations on SOEs have seen some adjustments through the years due to the country's changing political economy, especially after the 1997 financial crisis and the series of political reforms that affected various economic sectors. State-owned enterprises, in particular, operate in an area where political interests and lively debates have long been persistently affecting their economic performance in a globalising national market.

Against such backdrop, this chapter provides an overview of the national regulatory framework that governs SOEs in Indonesia and the TPP. In particular, it will assess the extent to which the TPP agreement potentially disciplines the operation of SOEs in Indonesia in terms of their function in the economy and how they respond to the evolving international trade laws. It also analyses the SOE Chapter of the TPP agreement from an economic-legal perspective and compares its stipulations with that of the equivalent national legal framework currently in effect.

2. Definitions and scope of applications

State-owned enterprises in Indonesia were established by Article 33 of the Constitution, which stated that: 'all resources in the country shall be utilized for the welfare of all Indonesians'. The legal basis of SOEs in Indonesia can be traced back to Law No.19/1960 (on State Companies). The Law defined state companies as the production units to provide services and public needs, and seek profit. The objective was to support national economic development while serving the public's need and the company's growing priorities.

A subsequent Law No. 9 (Amd)/1969 (on Types of State Companies) categorised three types of SOEs in Indonesia: (i) Perusahaan Jawatan (Perjan), which refers to facilities that derive their capital from the government and exist to provide public service; (ii) Perusahaan Umum (Perum), which are state companies providing goods and services that serve the public interest, but at the same time seeking profit; and (iii) Perusahaan Perseroan (Persero), which are companies owned in whole or in part by the government, but exist to seek profit.

Presidential Decree no. 3/1983 (on Management of State Companies) assigned the Ministry of Finance as the major shareholder of the General Meeting. The supervision board, meanwhile, was under the Ministry of Finance and the Technical Ministries.

In the context of financial management, the Decree defined a Perjan as one whose operational costs are funded from the national budget. Meanwhile, Perum and Persero are state companies whose budgets are separate from the state budget (Fitriningrum, 2006).

Since 1998, there has been an emerging new paradigm on SOEs in Indonesia. Presidential Decree No.12/1998 on Perseroan Terbatas (limited liability company) and Presidential Decree No.13/1998 on Perusahaan Umum (public company) stipulated the separate functions between shareholder and regulator, and the centralisation of supervision.

Such was followed, through Law No. 19/2003, by the establishment of the Ministry of State-owned Enterprises, whose function is to represent the government as the state shareholder for Persero and stockholder for Perum. The Ministry was also established to empower SOEs in the future through a system where the government owns a share using a holding company.

A detailed regulation on SOEs could be found in the more recent Law No. 19/2003 (on State-owned Enterprises). According to the Law, an SOE is a company where all or part of the stock is owned by the government through direct equity allocated from the government asset (Article 1). The Law recognises three kinds of SOEs:

i First, the joint-stock state company (Persero), where the government has at least a 51 percent ownership for profit-making purpose (Article 1.2);

ii   Second, the open joint-stock state company (Perseroan Terbuka), whose stocks meet certain qualification of public offering according to regulations in the stock market (Article 1.3);

iii Third, the public state company (Perusahaan Umum), where all its stocks are owned by the government, and whose purpose is to provide high-quality goods and services as well as to make profit according to the company's management principles (Article 1.4).

According to Law No. 19/2003, the main objective of the SOEs is to contribute to the national economic development in general and national income in particular, where profit making is a core function. Another objective is to deliver public expediency by providing superior goods and services to customers for public livelihoods. State-owned enterprises pioneer economic activities not implemented by the private sector and cooperatives and provide supervision and support to economically weak groups, cooperatives, and society (Article 2). Their capital comes from the state's separate asset such as the national budget, capital reserve, and other sources (Article 4.1). The state equity is allocated from the national budget to joint-stock state companies and public state companies through a government regulation (Peraturan Pemerintah).

On 25 October 2005, the government of Indonesia issued three government regulations to implement the SOE Law, namely: (i) Government Regulation No. 43 of 2005 (Regarding Merger, Consolidation, Acquisition, and Change of Form of State-owned Enterprises); (ii) Government Regulation No. 44 of 2005 (Procedure for Participation and Administration of State Capital in State-owned Enterprises and Limited Liability Companies); and (iii) Government Regulation No. 45 of 2005 (Establishment, Management, Supervision, and Dissolution of State-owned Enterprises).

Indonesian SOEs that will be subjected to TPP arrangements include (i) SOEs controlled by the government (more than 50 percent capital owned or where the government has the authority to appoint more than 50 percent of the board of commissioners); and (ii) SOEs with an annual commercial revenue above Special Drawing Rights (SDR) 200 million (or around IDR 4 trillion). Under such scope, 81 SOEs are not subject to the TPP stipulations, whereas 38 SOEs will be on the list (Shauki, 2016). Among the SOEs within the TPP scope are PERTAMINA (Indonesia Oil Company), PLN (National Electricity Company), Telkom (telecommunication company), Bank Mandiri, and Bank BRI (i.e. Indonesian major banks).

Generally, SOEs in many countries are legally structured like private corporations. They have:

i   Ministerial shareholders (usually the Portfolio Minister and the Minister of Finance or of SOEs) set the performance indicators and appoint the board of directors;

ii   A board of directors drawn from the private sector, paid at private sector rates;

iii A chief executive appointed by and accountable to the board, usually drawn from the private sector and paid at private sector rates;

iv   The chief executive is the employer of all other staff, who are treated as private (nor public) sector workers; and

v   State-owned enterprises report annually. A central monitoring unit oversees financial and non-financial performance and parliamentary committees can seek testimony.

According to the Indonesian SOE Law, the Ministry of State-owned Enterprises and the president have the authority to appoint the members of an SOE's board of directors. This board is fully responsible for the management of the SOE's interest and goals as well as represents the SOE in or outside the court.

Meanwhile, the Ministry of State-owned Enterprises is also appointed to represent the government as the state shareholder in a Persero and the stockholder in a Perum. Management of SOEs is in the hands of the director, whereas monitoring activities are under the purview of commissioners and the monitoring board. In implementing their tasks, members of the board must follow the organisational statutes and laws and must implement the principles of professionalism, efficiency, transparency, independence, accountability, responsibility, and appropriateness (Article 5.1 to 5.3). The Ministry of State-owned Enterprises has the responsibility of assisting the president in formulating policies and coordinating in the SOE sector (Article 14).

3. Commercial considerations and non-discriminatory treatment

Per TPP Articles 17.4.1 [a] and 17.4.2 [a], 'commercial considerations' refer to the terms and conditions in the purchase or sale of goods and services (such as price and quality, and other factors that would be normally taken into account in the commercial decisions of a privately owned enterprise). All parties are also obliged to ensure that SOEs and designated monopolies treat goods, services, and enterprises of another party on a non-discriminatory basis (Articles 17.4.1 [b][c] and 17.4.2 [b][c]).

3.1. Monopolistic practices and unfair business competition

Law No. 5/1999 (on Indonesian Competition) covers issues on monopolistic practices and unfair business competition. This law has been interpreted differently by varied stakeholders. Some Indonesians believed it to be a tool for authorities to redistribute assets from large powerful conglomerates back to the people. Others believe that the government designed the law to protect small businesses from aggressive competition from larger enterprises. Foreign enterprises, meanwhile, may view the law as a way to open up Indonesian markets (Juwana, 2002).

According to Articles 2 and 3, the objective of the Competition Law is to maintain public order, improve efficiency, improve people's welfare, create an atmosphere of fair competition, inhibit monopolistic practices and unfair business competition, and realise effectiveness and efficiency in all business segments.

Several objectives of the Indonesian Competition Policy concentrate on public welfare – that fair business competition and equal opportunity for small, medium-scale business can be made possible by protecting consumer welfare and maximising national efficiency (Pardede, 2005).

There are four aspects of monopolistic practices and unfair business competition that are regulated in this Law No.5/1999. First, prohibited contracts. This covers rules on oligopoly, price fixing, market allocation, boycott, cartel, trust, oligopoly, vertical integration, exclusive dealing, and trans-national agreement that may lead to unfair practices (Article 4.1, Article 4.2, Article 16). Second, prohibition of conducts, which covers monopolisation, market control/domination, predatory pricing, misleading of production cost, conspiracy (Article 15 to Article 24). Third, abuse of dominant position. Scope of abusing a dominant position, categories of businessperson(s) having a dominant position, interlocking directorship, concentration of shares ownership, merger, consolidation and acquisition, provisions on thresholds conducting and notification procedures (Article 25 through Article 29). Fourth, competition authority. This is concerned with the presence of Commission for the Supervision of Business Competition of Republic of Indonesia (KPPU), which holds significant power in the implementation and enforcement of the Competition Law; the power and authorities conferred upon the KPPU; the right to undertake a preliminary investigation or examination, as well as determining administrative sanctions for businessperson found guilty of violating the law the right conduct examination which is based on its own investigation (without any report from any parties) (Article 30 through Article 37).

The Competition Law includes regulations on some exemptions from its scope such as (i) contracts implementing pre-existing law; (ii) contracts concerning intellectual property rights, trade secrets, and franchises; (iii) contracts on technical standardisation that do not restrict competition; (iv) contracts that do not require resale or redistribution at a subsequently lower price; (v) research contracts designed to promote or improve the general welfare of Indonesian citizens; (vi) government-ratified international contracts; (vii) export contracts that do not affect domestic markets; (viii) small businesses; and (ix) cooperatives that exclusively serve members (Article 50).

3.2. *Rules on procurements of goods and services*

Presidential Decree No. 80/2003 (on Government Procurement) includes terms and conditions on the purchase or sale of goods and services.[2] Foreign companies carrying out works must collaborate with local firms via partnerships, subcontracting, and other forms if there are local companies that meet the required capabilities in the relevant field. Multinational bidding consortiums are not restricted to submit a bid; however, such consortiums must take into account the minimum value of the works and special terms.

In addition, the Ministry of State-owned Enterprises Decree Number Per-05/MBU/2008 (on General Guidelines for Procurement) recommends that SOEs use domestic products, national architecture, and engineering, and support small enterprises with reference to responsible market quality and pricing. This directive is meant to drive domestic industrial development as well as synergy among different SOEs and their subsidiaries. It applies to all goods and services procured directly by SOE, financed by their own budget or other budget, including those coming from international aid guaranteed by the state (Article 2).

In Indonesia, SOEs write their own procurement policies. With the exception of the Bank Indonesia, SOEs draft the board regulation on procurement of goods and services and can implement such regulation without any approval from relevant ministries. Note that the guidelines for the procurement of goods and/or services by the state may potentially contradict Law No. 5/1999 on Business Competition. Based on the State-owned Enterprise Minister Regulation No. Per-15/MBU/2012, it is possible to pose entry barrier to private businesses because as a legal entity, SOEs should give priority to another SOE, or a subsidiary and/or affiliated company of SOEs (Rakhmawati, 2017). Such domestic regulatory inconsistency needs to be addressed accordingly.

4. Restrictions on Non-Commercial Assistance (NCA)

In Indonesia, SOEs have long enjoyed privileges from the government such as capital injection.[3] Non-commercial assistance to SOEs potentially threatens the principle of market competition. The TPP Chapter defines 'non-commercial assistance' as meaning 'assistance to a state-owned enterprise by virtue of that state-owned enterprise's government ownership or control'. Here, 'assistance' means: (i) direct transfers of funds or potential direct transfers of funds or liabilities (such as grants or debt forgiveness, loans, loan guarantees, or other types of financing on terms more favourable than those commercially available); or (ii) goods and services other than general infrastructure on terms more favourable than those commercially available. The term 'by virtue of that state-owned enterprise's government ownership or control' refers to a situation where an SOE receives materially favourable treatment as a subject to government assistance or where government assistance is available only to the SOE (Article 17.1). Such non-commercial assistance covers prohibition of adverse effects, prohibition of injuries, exceptions and exemptions. The scope of regulations on non-commercial assistance is expanded to cover subsidies in trade in services and investment, which is outside the World Trade Organization's rule (Kawase, 2016).

Government Regulation No. 44/2005 (on Capital Participation) distinguishes between state capital participation in SOEs and ordinary companies derived from three different sources, namely: (i) the state budget or APBN, (ii) capitalisation of reserves, and (iii) other sources. Recently, the government of Indonesia issued the Presidential Decree No. 82/2015 (on Guarantee by Central Government to Infrastructure Financing through Direct Loan from International Financial Institutions to State-Owned Enterprise). This government guarantee will be issued to international development finance institutions (i.e. multilateral and bilateral foreign financial institutions such as JBIC, the Asian Development Bank, and the World Bank) with respect to loans (i) made by those institutions to 'Eligible Borrowers', and (ii) which are for the funding of 'Qualified Infrastructure Projects'. [4]

Generally, government regulations that currently apply to various develop-ment sectors provide certain forms of privilege to Indonesian SOEs. Attempts to harmonise existing domestic regulations with what the TPP agreement requires must be carefully examined to ensure that there are no significantly unfavour-able consequences. For example, the Indonesian government's regulations on the provision of subsidy on state infrastructure may need domestic consideration, particularly to conform with the clause on non-commercial assistance (Box 12.1).

Box 12.1   Subsidy for Pilot Railway Transportation Service

Presidential Decree No. 53/2012 (on The Obligation of Public Service and Subsidy of Pilot Project in Railway Sector, Budget for the Utilization of State Railways Facilities, Maintenance and Operation of State Railways Infrastructure) provides a subsidy for pilot transportation services. In Arti-cle 7, it states:

i   In order to provide affordable railway transport services to the Indo-nesian people, the government subsidises pilot transportation costs operating within a certain period in new regions or areas that were already provided with railways but not yet commercially variable.
ii   Under conditions where consumers are not able to pay for tariffs implemented by the provider of a pilot railway service, the Minister of Transportation, in coordination with the Minister of Finance, shall review the tariff.
iii The gap between operational cost and income of providers of railway transportation services should be addressed by the government in the form of subsidy of pilot transport services.
iv   The Ministry of Transportation determines of cost to be counted in the provision of pilot railway service for enterprises after obtaining consideration from the Minister of Finance.

Furthermore, Presidential Decree No. 124/2015 reinstated the need for the government to have certain public service obligations. The Minister of Transportation determines the procedure of tariff measurements in the provision of public service obligation by Railway Enterprises (Article 2). In Article 4, the Minister of Transportation assigns SOEs in the Railway Sector with certain public service obligations. In implementing their tasks, SOEs may collaborate with other enterprises.

Source:
Presidential Decree No. 53/2012 Article 7.1–7.4.
Presidential Decree No. 124/2015 Article 2, 4, and 9.

5. Ensuring transparency

SOEs operate between bureaucracy and the public realm. Ideally, they should be able to accommodate the public's rights to utilise and protect various strategic natural resources or man-made resources. State authority on these strategic resources must be read as public authority, and state ownership shall also be seen as representing the public. Transparency, therefore, is seen as a reflection of corporate culture as well as good governance (Abiyoga, 2007).

In Indonesia, there is, however, public concern over SOEs' level of transparency. The TPP requires each party to make a list of its SOEs and designated monopolies and have this publicly available on its official website or provided to other parties (Article 17.10.1 and Article 17.10.2). Also, upon request from another party, information concerning a specific SOE or designated monopoly (e.g. the percentage of shares owned by the government, the government titles of any government official serving as an officer or member of the board, annual revenue and total assets over the most recent 3-year period) and information regarding any government policy or program for non-commercial assistance (e.g. the form of the non-commercial assistance, the names of the agencies providing the non-commercial assistance, the amount of the non-commercial assistance) must be provided (Articles 17.10.3 through 17.10.7). This issue has been under public scrutiny due to past records of misuse of authority that resulted in the accommodation of vested interest at the expense of the Indonesian public.

5.1. *Corporate governance policy*

Transparency regulations on SOE is part of national policy reform. In a 2014 study by the Institute for Reformation of State-owned Enterprises (iReformbumn), its SOE Transparency Index showed that out of 138 listed SOEs, only four were categorised as transparent, while 64 were deemed relatively transparent, 63 were less transparent, and seven were not transparent. This study recommended that the government require all SOEs to share all public information as stipulated in the Freedom on Information Law (Law 14/2008) (Infomoneter, 2014).

This transparency problem may be at the personnel level and at the enterprise level. Law 19/2003 stipulated that in implementing their tasks, the Board of Directors must follow the SOE's articles of associations and regulations as well as conform to the principles of professionalism, efficiency, transparency, independence, accountability, responsibility, and appropriateness (Article 5).

At the enterprise level, State-owned Enterprise Ministerial Decree Number 08/MBU/06/2015 (on Guidance for Reporting the Utilization of State Investment in State-owned Enterprise and Limited Liability Company) requires SOEs or limited liability companies to report any use of state investment during the general shareholders' meetings of their subsidiaries (Article 3.1). They must also report the use of state investments to the Ministry of State-owned Enterprises, per the guidelines (Article 3.2).

Ministerial Decree No. PER – 01 /MBU/2011 (on Good Corporate Governance in SOEs) postulates some principles:

i   Transparency: openness in the decision-making process and in sharing material and relevant information about the company;
ii Independence: a situation where the company is managed in a professional manner without any conflict of interest and influence/pressure from any party that does not comply with the legislation and the principles of corporate health;
iii Accountability: clarity of function, implementation, and accountability so that the entity operates effectively;
iv Responsibility: capacity to manage the company based on rules and sound corporate principles and values;
v   Fairness: fairness and equality in the provision of rights of stakeholders.

Government Regulation No. 43/2005 (on Mergers, Consolidations and Acquisitions and Change of Forms of State-Owned Enterprise) sets out the basic rules on the merger, consolidation, and acquisition of BUMNs.[5] This regulation covers only mergers or consolidation between SOEs. In case of a merger or consolidation between an SOE and a limited liability company, the limited liability company should presumably follow the general procedures for the business integration of limited liability companies as set out in Government Regulation No. 27 of 1998 Regarding Mergers, Consolidations and Acquisitions of Limited Liability Companies.

In the event of an acquisition, the government regulations cover the process of acquisition by an SOE of the majority shares of another SOE or limited liability company. The corporate merger/consolidation of SOEs must be stipulated in a government regulation after the proposal prepared by the Minister of State-owned Enterprises has been discussed with other relevant ministers (e.g. the Minister of Finance and other technical ministers related to the business of the particular SOE) and approved by the Indonesian president. The transaction must also be approved during the general meeting of shareholders (for a Persero) or by the SOE Minister (for a Perum) (Soewito, 2016).

Such a business event should not be detrimental to the interests of the BUMN, minority shareholders, employees (e.g. it should avoid mass terminations), creditors, business competition, or the public. In addition, a Persero should also follow the applicable procedures for the merger, consolidation, and acquisition of ordinary limited liability company. This means that the directors of the BUMN must prepare a joint proposal and plan for the business combination, notify creditors, publish a newspaper announcement, and perform other actions required under Government Regulation No. 27 of 1998 for the corporate action to take effect. The procedures applicable to a Perum are similar to those for a Persero.

To increase public accountability, Government Regulation No. 45/2005 (on the Establishment, Management, Monitoring, and Dissolution of State-Owned Enterprise) covers the establishment of a new BUMN, the conversion of a business unit, a change in legal form, and the creation of a new entity resulting from a consolidation. The SOE's establishment should be formulated in a government regulation that also sets out the standard articles of association of the SOE.

The dissolution of an SOE must be stipulated in a government regulation, too. This regulation will ensure that the SOE is independent of any political interest. Candidates for the position of director of a BUMN should pass the fit-and-proper test and enter into a management contract. Government regulations prohibit directors and commissioners of a BUMN from holding any director position in other BUMNs or companies, from holding any conflicting positions, and from becoming officials of any political party or members of parliament.

5.2. Transparency on procurement

Presidential Decree No. 80/2003 (on Government Procurement) requires a contracting authority to publicly announce goods and (general) services procurement activity through a nationally circulated and/or provincially circulated newspaper (Article 4). Confidential goods and (general) services procurement plans for departments/institutions/commissions/Bank Indonesia/regional government/state-owned legal entity/SOEs/regional-owned enterprise must be publicly announced as well on the national procurement website. The previous provisions may be waived for defence materials and equipment for the Department of Defence/Indonesian Armed Forces, as determined by the Minister of Defence/Commander-in-chief of the Indonesian Armed Forces/Forces Chief Staff (Article 42.3).

6. Debates on SOEs' disciplines

In public debates, optimists have advocated the numerous benefits of participating in the TPP. These benefits include an improved legal and institutional framework for conducting trade and resolving trade-related disputes, opportunities to move up the value chain from raw materials to finished goods exports and access to an enormous, open market for selling finished goods.

There are at least three issues that might shape the debate on Indonesia's response to strict disciplines on SOEs under the TPP agreement. First, the high commitment towards liberalisation may possibly have a deeper impact on SOEs. As Wicaksono (2009) argues, the government of Indonesia needs to critically balance the commercial aspects of SOE with globalisation, the demands of domestic constituents, and democratisation of Indonesian economy that consider various economic groups that are not necessarily represented in the negotiation process. Issues with both political and commercial concerns will continue to drive discussions on the future of SOEs in Indonesia.

Second, it is foreseeable the potential threats to protectionist policies such as government tender and local content, dispute settlement mechanism regarding investment, government procurement, labour, environment, and small enterprises. In particular, there are concerns on the implementation of dispute settlements that allows investors to bring claims of breaches of investment protection.

Some SOE received special rights by the government as sole operator on several sectors by monopolisation and concession.

Third, there is an emerging view to maximise the benefits from the Regional Comprehensive Economic Partnership (RCEP), given its more flexible scope or agreement, the possibility to protect sensitive products, and the absence of any discipline on government procurement. The Association of Southeast Asian Nations describes the Comprehensive Economic Partnership as 'a modern, comprehensive, high-quality and mutually beneficial economic partnership agreement establishing an open trade and investment environment in the region to facilitate the expansion of regional trade and investment and contribute to global economic growth and development' (Jakarta Globe, n.d.). Proponents argue that Indonesia also has a bigger role in the Comprehensive Economic Partnership rather than in TPP (Hermansyah, 2015).

7. Conclusion

This chapter discussed the SOE Chapter of the TPP agreement from an economic-legal perspective. Indonesia needs to carefully define the reach of the Agreement to prospective SOEs operating inside the country. Public data needed to build international credibility is unavailable, although this has to be taken within the context of other member or/and prospective member countries' disclosure policies. Indonesia's government, through its regulatory instruments, should request that the TPP agreement push for simultaneous data sharing that is well coordinated, transparent, and accurate to avoid the undesirable consequences of information asymmetry among TPP members.

When it comes to commercial considerations and non-discriminatory treatment, Indonesia needs to carefully review the relations and congruence among domestic trade-related regulations. In particular, contradictory regulations create ambiguity in Indonesia's position on TPP issues. This is, in fact, currently not discussed seriously. It is simply assumed – albeit erroneously – that within the domestic sphere, there are already coherent and consistent trade-related regulations at various levels.

On the issue of restrictions to non-commercial assistance, the picture is not that straightforward. That is, there are some difficulties in presenting a comprehensive picture on the types of assistance provided by the government to SOEs across sectors. The nature of non-commercial assistance is very diffused, often intermingled with specific national interests that are not necessarily negotiable to international business stakeholders.

On the topic of transparency, Indonesians are strongly demanding for improved public disclosure, thus providing a constructive environment for harmonising the stipulations in the SOE Chapters with Indonesia's national regulations, particularly on corporate governance, corruption, privatisation, and transparency in procurement. In this context, how Indonesian regulators will link domestic and international goals regarding transparent and accountable trade-related measures – one that will serve the public's interest – will be a crucial agenda in the future.

Notes

1 Lecturer, Department of International Relations, Faculty of Social and Political Science, Universitas Gadjah Mada. The author can be reached at ranihps@ugm.ac.id.
2 Goods or services to be procured are of two types: (i) goods and (general) services; and (ii) consultancy service. Participation of foreign bidders is subject to the following procurement values: (i) for contract of works above Rp 50 billion; (ii) for provision of other goods and (general) services above Rp 10 billion; (3) for consultancy services above Rp 5 billion (Article 42, paragraph 1).
3 In the Revised State Budget Draft, the state will provide the Healthcare and Social Security Agency (BPJS Kesehatan) with a capital worth Rp 68.6 trillion (US$5.1 billion), increasing by Rp 20.2 trillion (US$1.5 billion) from that earmarked in the 2016 State Budget at Rp 48.3 trillion (US$3.6 billion). As many as 24 SOEs will receive fresh capital, including state power company PLN, which will receive Rp 13.56 trillion (US$1 trillion). The fund is earmarked to support the realisation of the 35,000 MW power plant project.
4 In the Decree, an 'Eligible Borrower' is defined as any State-Owned Enterprise ('BUMNu') in sound financial condition with the capability to fulfil its financial obligations, which is 100 percent owned by the government or wholly owned by (i) the government, and (ii) another BUMN which is 100 percent owned by the government; or the State-owned Infrastructure Financing Company – which channels loans through to BUMNs, provided that it is in sound financial condition with the capability to fulfil its financial obligations (Article 4.1[a][b]). A qualified infrastructure project is defined as any infrastructure project which is included in lists of infrastructure projects that are maintained by the Committee of Acceleration of Procurement of Priority Infrastructure; maintained by ministries/non-ministry government institutions, or in line with the Mid-Term National Development Plan based on a statement letter from the Head of the National Planning Development Agency (Bappenas) (Article 4.1[c]).
5 A merger is defined as a legal action undertaken by one or more BUMNs to merge with another existing BUMN, with the merging company being dissolved. In a consolidation, two or more BUMNs combine to form a new BUMN, while the consolidating companies are dissolved. In neither case is a liquidation required beforehand.

Bibliography

Articles

Abiyoga, B. (2007), *Keharusan Transparansi BUMN*. Online. Available at www.anti korupsi.org
Fitriningrum, A. (2006), 'Indonesia Experiences in Managing the State Companies', Paper presented at the OECD-ASIAN Roundtable on Corporate Governance Network on Corporate Governance of State-owned Enterprises. Singapore, 15 May.
Hermansyah, A. (2015), 'State-enterprises Under Threat If Indonesia Joins TPP: Experts'. *The Jakarta Post*, 29 November 2015.
Jakarta Globe (n.d.), 'Between Two Giants: Indonesia's Economy in the Balance'. Available at http://jakartaglobe.beritasatu.com/news/two-giants-indonesias-economy-balance/
Jakarta Globe (n.d.), 'Indonesia and the Trans-Pacific Partnership: To Join or Not to Join?' Available at http://jakartaglobe.beritasatu.com/opinion/indonesia-and-the-trans-pacific-partnership-to-join-or-not-to-join/

Juwana, H. (2002), 'An Overview of Indonesia's Antimonopoly Law', *Washington University Global Studies Law Review*, 185. Available at http://openscholarship. wustl.edu/law_globalstudies/vol1/issI/9

Kawase, T. (2016), 'Disciplines on State-owned Enterprises Under the Trans-Pacific Partnership Agreement: Overview and Assessment', March, Paper presented at the ERIA Kick-Off Workshop on 21st Century Regionalism, Mega FTAs, and Asian Regional Integration: Implications of TPP for ASEAN Countries. Bangkok, 5 June.

Marisi, N.B., H. Juwana and A. Nasution (2015), 'Role of Authorities in Supervision of Management of Privatized State-Owned Enterprises through Capital Market', *OSR Journal of Humanities and Social Science* (IOSR-JHSS), 20(12), pp. 37–41.

Pardede, S. (2005), 'Development of Competition Policy and Recent Issues in East Asian Economies (The Indonesian Experience)', Paper presented at the 2nd East Asia Conference on Competition Law and Policy. Bogor, 3–4 May.

Rakhmawati, C.S. (2017), 'Peraturan Menteri Bumn Nomor Per-15/Mbu/2012 Tentang Pedoman Umum Pengadaan Barang Dan Jasa Bumn Dalam Perspektif Hukum Persaingan Usaha', *Business Law Review*, 2, pp. 39–54.

Shauki, A. (2016), 'Implikasi Akses TPP pada BUMN: Dampak Ekonomi dan Usulan Strategi Reformasi', Policy Dialogue Series. Australia Indonesia Partnership for Economic Governance.

Soewito Suhardiman, E.K. (2016), *New Regulations on State-Owned Enterprise.* Available at www.mondaq.com/x/39590/Corporate+Commercial+Law/New+R egulations+on+State+Enterprises (accessed 3 October 2016).

Wicaksono, A. (2008), 'Indonesian State-Owned Enterprises: The Challenge of Reform', *Southeast Asian Affairs*, pp. 146–167.

Wicaksono, A. (2009), 'Corporate Governance of State-Owned Enterprises: Investment Holding Structure of Government-Linked Companies in Singapore and Malaysia and Applicability for Indonesian State-Owned Enterprises', Dissertation at the University of St. Gallen, p. 230.

Laws

Constitution of the Republic of Indonesia 1945. Law No. 5/1999 on Indonesian Competition Law (Ban on Monopolistic Practices and Unfair Business Competition).

Law No. 9 (Amd)/1969 on Type of State Companies.

Law No. 14/2008 on Freedom on Information.

Law No. 19/1960 on the State Companies. Law No. 19/2003 on State-owned Enterprises.

Law No. 31/1999 on the Eradication of the Act of Corruption.

Government Regulations

Government Regulation No. 6/2000 on Perusahaan Janata (Perjan).

Government Regulation No. 33/2005 on Privatization of Liability Company Government Regulation No. 59/2009 on Changes in Government Regulation No. 33/2005 on Privatization of Liability Company.

Government Regulation No. 43 of 2005 Regarding Merger, Consolidation, Acquisition and Change of Form of State-owned Enterprises.

Government Regulation No. 44 of 2005 on Procedure for Participation and Administration of State Capital in State-owned Enterprises and Limited Liability Companies.

Government Regulation No. 45 of 2005 on the Establishment, Management, Supervision and Dissolution of State-owned Enterprises.

Presidential Decrees

Presidential Decree No. 3/1983 on Management of State Companies.

Presidential Decree No. 12/1998 on Perseroan Terbatas (limited liability company).

Presidential Decree No. 13/1998 on Perusahaan Umum (public company).

Presidential Decree No. 53/2012 on The Obligation of Public Service and Subsidy of Pilot Project in Railway Sector, Budget for the Utilization of State Railways Facilities, Maintenance and Operation of State Railways Infrastructure.

Presidential Decree No. 80/2003 on Government Procurement.

Presidential Decree No. 82/2015 on Guarantee by Central Government to Infrastructure Financing through Direct Loan from International Financial Institutions to State-Owned Enterprise.

Presidential Decree No. 124/2015 on the revision to Presidential Decree No. 53/2012 on The Obligation of Public Service and Subsidy of Pilot Project in Railway Sector, Budget for the Utilization of State Railways Facilities, Maintenance and Operation of State Railways Infrastructure.

Other Regulations

Commission for the Supervision of Business Competition of Republic of Indonesia (KPPU) Regulation No. 1 of 2006 on Procedure of Case Handling in the KPPU.

Ministerial Decree No. PER – 01 /MBU/2011 on Good Corporate Governance in SOEs.

State-owned Enterprise Ministerial Decree Number 08/MBU/06/2015 on Guidance for Reporting the Utilization of State Investment in State-owned Enterprise and Limited Liability Company.

Index

Note: **Boldface** page references indicate tables. *Italic* references indicate figures and boxed text.

For Product Safety Concerns and Information please contact our EU
representative GPSR@taylorandfrancis.com
Taylor & Francis Verlag GmbH, Kaufingerstraße 24, 80331 München, Germany

www.ingramcontent.com/pod-product-compliance
Ingram Content Group UK Ltd.
Pitfield, Milton Keynes, MK11 3LW, UK
UKHW021012180425
457613UK00020B/915